For Matthew,
With admiration
anticipation of
Best r

Ruined by Design

Literary Criticism and Cultural Theory

WILLIAM E. CAIN, *General Editor*

For a full list of titles in this series, please visit www.routledge.com

Ruined by Design

Shaping Novels and Gardens in the Culture of Sensibility

Inger Sigrun Brodey

Routledge
Taylor & Francis Group
New York   London

First published 2008
by Routledge
270 Madison Ave, New York, NY 10016

Simultaneously published in the UK
by Routledge
2 Park Square, Milton Park, Abingdon, Oxon OX14 4RN

Routledge is an imprint of the Taylor & Francis Group, an informa business

© 2008 Taylor & Francis

Typeset in Sabon by IBT Global.
Printed and bound in the United States of America on acid-free paper by IBT Global.

Library of Congress Cataloging in Publication Data
Brodey, Inger Sigrun.
    Ruined by design : shaping novels and gardens in the culture of sensibility / by Inger Sigrun Brodey.
        p. cm.—(Literary criticism and cultural theory)
    Includes index.
    ISBN-13: 978-0-415-98950-3
    ISBN-10: 0-415-98950-7
    1. Sentimentalism in literature.   2. English fiction—18th century—History and criticism.   3. French fiction—18th century—History and criticism.   4. German fiction—18th century—History and criticism.   5. Emotions in literature.   6. Sympathy in literature.   7. Gardens in literature.   8. Ruins in literature.   9. Picturesque, The, in literature.   10. Emotions (Philosophy) I. Title.
    PR858.S45B76 2008
    823'.509353—dc22
    2008005413

ISBN10: 0-415-98950 (hbk)

ISBN13: 978-0-415-98950-3 (hbk)

Contents

List of Figures

Preface

Many of us have known 1960s flower children or hippies who in younger days decried those in traditional positions of authority in commerce or academia, only to rise to similar positions of power and authority in the 1980s or '90s. This book explores the culture surrounding a late-eighteenth-century character who is analogous to the ex-hippie in a management position: namely, the "man of feeling" who eschews all appearances of conforming to convention including narrative conventions, yet wishes to narrate his own life with authority. Like the American hippie culture of the 1960s, the European fashion of sensibility in the 1760s also elevated spontaneity over control and bred an idealism that self-consciously defined itself in opposition to commercial interests, conventional institutions, orthodox approaches to religion, militarism, consumerism, materialism, and patriarchal or centralized authority. Both movements claimed to establish a morally superior counter-culture and a morally superior form of 'failure.' The man of feeling was characterized, like the hippie, by embarrassment over conventional measures of success for "men of the world," including discomfort with authority, wealth, and influence.

Yet what of authorship? The culture of sensibility features a wide-spread reconsideration of the nature of the relationship between authorship and authority. Authorship, in mid-to-late eighteenth-century Europe, was still associated with the Enlightenment "man of letters," an elite and traditional source of masculine authority, rather than primarily with the burgeoning self-expression of the middle class. Thus, the "man of feeling" needs to distinguish himself from both the "man of letters" as well as the "man of the world." The result is a perplexing difficulty for the "man of feeling" as he aspires to write, publish, influence, and even express himself or survive in the face of the banal requirements of daily life and unchanging institutional expectations of society, particularly when the aesthetic ideals of sensibility are defined in opposition to the very qualities generally required of authorship, including conscious control, active calculation, or the ability to compose, revise, cohere, complete, or publish. In his pursuit of artlessness, the man of feeling needs to reformulate authorship and the novel in particular in order to tell and publish his story without appearing to wish to do so.

Ultimately the hippie and the man of feeling are both rebels who disdain authority, yet also succumb to its practical benefits. Are their internal tensions and seeming contradictions simply signs of a natural process of maturation or do they signify something more pernicious? This contrast between ideals and reality is paradoxical and even humorous at its best, hypocritical or even dangerous at its worst. When does this dilemma lead to hypocrisy or to an excuse for subterranean exertions of control or authority—a form of Tocquevillian soft tyranny? It can be seductive to laugh at the fallen idealist, and there is something deeply interesting about the revelation of the hypocrisy of a person who has claimed moral superiority. And yet, perhaps it might be important to express ideals even though they are difficult—or impossible—to maintain.

To some extent, one's answers to these questions depend upon one's opinions about the perfectibility of human nature—that is, on "natural goodness" or the existence of "moral sentiments," much debated issues in Enlightenment moral philosophy. These are some of the ethical dilemmas that continue to concern the man of feeling and others involved in the culture of sensibility in the second half of the eighteenth century in Europe, and they underlie the aesthetic fascination with ruination. The ruin, like the exposed hypocrite, provokes multivalent responses and begs questions about the perfectibility, duration, and import of human achievement, as well as the fate of private ideals in public life.

The rich material and literary manifestations around authenticity and authority within the culture of sensibility offer an unusual response to issues that reappear throughout various moments in history—whether in ancient quarrels between poetry and philosophy, historical tensions between lyric and epic traditions in literature, or aesthetic debates around the relative merits of organicism and mechanism in art. While I return to some more contemporary aesthetic and social examples in the conclusion of this book, the eighteenth-century culture of sensibility provides an interesting locus for conflicts surrounding idealism and the hope for human perfectibility. Amid a bewildering atmosphere of utopian aspirations as well as violent destruction, novelists and landscape architects within the culture of sensibility manage to create structures that simultaneously appeal to anti-authoritarian ideals and love of spontaneity, yet also appease more authoritarian (or pragmatic) impulses, such as the desire to maintain control of their audience's responses. This ambivalence, or insecurity regarding authority, is thus based on conflicted—or perhaps realistically mixed—views of human nature.

There are many ways of interpreting the eighteenth-century fascination with ruins: scholars have read ruins in the light of nation building, of historiography, of the invention of the Gothic, and in connection with romanticism, just to name a few. None of these, however, are the focus of this work. This book describes a structural parallel between the fake ruins or follies popular in the eighteenth-century "English" garden and the purposeful fragmentation and other innovative literary devices of the novel of sensibility (whose popularity roughly coincides with the follies). Here the focus is to understand the self-conscious aesthetic of the culture of sensibility, where artists, authors, and architects use ruination and fragmentation more generally as an expression of the dilemma described above—that is, ruination expresses an anti-authorian ideal, flaunting the lack of centralized completion and inviting the audience's role in (re)construction. Yet these forms nonetheless reluctantly, implicitly, and paradoxically rely on the presence and authority of monumental institutions and centralized authority and their creators. They give the appearance of allowing freedom of interpretation while taking numerous precautions against faulty readings. I thus argue that the purposeful re-creation of ruin is part of a self-conscious literary and aesthetic mode or fashion at the heart of the culture of sensibility, present from Burke's conception of "obscurity"; to the primal tones of Herder's "wilde Mutter"; to the extravagantly torn and imbedded fragments in novels of sensibility; to laboriously constructed follies in gentlemen's estates; to the voluptuously exposed corpses and gravestones of the fallen fictional men and women of sensibility. The Werthers, Julies, Harleys, and Clarissas all testify to not only the inauthenticity of control but also the moral superiority of ruin: they are popular martyrs to the cause of sensibility.

SCHOLARSHIP ON SENSIBILITY

The culture of sensibility, which flourished in the second half of the eighteenth century across much of Europe, has recently become a growth industry within eighteenth-century studies. Many works have studied the picturesque, the literature of sensibility, sentimentalism and its roots in new approaches to epistemology and in anatomical theories. Recent scholars have looked at its connections to medicine, science, philosophy, and other domains. In the last decade, critics such as G. J. Barker-Benfield, Barbara Benedict, Stephen Cox, Markman Ellis, Claudia Johnson, John Mullan, Jessica Riskin, Janet Todd, and Ann Jessie Van Sant, have built on earlier insights by R.S. Crane, Samuel Brissenden, Louis Bredvold, and Jean Hagstrum (to mention only select English-speaking critics), and have begun developing and illustrating a broader cultural context for the novel of sensibility. Barker-Benfield, for example, used socio-economic history to show the broader implications and function of the novel of sensibility and was one of the first to legitimate the term "culture of sensibility." Ellis continued the same project, weaving together issues in moral philosophy, theology, commerce, and psychological theory to explore the effects of the culture of sensibility on the eighteenth-century understanding of gender, in particular. Van Sant, in particular, by building intriguing parallels between scientific experimentalism and the novel of sensibility, exposes some of the seemingly sadistic and hypocritical aspects of sensibility in Europe.

Sensibility as a movement or "culture" requires, I would argue, a treatment that is both interdisciplinary and international. This study also incorporates French and German texts, allowing for the fact that the culture of sensibility defied national as well as disciplinary boundaries. Sensibility was in fact one of the earliest pan-European fashions, necessitating a consideration of multiple European cultures.

This work also builds upon what Ellis refers to as "the mutually informing nature of philosophy, theology, science and political economy in the eighteenth century"; in this volume, the disciplinary boundaries of the "culture of sensibility" (Barker-Benfield's term) are expanded to encompass landscape gardening and architecture, as well as the philosophy of language. I will include evidence not only from philosophers and theorists, but also from pattern books, how-to manuals, and popular rhetorical guides. By pursuing the cultural significance of paradoxical constructions in architecture as well as literature, this book develops the narrative strategies that identify the novel of sensibility by drawing upon a broader context of landscape gardening, philosophy of language, and moral philosophy. In relation to many contemporary accounts of the culture of sensibility, this study will have less emphasis on economics, science, and political history, and more attention to individual novels, landscape gardening, landscape architecture, and popular guidebooks concerning language and rhetoric.

In many ways, the cross-disciplinary comparisons that I have suggested here are reminiscent of the "history of ideas" approaches of J. G. A. Pocock or Arthur O. Lovejoy, approaches that have come under fire from recent critics of sensibility. Markman Ellis, for example, despite his own contribution to a broader cultural context for the "novel of sensibility," also indicates a suspicion of the "history of ideas" approach. Ellis makes the point that although the history of ideas approach has lent importance to the study of sentimental texts by linking them with the canonical texts of eighteenth-century ethical philosophy, it has also compromised our understanding of sensibility in a number of ways. For Ellis, these include: (1) the failure to treat the significance of the act of *reading* novels of sensibility, (2) the disregard for generic differences, such as the literary character of the novels, and (3) the tendency to treat literature primarily as a tool for disseminating philosophical ideas, thereby attributing both historical priority and causal influence to philosophy. Critics such as Ellis and Barker-Benfield therefore react against traditional intellectual history in favor of cultural history or cultural studies, expanding their 'texts' to include chamber pots, undergarments, and conduct books. This is appropriate since sensibility was both high culture and cult, philosophy and fad, and morally ambivalent, as Mullan, Van Sant and others have shown. By interweaving a range of disciplines representing both "high" and "low" culture—namely, landscape gardening, grammar books, the novel, and other elements of material culture, as well as moral philosophy and philosophy of language, the current study hopes to move beyond argument based on New Historical homology to suggest a broader web of meaning (to borrow from Clifford Geertz) that helps give coherence to the culture of sensibility.

Many of those recent critics who have attempted cross-disciplinary studies of the mid-to-late eighteenth century without the context of a culture of sensibility have experienced difficulty accounting for the surprising similarities among the disciplines they are studying, even when those similarities are precisely the point of their study. Ann Jessie Van Sant, for example, in her comparison of the psychological model of sensibility with the novel, apologetically claims no more than "analogy" and a surprising "coincidence between the rhetoric of pathos and scientific presentation." While it is indeed difficult to avoid similar terminology, analogy may ultimately fall short in describing the relation between these modes of thought, and could be understood as an anachronism, since an analogy requires a paradigmatic and disciplinary separation not historically characteristic of eighteenth-century thought.

One might ask what is the particular relevance that drives the interest in sensibility for scholars today. Sensibility is arguably the most revealing of cultural movements in the second half of the eighteenth century. It was a hugely innovative time period for narrative forms—especially the young genre that we (somewhat anachronistically) name the novel—and also provides a treasure trove for the psychoanalytic and gender issues that have come to the forefront of literary criticism in the past two decades.

While portraying a new type of self-conscious, feminized, and highly idealized male hero, sensibility is also deeply involved with sadistic sides of human nature. For example, its aesthetic relies on the innate curiosity, if not pleasure, one feels in response to others' suffering. Men and women of sensibility take additional pleasure in witnessing and recounting scenes of suffering in order to prove their own worth and ability to sympathize. When combined with the gendered studies of sensibility or sentimentalism, one cannot help but be astonished by the importance of female suffering in the late eighteenth century—the assumption that young, beautiful women are somehow particularly "interesting" and attractive when they are in distress. Ultimately, the cultural fascination with ruination involves the active pursuit of human suffering and ruin in order to achieve its aesthetic objectives.

DEFENDING SENSIBILITY

However one refers to or defines the most popular European literary taste of the second half of the eighteenth century, the literature of this period has not fared equally well in the hands of critics. The term 'Preromanticism' itself is vaguely derogatory; it suggests a *pseudo*-Romanticism, inferior content, or a period not worthy of the name of what succeeded and surpassed it: "a trough between two creative waves," in D. J. Enright's words, or the "the swamps between the Augustan and Romantic heights," according to

Janet Todd.[1] Partly because of the tendency toward definition by hindsight, the mid-to-late eighteenth century writings associated with the culture of sensibility have not generally been afforded a great deal of respect. Even Jerome McGann, elsewhere a defender of the literature of sensibility, confesses that "so far as high culture is concerned . . . these traditions remain something of an embarrassment."[2]

While attracting unparalleled scholarly interest in the last decade, the literature of sensibility oddly also remains a source of scholarly embarrassment. In fact, it has become a tradition for studies of sentimentalism or sensibility to begin with an apology for the quality of the literature that they treat. This treatment does not merely occur in modern times among readers who tire of sensibility's lachrymose exhibitions of virtue in distress. Dr. Johnson, for example, whose literary prominence overlapped with the culture of sensibility, complained of "the fashionable whine of sensibility." And indeed, the literature of sensibility consistently emphasizes excess over moderation: façades of exquisitely melancholy and chaste tears loosely cover a materialism and an eroticism that can be slapstick, hypocritical, or even sadistic in nature. Its internal tensions propel it to extremes and to hypocrisy, rather than to moderation or even to the resignation offered by aporia. These characteristics underlie some of the most interesting and revelatory aspects of sensibility, however, which have generated psychoanalytic insights as well as important contributions to gender studies. Yet perhaps some of the provocative features of sensibility also provide the foundation for contemporary scholarly embarrassment and defensiveness regarding the subject matter. Scholars habitually distance themselves from this literature, just as the fictional editors in the novels effectively serve to distance the authors from the most histrionic characters. Many literary historians who write about sensibility through the lenses of Romanticism have considered it lacking in luster, particularly in contrast to the magnificent periods that flank it: the bright and sparkling reign of neoclassical or Enlightenment prose and the darker splendor of Romantic verse.

Sensibility has received especially negative treatment at the hands of critics in relation to Romanticism. In this context, critics frequently use such terms as "half-hearted" or "weak" to describe sensibility. Marilyn Butler describes sensibility as a "weak trial run for Romanticism"; D. J. Enright writes that "between the self-assured work of the Augustans and the energetic and diverse movements of the Romantic revival came a period of half-hearted, characterless writing."[3] Marshall Brown describes Preromanticism as "a problem, rather than an ambition," while Robert W. Jones echoes Barbara Benedict's suggestion that sensibility is best understood, "not as a confidently accepted cultural norm, but as an anxiously attended-to set of problems."[4] Similarly, Markman Ellis' English politics of sensibility are "the politics of an emerging middle class," eager to demonstrate its own liberality and progressive munificence in issues such as the anti-slavery movement, yet "unwilling to engage with revolutionary change."[5] These phrases ("weak," "half-hearted," "characterless," "problem," "anxiously attended," etc.) all suggest in different ways that critics have been struck by a weakness or deficiency in sensibility: it may be again that the seemingly half-hearted revolutionary spirit of the failed man of feeling may be overly reminiscent of the suit-clad hippie in a management position—the sense of disappointment that revolutionary ideals were not accompanied by an equally impressive commitment to action. Indeed, sensibility seems to promote the idea that defeat is somehow a prerequisite for true feeling.

This book can be seen as a rumination upon the cost and limits of a cultural ideal that rests upon the admiration for ruin—whether that ruin is geological, architectural, narrative, or personal. By exploring some of the contradictory impulses at the heart of the culture of sensibility—impulses that lead to the creation of innovative narrative and architectural structures—I hope to illuminate some of the insights that the culture of sensibility offers, even to contemporary audiences, wary of its sudden excesses.

Acknowledgments

I have presented parts of the book in a range of formats, as the central theses evolved. My first attempt at comparing the follies and authors of the culture of sensibility won the award for the best non-plenary paper presented at the annual meeting of the Midwestern American Society for Eighteenth-Century Studies, where Thomas Bonnell kindly encouraged its further development. The hallmarks of sensibility mentioned in the Introduction are treated more extensively in my essay "Preromanticism, or Sensibility: Defining Ambivalences."[6] The Jane Austen sections draw on two published articles and one book essay.[7] I have also had the opportunity to test my ideas in a variety of public fora, particularly the 2003 Leon and Thea Koerner Foundation Lecture in the Liberal Arts at Simon-Frasier University, entitled "The Architecture of Distress: Jane Austen, Follies, and the Cult of Sensibility" and a plenary address at the 2001 Annual General Meeting of the Jane Austen Society of North America, entitled "Entertaining Grief: Jane Austen and the 'Luxury of Distress.'" I thank June Sturrock and Kimberly Brangwin, the respective organizers of these conferences, who encouraged me in developing, expanding, and synthesizing these ideas and thus indirectly helped me complete this book.

I have been very fortunate in the generous support of academic and private organizations that have helped to fund this research, beginning with a five-year Mellon Fellowship in the Humanities from the Woodrow Wilson Foundation to pursue my Ph.D. at the University of Chicago. The American Society for Eighteenth-Century Studies helped me, not only with the award mentioned above, but also with a Ruth and Gwin J. Kolb Annual Travel Grant for research at the British Library and the British Museum. The Earhart Foundation helped me on two occasions, first with an Earhart Foundation Dissertation Fellowship, and later with an Earhart Foundation Research Fellowship Grant. And finally, the University of North Carolina at Chapel Hill generously provided a Spray-Randleigh Faculty Fellowship as well as an Arts and Sciences Junior Sabbatical for the completion of this project.

My thanks extend to many more individuals than I can mention here, but particularly to those who have provided helpful advice and who have read or listened to ideas about much earlier versions of the project: Douglas Den Uyl, Denise Despres, Timothy Fuller, Gwin Kolb, Françoise Meltzer, Charles Rosen, Barbara Maria Stafford, Stuart Tave, Stuart Warner, and Anthony Yu. Saul Bellow, Gwin Kolb, and Wayne Booth did not live to see its completion, but were each very helpful to me in its inception.

Several friends have been helpful both in suggesting additional resources and in encouraging me not to allow this book to remain a fragment, purposefully or not. These friends include: Katharine De Baun, Francis DuVinage, Russ Geoffrey, Susanne Grumman, Joän Pawelski, Astrida Orle Tantillo, and especially Debra Romanick Baldwin, whose critical eye is ever a blessing. In the words of E. B. White, "it is not often that someone comes along who is a true friend and a good writer," yet Debra, in particular, is both.

Of my current colleagues at UNC-Chapel Hill, I would particularly like to thank Jan Bardsley, Marsha Collins, Lilian R. Furst, Darryl Gless, William Harmon, Edward Donald Kennedy, James Peacock, and James Thompson—all of whom have read parts of the manuscript and have been very supportive of this project, along with the rest of my colleagues in Comparative Literature and Asian Studies.

On an even more practical note, this manuscript would never have been completed without the Medici on 57th Street in Chicago; the Wallingford Tully's in Seattle; Strong's Coffee Shop, Foster's Market, and Three Cups in Chapel Hill; nor without help from Breanne Goss, Diana Pitt, Dustin Mengelkof, and Emily Bunner. Jessamine Hyatt and Diana Pitt also provided valuable assistance in checking my translations, and Rasmi Simhan was invaluable in helping with the illustrations and permissions. Lori Harris heroically created the index, and Erica Wetter, Liz Levine, and Eleanor Chan made the final steps of publication proceed (nearly) painlessly.

Finally, I would like to thank my parents, whose support enabled me to gain confidence in my intellectual pursuits, and whose dedication to symmetry and order helped shape my sense of aesthetics. My husband and children have given me additional appreciation for qualities associated with the culture of sensibility, including the beauties of disorder and irregularity. To paraphrase Jane Austen, having experienced order early in life, I learned to appreciate disorder later.

This volume is dedicated to Benjamin, who has endured many of the pains of this project and who proves that it is possible to have both sensibility and an M.D.

Introduction
Sensibility and its Discontents

Sensibility of soul, which is rightly described as the source of morality, gives one a kind of wisdom concerning matters of virtue . . .
People of sensibility . . . can fall into errors which Men of the world
would not commit; but these are greatly outweighed by the amount
of good that they do.

—Chevalier Louis de Jaucourt[1]

—Dear sensibility! source inexhausted of all that's precious in our
joys, or costly in our sorrows! . . . Eternal fountain of our feelings!—
this is thy divinity which stirs within me—that I feel some generous
joys and generous cares beyond myself—all comes from thee, great—
great SENSORIUM of the world!

—Laurence Sterne

The word 'sensibility' had a glorious past. It is largely gone from our vocabulary today, where we use the word to mean little more than 'emotional
viewpoint'; however, during the latter half of the eighteenth century, sensibility could inspire enthusiastic encomia and designate the essential spark
of life, virtue, and humanity. Both epigraphs above describe the "man
of feeling" and his overriding virtue, sensibility: one is an entry in Denis
Diderot's *Encyclopédie* (1765), the other a soliloquy by Parson Yorick in
Laurence Sterne's novel *A Sentimental Journey through France and Italy
by Mr. Yorick* (1768). In both cases, the authors equate the ability to feel
deeply with a virtue surpassing any achieved through discipline or reason,
even if (or perhaps *especially* if) it leads to ridicule in the eyes of the world.
It designates a moral superiority defined in opposition to more traditional
mores and societal standards of success.

In these passages, then, as univocal as they may at first appear, one can
see the conflicting impulses of the culture of sensibility at work. We see the
joyful and optimistic assertion of natural virtue—even a natural virtue with
a basis in the human body—yet also a sadness based on the reception that
such virtue receives in society, where sentimental actions are interpreted as

"errors." In other words, there is the hope, on the one hand, of universal access to sensibility and the euphoric description of the "source inexhaustible of all that's precious," effectively denying any necessity for other sources of virtue. At the same time, there is also the disturbing evidence that the majority not only lack "generous" feeling but also misunderstand those who possess it. As the passages suggest, this internal tension does not tend to lead to moderation in the culture of sensibility; in fact, it frequently leads to defensiveness or self-righteous declarations.

It is not only the external world that lacks sensibility: the second passage reveals a second underlying fear that "generous cares beyond myself" are difficult to achieve, even for the man of feeling himself—a fear that altruism cannot actually exist in the face of human solipsism. Sterne's phrase "beyond myself," spoken by Parson Yorick, exhibits the defensive tone of sensibility—suggesting both the general absence of "generous cares" and sensibility's foundational insecurity. It is thus defensive optimism that frequently leads to sensibility's characteristically demonstrative outbursts of enthusiasm. Conveniently, sensibility's totemic tears express both joy and sadness and thus provide the single most common signifier of virtue within the culture of sensibility. The bi-valence of tears and sensibility's penchant for tragicomedy enable authors to avoid taking a stand on the difficult issue of just how natural, how powerful, and how pervasive such generous care for others actually is.

The same impulses that shape sensibility's unremitting portrayal of virtue in distress, as well as its weeping, high-blown expressions of sentimentalism in passages such as those above, also inform the aesthetic and ethical position that shaped much of the literary art and material culture of the late eighteenth century. As a direct "sensorium," or private, spontaneous source of morality requiring no education or other external sanction, sensibility provided a way of justifying the individual's independence from the authority of reason and lack of need for centralized political power, as well as justifying a liberation from social and ethical norms. Yet the concept of sensibility grew to entail precise norms of its own—as well as a moral and aesthetic, if not political, authority of its own—that permeated Europe during the second half of the eighteenth century.[2]

PLACING SENSIBILITY

The exaggerated pathos of sentimental literature invites theatrical displays of streaming tears and drenched handkerchiefs and seems to warrant the epithet "*cult* of sensibility," a derogatory term sometimes used to refer to the literary, artistic, and philosophical culture surrounding the "man of feeling" in the latter half of the eighteenth century.[3] The term "cult" both indicates the extreme devotion of adherents to the aesthetic surrounding sensibility, and simultaneously marks it as a secret and seemingly arbitrary sign system

Le Barbier l'aîné del.   1786.   Delvaux sculp.

O Rousseau ! ô Richardson, où êtes-vous !

Figure 1

to which adherents pay homage. Figure 1, for example, a frontispiece from a novel of sensibility, written in French, which imitates Laurence Sterne's *A Sentimental Journey,* includes many of the most common signifiers of sensibility: rags, beauty, a tear-drenched handkerchief, and a "philanthropic posture" on the part of the traveler who witnesses a tearful, bittersweet scene. The prospective reader of François Vernes' *Le Voyageur Sentimental* (1786) therefore knows from the frontispiece alone the philosophical, moral, and aesthetic position that the novel espouses. The caption, "Ô Rousseau! Ô Richardson, où êtes-vous?" [Oh, Rousseau! Oh, Richardson, where are you?] suggests that the names of these authors of the culture of sensibility have received cult status, so that their names alone can function as signs of sensibility even *within* the fictions. The devotion to sensibility and its signs can perhaps be measured by the number of poems and paintings entitled "Sensibility" that appeared in the second half of the century as well.

Beyond placing sensibility in the second half of the eighteenth century, there has been little agreement about the exact dates to attach to the cultural movement, apart from saying that it is "linked to both the Enlightenment and Romanticism but distinct from them."[4] Geographically diffuse and lacking a specific manifesto or concrete set of goals, the culture of sensibility may indeed seem overly amorphous to deserve a single epithet; Northrop Frye's term "the Age of Sensibility," more recently resurrected by Jessica Riskin, may appear to oversimplify the issues of periodicization. Many scholars have used terms like the culture of sensibility (G. J. Barker-Benfield), the counter-culture of sensibility (Syndy M. Conger), the cult of sensibility (Janet Todd), or simply spoken of sensibility as a single movement for the purposes of argument (Louis Bredvold).[5] On the one hand, there are scholars who are engaged in extending the earlier boundary to accommodate what they view as central features or exemplars of sensibility: such scholars have described sensibility as a subset of Enlightenment, including Riskin's recent work on medical discourse in sensibility, where she convincingly argues that French and American Enlightenment thought was imbued with the language and philosophy of sensibility. Other scholars, on the other hand, are engaged in extending the later boundary, not only those who prefer the term Preromanticism to sensibility, but also scholars such as Julie Ellison, who has claimed that Romanticism itself is an episode within sensibility. For the purposes of this study, I have focused on literary texts and other artifacts constructed between 1750 and 1800 to allow for samples of sensibility at its prime, as well as a glimpse of its subsequent decay.

In Germany, Preromantic movements in music have been separated into "Sturm und Drang" (represented by artists such as Joseph Haydn) and the "Empfindsamer Stil" (represented by artists such as C. P. E. Bach). There is a similarly complex relationship between "Sturm und Drang," the "Früh Romantik," "Empfindsamkeit," and the Jena school of Romanticism in literature and philosophy. While it will not be a goal of this volume to untangle this web of movements, most scholars would name the "Sturm und Drang" or "Storm and Stress" movement as the most conspicuous manifestation of Preromanticism in German literature, featuring the extremely influential *Die Leiden des jungen Werthers* [*The Sorrows of Young Werther*] by Goethe (1774).[6] In France, Preromanticism also has numerous manifestations, including "Sensibilité," the *roman sensible,* and the *comédie larmoyante,* exerting influence over French literary styles in both the novel and theater.[7] In English literature, Preromantic manifestations include both sensibility and the Gothic (or Gothick)—largely overlapping, yet seemingly distinguishable movements.[8] In fact, the novel of sensibility postulated here encompasses the literature which Patricia Meyer Spacks divides into two groups in her recent book, *Novel Beginnings*: the novel of consciousness and the novel of sentiment. It is not possible here to distinguish between these many Preromantic cousins, nor is it a central purpose to establish the culture of sensibility in relation to the broader historical movement of Romanticism; instead this study will focus on sensibility, primarily in the English novel of 1750–1800, but also as sensibility is manifested in the prose fiction of French "Sensibilité" and of German "Sturm und Drang." Representative novelists include Laurence Sterne, Henry Mackenzie, Charlotte and Henry Brooke, Charlotte Smith, Frances Sheridan, and Mary Wollstonecraft in England and Scotland; Johann W. Goethe, Jean Paul (Johann Paul Friedrich Richter), E. T. A. Hoffman, Wilhelm Heinse, and Karl Philipp Moritz in Germany; and Jean-Jacques Rousseau, l'abbé Prévost, Jean-François Marmontel, and Bernardin de Saint Pierre in France.

If it is true that from mid-century to the 1770s, the culture of sensibility was predominantly shaped by the novel of the time, then it is also the case that it was largely shaped by *foreign* novels in translation. In the recent *Encyclopedia of the Romantic Era,* for example, Gary Kelly argues that it was the translation into English of Rousseau, Prévost, and Bernardin de Saint-Pierre (among others) that spurred sensibility in England, while Robert J. Frail argues that it was the translation of Defoe and Richardson (along with the poets Thomson and Young) into French that spurred Preromanticism in France. In fact, as French "Anglomanie" intensified after 1750, English novels appeared by the hundreds and such frenchified English novels were often called "le genre triste."[9] François Vernes' *Le Voyageur Sentimental* (1786) exemplifies this cultural ebb and flow: a clear imitation of Laurence Sterne's *A Sentimental Journey* (1768), it was first published in France, then translated into English, and became popular in England as *Louis and Nina* (1789).[10] As novels of sensibility swept Europe in the 1760s and 1770s at the height of the movement, Werther and Julie became household names in England, and Clarissa and Yorick became familiar presences in Germany and France, as well as in England. Within the literature of sensibility, the dominant genres tended to be poetry, drama, and especially the budding novel. Interestingly, most literary studies of sensibility have focused on poetry, neglecting the innovations shaping narrative prose during the eighteenth century.

One of the most apparent features of the eighteenth-century novel is the experimentation with fragmentation: one can readily find novels ending mid-sentence, "fragments" published by fictional editors, radical experimentation with typography and the printing press, and the generally episodic character of plots in the first half of the century. Fragmentation takes on a new tone in the second half of the century, when the culture of sensibility starts defining narrative closure and even plot-driven engagement as antithetical to sensibility. The reader of Mackenzie's *Man of Feeling,* for example, is taught that readers of sensibility are expected to differentiate themselves from those who "may have expected the intricacies of a novel": instead of being driven by an anticipation of the resolution of intricate plots, the reader of sensibility will be satisfied with "mutilated passages" or "a few incidents in a life undistinguished, except by some features of the heart."[11] In novels of sensibility, the basic narrative unit changes to the episode or fragment—the discrete image, tableau, or situation that evokes feeling rather than eliciting a desire for sustained narrative or closure. The structural manifestations of sensibility in the novel thus include the non-narrative features that purposely create gaps and fissures for readers to fill.

The other most apparent arena for experimentation in the novel is the role of the narrator and its relation to the author's voice. The increased use of the self-conscious narrator is particularly significant for understanding the growing self-reflexivity and concerns about the difficulties of self-representation that helped shape narrative techniques of the literature of sensibility, including first-person narratives, imbedded letters, fictionalized memoirs, self-conscious narrators, imbedded tableaux, and content with a deeper psychological edge. Basically, the idea of authorial omniscience becomes inimical to sensibility; such omniscience, as a form of inauthentic control or central authority, ceases to carry either credibility or prestige. The skepticism surrounding omniscience elicits further literary innovation, particularly in narrative prose rather than lyric poetry or drama.[12] For example, authors experiment with ways of distancing the story from the seeming artifice of the narrator; at times the paradoxical technique is to highlight artifice for the sake of achieving a shared sense of authenticity. Unlike lyric poetry, where there tends to be less distinction between narrating and experiencing voices—less distinction between the personae of protagonist, narrator, and implied author—the novel invites the performance of a theater of self-consciousness, suitable to the self-reflexive nature of sensibility.[13]

As McGann describes it, sensibility is "a momentous cultural shift whose terms . . . all but founded the novel, and . . . produced an upheaval in the way poetry was conceived and written."[14] This is however not a new opinion: scholars as diverse as Arthur Lovejoy, Erwin Panofsky, Christopher Hussey, M. H. Abrams, Martin Battestin, Michel Foucault, Charles Rosen, and Charles Taylor, have all located a highly significant aesthetic and philosophical watershed at the midpoint of the eighteenth century. Although the interpretations of this shift vary, all these authors describe the movement away from a confidence in neoclassical symmetry and order towards a new interest in asymmetry and irregularity, whether this be manifested in the growing importance of the passions and autobiography in moral philosophy and conceptions of the self; the vogue for the English garden across Europe; the renewed interest in mountains, cliffs, and fossils; chromaticism and dissonance in music; or the growing importance of spectatorship and acting, even in theology. In the aesthetic terms of Edmund Burke, or of landscape gardening, sensibility is involved more with the serpentine curves and studied irregularity of the picturesque than with the awe-inspiring and precipitous sublime: it does not yet open up the realm of the monstrous, characteristic of Romanticism *per se*.[15]

The developments in the novel thus relate to concurrent trends in moral philosophy, philosophy of language, and aesthetics. The rise of empiricism, the growing distrust of unaided reason, the elevation of the passions—especially as guides to moral behavior, and a new faith in the natural goodness of mankind, as well as an increasing emphasis on the faculties of sympathy and imagination—combined to shape the drastically new moral self which accompanied sensibility. Each of these features reflects an underlying philosophical insecurity that is expressed in a number of ways: in the contradictory assertions of optimism and pessimism, in odd combinations of radicalism and conservatism, and in ambivalence about whether order and system are fundamentally desirable and necessary or destructive forces in their own right.

Taken in this context, the remarkable innovations in narrative form show how the ruin as dominant motif of the period affected the history of the novel as well as many other aspects of material culture.[16] Just as authors of novels of sensibility develop a new cluster of narrative techniques that are suitable for embracing ruination and working against traditional narrative authority located in an omniscient narrator, landscapers of the gardens of sensibility also develop similar strategies to engage their viewers. Gardens have their own narratives, their own syntax, as we will see, and as taste in narration changes, the new aesthetic affects both art forms. The central purpose of this book is thus to illustrate a structural parallel between the shape of the novel of sensibility and the shape of the landscape architecture of the English garden—both of which reveal a similar ambivalence regarding the nature and necessity of externalized authority. By connecting the visual and verbal landscapes of sensibility and positing a "rhetoric of ruins" that applies to the novel of sensibility as well as to the so-called English landscape garden, this book will show not only that viewing a ruined tower or a melancholy object in an English garden shares emotional effect, dynamic, and structural strategies with the act of reading a novel of sensibility, but also that these similarities stem from a common drive to *fragment* works of art.

Completion and explicit authority or control were rendered not only suspect and aesthetically unpleasing, but also morally inferior by the fundamental philosophical stance of the culture of sensibility. This framework helps us understand the development of the curiously truncated, artificial ruins, called follies, that started appearing in pleasure gardens all over northern and central Europe, as well as the remarkably innovative narrative strategies developed by novelists of sensibility that include multiple frames of fictional editorship. Purposeful ruination, therefore, is one prominent technique within the culture of sensibility that shaped composition in both literature and landscape gardening. Both architects and authors addressed twin goals: to create a "publishable," coherent monument or volume and also to fragment their creation. They thereby both mask the creator's role and evoke greater emotional participation in the reader or viewer, appealing to insecurity and contradictory impulses through their paradoxical constructions.

This simultaneous optimism and pessimism regarding human possibilities results in important literary and architectural experimentation during the culture of sensibility. Ambivalence takes on new importance in this context, particularly ambivalence regarding the possibilities of human enterprise. The new structures—fragmented narratives imbedded with multiple tableaux and multiple fictitious editors on the one hand, and fictitiously ruined buildings called follies or fabriques on the other—represent optimism and pessimism in a way that appears mutually contradictory.

The novel of sensibility and the folly thus share a number of traits and purposes that will inform the argument of the subsequent chapters. They both reflect the attempt to imbue ruination with moral superiority that is portrayed in Chapter One, as well as a cultural mistrust of language itself— whether of its abuse or of its natural inadequacies. Both structures also appeal to the contradictory desires for monumentalism and for ruination that become the subject of Chapter Two; they also reflect an ambivalence regarding the authority to construct and about authorship in general; and they involve a pretense about their original (fictitious) discovery, rather than purposeful construction. Understood from a literary perspective, both structures reflect a societal preference for a myriad of non-narrative and anti-narrative techniques that can temper narrative drives and involve readers and spectators in an active role, completing and interpreting the fragments as co-authors or co-architects—the subject of Chapter Three. We also consider how each structure paradoxically develops an elaborate pedagogy of its own, teaching readers and viewers how to see and to feel. A common thread among these shared traits is the philosophical insecurity of the culture of sensibility—trustful in theory yet suspicious in practice—even of the motives of its own adherents (and readers). Finally, in Chapter Four, we consider the social cost of this purposeful ruination when it includes human ruin and gives aesthetic preference to women in distress. Before proceeding to the structure of the folly and the novel of sensibility, however, it is important to describe the role of the "picturesque" in establishing changing cultural and aesthetic expectations of the landscape garden, the characteristic psychology of the man of feeling who inhabits both the English garden and the novel of sensibility, and the challenges of narrating sensibility.

COMPOSING THE PICTURESQUE

Whereas twentieth- or twenty-first-century critics would think of landscape gardening, philosophy, and novel writing as very separate realms of discourse, involving different agents, this was generally far from the case in the eighteenth-century. Alexander Pope's gardening style influenced subsequent garden design as much or more than his poetry influenced future poetry; Adam Smith, in addition to achieving fame across Britain and Europe for his *Theory of Moral Sentiments,* also subscribed to the newest publications of William Chambers on oriental gardening and spoke about gardening and architecture styles in his lectures; Capability Brown, one of the most well-known commercial landscape gardeners, conversed with Hannah More, poetess of sensibility, about the similarity of their arts and respective "compositions"; Jane Austen read the writings of William Gilpin, popularizer of the picturesque style of drawing and traveling, and featured contemporary debate over landscape gardening in her juvenilia and novels; and historian-politician Horace Walpole was at least as well known for his thoughts on gardening and his own architectural follies as he was for his political opinions. In short, novels, poets, philosophers, and politicians in the second half of the eighteenth century showed great interest in and knowledge of landscape gardening, and landscape gardeners conversed with poets, philosophers, and kings in their turn, widely published illustrated plans of their gardens, writing influential and popular treatises, and affording a common topic of conversation among the middle classes, regardless of whether the conversants could afford the landscapers' expensive services.

In a remarkable passage, the landscaper Lancelot "Capability" Brown reports a conversation with Hannah More, poetess of sensibility, about the similarities between their art forms. Brown, one of the most well-known landscapers in the "English" style that dominated England and Europe during the mid-to-late eighteenth-century, describes his art in terms of authorship and punctuation. Rather than referring to God's having composed landscape in authoring the Book of Nature, Brown says that he himself 'composes' a landscape much as More would a verse or a sentence: "Now there, said he, pointing his finger, I make a comma, and there, pointing to another part (where an interruption is desirable to break the view) a parenthesis—now a full stop, and then I begin another subject."[17] Elsewhere Brown writes that he has a "Capability" of improving landscape to tell a story just as authors shape individual scenes in a novel.[18] Brown's comments attribute to gardens a syntax and narrative; he assumes the viewer's active participation and expectations that are capable of punctuation and fragmentation.

Although Pope had claimed that the word 'picturesque' was first adopted from the French, modern scholarship has shown that it first came to English through the Italian language and Italian painters, and achieved its full meaning in England circa 1740. Christopher Hussey, an early historian of the picturesque aesthetic, describes the designation as follows: "The relation of all the arts to one another, through the pictorial appreciation of nature, was so close that poetry, painting, gardening, architecture and the art of travel may be said to have been fused into a single 'art of landscape.' The combination might be termed 'The Picturesque.'"[19] Subsequently codified in the 1770s by William Gilpin and later elaborated by Sir Uvedale Price and Richard Payne Knight, the picturesque achieved a prominence in theoretical debates after the 1760s and 1770s that lasted well into the nineteenth century.[20]

The so-called *"cult* of the picturesque" celebrated obscure, concealed, and ruined scenes in nature that could evoke strong feelings in viewers trained in "picturesque travel." Thus the picturesque fondness for commanding vistas, crumbling ruins, and irregular terrain achieved totemic power and shared much of the culture of sensibility's philosophical and cultural heritage. In garden architecture and landscape gardening, the category of the picturesque grew alongside the preference for the irregularity and informality of the English garden over the French baroque garden. Depending on the garden and its owner, picturesque gardens might also be called English gardens, modern gardens (coined by Horace Walpole), natural gardens (terms used by both Walpole and Jean-Marie Morel), informal gardens, or irregular gardens (the latter term sometimes confused with rococo style).[21]

In the arts, 'sensibility' and 'sentimental' refer primarily to written works of poetry and novels evoking sympathy and melancholy in the reader, while the 'picturesque' usually refers to visual scenes, whether natural or artificial, that evoke strong feelings in the viewer. And yet in some domains, such as music, both terms could be used to designate characteristic styles. The unity of the arts, however, was asserted from all corners of the culture of sensibility—not only by such 'sentimental' thinkers as Lessing, or in Capability Brown's remarks above, but also in sensibility's own attempt to escape from language's linearity into a more visually-based, emotive, 'natural' language. In addition, adherents of both "cults" used visual imagery and tableaux to train the eyes of followers—whether to identify picturesque scenery or exhibitions of true sensibility. These all suggest that sensibility and the picturesque were intimately intertwined. The novel of sensibility strove to be "picturesque" just as the picturesque movement relied heavily on the moral aesthetic of sensibility.[22] Surprisingly, there has been almost no attempt to compare these two "cults" and to consider whether they were perhaps representative of broader characteristics of a common *culture* of sensibility.[23]

SEEKING AUTHENTICITY

Whether we examine Shaftesbury's gentleman of taste; Hume and Smith's man of sympathy or moral sentiments; Rousseau, Voltaire, and Diderot's "homme naturel"; Mackenzie's man of feeling; Sterne's sentimental traveler; or Goethe's "schöne Seele," the new literary hero of the culture of sensibility exhibits certain essential attributes: these include an unspoiled natural virtue based on an unusually deep capacity to feel, a susceptibility to sights of beauty or suffering, a lack of worldly success or recognition, and a sense of isolation stemming largely from the insufficiency of conventional language to convey his emotions. The traits are all secondary to the suspicion of centralized authority, whether construed in political, psychological, cultural, religious, or aesthetic terms, and the desire to achieve an authenticity defined in opposition to conformity to authority. Together these traits help shape the ethics, epistemology, and attitudes towards friendship and intimacy, as well as attitudes towards language exhibited within the culture of sensibility. They help us identify a family resemblance among men of feeling and women of sensibility.

The protagonists of sensibility reject reason as a guide to moral behavior; instead their authors show that their purity and feelings (especially sympathy) are superior guides to moral behavior. This results in a new psychology that relies on contested notions of natural goodness. In direct opposition to classical and Enlightenment thought, feeling takes the place of reason as the supreme human faculty; feeling rather than reason thus provides the only hope of community within the tenets of sensibility.

After John Locke establishes to an unprecedented degree the importance of the senses and the passions to the process of "thinking," [24] Anthony Ashley Cooper, the third Earl of Shaftesbury, often taken as the official philosopher of sensibility, began to substitute an 'ethics of feeling' for the dominant 'ethics of rationalism.' Confident that human beings could achieve both virtue and happiness by harmonizing their passions and by cultivating the delicacy and aristocratic nobility of "taste," Shaftesbury showed the limits of faculties like judgment, unaided reason, and conscience based on discipline: "After all," he wrote, "'tis not merely what we call principle, but . . . taste which governs men . . . Even conscience, I fear, such as is owing to religious discipline, will make but a slight figure where this taste is set amiss." [25] Accordingly, weakness of discipline, principle, and conscience and their inability to spur appropriate action become key themes in the literature of sensibility.

Following Shaftesbury, philosophers such as Hume, Smith, and Rousseau all carefully exclude unaided reason from their discussion of virtue; they achieve this by displaying the inherent weakness of unaided reason and by taking additional steps to raise the passions to an exalted status previously held exclusively by reason. Hume, for example, writes that only passion can oppose passion, just as "morality . . . is more properly felt than judg'd of." [26] The most shocking aspect of Hume's philosophy was not so much his claim that reason generally does not control the passions or ethics, but rather his refusal of the idea that reason *should*. Law, reason, and discipline cannot move us to virtue; only such *virtuous passions* as sympathy and benevolence can do so: "Our sense of duty always follows the common and natural course of our passions." [27]

In order to endow itself with greater authority, the ethics of feeling borrows the phraseology of the rationalist philosophy it contradicts:

Conscience, conscience! Instinct divin, immortelle et céleste voix, guide assuré d'un être ignorant et borné, mais intelligent et libre; juge infaillible du bien et du mal, qui rends l'homme semblable à Dieu; c'est toi qui fais l'excellence de sa nature et la moralité de ses actions; sans toi je ne sens rien en moi qui m'élève au-dessus des bêtes, que le triste privilège de m'égarer d'erreurs en erreurs à l'aide d'un entendement sans règle, et d'une raison sans principe.

[Conscience! divine instinct, immortal and celestial voice; the certain guide of a being which, ignorant and limited, is yet intelligent and free . . . without thee I feel nothing in myself which can raise me above the beasts except the melancholy privilege of wandering from error to error with the help of an unruly understanding and an unprincipled reason.][28]

In order to achieve this socialization and normatization of the passions, a singular noun—'feeling' or 'sensibility'—replaces the chaotic plurality of the term 'passions,' with the desired appearance of concord or even unanimity. And conversely, instead of referring to the singular faculty "Reason," authors begin to speak of plural thoughts called "reasons"— namely, rationalizations or cold, selfish, and ultimately divisive arguments leading to the fragmentation of society, rather than providing a unifying recourse to the common language of logic and truth.[29] The latent question of whether this change is a superficial delusion or an actual refinement intensifies the philosophical insecurity of the culture of sensibility.[30] In other words, it is unclear how the passions show themselves worthy of this new 'liberation' from externalized sources of authority and why this inner impulse does not degenerate into random subjectivity, solipsism, or utter chaos. The novels of sensibility in the following chapters illustrate the tenet that the passions alone can establish unity among kindred, sensitive souls. Whereas in *Genesis* and for the ancients, in other words, reason was a shared source of public unity while passions caused discord and atomization, after what Charles Taylor refers to as the "Deist shift" of the mid-eighteenth century, the only authentic source of unity was accessible largely through the passions. Feeling, rather than *logos,* becomes the human characteristic that separates us from beasts, and even becomes the source of community.

Reason, in the passage cited above, is now the "unprincipled" and wayward force which leads mankind "from error to error" and does nothing to "raise [men] above beasts." The same words could equally well have been applied, even fifty years earlier, to passion. Such substitutions demonstrate sensibility's philosophical insecurity in that the appearance of revolutionary thought is qualified by or muted by the limited change in syntax, suggesting a fearful retention of the older paradigm. What I call "philosophical insecurity" is thus a complex of doubt, assertion, and denial: it is a vocal clinging to optimism regarding human nature, or government, or the nature of authority that in its very enthusiasm reveals an underlying (and stimulating) layer of doubt.[31]

Underlying sensationist thought and the search for alternatives to reason as a regulating force, are larger philosophical and political issues—particularly a hidden fight against externally imposed authority in favor of the authority and primacy of individual experience.[32] Sensationist thinkers such as Condillac, responding to empiricist philosophers such as Locke, attempt to confound various sources of arbitrary power (in France, especially the Roman Catholic church). Implicit in the debates over psychology and the passions is also a debate over governmental structure—the state as the soul "writ large."

Disengaged reason and the laws of logic come to represent Hobbes' "common power" to keep all citizens in awe. If private, untutored "sensoria" can provide a moral foundation, then the spontaneous order of the soul can be used to justify freedom from governmental intrusion, and liberation from the tyranny of externalized reason can free one from the necessity of obedience to doctrine. Within the literature of sensibility, therefore, logicians are inevitably villainous—and represent a form of tyranny or social destruction.[33] Within sensibility's rhetoric, to rebel against logic is tantamount to making a broader claim against the injustices of society's institutions.

Reason's fall from favor is also directly related to the decline of 'prudence' as a virtue.[34] The steady devaluation of "the colder homilies of prudence"[35] during the last half of the eighteenth century shows that not only did behavior guided by reason come to be seen as a psychological impossibility, but to attempt such control became positively disreputable (as witnessed by Marianne Dashwood's dispute with her sister Elinor in Jane Austen's *Sense and Sensibility*). The dominant psychological models exhibited in the culture of sensibility thus exhibit a fear that authority, authentic feeling, and virtue cannot coexist in any given individual, as well as doubt as to whether virtuous individuals can ever conform their expressions to the political and social conventions of society without sacrificing their own authenticity and, therefore, their virtue. Prudence, or reasoning about potential behavior in general, became linked to Machiavellianism and to hypocrisy. Reason, established etiquette, logic, self-conscious moderation, and mathematical proportion eventually came to be seen by devotees of sensibility as enemies of the "right inner impulse" that would only be quenched or diffused by such censorship. Eventually, as we shall see in Goethe's *Werther,* any form of control becomes, not only aesthetically unappealing, but inauthentic and therefore morally reprehensible. Thus when Sedaine entitles his *comédie larmoyante* "Philosophe sans le savoir" or "The Unwitting Philosopher," he is not only referring to a particular character in his play, but also alluding to a popular notion within the culture of sensibility: immediate sensation and intuition lead to greater wisdom and virtue than discursive thought or study.[36]

The importance placed on independence from institutional authorities also shows itself in the consistent preference for rural simplicity over urbanity and consumerism, and for original genius over formal education. Across the genres of literature, one can see a growing emphasis on nature, natural simplicity, the ordinary, and everyday rustic life. The new moral aesthetic left no room for more urban forms of virtue: urbane sophistication was untrustworthy; erudition was formed for abuse; civility was another form of dishonesty; and those with education were seen as most skilled in deception. Sensibility thus coincides with a dramatic rise in folklore movements across Europe and Britain. Three works—in the French-speaking world, Rousseau's *Discours sur l'origine et les fondements de l'inegalité parmi les hommes* [Discourse on the Origins of Inequality among Men] (1755); in England, Thomas Percy's *Reliques of Ancient English Poetry* (1765); and in Germany, Herder et al's *Von Deutscher Art und Kunst* [Of German Style and Art] (1773)—were especially significant in building a vogue for folk culture and folk literature.[37] Some authors, most notably James Macpherson in his *Poems of Ossian* (1760–63), were so eager to include examples of ancient, untrained, natural simplicity and virtue that they resorted to forgery in order to claim the historical authenticity of their texts and protagonists. Others took to the fields to find poems written by talented milkmaids (such as Hannah More's "discovery" of Ann Yearsley, who wrote under the pseudonym Lactilla, Milkwoman of Clifton).

These changes aim to accord virtue equally to all, regardless of class, religion, or education. Sensibility's ethics emphasize the most universal basis of virtue: the body. Because of the notion of a biological basis of emotion and sympathy, the faculty of sight is thus endowed with ethical, didactic, and emotional power—a direct vehicle of communication to other sensitive souls. Rather than by his actions or his principles, the man or woman of feeling is judged by the degree to which his or her nerves are moved by external stimuli such as sights and tales of virtue and suffering. The fall of disengaged reason, the internalization of virtue, and the new emphasis on the spontaneous overflow of passion enable Shaftesbury (and Marianne Dashwood) to claim that a good man "never deliberates . . . or considers of the matter by prudential Rules of Self-Interest and Advantage. He acts from his Nature, in a manner necessarily, and without Reflection."[38] In contrast to Enlightenment or neoclassical thought, where vision's goal is to perceive a rational, eternal order, and in contrast to Romantic thought, where the "inner eye," or what the imagination "sees" often seems more significant than what the eye could witness in daylight, sensibility's use of sight focuses on *affect*—especially the possibility of sympathy evoked by visions of suffering. In fact, this psychology that stresses the ethical, didactic, and emotional effect of the faculty of sight rests upon the foundation of the sensory origin of ideas, first made popular by John Locke, and propagated in literature through the works of Samuel Richardson, Jean-Jacques Rousseau, Laurence Sterne, and others.

If vision looms large as a sense that enables the sensitive soul to sympathize with others, then the nerves figure even more prominently as the conveyors of emotion within the sensitive soul's anatomy. Potential for virtue, in other words, seems to have been proportionate to the functioning of one's nervous system. As a number of excellent studies have shown, preoccupation with bodily mechanisms of emotion and experience stem from Enlightenment materialist epistemology, and much discourse in philosophy and natural science was devoted to finding the biological basis of emotion, particularly as located in the nerves and senses. As a result, novels of sensibility are sprinkled generously with visual tales and tableaux of suffering to serve as stimuli for the virtuous feelings of protagonist and reader alike.

"Far more penetrating than the intellect alone," sensibility's ideal again conveys the notion that reflection no longer has direct contact with the will, and that the passions and nerves carry more potent (eventually even more accurate) information than reasoning. Mary Wollstonecraft describes sensibility as "the result of acute senses, finely fashioned nerves, which vibrate at the slightest touch, and convey such clear intelligence to the brain, that it does not require to be arranged by the judgment."[39] Reliance upon judgment and obedience to rules betoken lack of feeling and lesser worth. Mary Wollstonecraft's Maria, for example, is "too much under the influence of an ardent imagination to adhere to common rules."[40] In another, earlier context (for example in Johnson's *Rasselas*), this description would have been an insult, yet within the culture of sensibility, it is high praise.

Depending on the individual authors, independence from external authority takes on different meanings and can be construed in political, aesthetic, cultural, or religious terms. Authors stress the inadequacies of old hierarchies, praise a reliance on self-taught knowledge, and promote skeptical irreverence towards theories and institutions. In French literature, this often takes the form of freedom from Classicism and its aesthetic regulations, as well as from traditional religious and social constraints. In Germany, it can be seen, for example, in the growing popularity of Pietism, a brand of Protestantism that emphasizes direct communication with a personal deity in preference to mediation by institutions and clergy. These reformist or oppositional aspects of sensibility have led many authors to place sensibility squarely in the camp of French revolutionaries, as did Edmund Burke and other anti-Jacobins in England in the 1760s-80s.[41] The contradictory impulses and philosophical insecurities of sensibility make its political allegiances more difficult to assess, however, as testified by the fact that Burke himself evinces sensibility's moral aesthetics in his writings.[42] The cult of the picturesque has been similarly difficult to pinpoint in its political leanings.[43]

Behind this pursuit of originality and independence from authority and traditional institutions, as I have mentioned, is the haunting dream of natural human goodness and the desire to prove Hobbes wrong in his pessimistic description of human nature. For at least a century beforehand, authors were haunted by Hobbes' challenge to natural sympathy: "Let [any man] consider with himself, when taking a journey, [whether] he arms himself, and seeks to go well accompanied; when going to sleep, he locks his doors; when even in his house, he locks his chests . . . ; what opinion has he of his fellow subjects, when he rides armed; of his fellow citizens, when he locks his doors; and of his children, and servants, when he locks his chests."[44] In our everyday actions, Hobbes suggests, we continually reveal our lack of faith in human goodness.

In contrast, David Hume pens the following rhetorical question: "Would any man, who is walking along, tread as willingly on another's gouty toes, whom he has no quarrel with, as on the hard flint and pavement?"[45] And while Hume, like Shaftesbury, wants the answer to be an emphatic and heartwarming "no," the literature and indeed history of the time suggest otherwise, and his rhetorical formulation allows for an element of doubt as well. In fact, according to the odd workings of the moral-aesthetic associated with sensibility, the sight of human suffering or of architectural ruins of ancient grandeur can paradoxically enhance the viewer's sense of human goodness. Similarly, in more philosophical writings, writers of sensibility frequently minimize the threshold for virtue in their euphoric optimism; yet the same authors also idealize the beauty and, more tellingly, the rarity of this goodness with an almost disabling pessimism. As a result, the beautiful Shaftesburian soul, or in Germany "die schöne Seele," is often distinguished precisely by its rarity and isolation in the midst of a Hobbesian universe.

The enemies to virtue have changed, in other words, along with its redefinition in sensibility's new Adam. Sterne, for example, emphasizes the physical basis of natural goodness—the common conception that the physical impulses of sensibility are imbedded in human nature, and are the key to sociability and brotherhood.[46] They do not need a "common power" to bring them into action; rather they are naturally effective for the common good. Sterne's Yorick claims, for instance, that he hopes he will continue to be "in love with one princess or another" the rest of his life, for he is convinced that "if [he] ever do[es] a mean action, it must be in some interval betwixt one passion and another . . . The moment I am rekindled, I am all generosity and good will again."[47] The sensual, if not erotic, passion that prompts many of Yorick's digressions is not the locus or origin of sin in Sterne's world, for each digression betokens fellow-feeling, whether or not it includes an erotic admixture. In a sense, then, the smooth-functioning of the sensitive and moral self becomes the new microcosm of providential order, which itself expands to incorporate the irregularities of nature and even economics.

The American and French revolutions, occurring as they did during this period, provided a test case for Hobbes' and Hume's theories, and were therefore viewed with particular interest, since they presumably served as an indicator of individuals' and states' ability to govern themselves and regulate selfish passions without a "common power" in place. The more capable human beings are of creating order without external authority, or the more naturally good human beings are, the easier it is to deny Hobbes' theory and its ramifications. The revolutions' mixed results—the relative success of the American Revolution and the Terror following the French—fueled both the hopes and fears of sensibility and prevented the possibility of using contemporary political experiments simply to prove Hobbes right or wrong, resulting in a profound ambivalence about the nature and necessity of authority.

The rarity or scarcity of natural goodness and authentic feeling was denoted in a number of ways, including the drive to look further and further afield for its exemplars. Eventually, the published accounts and illustrations of Captain James Cook's and Louis Antoine de Bougainville's initial voyages to the South Pacific gave additional fodder to the hope of finding untainted natural goodness elsewhere, if not at home. Finally we end up with an ironic return to a universe that seems strikingly Hobbesian, as the "sensitive soul" or man of feeling becomes increasingly rare and embattled.[48] Authors of novels of sensibility thus felt pressure to portray heroes who were also victims of society—Shaftesburian souls, forlorn in a Hobbesian universe. In other words, sensibility reacts against civilization, its unnatural hierarchies, and artificial aristocracy, yet it also establishes a new, elaborate, exclusive aristocracy of its own.

NARRATING FAILURE

If one of the primary features of the psychology of the man or woman of feeling is the assumption of the impossibility of the coexistence of authority, authentic feeling, and virtue in any given individual, a second feature is a doubt in the possibility that virtuous people can conform their expressions to the political and social conventions of society. According to this notion, good men do not tend to rise to positions of political or social power, partly because they are too authentic to make good orators. Generally the protagonist is a "sensitive soul" or a "man of feeling" who is placed in conflict with either "men of the world" (who think mostly of worldly gain), or the prototypical Enlightenment "man of letters" (who argues with great faith in reason, but little heart). Unlike protagonists in many other cultural movements, his virtue is actually underscored by his weakness in other traditional roles: he possesses neither prudence, public authority, oratorial powers, martial skill, nor physical prowess. When he addresses broader political or societal problems (such as Harley's reflections on India and the Jamaican slave trade, or Werther's on the treatment of insanity), he does so silently and with no external effect. We will return in Chapter Four to the issue of whether female protagonists of sensibility are equally able to satisfy this moral aesthetic; suffice it to say for now that the male protagonists were more striking because the role of 'man of feeling' was more overtly opposed to normative conceptions of masculinity, whereas many of the characteristics described here were stereotypically considered as 'feminine' traits.

Fictional heroes and heroines in the second half of the eighteenth century frequently share great difficulty expressing their deep, naturally virtuous feelings in the conventional public language of society. The one who writes well or writes clearly must also be guilty of artifice or vice—manifestations of the mortal sin of "lack of feeling." We can therefore also have a character like Werther, who complains repeatedly about his inability to express himself: what may at first sound modest, is actually self-congratulatory, for only one whose feelings are naturally deep, mercurial, and bountiful can "outrun" words. A strong sense of this new sin is common among many of the authors treated in this volume: Diderot, Rousseau, Bernardin, Sterne, Mackenzie, Goethe, and Austen. Rousseau, Voltaire, and Diderot's noble savage, Mackenzie's man of feeling, Sterne's sentimental traveler, and Goethe's Werther, all share a great difficulty expressing their deep, naturally virtuous feelings in the conventional language of society.[49] In fact, their difficulty speaking becomes a measure of their sensibility: in being men of feeling, they are explicitly *not* men of words.

The man of feeling or the woman of sensibility, far from being a good orator, has feelings so keen and delicate that words inevitably fail to do them justice. As the narrator of Henry Mackenzie's *Man of Feeling* writes: "We would attempt to describe the joy which Harley felt on the occasion, did it not occur to us, that one half of the world could not understand it though we did; and the other half will, by this time have understood it without any description at all."[50] In such passages, the necessity of speech can function as a gesture of exclusion or despair. Rather than being simply an attempt to gain understanding or community through explanation, the very urge to explain reveals a lack of transparency as well as of intimacy. Because of a growing distrust of the referential and communicative powers of language, spectacle and fragmentary communication are sought as an antidote to solipsism, melancholy, and madness.

Yet the philosophical suspicion of oration (and narration) goes even deeper. Under the residual influence of Locke and Condillac, Diderot, Rousseau, and Herder showed that by allowing feelings to be passed through the ordering, but stultifying funnel of discourse, we lose the authenticity of the instantaneous "flash" of feeling. To protect the authenticity of original emotions, sensibility constantly pushes its heroes and heroines towards silence, or draws readers' attention to what is either not said, only partially said, or said in an unfelicitous, desultory, or solecistic manner. Thus, the culture of sensibility seeks to represent through gestures, visual art, and fragmentation what can no longer be articulated through syntactic completion, or with a reliance on logic and discursive reason.

Silence, *per se*, does not satisfy the moral aesthetic of sensibility, and indeed, none of its heroes or heroines are entirely mute (in fact, some are quite garrulous in their own way). Its significance rests in its multivalence, as with the other figures of ruin and tears. Simple silence could convey a dearth of thought or feeling, as well as an abundance. Sensibility's vocabulary is located, paradoxically, in the gaps between words—the sighs, hesitations, stammerings, and fragmentation that demonstrate an individual whose expansive feelings are constrained but refuse to be corrupted by the "artificial" language of society—and in follies, or crumbling monuments, built purposely to arouse greater emotion in viewers as they imaginatively recreate the missing parts of the monument. There must, therefore, be speech for the gaps to punctuate, as well as walls for cracks to puncture. The hero of sensibility and the reader of novels of sensibility must both be adept at the rhetoric of ruins.

DEFINING AMBIVALENCE

In the preceding pages, we have considered the distrust of reason argued most persuasively and rationally by philosophers; the insistence upon natural goodness accessible to all, yet which is poignantly rare and fragile; and the lengthy and voluble, if fragmented, explanations of the insufficiency of language for communication. As this book seeks to establish, sensibility's contradictory impulses consist in a persistent tension between extreme optimism and fearful pessimism, between revolutionary fervor and nostalgic conservatism, between democratic and authoritarian impulses, between egalitarianism and elitism, between virtue as natural and virtue as highly cultivated, between ruins and carefully constructed buildings, and between fragmentation and narrative closure. In most of these cases, sensibility started as a reaction against Enlightenment confidence in the powers of reason and education, but ultimately resulted in an ironic reversal, showing the continuity of family traits by pursuing similar goals under different terms. Literary didacticism, too, continues in masked form—transformed into a pedagogy of seeing and feeling, rather than a pedagogy of abstract reasoning.

As the passions grow reasonable and even moral, the need arises to *cultivate* rather than suppress them. We will see the effects of this trend in the pedagogy of seeing and feeling emphasized both in landscape gardening and the sentimental novel. Sensibility's moral psychology brings with it an emphasis on receptivity or sensitivity to external behavior and sights, whether the landscape garden, the Alps, or the sight of human suffering at home. The new aristocracy and pedagogy of feeling indicate the underlying ambivalence about whether sensibility itself was profoundly "natural"— that is, whether it is defined in opposition to the corrupted, "artificial," cold ways of society, or whether it is a product of great aesthetic refinement.

In other words, despite the moral sense school's attempts to portray virtue as increasingly natural and accessible, virtue actually became rarer and more fragile as the culture of sensibility progressed. Returning again to the epigraphs above, sensibility emphasizes quotidian virtues, accessible to all on the one hand, and on the other, rarity and heroism enter because people of sensibility are defined as being at odds with the presumably more commonplace "men of the world" and "fall into error," if not into ruin. The conflict implied in the epigraph above foreshadows the fate of this new character—one that almost always ends either in ruin or impotence when faced with "men of the world."

In short, the culture of sensibility exhibits a profoundly ambitious and exuberant hope in the natural goodness of human nature and in human attempts to regain a natural innocence, community, and mutual transparency—an exuberance that is simultaneously spurred on and held in check by its haunting fear of human depravity and inescapable isolation.[51] And while such an internal tension might describe other "transitional" moments in history, the culture of sensibility demonstrates innovative responses to its philosophical insecurity in its art, literature, and philosophy.[52]

There are certain philosophical advantages to the dialectic tension within sensibility, which stems from its defensive insecurity. The lack of Romantic or revolutionary univocalism, in other words, is not necessarily a weakness. While sensibility's conflicting impulses may seem hypocritical at times, its heartfelt ambivalence not only distinguishes it from Romanticism, but is also at least partly an enlightened response to the events of the French Revolution and subsequent Terrors.[53] Simultaneously intrepid and fearful, sensibility is an interesting experiment in combining both optimistic revolutionary fervor and conservative nostalgic concerns for order and stability without falling into either disastrous extreme—in political terms, avoiding both anarchy and totalitarianism. Their very ambivalence, built into the structure of these cultural artifacts, may be a key reason that these novels merit serious critical treatment.

MAPPING RUIN

The appeal of ruins in the mid-to-late eighteenth century was based on far more than antiquarian impulses. Chapter One locates ruin mania within a broad desire to rewrite *Genesis* and to debunk Hobbes' pessimism about human nature. Thus we find the roots of the new appreciation of ruins already in the pervasive ideas of natural human goodness. The smooth functioning of the passions allows the self to become the microcosm of providential order, and this order expands to incorporate the irregularities of nature. As passions grow both beautiful and moral, so do volcanoes and the jagged cliffs of the Alps. The attitude towards the irregularities of nature shows itself in the changing view of mountains, cleansed of their postdiluvian reputation. Authors thus reclaim *Genesis* with multiple desires: to combine utopian ambition with a desire to reverse the ethical and aesthetic judgments based on old testament readings and on skeptical philosophies such as Hobbes', while still retaining the sanction of biblical authority.

Chapter Two turns from the general topoi of irregularity and ruination to a particular kind of ruin: the folly. In focusing on the mutually illuminating juxtaposition of the fascination with these fake ruins on the one hand, and the purposeful fragmentation of the novel of sensibility on the other, this chapter draws parallels between the architectural style of Thomas Whately and the "rhetoric of ruins" employed by Laurence Sterne and J. W. Goethe. For architects, the building of fake ruins is problematic in that it challenges one central aspect of their traditional vocation—to build structures that will stand the test of time intact. Instead the architect must aim for deliberate failure. It is also a reversal of the architect's usual role as creator: in building an artificial ruin, creation must disguise itself as discovery, as the architect poses as archaeologist. It is true that, in some sense, all architects use the past, but seldom do they impersonate the hand of time and intentionally unmake what they themselves have made. They must mask the traces of their own artistry and industry, with ruination, irregularity, and the mark of time. Follies and novels of sensibility thus both express the desire for order and system coexisting with the relish of spontaneity, or the desire for narration that seeks to hide all traces of narrative authorship.

Chapter Three delves further into the ethical and political implications of the pursuit of the language of nature—whether in landscape gardening and architecture or in the novel. In particular, this chapter treats the cultural and philosophical significance of the use of fictional editors in novels of sensibility and the political implications of the narrative techniques, such as the use of (seemingly insignificant) dashes and asterisks within the narratives. In the process, it sheds light on the importance of spectatorship in the landscape garden and literature of the culture of sensibility, an obsession that culminates in the perceived need for hermits and mannequins to pose as ideal spectators and spectacles, and the false promise of transfer of authority and authorship to readers and viewers when they prove less tractable than mannequins.

Chapter Four focuses on human ruin and sensibility's moral ambiguity regarding suffering. By studying the issue of female narration and the role of an aesthetic category called the "interesting" in sensibility, we can see sensibility's codes of authenticity leading to sadistic extremes, anticipated and ridiculed by Jane Austen. Building on Austen's admiration for one of the founders of the "picturesque" movement, William Gilpin, her multiple allusions to Goethe and Rousseau, and a study of her narrative technique, this chapter reveals how Austen inherits elements of the culture of Sensibility—such as its ambivalence towards authority, completion, and eloquence—and adapts them to suit her own didactic purposes. As an examination of the pursuit of "natural acting" suggests, the paradoxes of sensibility's artificial efforts at appearing natural implode upon themselves, and reveal a fad that extravagantly pursues primitivism and fetishizes female suffering with only the pretense of sympathy, let alone the desire to relieve pain.

1 Redeeming Ruin

And they said, Go to, let us build us a city and a tower, whose top *may reach* unto heaven; and let us make us a name, lest we be scattered abroad upon the face of the whole earth.

—*Genesis* 11:4

There are certain combined looks of simple subtlety— where whim, and sense, and seriousness, and nonsense, are so blended, that all the languages of Babel set loose together could not express them . . .

—Laurence Sterne

Upheaval characterizes many areas of mid-to-late eighteenth century European life. It was not only a time for self-conscious new beginnings, but also a time for recovering (and at times inventing) origins of all kinds—whether the original human language, the state of nature, or the geography of the antediluvian Earth. Events and scientific discoveries reinforced the sense of significant beginnings and endings into a form of millenialist self-importance. Examples include the eruption of the American and French Revolutions and resulting experimentation in nation building; the growing age of exploration and naval discovery; the dawn of the microscope and drastic improvement of the telescope, revealing new worlds both far away and close at hand; and the discovery of the ashen, fiery fates of Pompeii and Herculaneum; as well as the more immediate devastation resulting from the Lisbon earthquake of 1757. It was a time of optimism in widening human achievements and utopian fantasies, as well as sullen reminders of the fragility of peace, innocence, and even civilization itself.

Despite the Lisbon earthquake and the presence of recent ruination from civil war and other natural and human disasters, irregularities and jagged edges became increasingly valuable in the novels and gardens of sensibility. A particularly vivid example is an English garden in Germany—the Garden of Wörlitz, which included two artificial volcanoes

Figure 2

that were added between the years of 1788 and 1792. These volcanoes had lamps and sound effects to enhance the simulated eruptions. These fake eruptions could be seen and admired from great distances (see Figure 2). Such a demonstration suggests not only tolerance of ruin, but also the purposeful mimicking of destruction.

This elaborate domestication of wildness provides an excellent example of the human ambition to frame the terrifying forces of nature for our own aesthetic purposes, even if it means artificially recreating the wildness in order to frame it within the garden as a whole. Unconsciously subscribing to the mental habit of sensibility, including its insecurities, perhaps, landowners and patrons in the culture of sensibility frequently attempt to rise above chaos and above human limitation through art and material culture—even if they must recreate chaos to seek this end.

In his immensely influential *Sacred Theory of the Earth* (1684), written half a century before the first flowering of the literature of sensibility, Thomas Burnet planted some of the seeds of the incipient appreciation of fragmentation and irregularity. In *Theory*, Burnet attempts to explain the phenomena of *Genesis* through scientific language. He describes the original state of God's created Earth, the "Mundane Egg": "In this smooth Earth were the first Scenes of the World, and the first Generations of Mankind; it had the beauty of Youth and blooming Nature, fresh and fruitful, and not a wrinkle, scar, or fracture in all its body; no Rocks or Mountains,

Figure 3

no hollow Caves, nor gaping Chanels, but even and uniform all over . . . 'Twas suited to a golden Age, and to the first innocency of Nature."[1] Subsequently, Burnet movingly portrays mountains as antediluvian reminders of the fallen state of humanity and as decrepit, if awe-inspiring, ruins of the original, smooth perfection of God's creation (Figure 3).[2]

Burnet's thesis regarding the origin of mountains influenced many prominent philosophers in the culture of sensibility, particularly Shaftesbury. His "physico-theological" account was remarkable for using geology rather than allegory as the key to access scriptural truth, for using scripture to look at Nature in terms of its ancient wholeness (anticipating the revisionist aesthetics of sensibility and Romanticism) and for suggesting that we have first-hand access to Eden: "we have still the broken materials of that first world, and walk upon its ruins." Burnet's thesis, strengthened by other aspects of the subsequent culture of sensibility, eventually lent the Alps new glory in their own right (even in their deplorably fragmented state). What were, in the mid-seventeenth century, "Warts, Wens, Blisters, Imposthumes" and "Nature's Shames and Ills," had become "temples of Nature built by the Almighty" and "natural cathedrals, or natural altars."[3]

The redemption of ruination and natural irregularity begs important questions for the culture of sensibility: are the psychological and social equivalents of jagged cliffs, volcanoes, and tempestuous storms equally admirable in human nature? Is it possible that a new confidence in the disruptive, mercurial elements of the self coincides with a new appreciation for irregularity in art and the increase of chromaticism and dissonance in music? If so, then not only are Sterne's Yorick's tingling nerves and fibers key to his virtue, but his passionate eruptions may be as well. The Terror following the French Revolution complicated the new admiration of the passions and its accompanying confidence in human self-determination. Rousseau, Goethe, Herder and other authors attempt to create or reclaim authorizing origins that satisfy emerging democratic impulses by establishing the possibility of self-sufficiency without isolation, of self-government without chaos, and of virtue without external regulation.

Authors within the culture of sensibility, including Rousseau, Goethe, and Herder, reappropriate the stories of the first fourteen chapters of *Genesis* in hopes of validating natural virtue, spontaneity, and irregularity: they reinterpret the expulsion from Eden, the fall of Babel, and the flood by asserting natural goodness; they reclaim the fallen world, its ruins, and its irregularities; and they establish the ethical and aesthetic superiority of ruination—as well as a new pedagogy and new hierarchy under the pretense of eradicating hierarchical relations.[4] There is of course nothing new about reinterpreting Biblical authority to support particular arguments about political or moral philosophy. Thomas Hobbes, for example, uses *Genesis* in his 1651 masterpiece, *Leviathan,* to argue for unlimited sovereign power. In his interpretation of the fall and expulsion from Eden, Hobbes makes an explicit connection to the need for sovereign power to be absolute. Not only do human beings have inescapably selfish tendencies, as well as the "restless desire for power after power, that ceaseth only in death"—tendencies that are displayed whenever there is no "common power to keep them all in awe," but, quoting *Genesis* 3.5 and 3:11, he writes: "it [is] clear that the commands of them that have the right to command, are not by their subjects to be censured, nor disputed." He concludes: "So it appeareth plainly, to my understanding, both from reason and from Scripture, that the sovereign power, whether placed in one man, as in monarchy, or in one assembly of men, as in popular, and aristocratical commonwealths, is as great, as possibly men can be imagined to make it."[5] Despite the fact that it predates the culture of sensibility by more than a century, Hobbes' *Leviathan* provides a theory that devotees of sensibility loved to hate (just as seventeenth-century Latitudinarians had hated it).

Half a century later, in his *Second Treatise on Government* (1690), John Locke relies on textual evidence from *Genesis* to propose a natural human right to private property and a natural inclination towards society. According to Locke, God gave Adam and his descendants the earth—the first emergence of property. The difficulties emerging from property, were, according to Locke, somewhat remedied by the natural human sociability described in *Genesis* 2:18: "God having made man such a creature, that in his own judgement it was not good for him to be alone, put him under strong obligations of necessity, convenience, and inclination to drive him into *society,* as well as fitted him with understanding and language to continue and enjoy it."[6]

Whereas these seventeenth-century authors do not limit God's authority, Rousseau and other eighteenth-century authors involved in the culture of sensibility draw on *Genesis* in order to increase the human sense of self-determination. "La religion nous ordonne de croire que Dieu lui-même ayant tiré les Hommes de l'état de Nature . . . , ils sont inégaux parce qu'il a voulu qu'ils le fussent; mais elle ne nous défend pas de former des conjectures tirées de la seule nature de l'homme et des êtres qui l'environnent, sur ce qu'auroit pu devenir le genre-humain s'il fût resté abandonné à lui-même." [Religion commands us to believe that since God Himself took men out of the state of nature immediately after the creation, they are unequal because He wanted them to be so; but it does not forbid us to form conjectures, drawn solely from the nature of man and the beings surrounding him, about what the human race might have become if it had remained abandoned to itself.][7] Rousseau's separation of belief and conjecture leads to a concomitant separation of scriptural origins and self-actualizing origins.

The eighteenth-century tendency to reinterpret Biblical authority concerning human nature while still wishing for Biblical sanction recalls sensibility's philosophical insecurity. While rebelling, theoretically, against God's Old-Testament authority, the authors in this chapter nonetheless require Biblical authority to make their point. In other words, the point is not so much to prove *Genesis* wrong, as to reinterpret or reappropriate *Genesis* for the purposes of the culture of sensibility. But the desire to reclaim *Genesis* for the culture of sensibility, rather than to disregard it, is itself an expression of philosophical insecurity, using optimism about human nature to assert independence from traditional religious authority, while only half suppressing a lingering fear that human nature may indeed be fallen. Philosophers representing the culture of sensibility felt torn between Christian views of original sin or selfishness and Hobbesian views of human isolation and solipsism on the one hand, and the hope and desire to believe in natural goodness, transparency, self-determination, and the possibility of earthly community and meaningful intimacy, on the other. In order to reclaim *Genesis*' authority to accord with democratic impulses and a sense of natural goodness and transparency, authors influential for the culture of sensibility revise Old Testament stories to diminish the prevailing sense of sin, hierarchy, and of a single, omniscient authority external to the individual agent. As altered myths are sought, and faith diminishes in the classical or Judeo-Christian conceptions of reason and virtue, new popular mythologies "abduct" (in Roland Barthes' terms) signifiers already laden with meaning from familiar and loved cultural contexts into alluring new "mosaic[s] of signs."[8]

As we see in this chapter, authors reappropriate *Genesis* in hopes of validating natural virtue, spontaneity, and irregularity by reinterpreting the expulsion from Eden, the fall of Babel, and the effects of Noah's flood. Prominent authors expound upon the benefits of Noah's flood, which changed the configuration of the earth's surface in favor of irregularity and picturesque adornment and the beauty of the Alps, previously seen as ruins of the Flood and thus reminders of human fallen nature. They also describe an Adam and Eve who withstand original sin and instead can exhibit natural goodness, rely on intuition, and achieve mutual transparency. They question God's felling of the Tower of Babel, yet claim the ability to recreate the original, universal human language of the passions, as well as to recreate new gardens of Eden that allow the new Adams and Eves to indulge in their innocent passions and that enable landscape to speak "the original language of Nature." While the search for the origin of language and the "Ursprache" by no means originated in the second half of the eighteenth century, it did however change its character from searching for the rational, philosophical perfection desired by Leibniz to the uncensored authenticity of the "wilde Mutter" described by Herder.

In other words, as this chapter progresses from archaeological and geological ruin, to purposeful fragmentation in landscape gardening, to attempts to reclaim the language of nature in human conversation, we will see that these seemingly disparate traditions evince a similar objective. In these disparate domains, a similar dynamic takes place: the culture of sensibility tacitly redeems and elevates an aesthetic of ruination and fragmentation as a symbol of new hope in human nature and new democratic aspirations. The devastation described in *Genesis* is reclaimed in favor of the picturesque, while God's jealous authority is dampened in favor of decentralization and in order to give human beings a less subordinate position *vis-à-vis* God. Yet the frames and the sheer artifice of the resolutions still reveal the doubts haunting sensibility's more revolutionary ideals.

TOURING RUIN, COLLECTING RUIN

Most eighteenth-century Grand Tours led to Rome via the Alps and the Appenini, which were also described as "*Ruins* of a broken World"—that is, of an antediluvian glory.[9] In fact, in eighteenth-century portrayals, ruins and mountains often blend almost indistinguishably, their interpenetration revealing their kindred, ruined nature as well as the overriding importance of an aesthetic of irregularity, disproportion, and fragmentation. Geometric forms and right angles are thus "naturalized" into irregular shapes, as they are overtaken by time and weeds.

This interest in ruins did not originate in the eighteenth century: several popular mid-seventeenth century European painters such as Nicolas Poussin, Claude Lorrain, and Salvator Rosa, as well as numerous poets across Europe, had already helped familiarize the public with ruins as a symbol of *memento mori*. By enhancing their religious and secular paintings with broken arches and porticos as backdrops, they brought Roman ruins "into every cultivated home." In the mid-eighteenth century, however, the fascination with ruins reached manic proportions,[10] and they became a favorite subject for artists and poets throughout France, England, and Germany. Ruins figured prominently in the works of painters such as Gabriel de Saint-Aubin, Hubert Robert, Joseph Vernet, J.H.W. Tischbein, and even the American Thomas Cole. The celebrated engraver Giovanni Battista Piranesi also helped spread the interest, and poets such as John Dyer, William Cowper, Oliver Goldsmith, Johann Wolfgang von Goethe, and William Wordsworth all found the rhetoric of ruins integral to their art.[11] Some well-known painters, such as Hubert Robert and Jean-Honoré Fragonard both consulted on and built artificial ruins in actual estates as well as painted them in their landscapes. Denis Diderot even writes of "la poétique des ruines" which expresses the mood of sensibility.[12]

Men of feeling themselves invoke these painters, as Harley's narrator does in the *Man of Feeling*: "Harley looked on [Edwards] with the most earnest attention. He was one of those figures which Salvator would have drawn; nor was the surrounding scenery unlike the wildness of that painter's backgrounds . . . A rock, with some dangling wild flowers, jutted out above where the soldier lay; on which grew the stump of a large tree, white with age, and a single twisted branch shaded his face as he slept" and so forth for over half a page of minute description, first of the fragmentation, sparsity, and ruggedness of the natural setting, then an equally detailed description of the similarly rugged 'topography' of Edwards' face, which "had the marks of manly comeliness impaired by time; his forehead was not altogether bald, but its hairs might have been numbered." [13]

The ruin industry in mid-eighteenth-century Europe and England and the renowned eighteenth-century "antiquarian impulse"[14] was spurred not only by the Grand Tours to Italy and Greece, but also by the archaeological excavation of ruined Roman cities, notably Pompeii and Herculaneum. These new discoveries brought ruins to the attention of the public eye. Yet, the sources of interest and emotions raised by the destructive forces of ruination were diverse: on the one hand, close contact with vast volcanic destruction intensified philosophical and theological skepticism within the culture of sensibility, yet on the other hand, the vast grandeur of Roman civilization increased interest in ancient achievement. Fossils, especially those excavated from volcanic fields in Italy,[15] provided glimpses of an unrecorded past and drew new interest in Biblical accounts of creation and destruction. In the process, the forces that caused great destruction were redeemed as legitimate arenas of human inquiry.

After having been seen as an ugly reminder of fallen nature, volcanoes, hurricanes, and earthquakes actually grew to be a popular area of study. Whereas, in his 1743 *The Antediluvian World,* Francis Walsh still agrees with Burnet that "this terrestrial Globe as it now appears, is not the first and immediate Work of the Hands of the Almighty, considering its outward Face, Shape and Form, as a thing not suitable to his immense Power, and infinite Goodness, being such an irregular, disordered, and incommodious Piece,"[16] the anonymous author of a 1764 volume of *The Beauties of Nature and Art Displayed, in a Tour through the World* strikingly dedicates a full chapter to "An Historical Account of the most remarkable Earthquakes, Inundations, Fires, Epidemic Diseases, and other Public Calamities . . .," in addition to the sections on "remarkable Mountains, Caves, and Volcano's [sic]."[17] In the latter volume, these destructive forces are included, notably, among "The Beauties of Nature." The topic of these volumes was not idiosyncratic: in the latter decades of the eighteenth century, a flurry of volumes address the geological origins of Earth, physicotheological interpretations of creation,[18] reinterpretations of the first three books of *Genesis,* as well as countless studies of volcanoes and islands as "fragments" from Iceland to Japan.

The titles of some of these volumes demonstrate the Enlightenment confidence applied to these new areas, such as *Sacred Scripture: Theory of the Earth from its First Atom to its Last End* (1798).[19] There was, in other words, a fascination with the grandeur of earth's natural forces and also a popularly driven desire to explain and control these forces—or at least to simulate or domesticate them. William Hooper, M.D., for example, demonstrates the Enlightenment techniques applied towards sensibility's new topoi in his *Rational Recreations, in which the Principles of Numbers and Natural Philosophy are Clearly and Copiously Elucidated by a Series of Easy, Entertaining, Interesting Experiments.* Here, Hooper shows simple household experiments to create one's own volcanoes and earthquakes, and to simulate artificial lightning and other impressive spectacles of nature. Armed with only fifty pounds of a powder made from fresh iron filings and pure sulphur, anyone can create a "true" volcano: just bury it a foot deep under the earth, and "in about eight hours the ground will begin to heave and swell, . . . it will send forth hot sulphureous steams, and at last, bursting into live flames, will form a true volcano."[20] Simulation thus provides the impression of control.

The British Museum also exhibited a particularly impressive display that included a study of volcanoes, samples of basalt rocks and hardened lava from Mt. Vesuvius, as well as a darkened room with lighting behind a transparent painting to simulate a volcanic eruption. It was in fact, this display in 1775, that (along with his Grand Tour, numerous trips to English gardens, and acquaintance with Laurence Sterne) inspired Prince Leopold III Friedrich Franz von Anhalt-Dessau to build his island with artifical volcanoes at Wörlitz.[21] Philosophical debates were heated between "Volcanists" and the "Neptunists" as to the exact role of volcanoes in creation of the Earth, and these debates also informed the choices Franz made in the English Garden at Wörlitz. In choosing to devise a staging of the volcano as a "constructive natural force," Franz was taking the part of the Volcanists who argued that the volcanoes aid in the process of an ongoing, decentralized model of creation, as opposed to the Neptunist argument that accords more with traditional readings of *Genesis* and focused on one, central, historical creative act (125–128).

The example of Wörlitz is significant for many reasons. The English garden of Wörlitz grew to encompass much of the small principality itself, and became known as the "Gartenreich" or "the Garden Kingdom." Franz very self-consciously designed his garden for didactic purposes using the vocabulary of eighteenth-century debates from within the culture of sensibility. In particular, he drew upon the parallels between political thought and landscape gardening: just as he viewed his own state as a "Model for non-state-centred reform"[22] and "minimum state intervention," he wished to differentiate himself from neighboring principalities with less liberal politics. For this purpose, he adopts the language of the English Garden and of its characteristic fragmentation and decentralization. One of the purposes, then, of re-creating volcanoes was as a symbol of the power of natural forces to create regularity without external control—to create spontaneous order, symbolized by the crystalline, precise architectural columns formed by basalt. To this humanistic end, Franz also displayed a Volcanist text upon a table carved out of lava.[23]

Countless other well-known, mid- and late-century intellectuals, such as Addison, Gray, Walpole, Gibbon, Goethe, and Humboldt, to name a few, indulged in the aristocratic taste for "Grand Tours" and made their pilgrimages to Rome. The often life-changing effects wrought upon these authors by the sight of the ruins of Rome led to a desire to appropriate the ruins and thereby to perpetuate their aesthetic effect at home. Goethe, for example, (who commented on the Neptunist-Volcanist debate in his *Faust*) gathered as many fragments of classical culture as possible during his Grand Tour. The sculptured ornaments that he could not physically transport (because they were not yet sufficiently ruined), he had cast in gypsum: "It is necessary to acquire these invaluable treasures," he wrote, "I am modelling them in clay, in order to appropriate everything."[24] The famous full-length portrait of Goethe by Tischbein (Figure 4) shows the patronizing tendency towards not only appropriation but also domestication of the wild and ruined objects dislocated and framed within walls or boundaries of French, German, or English landscape gardens or estates. Goethe's posture, reclining and dominating the landscape, suggests a comfortable admiration from a superior position. Not only does he admire the objects, he appears to hoard and even recline upon them. The attitudes towards the new appropriations reinforce the insecurity characteristic of the culture of sensibility: on the one hand they lend an aristocratic and colonizing sense of conquest to their possessors, whether in real or artificial artifacts. On the other hand, they serve as a reminder of the hidden destructive power of nature and reminders of the authority and biblical omnipotence of God.

In Britain, *Ruinenlust* led not only to the importation of these classical ruins, fragment by fragment, but also, together with a developing sense of nation and of local history, to a growing aesthetic appreciation of—and search for—local ruins. As specific claims to classical connections were gradually abandoned, interest grew, not only in ruined Gothic churches such as Tintern Abbey, but also in ancient pagan structures such as Stonehenge.[25] The love of local, mostly Gothic, ruins inspired countless literary and artistic responses as well. To see this, one need only consider the number of poetic and pictorial tributes to Tintern Abbey, the growing taste for the Anglo-Saxon elegies of pagan Britain, or the

Figure 4

Ossianic cult of primitive landscape moods and imitations of Stonehenge (such as the Ilton 'Stonehenge' in Yorkshire) that followed the publication of James Macpherson's *The Works of Ossian, Son of Fingal* (more commonly called *The Poems of Ossian*), begun in 1760.

Estate holders aspiring to current fashions imported columns from ruined classical monuments and adapted them into objects of interest in the landscape surrounding their estates. Whereas sixteenth and seventeenth-century architects had been known to use occasional antique effects like dropped keystones or broken pediments as an extension of rustification, eventually fake ruins became a favorite form of architecture in the eighteenth century.[26] The taste for artificial ruins is especially ironic given the fact that ruins had been chosen as a favorite subject for painters in the "picturesque" style because the decaying buildings were thought to blend so *naturally* into the countryside—that is, because human artifice appeared to have been reclaimed or 'naturalized' by nature.[27]

Fake ruins, or purposely truncated monuments sometimes known as *fabriques* or "follies," reached a high level of notoriety and popularity in what is today Britain, France, Germany, Belgium, Poland, Austria, Sweden, Norway, Denmark, Russia, and the Netherlands. All of these areas had significant English-style gardens with follies before 1800.[28] Hubert Robert, a prominent painter of ruins, also became involved in designing actual landscape gardens, including the tomb of Rousseau at Ermenonville; the follies at Méréville and Betz; and Marie Antoinette's hamlet near Versailles, Le Petit Trianon. Several of these gardens and follies still remain intact today.[29] Later, private individuals arranged authentic ruins into inauthentic forms, suggesting local monuments that had never existed, such as those at Ruinenberg, part of the gardens at Sanssouci in Potsdam. Most follies were constructed anew, without access to such expensive architectural fragments fresh from the Campagna, but often with the assistance of some ancient stones or bricks from a nearby ruined castle or abbey that did not have the benefit of an appropriately picturesque location. An example of such a folly would be Sanderson Miller's Gothic sham castle at Wimpole Park, designed in 1750 for Lord Chancellor Hardwicke and built between 1768 and 1772 (Figure 5). The ruins are still visible today, with the large column serving as a view tower.

Barbara Jones defines the folly as "a useless building erected for ornament on a gentleman's estate."[30] One might well wonder what could have induced numerous landowners across Europe in the late eighteenth century to spend large amounts of money constructing these artificially ruined buildings and monuments for their garden estates. In the hands of ancient-regime architects, ruins were often invoked to represent ancient authority: Louis XIV had imported Roman columns *en masse* from Leptis Magnus and grandly put them to use to assert both the ancient basis of his authority and the unlimited nature of his rule. Wherever their location in the culture of sensibility, ruins' appeal rests in double meanings,

Figure 5

intensified by interest in origins and biblical accounts of destruction. In subsequent chapters, we will see that the desire to reappropriate *Genesis* to sensibility's mental habit of ambivalence is also reflected in the desire to find innovative narrative structures for the novel. In all these arenas, the domestication and secularization of ruination, fragmentation, and the irrational aspects of human nature enable viewers (or owners) to feel increased control over cataclysmic events.

CONSTRUCTING EDEN, OWNING EDEN

As the culture of sensibility was preoccupied with reclaiming *Genesis* for its own moral, political, and aesthetic purposes, gardens, too, were reclaimed for secular purposes and separated from their previous status as sacred emblem. Traditionally, as John Prest's interesting study shows, European gardens were modeled after Eden. The garden was square and divided into four quadrants representing the four corners of the world, and in it were planted only the most civilized of plants; erratic and undisciplined flora, such as wildflowers, were disdained. Gradually, as the eighteenth century progressed, gardeners introduced a greater variety of plants and relaxed the strict separation of garden from lawn; the geometric design was nearly completely discarded in the English garden. In so far as most sixteenth- and seventeenth-century European gardens imitated the original garden in *Genesis,* the forbidden tree representing God's authority tended to be in the center of the garden.[31] And since the French style celebrated centralized authority, many seventeenth and eighteenth-century depictions of the Garden of Eden, such as the ones in Figure 6 and 7, used French-style baroque gardening (complete with geometrically arranged parterres) to represent the degree of order and harmony under God's absolute dominion. On the estates of noble and wealthy landowners in France and England, French gardens in the baroque style, however, substitute worldly political authority for divine authority.

The theological and political significance of the shape of gardens was manipulated on both sides of the British Channel, and even on both sides of the Atlantic. In England, the attempt to re-create the Garden of Eden gained new strength and form in the culture of sensibility, as garden walls and the visible fences of the enclosed garden (*hortus conclusus*) were eliminated, and the variety of plantings greatly increased. Prest remarks that as "men's attitudes towards nature changed, . . . gardeners, who had burst the bounds of the *hortus conclusus* either in an optimistic attempt to overcome the consequences of sin, or with the intent to reduce a rebellious people to subjection, began to stress the idea that nature likes variety."[32] With the more redemptive view of nature and human nature, plants such as wildflowers that had been deemed inappropriate or too 'fallen' for the garden, now were reclaimed as suitable to adorn garden landscapes. Similar thoughts led Horace Walpole to praise the garden design of landscape designer Lancelot 'Capability' Brown: "With one lost Paradise the name/ Of our first ancestor is stained;/ Brown shall enjoy unsullied fame/ For so many a Paradise regained."[33] As the postlapsarian and postdiluvian world was reclaimed, the language and content of nature was also decentralized to make it suitable for a more democratic Adam.

The picturesque also mixes older authority with newer ideals, attempting "to win traditional sanctions for a new experience."[34] By the time William Gilpin, one of the mid-eighteenth-century founders of the cult

LA SCENA SI FINGE
NEL TERRESTRE PARADISO.

Iafcuna delle Scene porta in fronte vna figura efpri-
mente al viuo gli affetti , e le cofe che fi contengo-
no in effa . Il gentilifsimo Signor Carlo Antonio
Procaccino , che gentilmente procaccia appunto à
fe fteffo con la cortefia, e con la Virtù la via dell'immortalità;
fece le figure , & honorò doppiamente l'Autore co'l fuo Ri-
tratto, eternando fe fteffo, fe non l'Opera, che poco merita, &
vccidendo la Morte con lo ftrale finifsimo del fuo pennello .

Figure 6

of the picturesque, wrote his essays on the picturesque, the aesthetics of
irregularity had boosted the status of ruins and mountains from shame-
ful reminders of fallen nature to an exalted symbol of authenticity, feeling, and the language of nature.[35] Gilpin not only helped create a British
counterpart to the Alpine travel growing so popular on the continent,

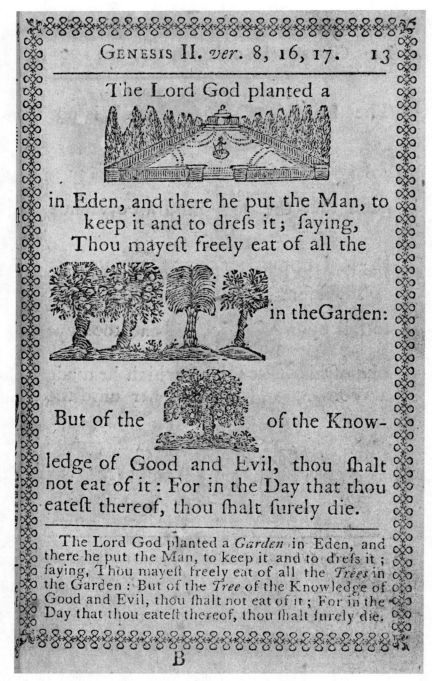

GENESIS II. *ver.* 8, 16, 17.   13

The Lord God planted a

in Eden, and there he put the Man, to keep it and to drefs it; faying, Thou mayeft freely eat of all the

in the Garden:

But of the   of the Knowledge of Good and Evil, thou fhalt not eat of it : For in the Day that thou eateft thereof, thou fhalt furely die.

The Lord God planted a *Garden* in Eden, and there he put the Man, to keep it and to drefs it ; faying, Thou mayeft freely eat of all the *Trees* in the Garden : But of the *Tree* of the Knowledge of Good and Evil, thou fhalt not eat of it ; For in the Day that thou eateft thereof, thou fhalt furely die.

B

Figure 7

but he also encouraged the picturesque admiration for irregularity and ruination and taught his readers how to capture picturesque and rugged prospects on paper when wartime conflicts made continental travel less feasible. For example, in one essay, he uses an illustration of a landscape with only smooth surfaces to depict a "scene without picturesque adornment" (Figure 8), a scene that resembles Burnet's portrayal of the earth's pristine original condition as "mundane egg." In Figure 9, Gilpin shows how, by swiftly adding a few irregularities such as bumps, broken tree stumps, rocks, or ruined abbeys, the scene can become gratifyingly "picturesque," thus "improv[ing] upon nature": the postdiluvian world can thus be aesthetically enhanced through additional irregularities or small reenactments of the flood, purged of any ethical significance. Eventually, topographical irregularity or variety becomes one of the most general characteristics of the picturesque that Uvedale Price tries to encode as a new aesthetic category mediating between the beautiful and the sublime. According to picturesque principles, a degree of wildness and irregularity was thought to lend sympathetic interest to a painting or to natural scenery, whether in the form of crumbling cliffs, architectural ruins, or banditti.

A term that now means little more than something that would look nice on a post card, "the picturesque" once invoked a contested field of aesthetics and wielded extensive influence on not only poetry, fiction, landscape improvement and gardening, as we are discussing here, but also on tourism, ecology, and politics; it provided a "point of intersection in discussions of science,

Figure 8

Figure 9

ecology, theories of association, and the psychology of perception."[36] While its special meanings are still the subject of intense debate among scholars, the importance of the picturesque to general eighteenth-century aesthetics seems difficult to dispute.[37] Just as the irregular terrain of the postdiluvian world rose in public esteem with the rise of the culture of sensibility, smoothness of any kind in the garden grew offensive for picturesque theorists such as Gilpin and Uvedale Price. "Turn the lawn into a piece of broken ground: plant rugged oaks instead of flowering shrubs: . . . give it the rudeness of a road: mark it with wheel-tracks; and scatter around a few stones, and brushwood; in a word, . . . make it *rough;* and you make it also *picturesque.*"[38]

It is then fitting that the new Adam entailed by the culture of sensibility requires a new garden—one that has "lep't the fence," has done away with the traditional walled or fenced garden, emphasizes irregularity, and deemphasizes the hierarchical authority of God. Sensibility and the picturesque thus both attempt to recapture a fallen world to engage the interest, sympathy, and moral engagement of viewers or readers.[39] As the movement grew, the "English" gardens and the picturesque school came to be the perfect setting for the unfolding of the inner drama of the Shaftesburian soul trapped in a Hobbesian world, or for the lone and virtuous spectator with exquisite sensibility, who therefore could properly appreciate the landscape and its picturesque settings and artifacts. The garden becomes a status symbol for the prestige associated with sensitive souls.[40]

Not only status, but also politics figured prominently if not always overtly in discussions of the differences between English and French gardening styles, and frequently involve responses to the American and French revolutions. There is evidence that landscape gardening (tied to agricultural law, enclosure acts, and merchant conditions, for example) became a party issue separating Tories and Whigs, as well as enemies and supporters of the American and French revolutions. Edmund Burke invokes the same aesthetic assumptions when he refers to Thomas Paine's "geometric principles of government" and in relation to the domestic importation of views generated by the French Revolution in particular. The irregularity of 'natural' gardens contrasted not only with absolute monarchies of Europe, but also with domestic Jacobin thought. Samuel Kliger, one of the first scholars to write of these connections, writes of the pattern of ideas "that equated political liberty with a taste for 'natural' art and tyranny with formal art." Kliger quotes John Aikin as saying "Even moral ideas are brought in to decide the preference; and a taste for nature is said equivalent to a love for liberty and truth; while the votaries of art are pronounced slaves to formality and constraint."[41] Similarly, on the other side of the Atlantic, Washington Irving recounts a conversation with an English squire defending his father's formal garden, where "grounds were laid out in the old formal manner of artificial flower-beds, clipped shrubberies, raised terraces, [etc.]": "[My father] admired this fashion in gardening; it had an air of magnificence, was courtly and noble, and befitting good old family style. The boasted imitation of nature in modern gardening had sprung up with modern republican notions, but did not suit a monarchical government; it smacked of the levelling system."[42] To glory in 'natural' appearance and its liberal or levelling associations could only be done by ignoring the artificial means through which they were achieved.

When Burke wrote of the "fetters" of the garden in his *Philosophical Enquiry into the Origin of Our Ideas of the Sublime and Beautiful,* his mind was not far from politics; when Pope wrote scathing essays attacking the art of topiary, he was arguing about more than horticulture; and when Addison champions gardens that allow prolific flowers "in their natural Luxuriancy and Disorder . . . [that] they could [never] have received from the Checks and Restraints of Art,"[43] he has French autocracy in mind, as well as domestic importations of French style, whether in gardening, art, or politics. According to John Dixon Hunt, Pope and Addison also have Lockean associationist psychology in mind: it would seem that according to these authors, irregularity, variety, and surprise (a subsidiary of irregularity that presumes the audience's anticipation of regularity) protect liberty of mind and feeling, as well as civic liberty. French gardens, regardless of their location, typically used a large château as the center of the geometrical patterns. We see a version of this style reflected in the Avenues at Hampton Court (Figure 10), as well as in the more prototypical French garden of Versailles, designed by André Le Nôtre.

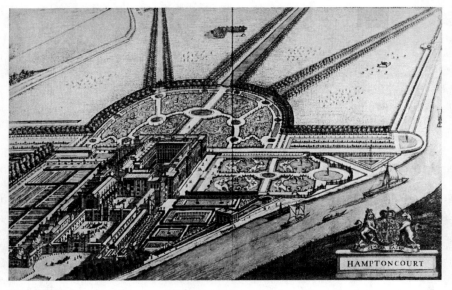

Figure 10

In the baroque garden, cultivation, order, and control would symbolically emanate from the central château and suggest the relative importance of the landowner, as well as the literal extent of his political authority. While often equally involved with the display of worldly authority and possessions, "English" gardens tended to be less public and far less geometrical: they were often designed to be viewed *from* a manor house, rather than using the manor house as the principal prospect. The synoptic, bird's-eye view of the estate demonstrates how the estate claims surrounding territories in the progression of its avenues, symbolically reinstates order, and explicitly separates civilization and wilderness.

It is appropriate that at the same time, illustrations of landscape gardens change from being presented from a bird's-eye (or God's-eye) view to a more subjective, lateral view from the perspective of an individual walking through a garden (compare, for example, Figure 10 against the perspective of Figures 11–13). Prest and Pizzoni both note the diminishing use, in the eighteenth century, of a central vanishing point and a bird's-eye view to represent the "boundless garden" and correspondingly boundless authority of the owner of great estates that could visually "subordinate" all neighboring villages (see Figure 10).[44] Although somewhat later, Hunt also reports of the 1809 Volksgarten in Vienna that was "laid out in open regular French style, largely in the interests of controlling large crowds."[45]

Both symbolically, visually, and practically, the French garden came to represent a more authoritarian or hierarchical perspective of the individual in the garden, whereas, the English garden was more suited to the strong inclination towards a belief in natural goodness characteristic of the culture of sensibility and useful for establishing the claim that democracy could function justly and peacefully without external restraints. And while Repton warns against excessively political or factional interpretation of landscape gardening, he nonetheless formulates the prevalent political readings of the salient difference between English and French gardening. As Repton idealistically describes it: "I cannot help seeing a great affinity betwixt deducing gardening from the painters' studies of wild nature, and deducing government from the uncontrolled opinions of man in a savage state. The neatness, simplicity, and elegance of English gardening, have acquired the approbation of the present century, as the happy medium betwixt the wildness of nature and the stiffness of art; in the same manner as the English constitution is the happy medium betwixt the liberty of savages, and the restraint of despotic government; and so long as we enjoy the benefits of these middle degrees betwixt extremes of each, let experiments of untried theoretical improvement be made in some other country."[46] It was based on this shared aesthetic that Franz imported the English style of gardening to Germany at Wörlitz.

In the baroque (French) garden, intruders or anything out of order could be easily detected, and there was no escaping the central eyes of the landowner. In his poem *Liberty* (1735), James Thomson avails himself of this association when he equates political tyranny with the gardening styles of France:

> Those parks and gardens, where, his haunts betrim'd,
> And Nature by presumptuous Art oppress'd,
> The woodland Genius mourns.
> . . . .
> Detested forms! that, on the mind imprest,
> Corrupt, confound, and barbarize an age. [47]

"Presumptuous Art," or the marks of the scissors, as Hunt demonstrates, were equated with the oppressive rule of the autocrat.

There is, of course, another great irony in that the natural garden is enabled by an agricultural revolution where enclosure acts enabled landowners to consolidate large contiguous blocks of land around their house and park.[48] Eden turns out to exist only at the expense of a good many commoners. Additionally, the English garden has its own forms of artifice and masks the "presumptuous Art" through anti-utilitarianism, an affective focus, and the emphasis on the individual viewer's experience. In both the English garden and its baroque nemesis, therefore, "art" is the enemy. It is interesting that artifice is a critique leveled at both styles in eighteenth-century discourse: one explicitly critiqued as "presumptuous," the other as hypocritical. One is critiqued for excessive artifice, the other for pretending it has none.

One of the transitional forms between the French and English garden was the "emblematic" style,[49] which involved direct quotations and literary allusion to classical and medieval texts, engraved on stones, urns, and benches for more directed associations. Such inscriptions were eventually disapproved of by gardeners such as Thomas Whately for being too explanatory rather than evocative—too tyrannical, in a sense. Whately, for example, complained of these overly literal (and overtly artificial) endeavors: "natural cascades have been disfigured by river gods; and columns erected only to receive quotations . . . All these devices are rather *emblematical* than expressive; . . . they make no immediate impression; for they must be examined, compared, perhaps explained, before the whole design of them is well understood." "Allusions should have the force of a metaphor, free from the detail of an allegory" (*Observations*, 150–1).

Within the fashion for English gardens, the literary emblematic style transitioned to a more emotional and loosely associative style. These associative gardens subsequently gained strength and meaning through the broader changes in the culture of sensibility. The Baroque's overt sense of order and human control was replaced by the emblematic garden's sense of erudite inclusion and nostalgia. Finally, the full-fledged English garden further emphasizes one's own experience, particularly a heightened sensitivity to one's surroundings. Whereas the emblematic garden frequently relies on written language, the later English garden emphasizes the affective powers of landscape without the aid of written language.

As we shall see in later chapters, elaborate stratagems arose to hide the marks of the shears or scissors from the view of the spectator. The result is not wildness, but a picturesquely regulated wildness, a compromise reminiscent of sensibility's insecurity and equivocation towards external sources of authority. Similarly, the appearance of mechanism was avoided in favor of organicism whenever possible; the experience of the individual gained more autonomy, as private spaces were created among the serpentine paths. While transition from a scientific mechanism to an organic appreciation of wholeness occurred in painting by the movement from an emphasis on line to an emphasis on color, lines and structure also became less permanent in the English garden: rather than meticulous mosaics or paths made of stone or brick, the new breed of gardeners used gravel, or suggested lines by planting rather than pruning.

In baroque styles of gardening, nature was often made to imitate architecture, using *trompe l'oeil* devices such as topiaries—trees and hedges pruned into geometrical forms of even the shape of knots, locks, and bridges. Such overtly artificial techniques highlight the control of the gardener's hands— they mark the presence of human authority and celebrate the transforming power of reason. The Topiary Arcade at Hartwell House, for example, first constructed in 1738, looks almost as though the hedges had been sliced into perfectly smooth planes rather than pruned; the sharply defined edges emphasize the machine-like perfection of the manual labor which proudly obliterates the naturally irregular surface of the bushes (see Figure 11). Balthazar Nebot emphasizes the man-made precision by portraying the talented gardeners and their sharp blades prominently in the foreground of the painting. In contrast, sensibility's more "natural" styles of gardening reverse the direction of imitation and often make architecture imitate nature: bridges imitate trees, rather than trees and hedges imitating bridges. For example, William Chambers camouflaged his "Ruined Arch" at Kew Gardens to resemble overgrown tree stumps and piles of rocks in order to hide from the viewer the arch's purpose as a transport bridge (Figure 12). By using organicism to hide and mask mechanism, sensibility reverses the prior trend. Not rejecting mechanism entirely, sensibility once again reveals its dual impulses: organicism is the new ideal, but mechanisms are trusted as the way of ensuring the properly organic appearances while retaining maximum utility. The goal: the appearance of Nature, but without inconvenience. See Figure 13 for example of a bridge made to look as rustic, precarious, and impractical as possible. François Nicolas Henri Racine de Monville had it built at Le Désert de Retz purely as a picturesque adornment, since he provided another hidden (practical, yet unscenic) entrance for supplies to the tower.

The "tyrannical" tendencies of the emblematic garden give a clue to an even greater irony regarding the English, "natural" garden: while applauding Nature's "escape[-] from . . . fetters," the degree of expense

Figure 11

Figure 12

Figure 13

and artifice required to create an English garden indicates that natural-
ness alone is distinctly not good enough to meet the aesthetic requirements. Apparently, while the language of nature itself grows more
trustworthy, it still requires much artifice, labor, and disguise to present this natural language in an appropriately affective manner. In later
chapters we will see that authors such as Thomas Sheridan and John
Walker describe the need for rhetorical training, if not actually training in acting, to learn how to convey natural feelings in speech: again,
nature requires cultivation to be sufficiently "natural." Gardenists strive
for order without the marks of the scissors as moral philosophers seek
natural goodness without external sources of authority, and novelists
and narrators in the novel of sensibility seek the appearance of lack of
control over their stories. The landscape gardens associated with the culture of sensibility emphasize the newer, liberated English gardens over
neoclassical mechanism, but in the process they reveal another arena in
which sensibility's half-hearted idealism leads to an ambivalence about
nature in its unimproved state.

RECLAIMING THE RUINS OF BABEL

One of the most prominent architectural ruins in the eighteenth-century
imagination is a mythical one: the tower of Babel. In its philosophy as well
as in linguistics, the culture of sensibility resonates with the fall of Babel.
Whereas before Babel, according to *Genesis*, "the whole earth was of one
language, and of one speech,"[50] Babel's fall symbolized not only the lost
"transparency" or immediacy of communication depicted by Rousseau
in his discourses, but also the loss of a singular, universal language and
of the possibility of homogeneous community. "They said, Go to, let us
build us a city and a tower, whose top *may reach* unto heaven; and let us
make us a name, lest we be scattered abroad upon the face of the whole
earth."[51] The ruins of Babel thus draw attention to the artificial nature
and fragility of human community and authority, especially in contrast to
divine omnipotence.

As the following verses suggest, the Old Testament God is jealous of the
godlike centralized power that the human beings seek: "And the Lord came
down to see the city and the tower . . . and the Lord said, Behold, the people
is one, and they have all one language; and this they begin to do: and now
nothing will be restrained from them, which they have imagined to do. Go
to, let us go down, and there confound their language, that they may not
understand one another's speech. So the Lord scattered them abroad from
thence upon the face of the earth: and they left off to build the city."[52] The
multivalent ruins of Babel can therefore represent either a humbling sight,
a reminder of the dangers of hubris and the limits of human achievement,
or remind the reader or viewer of a lost human innocence and intimacy,

mythically recorded in *Genesis,* as well as in Rousseau's own revision of *Genesis,* the *Discours sur l'origine et les fondements de l'inégalité parmi les hommes [Second Discourse]* (1754).

Older, more authoritarian explanations of the Tower of Babel, such as Hobbes', were no longer satisfactory: "All this language gotten, and augmented by Adam and his posterity, was again lost at the Tower of Babel, when, by the hand of God, every man was stricken, *for his rebellion,* with an oblivion of his former language. And being hereby forced to disperse themselves into several parts of the world, it must needs be, that the diversity of tongues that now is, proceeded by degrees from them."[53] Linguistic diversity is thus itself an emblem of decay. Rebelling against God's punitive assertion of authority, authors writing from within a culture of sensibility were nonetheless still unsure about the human ability to self-govern. The challenge to satisfy sensibility's dual impulses required an assertion of natural goodness and renewed human innocence; however, it also had to acknowledge a degree of Hobbesian corruption and chaos in the world at large. It attempted to balance liberal aspirations and conservative skepticism, liberty and traditional sources of authority, spontaneity and order in modern society, by reclaiming the authority and mythological power of *Genesis* on its own behalf.

Sensibility's reappropriation of the Babel story from *Genesis* helps shape mid-to-late eighteenth-century aesthetics, landscape gardening, and literature: on the one hand, authors of sensibility mourn the fall of language from an elevated position as well as the loss of community and mutual transparency. On the other hand, the same voices often also celebrate the "fortunate fall" of Babel. In the epigraph to this chapter, for example, Laurence Sterne has his Yorick of *A Sentimental Journey* exclaim that "there are certain combined looks of simple subtlety—where whim, and sense, and seriousness, and nonsense, are so blended, that all the languages of Babel set loose together could not express them."[54] Yet, for Yorick the limits of verbal language, as we shall see, enable him to progress in the translation of looks, gesture, and silence—languages that, according to him, express feeling more directly than words. The rubble of Babel, rather than being a reminder of God's central authority, becomes an indicator of the importance of individual language communities, for better and worse. Authors in a number of fields locate the possibility for the "progress of sociality" in extra-verbal communication.

Most mid-to-late eighteenth-century literary depictions of the fall of language from a position of trust and objectivity are composed so as to communicate this ambivalence—the bittersweet fact of Babel's fall. This ambivalence is apparent every time Goethe's Werther bemoans the shortcomings of speech to capture his emotions ("O Wilhelm, . . . Wie kann der kalte, tote Buchstabe diese himmlische Blüte des Geistes darstellen" [Oh, Wilhelm, . . . How can cold, dead letters represent this heavenly spiritual blossom?][55]), and every time Rousseau and his characters explain the impossibility of using words to communicate what they instinctively feel ("Que d'ardens sentiments se sont communiqués sans la froide entremise de la parole!" [What ardent feelings are communicated without the cold intrusion of speech!] [56]). Consider, for example, Harley's pastoral poem included within the pages of Henry Mackenzie's *Man of Feeling:*

> It [my passion] ne'er was apparell'd with art,
> On words it could never rely;
> It reign'd in the throb of my heart,
> It gleam'd in the glance of my eye. [57]

In this pastorale, Harley bemoans the fact that if he felt less, he might have been able to win his true love, but instead his strong passion only speaks the "language of nature" and is unheard. The throbbings of the heart are resistant to artifice, cannot rely on words for expression, and can only speak through "glances." In addition, Harley's use of the word "rely" suggests that a traditional safety net has disappeared or that a trust has been violated, again indicating a Rousseauist nostalgia for a time of greater transparency.

In these four passages, by Sterne, Goethe, Rousseau, and Mackenzie, we witness linguistic forms of the insecurities common to authors of sensibility: sadness over the shortcomings of language motivates, yet also tempers, the poignant appreciation of the powers of non-verbal communication; there is sadness over human isolation, yet also pride over heightened and natural sentiments such as longing or love that have not been sullied by direct expression in words, and therefore remain untainted by artifice. There is a lingering despair over limits of contemporary public language, along with hope that we may yet retrieve pre-Babelian transparency. It remains to be seen whether authors of sensibility reconcile themselves to Babel's ruin by asserting the dignity of that which words cannot express, or whether they purposely invoke Babel's ruins in order to separate themselves from accusations of cold rationality and to prove the authenticity of the feelings they describe or profess. In either case, they actively search for alternatives to words (especially narration and syntactic completion) and make frequent allusion to Babel's rubble.

Yet, we must not forget what Timothy Reiss has called a "period-dity"[58]—that Dr. Johnson's writings overlapped with Shaftesbury's as well as Rousseau's, and expressed a profound faith in reason, as well as the duty to protect precise definitions of words. To a great extent, this can be seen as his motivation behind his innovative *Dictionary of the English Language* (1755). In an *Idler* essay from 1759, for example, Johnson writes that: "Difference of thoughts will produce difference of language. He that thinks with more extent than another, will want words of larger meaning; he that thinks with more subtlety will seek for terms of more nice discrimination; and where is the wonder, since words are but the images of things, that he who never knew the originals should not know the copies?"[59] In other words, the precision and size of one's vocabulary in this taxonomical approach directly indicates the degree of one's perspicacity or ability to make fine discriminations. Since Johnson does not make the distinction between thought and feeling here, the implication is that the better one understands, the better one can communicate, regardless of the topic. Self-representation and communication can be improved through study, just as one's understanding of the external world can be improved by study.

In contrast, authors writing from the ostensibly anti-Enlightenment perspective of sensibility tend to claim that the limitation lies in language itself, as Goethe suggests: "sobald man spricht, beginnt man schon zu irren" [as soon as one speaks, one begins to err]. Suspicion is cast upon eloquence, oratorial speeches, analysis, definition, naming, logic, and what Mullan has called the "tyranny of explanation." In addition, the culture of sensibility suggests not only that language cannot do justice to the unfolding of the inner drama of the individual, but also that this drama may be better represented through feelings, gestures, and imagination, when unfettered by words or syntax. Babel's original success would have enabled human reason to "reach unto heaven"; however, its failure is an opportunity for the heart to establish a new universal rhetoric. In subsequent sections we will see how echoes of this "successful failure" resonate through the culture of sensibility, ultimately providing hope that a new basis for community and sociality might be found amidst the rubble of Babel, as well as new opportunities to exhibit authenticity. It seems that in the course of the eighteenth century, these alternatives to the failed Babelian project themselves become attempts at other, better towers, simply substituting new terms for the pursuit of the same mythical and Enlightenment project.

In this sense, there is no "perioddity" in the coexistence of Johnson and Rousseau, or in the coexistence of sensibility's mode of thought and the Enlightenment mode of thought. Sensibility's discourse depends upon Enlightenment discourse, not only as fodder for oppositional self-definition, but at the same time, an implicit respect for Enlightenment ambitions contributes to its contradictory impulses. In the following section, we will see this in the attempt to apply Enlightenment rational procedures, scientific method, and taxonomy to sensibility and feeling. We will witness linguists' attempts to systematize a universal 'language of true feeling'—using gestures, looks, intonation, and silence—to achieve what Babelian and Enlightenment endeavors had failed to achieve through the language of reason.[60] Meanwhile, novelists were struggling to define new notions of authorship and to represent *despite words* that which cannot be articulated *by words*. As we will see in subsequent chapters, some of the tactics they employ include visual representation, masking of authorship, imbedded oral tales, imbedded fragments, aposiopesis, and fictional editorial frames.

The new authority of the passions and of individual experience in general is essential for understanding sensibility's peculiarly distrustful attitude towards language. The tremendous attention paid to language in eighteenth-century England, France, and Germany largely corresponded to the energy spent defining the new moral self implied by sensibility. As the century progressed, the linguistic interest shifted focus according to the dominant conception of human psychology—especially according to the relative roles of reason and passion in thought. One can gauge this interest by the "massive . . . outpouring of dictionaries, secret code schemes, spelling books, grammar books, pronunciation books, and lectures" that appeared in England, for example, during the course of the century.[61] The degree of debate and attention suggests also that ideas about language were changing rapidly—and it is, indeed, easy to detect a significant difference between attitudes at the beginning and end of the century, as Aarsleff, Cohen, and Thompson all have demonstrated in different ways (Thompson using poetry, and the others through reference to eighteenth-century guidebooks and studies of language).[62] The change is, broadly speaking, from concerns about the *abuse* of language to an emphasis on the *limits* of language—from a distrust of speakers, to a distrust of words themselves. We will see that the growing distrust of words is not only intimately connected with the fall of reason from its position of moral authority, but also with the urge to reappropriate *Genesis,* the desire to change the nature of the authority wielded by God, the wish to confirm an ideal of human innocence, and the hope for community and communication.

In a *Spectator* essay from 1712, for example, Addison claims, "The Reader finds a Scene drawn in stronger Colours, and painted more to the Life in his Imagination, by the help of Words, than by an actual Survey of the Scene which they describe. In this case the Poet seems to get the better of Nature; he takes, indeed, the Landskip after her, but gives it more vigorous Touches, heightens its Beauty, and so enlivens the whole Piece, that the Images which flow from the Objects themselves appear weak and faint, in Comparison of those that come from the Expressions."[63] However, a half century later, in "Lines Composed a Few Miles Above Tintern Abbey" (1798), Wordsworth admits, "I cannot paint/ What then I was," reflecting a general shift in attitudes towards the adequacy of words.[64]

Looking back to the dominant modes of the mid-to-late seventeenth century, when Locke was writing, the extremely influential *Port-Royal Grammar* of 1660 looms large, stressing the ostensive referentiality of language: like many other studies in the mid-seventeenth century, it assumes, based on the Adamic model of *Genesis,* that words represent things, and that cataloguing language is actually a scientific process of cataloguing reality.[65] Largely through its taxonomy, language is a subject of study for philosophy and natural science, functioning as an index to the "Book of Nature," guiding us to a better appreciation of the natural order inherent in the external world.[66] In the *Port-Royal Grammar,* the disciplines of grammar and logic are considered as analogous if not identical, since the hidden order of language corresponds to logic and thought, as well as to external physical referents. This is the reason behind the curious combined occupa-tion "grammarien-philosophe" found in the *Encyclopédie*.[67]

When Locke casts doubt not only upon the taxonomical function of language, but also on its referential and communicative powers, as well as its epistemological utility, he separates himself from the authors of the *Port-Royal Grammar,* revealing the potentially dark "gap between sign and meaning"[68] and undermining the Adamic Biblical tradition.[69] By dis-cussing the difference between 'real' and 'nominal essence' and describing language's lack of ostensive reference, Locke opens the door for the subse-quent schism between two human languages: the "natural" and the "artifi-cial," a concept which, after Rousseau, becomes central to sensibility.

Locke's notion of double conformity reveals the potential for the sub-sequent development of his ideas in directions that he neither anticipated nor would have condoned. When we use words to communicate, we always seek what he calls "double conformity"—that is, conformity between our ideas and the words we use to describe them, as well as between our ideas and the things to which we would like them to refer. "Without this *dou-ble conformity of* [our] *Ideas,*" Locke writes, "[we] find, [we] should both think amiss of Things in [our]selves, and talk of them unintelligibly to others."[70] Not only does the passage suggest that there is a significant dif-ference between private and public language (Locke says elsewhere that "private" language never fails[71]), but it also opens the door for solipsism.[72] The suggestion that words actually pose a threat to understanding is a remarkable step away from language's earlier Adamic or taxonomical role, where the alliance between words, reason, and truth was undisputed.

Yet, Locke is terribly concerned about protecting "Language, which was to be the great Instrument, and common Tye of Society."[73] Although he introduces the splintering of language into private languages, he does so for the sake of public language (like Dr. Johnson in the subsequent cen-tury). He focuses on the imperfections of language with an eye towards its improvement and more *rational* use.[74] In other words, Babel fails privately but hope remains for a public resurrection or an improved tower. Not only does Locke seem to believe that language can be *improved,* he also claims that language naturally protects itself from linguistic and semantic anarchy through public meaning, which is created and preserved through a linguis-tic analogue to the "Social Contract": "common use, by a tacit Consent, appropriates certain Sounds to certain *Ideas.*"[75] Thus, public discourse serves as a corrective against the tendency to develop private languages and private meanings, a process Aarsleff calls "rectification."[76]

Etienne Bonnot, Abbé de Condillac (1714–1780), in his response to Locke, introduces a greater role for the senses in thought and therefore contributes further to the fall of unaided reason from its position of author-ity; Condillac also encourages the greater importance paid to language as part of the internal human drama which psychology seeks to describe. In his *Essai sur l'origine des connaissances humaines* [*Essay on the Origin of Human Knowledge*] (1746), he claims, for example, that when Locke derived *two* sources for knowledge—sensation and reflection—he had not gone far enough, and that knowledge actually has a single origin in sensation. According to Condillac, however, the primacy of sensation does not weaken the position of thought or reason, but rather allows for the *perfection* of thought and reason.

The crucial new element is the "linearity of speech." "Si toutes les idées, qui composent une pensée, sont simultanées dans l'esprit, elles sont successives dans le discours: ce sont donc les langues qui nous fournissent les moyens d'analyser nos pensées" [If all the ideas that compose a thought occur simultaneously in the mind, then they occur successively in speech: it is thus languages that provide us with our means of analyzing our thoughts].[77] Speech is, according to Condillac, "une méthode analytique" [a method of analysis]: thought does not exist over time, has no "succession dans l'esprit" [succession in the mind] without discourse, which decomposes (*décomposer*) our thought into as many parts as the ideas it contains." This is the beginning of the self-conscious internal drama that becomes so important to sensibility: as this decomposition happens, "nous pouvons observer ce que nous faisons en pensant, nous pouvons nous en rendre compte; nous pouvons par conséquent, apprendre à conduire notre réflexion. Penser devient donc un art, et cet art est l'art de parler" [we are able to observe what it is that we do when we think, we are able to explain it; as a consequence, we can also learn to direct our thoughts. Thinking becomes an art, and this art is the art of speech].[78] In drawing this distinction between the nature of thought and the nature of discourse—that thought is instantaneous and speech linear—Condillac opens the door for the evaluative differentiation between natural and artificial language.

Once thought and discourse are so different in nature, the "inexpressibility" of thought becomes an issue as well: Sensibility, as we will see with Rousseau, starts paying attention to what is left behind when thought is passed through the funnel of discourse. We can compare, for example, Condillac's description with the following passage from Diderot's *Lettre sur les sourds et muets* [*Letter on the Deaf and Dumb*]: "Notre âme est un tableau mouvant, d'après lequel nous peignons sans cesse: nous employons bien du temps à le rendre avec fidélité: mais il existe en entier, et tout à la fois: l'esprit ne va pas à pas compté comme l'expression. Le pinceau n'exécute qu'à la longue ce que l'oeil du peintre embrasse tout d'un coup." [Our mind is a moving picture from which we paint ceaselessly: we use much time trying to render it faithfully; however, it exists in its entirety instantaneously. The mind does not go *step by measured step* like expression. The brush executes *only* in the process of time what the painter's eye embraces in a *flash*].[79] The transition from thought to language is precisely the same process as the one described by Condillac, but Diderot reverses the values largely with the help of the important analogy to painting.

Decomposition has been transformed from a process of refinement to the practice of producing hopelessly inferior copies of a greater vision: "Que la diction la plus vive est encore une froide copie de ce qui s'y passe!" [Even the most animated language is still a cold copy of what occurs.][80] Diderot supports the movement away from perfectibility of reason and naming described in *Genesis* 2. The aesthetic reversal here will be especially important to sensibility and illustrates the fall of disengaged reason from its primacy: "step by measured step" is no longer ground for admiration, and the new praise ("éclair de genie," "tout d'un coup" or "in a flash") illustrates the elevation of speed, light, and especially potential energy, so memorably eulogized in Lessing's "fruchtbarer Augenblick" [the fertile moment] of the *Laokoön* (1766). In the novel, this aesthetic reversal and increased emphasis on anti-narrative "flash" diminishes the role of narrator, even of narrative itself. Narrative comes to be seen as plebian at best, and autocratic, inauthentic, or even vicious at worst.[81]

Studies such as Condillac's and Diderot's inspired interest in the "origins of language," for it was thought that such study would show whether speech or thought was prior—if not historically, then ontologically. Thus the "origins" fashion was directly related to the attempt to understand the psychological relation between reason, passion, and language. Rousseau's study of the origins of language transforms Condillac's ideas by sentimentalizing them. Ultimately, Rousseau's interest in his *Discourses* as well as his essay on language is psychological and moral rather than historical; the "return" to nature that he calls for in one, and reconstructs in the other, is synchronic rather than diachronic. He uses the language of *Genesis,* along with its structure and mythological force, to enhance his argument.

Addressing his reader in the second person, Rousseau invokes the universalist language of myth: "O homme, de quelque contrée que tu sois, quelles que soient tes opinions, écoute; voici ton histoire, telle que j'ai cru la lire, non dans les livres de tes semblables, qui sont menteurs, mais dans la nature, qui ne ment jamais . . . combien tu as changé de ce que tu étais!" [O man, whatever country you may come from, whatever your opinions may be, listen: here is your history as I believed it to read, not in the books of your fellow-men, which are liars, but in nature, which never lies . . . How you have changed from what you were!][82] He is not interested in the state of nature as a historical condition, but rather as a key to human nature. We must learn, he teaches, to listen to the infallible voice of nature or "conscience" in order for the individual to achieve "moral self-sufficiency and encourage him to live his life with eyes turned inward."[83] Reason plays little role in moral education; in fact, philosophy, as commonly conceived, is virtue's enemy rather than guide.[84] Science, philosophy, and analytical skills are worse than superfluous to the moral project of regaining natural goodness.

Rousseau encourages us, as Arthur Melzer writes, to search for and develop the natural within ourselves and to "prevent all false ideas of the higher [such as the repression or transcendence of man's lower, sensuous

nature] from corrupting or alienating us from our original natural goodness."[85] In this way he encourages a return to something closer to our natural (Edenic) existence, undoing or ignoring the ills of the Fall and expulsion
as *Genesis* described them.

> Les philosophes, qui ont examiné les fondements de la société, ont tous
> senti la nécessité de remonter jusqu'à l'état de nature, mais aucun d'eux
> n'y est arrivé . . . enfin tous . . . ont transporté à l'état de nature des idées
> qu'ils avaient prises dans la société: ils parlaient de l'homme sauvage, et
> ils peignaient l'homme civil. Il n'est pas même venu dans l'esprit de la
> plupart des nôtres de douter que l'état de nature eût existé, tandis qu'il
> est évident, par la lecture des livres sacrés, que le premier homme, ayant
> reçu immédiatement de Dieu des lumières et des préceptes n'était point
> lui-même dans cet état . . . La religion nous ordonne de croire que, Dieu
> lui-même ayant tiré les hommes de l'état de nature . . . ils sont inégaux
> parce qu'il a voulu qu'ils le fussent; mais elle ne nous défend pas de for-
> mer des conjectures tirées de la seule nature de l'homme et des êtres qui
> l'environnent, sur ce qu'auroit pu devenir le genre-humain s'il fût resté
> abandonné à lui-même.

> [The philosophers who have examined the foundations of society have
> all felt the necessity of going back to the state of nature, but none of
> them has reached it . . . All of them . . . have carried over to the state of
> nature ideas they had acquired in society: they spoke about savage man
> and they described civil man. It did not even enter the minds of most
> of our philosophers to doubt that the state of nature ever existed, even
> though it is evident from reading the Holy Scriptures that the first man,
> having received enlightenment and precepts directly from God, was
> not himself in that state . . . Religion commands us to believe that since
> God Himself took men out of the state of nature immediately after the
> creation, they are unequal because He wanted them to be; but [religion]
> does not forbid us to form conjectures, drawn solely from the nature
> of man and the beings surrounding him, about what the human race
> might have become if it had remained abandoned to itself.] [86]

In this interesting passage, Rousseau shows an ambivalence towards the
authority of *Genesis* as well as towards his philosophical project's need
for Biblical sanction. He relies on *Genesis* for confirmation of an original
Edenic state of human perfection and therefore relies upon a religiously
based sanction of his view of human nature. Yet while he uses *Genesis* as
an ontological starting point, he outdoes *Genesis* in his assertions of original purity and innocence, interpreting God's actions in *Genesis* as the first
source of our painful separation from our nature. While Rousseau tacitly
acknowledges God as the source of original purity, God is, more importantly for this passage, also the first source of "lumières et . . . préceptes"

[enlightenment and precepts]. As such, God actually contributes to our corruption as does civilization itself in Rousseau's account. Somewhat ironically, then, the Adam and Eve inhabiting the Garden of Eden before the Fall are insufficiently pure to represent Rousseau's model of innocence. Rousseau thus contributes potently to the culture (and the cult) of sensibility, as well as to a new conception of the self.

In his *Essai sur l'origine des langues* [*Essay on the Origin of Languages*], Rousseau uses the origin of language to reconstruct our alienation and decline from the natural state of innocence: he encourages the growing distrust of words by presenting them as tokens of this artifice and deadening convention which has alienated us from our natural goodness. Rousseau gives the distinction between "natural" and "artificial" language new fervor: the original speech, he claims, was the figurative, melodious language of the poets; however, "L'étude de la philosophie et le progrès du raisonnement ayant perfectionné la grammaire ôtèrent à la langue ce ton vif et passioné qui l'avoit d'abord rendüe si chantante." [Having perfected our grammar, the study of philosophy and the progress of reasoning now robs language of the lively and passionate tone that had initially made it so lyrical.][87]

Rousseau constructs a definite hierarchy among the communicative arts: music and drawing express feeling infinitely better than speaking,[88] and speaking much better than writing: "L'écriture, qui semble devoir fixer la langue, est précisément ce qui l'altère; elle n'en change pas les mots mais le génie; elle substitue l'exactitude à l'expression. L'on rend ses sentimens quand on parle et ses idées quand on écrit. En écrivant on est forcé de prendre tous les mots dans l'acception commune." [Writing, which seems as if it should fix language, is precisely what alters it; it changes not its words but its genius; it substitutes precision for expressiveness. One conveys feelings in speech and ideas in writing. In writing, one is forced to take all the words according to common usage.][89] One of the flaws of writing is thus that it obscures the speech act, transmitting neither intonation nor gesture. As Diderot explains: "Par la raison seule qu'aucun homme ne ressemble parfaitement à un autre, nous n'entendons jamais précisément, nous ne sommes jamais précisément entendus; il y a du plus ou du moins en tout: notre discours est toujours en deçà ou au delà de la sensation." [For the very reason that no man is identical to any other, we never understand precisely, and we are never precisely understood. There are degrees in everything; our speech always goes beyond or falls short of the sensation itself.][90]

Rather than reason and speech being the means to unity as taught by classical authors or in Locke's "Common Tye," now unity is present in sensations that defy expression as words. Or as Diderot wrote in his *Pensées détachées sur la peinture* (1776–1777): "Le sentiment est difficile sur l'expression, il la cherche; et cependant, ou il balbutie, ou il produit d'impatience un éclair de génie. Cependant cet éclair n'est pas la chose qu'il sent; mais on l'aperçoit à sa lueur."[91] [It is difficult to find the right expression for a feeling; we search for it, and, in the process, we either stammer or else, out of impatience, we have a flash of genius. However, this flash is not the thing we felt; but it can be glimpsed through the light of the flash.] As time wears on, stammering itself becomes a way to communicate genius.

Communication is by nature a public enterprise, and the public domain of speech remains hazardous to "l'homme naturel" in us all. In the task of (self-) representation in particular, one risks, on the one hand, a richly emotional isolation or solipsism in the pursuit of natural speech and, on the other, the tempering and therefore corrupting influence of convention and its public and "artificial" language. The unfortunate alternatives to which Rousseau's theory leads help establish the new and important role acquired by the rhetoric of silence during sensibility.

Others, like Herder, responded to the conflict between language and feeling with less pessimism, echoing tones of Babel's fortunate fall. In his interpretations of *Genesis* within *Über den Ursprung der Sprachen* [*On the Origin of Languages*], Herder demonstrates the more optimistic reading of the split between natural and artificial languages—or as Herder calls them, "innere" and "äußere Sprache" (inner and outer speech). The fall from Edenic Grace, for Herder, is less a catastrophe than a new beginning, humankind's great opportunity ("Möglichkeit"). His interpretation of Babel's fall is similarly optimistic. Although he agrees with Rousseau about the regrettable domestication of language from its "original wild mother of the human race" ("[die] ursprüngliche[-] wilde[-] Mutter des menschlichen Geschlechts") to "the child of reason and society" ("das Kind der Vernunft und Gesellschaft"),[92] he thinks that the grand passions of the few will pour forth nonetheless: "Unsre künstliche Sprache mag die Sprache der Natur so verdränget, unsre bürgerliche Lebensart und gesellschaftliche Artigkeit mag die Flut und das Meer der Leidenschaften so gedämmet, ausgetrocknet und abgeleitet haben, als man will; der heftigste Augenblick der Empfindung, wo und wie selten er sich finde, nimmt noch immer sein Recht wieder und tönt in seiner mütterlichen Sprache unmittelbar *durch Akzente*." [Our artificial language may have suppressed the language of nature so much, our bourgeois style of life and social courtesy may have dammed in, dried up, and re-channeled the tide and ocean of the passions so much as one will; the most powerful moment of feeling, wherever and however seldom it is found, still reclaims its right, sounding its mother tongue directly *through accents*.][93]

Like Rousseau and *unlike* Dr. Johnson, Herder claims that the acuity of the senses is inversely proportionate to the development of language; this lamentable loss is actually due to the great human capacity to adapt to different spheres of activity. According to Herder, it is a sign of human strength. In this way Rousseau and Herder delineate the dispute over just how *dark* the "gap between sign and meaning" or between language and feeling really is; it is not a dispute over whether the gap exists, but rather how one should react to it. Thus, for Herder, human and linguistic incompletion signifies freedom and potential rather than inevitable dissatisfaction. The catch is, however, that in order to achieve this optimistic reading, Herder must interpret "Sprache" as not necessarily verbal. In other words, purity still has a strong suggestion of incompatibility with grammatical and syntactic speech. As he writes in his *Kritische Wälder* (1766), rational language so weakens expression, that we are left with a language fit only for philosophy, not for poetry.

In contrast to Condillac, Rousseau and Herder both locate purity on the same side of the "decomposition" from thought to language as does Diderot—that is, to compose language is to allow it to decompose in the process. A split between the language of thought and the language of discourse, and therefore between "natural" and "artificial" languages, is implied in the very notion of origins studies. The natural language, associated more closely with a putatively pure *source* of expression (regardless of whether this source is defined as "thought" or "feeling" or "sentiment"), takes on features that are non-verbal, non-lexical, asyntactic, or non-grammatical. This is where the moral-aesthetic components of sensibility start to alter the discourse about language: "inexpressibility" becomes not only natural, but also expressive of greater sentiment. Subsequently, issues such as the ability to convey moral feeling, the moral ability to convey feeling, and the moral ability to feel all rise in prominence, as we shall see in subsequent sections. The opponent to "pure" language and sentiment in these tensions continues to be convention, including conventional regard for logic, grammar, syntax, and narration.

As we have seen, the same wary optimism that leads philosophers associated with the culture of sensibility to create theories of "moral sentiments" and to pursue natural goodness in the absence of traditional authority, religion, or disengaged reason, also leads linguists in the late eighteenth-century to search for a more "natural" form of language. This more natural language could not only reestablish greater transparency among human beings, but also help to rediscover a long-lost universal language supposed to predate *Genesis*' Tower of Babel. Frequently, in fact, these philosophers and linguists are the same individuals: prominent philosophers, such as Rousseau, Diderot, and Herder, give their reactions to the writings of Locke, and accordingly establish a new interpretation of the fall of the Tower of Babel, where the language of emotions is the most authentic one of all.

THE LANGUAGE OF TRUE FEELING

Natural language is not just posited within the culture of sensibility, but also didactically reconstructed in popular guidebooks on language, whose authors paradoxically teach their audiences what methods to use in order to achieve more natural and affective language. These how-to books attempt to undo Babel's damage to communication and community, and transform a nostalgia for wholeness into a redemption of fragmentation and incompletion.

During the 1770s and 1780s, the new emphasis on communication (as opposed to ostensive reference) spurs increasing attention to sounds, intonations, and gestures—the non-verbal elements of language. As emphasis upon "sentiment" grows, the question arises whether the heart speaks in the same "language" as the mind—that is, whether the language of reason can adequately express emotion.[94] Several popular British guides to speech and rhetoric from the 1770s and 1780s, including writings by John Herries, Thomas Sheridan, Hugh Blair, and John Walker, aim to help audiences regain the affective power of their speech, whether for the purposes of achieving political persuasion or expressing poetic feeling. "Vocal tones," the "melody of speaking," aspiration, pauses, looks, and gestures become worthy of attention because they are thought to be especially *affective,* and can thus aid in the goal of improved communication of sentiments or the alleviation of human isolation. As Walker writes, "pronouncing or hearing . . . sounds effectively leads us into the passion or sentiment of every speech," implying not only that sympathy and shared sentiment have become increasingly important goals, but that these goals may be served through better pronunciation.

Rather than the taxonomical usage of language assigned to Adam by God in *Genesis,* the analysis of language serves the purpose of attempting to overcome the division and opacity in human relations traditionally associated with the fall of the Tower of Babel. More specifically, the late-eighteenth century approach to language, especially as reflected in popular guidebooks of the time, works to further the hallmarks of sensibility described above, especially the attention to emotions over reason, and the emphasis on natural goodness or virtue. It also contributes greatly to the growing aesthetics of irregularity. Finally, the techniques used to achieve these ends underscore sensibility's philosophical insecurity: sensibility paradoxically relies upon Enlightenment techniques of systematization and standardization, frequently involving universal claims and a return to taxonomy. Conservative constructions and methods of inquiry thus continue to undergird its revolutionary claims.

In his *Elements of Speech* (1773), John Herries claims that accents and other non-verbal aspects of language are not only more natural, but also (or perhaps therefore) form the only universal language. Sounds, or the "infinite variety of vocal tones," he writes, "correspond[-] to every impression of the imagination and senses. This is the universal, untaught language of nature."[95] Hugh Blair echoes this idea in one of his widely read works: "Cries of passion . . . are the only signs which nature teaches all men, and which are understood by all."[96] And while Blair's Herderian "cries of passion" are only one example of the "variety of vocal tones" described by Herries, both authors emphasize that the "untaught" language of nature is not only closer to the original human language, but also more readily communicated and understood. They also claim that this non-verbal language is "universal," defying the punishment associated with Babel's mythical fall.

In addition, these guidebooks and others show the new importance of what had been considered arbitrary or erratic features of language. The illustrations included in late eighteenth-century guidebooks show an attempt to reproduce the irregularities of language by charting aspiration, plotting intonation curves, and diagramming pronunciation differences among dialects.[97] In Figure 14, we see one such attempt in John Walker's *Elements of Elocution* (1781): Walker uses this diagram to represent the "variety" of speech, or the "melody of speaking," in order to teach his readers to maximize the rhetorical powers of speech. By breaking his sentences to conform to the alpine zig-zags of the melody of speech, Walker symbolically makes words secondary to the music of language. And while the "melody of speaking" may seem both surprisingly regular *and* surprisingly jagged, the speaker's power as Walker portrays it, is the power of silence—the power to pause—to space out the words of one's sentences in order for the words to coincide with the appropriately rising or falling parts of the patterned music of speech. His regular depiction of irregularity thus belies the divorce of meaning and music or the loss of control and transparency that his teachings imply.

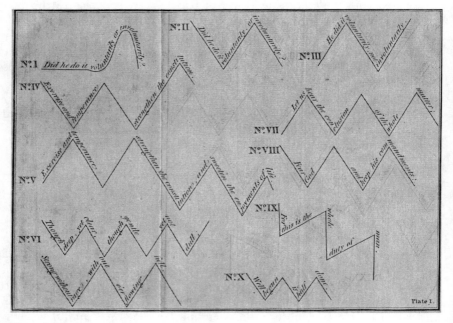

Figure 14

Walker's many popular works, including *The Elements of Elocution* (1781), *A Rhetorical Grammar* (1785) and *Critical Pronouncing Dictionary* (1791), show his attention to and the public's concern about understanding and overcoming idiosyncrasies in speech acts. In fact, such universalism at times appears quite didactic, as he gives advice to Scottish and Irish speakers on how their speech can sound more English in the latter volume. Having to work rather hard to create that which he claims to be natural, Walker exemplifies the aspect of the culture of sensibility that is a continuation of the Enlightenment impulse towards order and standardization, as well as sensibility's contradictory impulses. In drawing attention to the seeming irregularities of language, he echoes authors writing on the human passions or the rugged Alps with the intention of framing or reclaiming unsightly irregularities for the causes of order, virtue, and self-sufficiency.

One of Walker's claims to fame was his invention of "rhetorical punctuation" as an enhancement of "grammatical punctuation"—little markers to help designate tone (the eighteenth-century equivalent of emoticons). In *A Rhetorical Grammar* (1785), for example, Walker teaches how to speak with appropriate inflections and pauses to express a given "passion or emotion." Walker's goal was not the same as Locke's when the latter also suggested that studies of words are best complemented with illustrations.[98] While both authors are concerned with the accuracy of communication, all of Walker's main works suggest that the primary goal of speech is to affect the passions rather than to serve ostensive reference—to express rather than to classify. Nor was this tendency limited to Walker. Thomas Sheridan, another of the most popular authors of guides to speech, justifies the purpose behind his *Lectures on Elocution* (1796) accordingly: "Some of our greatest men have been trying to do that with the pen, which can only be performed by the tongue: to produce effects by the dead letter, which can never be produced but by the living voice, with its accompaniments."[99] Late eighteenth-century British linguists proclaim the written word "dead" and either seek to revive it or seek to communicate despite its limitations.

Of all these rhetoricians who emphasize affect, Thomas Sheridan most explicitly applies the Rousseauan distinction between artificial and natural language to the new practical concern about communication in his distinction between a "language of ideas" and a "language of emotion": the latter is more important since "the communication of these internal feelings was a matter of much more consequence in our social intercourse, than the mere conveying of ideas."[100] Again, the natural "tones" are what constitute the lost pre-Babelian transparency, a "universal language, equally used by all the different nations of the world, and equally understood and felt by all."[101]

These examples display the effects of the Deist shift as it applied to language studies. Even Sheridan's musical analogy in the previous passage is not analogous to the medieval Boethius' attempt to mirror cosmic order through music or song, but rather an attempt to find meaning within the individual's natural sense of music: through intonation and accent, speech's "accompaniments." Just as the passions, which for the Ancients had been an enemy to community, now offer the philosophical basis of both community and communication, so too the accents and the music of language, which had been distractions from meaning now are seen as offering hope for strengthened community and communication, if not universal transparency.

Like the Deist shift and the new psychology described above, this change in attitudes towards language had implications for moral philosophy as well. Not only was "natural language" or the "language of the passions" considered more natural and transparent in the context of the culture of sensibility, it was considered as an indication of greater virtue in a speaker. Hugh Blair, in his immensely popular work on rhetoric, *Lectures on Rhetoric and Belles Lettres* (1783), writes that "no kind of Language is so generally understood, and so powerfully felt, as the native Language of worthy and virtuous feelings. He only, therefore, who possesses these [feelings] full and strong, can speak properly, and in its own language, to the heart."[102] To a modern reader, the ethical terminology "worthy and virtuous" may seem misplaced in this passage, but just as the elevation of the moral authority of the passions and the new moral psychology would suggest, virtue tended strongly to reside with the "natural" language of the heart rather than with the colder, "artificial" language of the head,[103] again lowering the status of *logos* from that which it had in the New Testament. One of the new virtues required for successful oratory is "a strong and tender sensibility to all the injuries, distresses, and sorrows of his fellow creatures."[104] It also suggests a problem that is to haunt both the discourse on the picturesque and sensibility: the power to communicate feeling becomes an indicator of virtue itself, leading to a raised appreciation for actors, such as David Garrick and Lady Hamilton in England.[105]

This brings us back to the culture of sensibility's philosophical insecurity and the fortunate fall of the Tower of Babel—the problem of achieving, as Sterne writes, "generous cares beyond myself." The same failing (whether one sees this failing as linguistic, physical, or moral) in nature that causes isolation and misunderstanding among human beings also allows, within the culture of sensibility, the possibility of human sympathy. Adam Smith describes the failings of language that enable a spectator to feel sympathy with a "brother on the rack": "Though our brother is on the rack, as long as we ourselves are at our ease, our senses will never inform us of what he suffers. They never did, and never can, carry us beyond our own person, and it is by the imagination only that we can form any conception of what are his sensations."[106] Within Smith's *Theory of Moral Sentiments* (1754), the failure of complete identification between spectator and sufferer leads to the possibility not only of cooperation and therefore of society, but also to the possibility of virtue itself. How well the individual compensates for failed identification or transparency through vivid sympathy depends upon the sensibility of the spectator. The better the imagination or the more "exquisite" the sensibility of the spectator, the stronger his or her capacity to feel and the greater the capacity for virtue. Smith falls short of claiming that we regain transparency through spectatorship. In fact, he claims that it is easier to enter into the feelings of the sufferer if one also knows something of the context or narrative behind the suffering; therefore, some description of circumstances tends to be more helpful than "general lamentations" in exciting sympathy.[107]

High hope and claim of natural sympathy rests in what Sterne and others refer to as the "sensorium": Sensibility and feeling responses to spectatorship are key to communication. A similar argument is at work in Pratt's poem *Sympathy* (1781):

> Hail, sacred source of sympathies divine,
> Each social pulse, each social fibre thine;
> Hail, symbols of the God, to whom we owe
> The nerves that vibrate, and the hearts that glow;
>
> . . . .
> Thy heav'nly favours stretch from pole to pole,
> Encircle earth, and rivet soul to soul![108]

According to Pratt, sympathy is built by God into our very nerves and veins, unites the globe, and enables human community more than any other faculty or passion.

The central issue of the human capacity for sympathy is taken up by many other authors within the culture of sensibility. Thomas Sheridan's approach is more optimistic than Smith's, despite the fact that it begins with a similar problem—that mutual sympathy is necessary to society: "Tho' it be not necessary to society that all men should know much; it is necessary that they should feel much, and have a mutual sympathy, in whatsoever affects their fellow creatures."[109] Sheridan goes on to claim that this sympathy can be established without the aid of speech: "Visible language alone . . . shewn in the features and limbs of man, is of itself sufficient, without other aid, to every purpose of social communication." And again: "What inward emotion is there, which can not be manifested by these [the eyes and hands]? Do not the eyes discover humility, pride; cruelty, compassion; reflection, dissipation; kindness, resentment? Is there any emotion of fancy, is there a shade of ridicule, which they can not represent?"[110]

Sheridan describes the dynamic of this communicative act by suggesting that rather than punctuation marks, one needs "sensible marks," taking Walker's "rhetorical punctuation" one step further: "In order to feel what another feels, the emotions which are in the mind of one man, must also be communicated to that of another, by sensible marks . . . The sensible marks necessary to answer this purpose, can not possibly be mere words."[111] What we need to communicate emotion are "the true signs of the passions, which are, tones, looks, and gestures . . . The language, or sensible marks, by which the emotions of the mind are discovered, and communicated from man to man, are entirely different from words, and independent of them." Only this language, "the language of the animal passions of man," is "fixed, self-evident, and universally intelligible" and has "been impressed, by the unerring hand of nature, on the human frame."[112] Again these authors express the underlying insecurity common among authors writing from within the culture of sensibility: on the one hand, they wish to claim the universality of the natural language of tones and gestures, yet they also wish to teach us to adopt them in order to improve communication and lessen human isolation.

Only when he subsequently divides language into two types, the "language of emotions" and the "language of ideas," does the reader discover any hint of shortcoming in Sheridan's natural, non-verbal language of emotions: "It is not in the power of the language of emotions, to give us the least insight into the language of ideas." More optimistic than Smith, Sheridan nonetheless admits that knowledge of circumstances of suffering or reasons for suffering are inaccessible without narrative. Yet he differs from Smith in saying that this knowledge is not necessary for sympathy. In describing the effect of listening to a person speaking an unknown tongue, Sheridan concludes that: "Tho' we may perfectly understand the nature of his emotions and partake of his feelings, yet it is impossible, without an interpreter, to know the cause of them, or the particular ideas in the mind of the speaker, that gave them birth." Yet the language of ideas has, according to Sheridan, "no power of moving."[113] One of the ironies of this situation is that the lack of transparency among human beings can lead us to perform our feelings more overtly—or exaggerate them—in order to ensure their successful communication. The knowledge that we cannot see each other's motives can lead to defensiveness and also to acting, leaving open the possibility of even greater opacity through deception or misrepresentation.

There is an irony in the point at which authentic feelings need rhetorical training in primeval intonation and gesture in order to communicate authentically and successfully, when natural feelings need training in affect and gesture in order to be persuasive, or when special punctuation marks are required to communicate emotion. This irony reflects sensibility's philosophical insecurity and the persistent conflict as to whether transparency is natural or requires cultivation: the attempt to reclaim a prelapsarian innocence and transparency while relying on a scientific ambition for taxonomy, all the while haunted by a fear that Hobbes may have been right after all. To this paradoxical end, Sheridan invented "the Natural Mode of delivery," a movement he pioneered in opposition to the "Mechanical School" of rhetoric, which he viewed as excessively rule-bound. Again, we see a good example of the dual impulses of the culture of sensibility, as well as its seemingly high tolerance for paradox: whether one regards these methods as a *conscious* return to Nature, a *scientifically* inspired attempt to speak naturally; an *artificial* pursuit of transparency; or a *mechanistic* attempt to regain organic understanding of language, these linguists found a way to combine Enlightenment scientific methods with a hope of recreating a pre-Babelian natural transparency.

When novelists of sensibility apply these popular modes or conflicts to their novels, they tend to reflect them in content (as well as form)—sometimes with direct reference to the Tower of Babel. Among novelists of sensibility, Sterne in particular finds rich possibilities for artistic expression in the dark gap between sign and meaning, and this may be part of the reason why his work was received all over Europe as enthusiastically as it was, serving as a model for Goethe's *Werther,* among many other works. According to Sterne's sermons and fiction, the insufficiency of language provides a positive aesthetic and moral opportunity. While it does necessitate the translation of silence, looks, and gesture, it also allows the freedom of the listener to participate in the construction of meaning. Since the objective referents of words are unclear, they affect the listener or reader with greater imaginative force, resulting in a "successful failure." In *Sentimental Journey,* Mr. Yorick remarks: "If tone and manners have a meaning, which certainly they have, unless to hearts which shut them out—she seemed really interested, that I should not lose myself."[114] In this interesting little passage, Sterne's Yorick suggests that felicitous translation of "tone and manners" requires sympathy or the ability to listen to them with one's "heart."[115]

Sterne speaks in one of his sermons about the natural transparency that the language of gesture, look, and tone allows:

> In the present state we are in we find such a strong sympathy and union between our souls and bodies, that the one cannot be touched or sensibly affected, without producing some corresponding emotion in the other.—Nature has assigned a different look, tone of voice, and gesture, peculiar to every passion and affection we are subject to; and, therefore, to argue against this strict correspondence which is held between our souls and bodies,—is disputing against the frame and mechanism of human nature.—We are not angels, but men cloathed with bodies, and, in some measure, governed by our imaginations, that we have need of all these external helps which nature has made the interpreters of our thoughts.[116]

Sterne here inverts the Biblical story of the Tower of Babel: while he ostensibly supports the notion of original sin ("we are not angels"), his claim is that our fallen nature paradoxically allows an even stronger connection between our minds and our bodies. Rather than limiting the possibilities of virtue, he describes our reliance upon interpretation as enhancing the possibility of engaging our imaginations in communication—an antidote for human isolation. The "strict correspondence" he claims in this passage is quite doubtful; and indeed he shows the frequent failure of well-meant translation within the pages of *Sentimental Journey* as well as in

Tristram Shandy. Using the Deist language of Nature rather than reference to a Judeo-Christian God, Sterne argues for virtue based on reception or imagination rather than faith or knowledge.

One could say that the central locus of both the tragic and comic elements involved in the fall of Babel lies in the necessity of *interpretation* and self-representation in the absence of transparency: on the one hand, this is a cruel fact and on the other hand, it allows for increased creative expression, more active authorship, and increased participation by the interlocutor, spectator, or audience. The positive sides of the fall are greater freedom and creativity, while the negative are reminders of human isolation and inescapable solipsism—insecurities of the culture of sensibility. The popularity of late eighteenth-century linguistic and elocutionary studies may have been driven by such combined hope and fear: the defensive concern that listeners will misunderstand meaning as well as the hope that the art of rhetoric and elocution can help audiences regain mastery over speech acts.[117] Although these linguistic writings pay attention to irregularities (the peaks and valleys) of language that resist transcription into words, they analyze them in order to perfect the communicative act or to mitigate linguistic insufficiency: to decrease human isolation by (re)creating a natural language that increases mutual transparency.

In other words, as we have seen, philosophical insecurity underlies these authors' returns to linguistic claims in the ancient texts of *Genesis*. The culture of sensibility in France, Germany, and Britain in the late eighteenth and early nineteenth centuries represents one literary reaction to the dark gap between sign and meaning. Doubts about both the referential and communicative ability of language suggest that language is limited as a tool for both reason and emotions. Yet, hope in the natural power and social effects of sympathy abides and partially fills the lacunae left by the loss of a previous generation's unquestioning faith in objectivity, while authors devise a "language of feeling" that communicates through evocation rather than explanation, avoiding the censorship of reason.

Through the vehicle of Deism, through the doctrine of natural goodness, and through the cult of feeling, the man of feeling is relieved of his presumed subservience to God as heavenly monarch, to nature as normative or hierarchical, to reason in its externalized or disengaged form, to sin as an inescapable aspect of life, and by extension to earthly monarchs as well. As an example of this new deist Adam, eccentric as he may be, Sterne's protagonist Yorick from *Sentimental Journey* reveals the changing relationship with the divine. As his eulogy to "sensibility" illustrates, the source of Yorick's virtue is his sensibility, which he externalizes, objectifies, and almost deifies in the following, extremely sentimental passage quoted above. The encomium concludes with the additional claim, omitted in the epigraph above: the Sensorium "vibrates, if a hair of our heads but falls upon the ground, in the remotest desert of thy creation—."[118] This Godlike source of all virtue "vibrates" if a hair of our head is lost, unlike the New

Testament God who shows more mathematical propensities, numbering the hairs on our head.[119] This passage thus dramatizes the internalization of virtue; in fact, Yorick's eulogy of sensibility comes interestingly close to self-eulogy, reflecting a narcissistic tendency that runs through novels of sensibility and the culture as a whole, despite its aspirations to natural goodness and universal sympathy. At the same time, the context of the passage also dampens the idealistic content of the encomium and adds to Sterne's comic purpose, as the entire chapter "The Bourbonnois" is dedicated to the goal of sufficiently erasing the memory of the suffering Maria from his mind, so that he can enjoy the rest of his journey in this new region of France, some ninety miles southeast of Moulin, where he has encountered her.

The tensions between sensibility's idealistic aspirations and its intellectual inheritance inform sensibility's recreation of *Genesis* as well as its philosophical insecurity. Authors from a variety of domains implicitly revise *Genesis* to accord with new democratic ideals of decentralized government, but reveal their uncertainty about the practicality of these ideals. We will see in subsequent sections, for example, that a profound awareness of Babel's ruin ironically suggests new plans for tower-building. What follows includes: a pursuit of authenticity and immediacy that leads to new heights of artifice; a pursuit of innate goodness that leads to remote parts of the world; a pursuit of the "language of nature" that leads to vast redesigns of privately held lands; a quest for the "natural language of feeling" that leads to new forms of naturalistic acting; a desire for intimacy even when based on the principles of acting; and a new appreciation of the authenticity and immediacy of irregularity and fragmentation that leads to its conscious construction in picturesque landscapes, the "natural" mode of delivery, and in the novel of sensibility. These authors, gardenists, and architects attempt to recreate or retrieve nature in linguistics, landscaping, acting, and literature, even through recourse to great artifice.

2   The Anatomy of Follies

We must use the mallet, instead of the chissel:
we must beat down one half of it, deface the other,
and throw the mutilated members around in heaps.
In short, from a smooth building we must turn it into a rough ruin.

—William Gilpin

Why is it that a beautiful sketch pleases us more than a beautiful
painting? It is because a sketch has more life and less form.
As form is gradually introduced, life disappears.

—Denis Diderot

While on his Grand Tour to Rome, Addison comments upon both
"Buildings the most magnificent in the world, and Ruins more magnificent than they."[1] His comment suggests the interesting possibility that
ruins can exceed monuments in magnificence. For later eighteenth-century audiences, old symbols of authority and power, whether classic or
Gothic, have a particular appeal when they are weak and crumbling.
The intertwining of ruin and monument can demonstrate the late eighteenth-century's characteristically ambivalent attitude towards authority
and order. The "ideal" ruin must be grand enough in stature to suggest what it once *was,* and, at the same time, decayed enough to show
that it no longer *is;* grand enough to suggest a worthwhile conquest,
yet decayed enough to quell any doubts about who conquers. Ruins can
emphasize either permanence—that is, the enduring presence of the past
and its still-unextinguished glory—or the *im*permanence of the present
and, indeed, of all earthly glories. For this reason, they are capable of
evoking emotions as varied as national pride, melancholy, nostalgia, or
even utopian ambitions. Contradictory impulses undergird the fascination with ruins, which Rose Macaulay dubs the "ruin drama": "Half of
[the] desire is to build up, while the other half smashes and levels to the
earth."[2] Just like the famous glass of water which can appear either half-full or half-empty, a given ruin can also be seen as either half-remaining

or half-vanished—as either "comforting" or "horrifying," or more likely both at the same time.[3]

This multivalence of ruins is especially important in sensibility, for, as we have seen, there are similarly multivalent interpretations not only of human goodness, but also of the gaps between sign and meaning or between language and thought. For Rousseau, the emphasis was on the tragic loss of former glory, and for Herder, the loss signaled new possibilities: yet the fall of the tower of Babel was for each tragi-comedy. Their difference in tonality reflects sensibility's ambivalence concerning human nature: the emphasis upon *natural* human goodness was, ironically, defined in ways which made it seem just as rare, exotic, and difficult as the models of virtue it was meant to replace. The multivalence of ruins could thus suit the philosophical insecurity of sensibility: its hopeful idealization as well as cautious minimization, its optimism as well as pessimism, its utopian fervor as well as its nostalgia.

An unfinished, fragmented quality in art, the nonfinito,[4] which lends itself towards the reader's or viewer's participation, is quite central to eighteenth-century aesthetics in general, and profoundly influenced people's assumptions about the activities of reading and viewing.[5] Just as philosophers in the culture of sensibility associated natural language with non-linearity and disruption of syntax, numerous eighteenth-century authors support the notion that incompletion—whether visual or narrative in form—leads to greater imaginative or affective involvement of the spectator. Diderot, for example, consistently prefers sketches, outlines, and incomplete drafts to finished creations, as he suggests in the rhetorical question used as an epigraph to this chapter.[6] Just as syntactically fragmented and solecistic sentences connoted greater sensibility in the literature of sensibility—that is, deeper, more authentic, more "natural" expression of feeling—ruined buildings, too, were thought to be more expressive. Several authors within the Picturesque movement, particularly Thomas Whately in England (whose works were quite influential in France), wrote of architecture in terms of its associationist capacity to rouse emotion.[7] Just as, in discussions of language, it becomes important to discover how "natural" expressive language can best be achieved through gestures, tones, and other non-verbal aspects of language, a similar rhetoric of ruins was developing in the architecture associated with the English garden.

As the conversation between Capability Brown and Hannah More (where each discusses the art of "composition") suggests, gardens have their own narratives, their own syntax that can be disrupted for emotional or aesthetic purposes. As taste in narration changes, the new aesthetic affects both art forms. In the novel of sensibility, a new cluster of narrative techniques emerged, suitable for embracing ruination and working against traditional narrative authority located in an omniscient narrator. The ruins addressed in this chapter, then, are actual ruins that dotted the landscape of the English garden, as well as the fragmentation that became a liberating feature of the novel of sensibility. In both cases, authors and architects (or gardenists) create a delicate balance between the urge to narrate and the forces that disrupt, freeze, silence, or interrupt narrative—a tension between story telling and spectacle—in order to represent sensibility's subject and also to affect sensibility's reader or viewer.

NARRATING NATURE

The liberty of mind or feeling that the English gardens were also felt to support stemmed partly from the sensation of immediacy that they could evoke. There was a strong connection between the linguistic discourses about regaining "natural language" and the landscape gardeners' discourse over learning the "language" and "syntax" of Nature herself in order to affect the viewer immediately, without recourse to thought. According to William Gilpin, in an oft-quoted passage from his *Three Essays on the Picturesque*: "It is not from this *scientifical* employment, that we derive our chief pleasure. We are most delighted, when some grand scene, tho perhaps of incorrect composition, rising before the eye, strikes us beyond the power of thought—when the *vox faucibus haeret* [voice sticks in the throat]; and every mental operation is suspended. In this pause of intellect; this *deliqium* of the soul, an enthusiatic sensation of pleasure overspreads it, previous to any examination by the rules of art. The general idea of the scene makes an impression, before any appeal is made to the judgment. We rather *feel,* than *survey* it."[8] Gilpin describes pleasure in the non-discursive immediacy of experience, defined by the suspension of our natural urges to examine, judge, explain, or narrate. Natural language achieves immediacy by separation from discursive thought, analysis, contemplation, reflection, distance, and narration; similarly, the natural garden was by definition *un*-mediated by obvious signs of human control, rectilinear designs, cement paths, and other seeming impositions of authority.

Christopher Hussey describes the psychological advantages offered by the picturesque attitude towards incompletion: he notes that whereas the Elizabethan "regarded distance as little more than an inhibition to clear seeing," by the end of the eighteenth century, a poet could extol obscurity: "'Tis distance lends enchantment to the view/ And robes the mountain in its azure hue."[9] In this atmosphere, it is natural that ruins should become a favorite subject of the picturesque, because they are both formally and emotionally suggestive. The spectator cooperates in recreating the ruins just as one sympathetically recreates language (according to Burke), others' emotions (according to Smith), or the omitted words of 'men of feeling' at telling moments in the novel of sensibility. Partial destruction of monuments and edifices satisfies aesthetic demands, then, not by making the buildings more beautiful, but rather more picturesque. In avoiding the appearance of order, completion, or authority, ruins give the imagination more room to play.

The preference for unfinished structures, tied to a desire for greater spectatorial participation, was at times so strong that it led to the *preference* for ruin over monument: Following Addison, Wilhelm von Humboldt writes, for example, that "we are even vexed when a half-buried building is dug up; it is a gain for learning at the expense of the imagination."[10] Taking this one step further, Diderot writes in his *Salon of 1767,* "Nous anticipions sur les ravages du temps, et notre imagination disperse sur la terre les édifices mêmes que nous habitons." [We anticipate the ravages of time, and our imagination scatters over the ground even the very buildings that we inhabit.][11]

Thomas Whately describes the desired effect of ruins on spectators and imagination: "beautiful as objects, expressive as characters," suggesting that ruins facilitate an "expressive" form of communication towards the spectator. He describes the psychology of viewing ruins further in his *Observations on Modern Gardening* (1778):

> All remains excite an enquiry into the former state of the edifice, and fix the mind in a contemplation on the use it was applied to . . . They suggest ideas which would not arise from the building if entire. The purposes of many have ceased: an abbey, or a castle, if complete, can now be no more than a dwelling; the memory of the times, and of the manners, to which they were adapted is preserved only in history and in ruins; and certain sensations of regret, of veneration, or compassion, attend the recollection . . . Whatever building we see in decay, we naturally contrast its present to its former state, and delight to ruminate on the comparison. It is true that such effects properly belong to real ruins; they are however produced in a certain degree by those which are fictitious."[12]

The last line introduces an interesting suggestion, especially in light of sensibility's emphasis on origins, authenticity, and natural language. The fact that architects began to erect artificial ruins in many public and private parks suggests that impulses other than historical authenticity were involved: interest in the psychological effect of the ruins overshadowed the importance of their historical authenticity and perhaps also their symbolic meaning.

These monuments are, in fact, often more perfect in decay than in full form. In describing a piece of Palladian architecture that does not look suitably picturesque in a landscape, Gilpin gives useful, if somewhat ironic, advice on what measures need to be taken : "We must use the mallet, instead of the chissel: we must beat down one half of it, deface the other, and throw the mutilated members around in heaps. In short, from a smooth building we must turn it into a rough ruin."[13] Neoclassical smoothness and harmony are not the goal in the picturesque style, but rather an ambivalent roughness and incompletion, maintaining a largely complete (if "defaced") half to enable viewers imaginatively and emotionally to participate in the effect.

According to Whately, the gardenist should avail himself freely of the picturesque advantages of ruins in a landscape, regardless of whether they are real or artificial. As much as the suggestion would shock a contemporary archaeologist, Whately requires the architect to rearrange or move any authentic ruins in order to ensure the proper emotional effect on garden visitors.

> *Ruins . . . are . . .* peculiarly calculated to connect with their appendages into elegant groupes: they may be accommodated with ease to irregularity of ground, and their disorder is improved by it; they may be intimately blended with trees and with thickets, and the interruption is an advantage; for imperfection and obscurity are their properties; and to carry the imagination to something greater than is seen . . . Straggling ruins have a bad effect, when the several parts are equally considerable. There should be one large mass to raise an idea of greatness, to attract the others about it, and to be a common centre of union to all: the smaller pieces then mark the original dimensions of one extensive structure.[14]

As this passage indicates, the "expressive" character of ruins is dependent upon the organization of the fragments. There needs to be a center point in order to organize the imagination and emotions of the viewer to its imaginary "grand" completion. While the follies thus are useful because of their "irregularity," "imperfection," and "obscurity," the secret to their picturesque use is in the proper ordering, unifying, or regularizing of their arrangement, so that a dominant narrative emerges out of their seemingly anti-narrative existence.

The seeming preference for ruins over (intact) monuments nonetheless requires an intimation of a monumental quality in the original structure: in his statement about "straggling ruins," Whately makes it clear that ruination is not enough in itself, but that the ideal ruin in a landscape must suggest the grandeur of an original monument, even if only an imaginary one. (Hence the trend of allowing ruins to remain partially buried in order to enhance the imaginative scale of the original structure). Its degree of residual completion lends Tintern Abbey its picturesque quality, according to Whately. Enough remains of its original proportions that the spectator can easily imagine its original state; yet enough was destroyed to satisfy the desire for both ruination and spectatorly participation in its imaginary reconstruction. "In the ruins of Tintern Abbey, the original construction of the church is perfectly marked; and it is principally from this circumstance that they are celebrated as a subject of curiosity and contemplation. The walls are almost entire."[15] In Figure 15, Turner

Figure 15

emphasizes the picturesque qualities of Tintern Abbey by using multiple ruined archways that no longer support a roof or enclose a door. These archways function as window frames in his painting, framing layer upon layer of ruin, with the uppermost arch appearing to hold the entire abbey together. Sensibility's aesthetic model thus depends upon remnants of the imposing authority of the past, impressive for its very longevity and former strength.[16] The two sides of the ruin drama are ultimately inseparable;

they compose a double symbolic meaning, crucial for expressing the philosophical insecurities of the culture of sensibility.[17]

The contradictory impulses of the rhetoric of ruins somewhat uncomfortably combine the importance of authority with the beauty of decay, the "monumental" with the "ruined," or centripetal with centrifugal forces. While the appeal of ruins to sensibility's democratic impulses relies upon a degree of decentralization, successful interpretation, according to the architects, depends on a degree of centralization, albeit generally invisible. That is, the metaphysical peculiarity of ruins, like Friedrich von Schlegel's *Fragmente,* is that they involve something else which must not be present. The ruin, unlike the modern fragment which Schlegel describes, implies a former completion.[18] The *pathos* of the ruin depends upon the intimations of former grandeur—of a wholeness that has been lost. The more monumental the original (whether historical or imaginary), therefore, the greater is the effect of ruination and privatization. The viewer must be able to imagine a "finito" in order to participate in the pathos of the "non finito"—must imagine a former public presence to enjoy its decayed, and therefore privatized, exposed, and intimate state.

For the spectator, the task is to reconcile a present fragment with an absent wholeness, yet this can have multiple tonalities: is one recovering lost history or imaginatively completing a new ahistorical narrative to suit one's own desires? Paraphrasing Walter Benjamin for her own purposes, Susan Buck-Morss writes: "The *ruin* . . . is the form in which the wish images of the past century appear, as rubble, in the present. But it refers also to the loosened building blocks (both semantic and material) out of which a new order can be constructed."[19] In other words, Buck-Morss, along with Sophie Thomas and Elizabeth Harries, concludes that ruination tends to free people by drawing attention to the constructed character of the past, loosening the hold that history can have over us, again freeing the New Adam from previous legacies of history.[20] This suggests reasons behind the appeal of ruins to the explicitly democratic impulses of sensibility. Thus, in order to fulfill the aesthetic demands of sensibility, the monumental quality of a public edifice (the hypothesized original monument) needs to be ruined, feminized, and privatized in order to suit the emotive needs of the viewer and to suit the private residence of a man of feeling.

For these reasons, gardenists, architects, and novelists of the culture of sensibility seek unusual ways of incorporating "ruins" into their finished products—whether through the inclusion of actual architectural ruins and narrative fragments, or by using a variety of the anti-narrative devices that become essential to the novel of sensibility. Sensibility's contradictory impulses thus are apparent across visual and literary disciplines: for follies, in the tension between the urge to monumentalize and the urge to destroy; for novels, in a constant dialectic between the more traditional impulse to form a complete narrative with beginning, middle, and end and the impulse to devise "anti-narrative" techniques that interrupt narration for the sake of immediacy, intimacy, authenticity, or the appearance of virtue.

NATURAL LANGUAGE IN ARCHITECTURE

Whately's *Observations on Modern Gardening* was translated immediately into French by Montesquieu's protégé François de Paul Latapie; it had an enormous influence on architects and gardenists in France, especially the idea that one could rouse imagination and moods in the viewer through three-dimensional composition. Several French architects echoed his ideas in the last four decades of the eighteenth century and wrote of architecture in terms of its theatrical and emotionally evocative nature. One of the earliest of these authors, Jacques-François Blondel, wrote influentially on the emotionally, intellectually, and sexually expressive powers of architecture in his *Cours d'Architecture* (1771–77). Blondel taught his students to give each building a character by evoking particular responses in the viewer, and thereby engaging the viewer's imagination: "Nous allons donner l'idée précise que doivent produire à l'imagination des Spectateurs." [We will give the precise idea that they should produce in the spectator's imagination.][21] Thus his buildings could take on diverse and often gendered dramatic roles, from the "mâle, ferme, ou viril" to the "elegante ou delicate" to the "caractère naïf."[22]

As architects, these authors did not only wish to describe the 'natural' language of visual structure, but they also wished to devise and imitate it through artificial constructions. Blondel's pupil, Claude Nicolas Ledoux, follows in the theatrical vein, describing buildings as actresses assuming different stage presences: "Cette coquette habile, appuyée sur les doux arts de la civilisation, joue tous les rôles; elle est alternativement sévère ou facile, triste ou gaie, calme ou emportée. Son maintien impose ou séduit; elle est jalouse de tout, et ne peut supporter le voisinage qui l'offusque, ni la comparaison qui détruiroit ses charmes." [This clever coquette, aided by the sweet arts of civilization, plays all roles; she is alternatively severe or easy, sad or gay, calm or passionate. Her attitude imposes or seduces; she is jealous of all and can tolerate neither neighbors who obscure her nor comparisons that detract from her charms.][23] Drawing further on the analogy between architecture and speech, he writes: "L'Architecture est à la maçonnerie ce que la poésie est aux belles lettres: c'est l'enthousiasme dramatique du métier . . . Comme il n'y a pas d'uniformité dans la pensée, il ne peut y en avoir dans l'expression" [Architecture is to masonry what poetry is to literature: it is the dramatic enthusiasm of the profession . . . Just as there is no uniformity in thought, there can also be none in expression].[24] Using this rhetoric (or natural language) of architecture, architects can stage urban theater.[25] In Figure 16, Blondel displays an anthropomorphic understanding of the expressive powers of a Classical cornice in relation to a Palladian cornice,

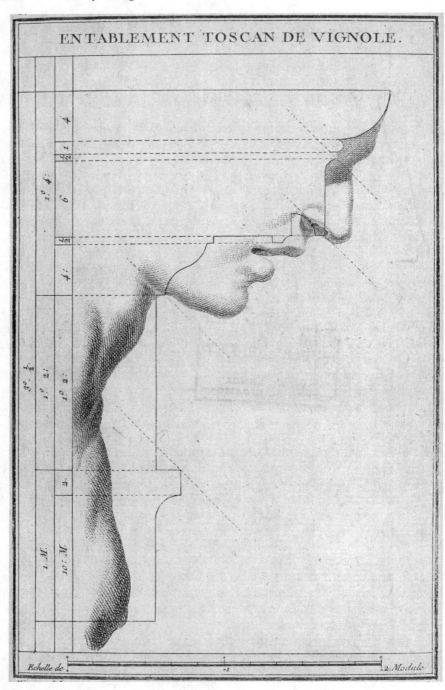

Figure 16

for example. The two dominant curves of the cornice have been interpreted as human brow and chin, and the other more angular turns have been softened to facilitate an anthropomorphic interpretation. Just as we saw with theories of language and rhetoric, however, there is a fine line between the claim to have found a more 'natural' way of communication and the use of this language for entirely artificial or even hypocritical purposes. The goal is still a return to a universal language; however, the implication is that silent visual language grows important because of failure of the spoken, or that paradoxically, theater becomes important for conveying natural effects.

Blondel's analogy to theater highlights the "non-linear," visual, and immediate, if not intimate, qualities of this architectural language. As reason, in moral philosophy, is changing from a static source of knowledge to an active process or energy (reasoning) and begins to resemble the passions, similar changes occur in architecture. In a sense, what was mythically lost through architecture at the Tower of Babel is thus to some extent reclaimed through a new understanding of architecture's communicative potential:

> The classical idea of architecture as a fixed language was . . . replaced by a situation where the observer made instantaneous communication with the building *sur place,* allowing it to work on his emotions and to declare itself to him in other ways. Meanwhile, he in his perceptions of the building, replied to it, and this response when governed by education and other resources could add to the artistic sum of the whole transaction.[26]

Blondel's ideas influenced Nicolas Le Camus de Mézières' *Le Génie de l'architecture, ou l'analogie de cet art avec nos sensations* (1780). Le Camus' work, also inspired by Condillac, as well as by Julien-David Leroy, was calculated to appeal to the associationist aesthetics of the culture of sensibility. Le Camus describes the experience of moving through a building as analogous to movement through a picturesque garden, with various theatrical tableaux giving rise to appropriate moods. In other words, the growing cult of the picturesque inspired Le Camus and others to see architecture, as well as nature, as theatrical and expressive—a new means of reclaiming a more natural language.[27] Viewing architecture, especially ruins, was thus an interactive experience—its transparency obscured only by the references to education and resources. It was tantamount to engaging in a sympathetic conversation, similar to what Hume and Smith prescribe in their moral philosophies. For Smith and Hume, imaginative sympathy, spectatorship, and theatrical dynamics are necessary precisely because direct, verbal communication of sentiment is impossible. Therefore, just as in "the rhetoric of ruins," such conversation is simultaneously a testimony to failure and a hopeful result—a reflection of the philosophical insecurity of authors within the culture of sensibility. One must engage in a social pursuit of meaning, whether it is "rectification" through conversation, or imaginative completion of fragmentary evidence.[28]

As the construction of follies becomes more popular and more mainstream, many volumes of pattern books appear with designs for building authentic-looking ruined classical temples, arches, colonnades, and island precipices, such as the various exotic examples shown with suggested dimensions in Gabriel Thouin's templates (Figure 17). In Figure 18, C. C. L. Hirschfeld offers a plan for a purposely ruined classical temple designed to be evocative in an outdoor park setting. While its footprint does not reveal its ruined nature, the lateral view suggests how one can use irregularity and artificial decay in the roofline to enhance its effect on the viewer. Figure 19 is especially interesting in regard to the domestication of the ruin. In this plan from Robert Lugar's *Architectural Sketches for Cottages, Rural Dwellings, and Villas, in the Grecian, Gothic, and Fancy Styles, with PLANS, suitable to persons of Genteel Life and Moderate Fortune* (1805), Lugar's "ornamental cottage" "contains rooms sufficient for a numerous and respectable family, partly formed in ruins, together with a chaise-house and stable, connected by a gate way."[29] A look at the floor plan confirms that the three-story ruin and two-story cottage are joined together as one living space, with more formal activities assigned to the cottage, while the more private spaces are reserved for the ruin. The partially ruined wall in front of the combined structures screens the more modern parts from view and ties both buildings together as though part of a larger castle complex. The fact that private rooms are assigned to the ruins of a grand tower emphasizes the privatization and domestication of ruin that accompanies the picturesque taste.

Pattern books for garden ornamentation were widespread across Europe and in the United States. Volumes such as Lugar's aimed to appeal to suburban landowners, landed gentry, and perhaps especially the newly wealthy merchant class eager to gain the prestige of a settled estate. By domesticating ruin, these landowners felt able also to imitate the effects of a large-scale park and to appropriate the ancient grandeur of ruins. In addition, within the culture of sensibility, it was fashionable to represent one's modern sensibility through the English style of the garden. Therefore, the picturesque style afforded these landowners simultaneous modernization and antiquation, both of which could be seen as symbols of status, if not virtue, particularly when combined in the same structures.

Meanwhile, architects, gardenists, and theoreticians, such as Whately and Gilpin, aggrandized the artistry needed to perfect the fake ruin. Gilpin writes: "to give the stone its mouldering appearance—to make the widening chink appear to run naturally through all the joints—to mutilate the ornaments—to peel the facing from the internal structure—to shew how corresponding parts have once united . . . are great efforts of art." Finally, he writes, the architect cannot achieve such masterpieces singlehandedly: "you must put your ruin at last into the hands of nature to finish," and induce the ivy and the "long, spiry grass" to encroach.[30] Accordingly, a new breed of architects specialized in this art of dissembling and disassembling the past.

Figure 17

Finally, one of the great ironies that result from the strict principles regulating the construction of follies (and the picturesque's rule-bound pursuit
of irregularity) is that it grew possible for sham ruins to be either *incomplete*
or *ruined*: Gilpin and Hirschfeld, for example, complain of follies that have

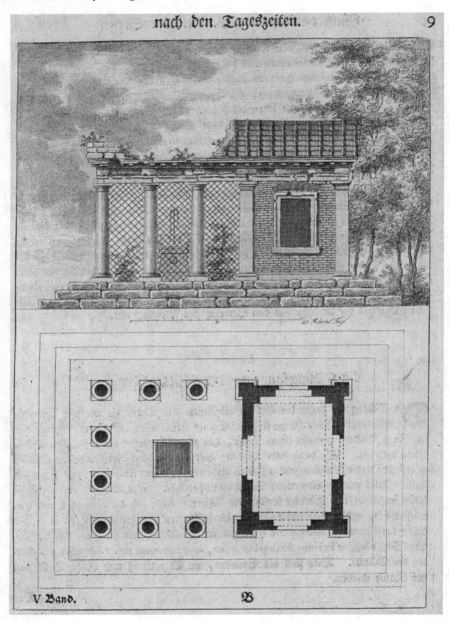

Figure 18

not been sufficiently overgrown with ivy, and which are therefore aestheti-cally incomplete. Ruins—even fake ones—can also be ruined when they crumble excessively and lose their picturesque proportions. In *A Poem on*

Figure 19

the Park and Woods of the Right Honourable Allen Lord Bathurst (1796), Edward Stephens complains of the ruined state of a favorite folly and its "crusted, mould'ring wall": "This pile the marks of rolling cent'ries wears, / Sunk to decay,—and built scarce twenty years."[31] Appropriately enough, the picturesque structure cannot hold; the fake ruin is overtaken by nature; the precarious balance asserted by the picturesque—and indeed by the contradictory impulses of the culture of sensibility—is destroyed. The fake ruin inherently and precariously balances in avoidance of two anathematic extremes: on the one hand, it seeks the more natural appearance, avoiding order, balance, and harmony, whether neoclassical, Palladian, or baroque in style; on the other hand, it must also rely upon traditional balance and order to avoid complete ruination.

NARRATING SENSIBILITY'S SELF

The apparent disdain for monumental façades appears in other domains of the culture of sensibility. As architectural façades in the garden grow preferable in a semi-ruined condition, and as a sense of order and closure grows aesthetically and morally suspect in the literature of sensibility (signifying shallow feelings and lack of moral refinement), omniscient narration and tidy endings also grow suspect. A distrust of syntax, of grammar, and of the referential and communicative power of words creates an unusual problem for the author of narrative fiction, since the very possibility of representation is thrown into doubt. The problem is only heightened when the dominant aesthetic of the period insists that deeply felt emotion must be incommunicable—when "les langues se taisent mais les coeurs parlent" [languages are silent, but hearts speak][32]—and when dominant linguists proclaim that passion "expresses itself most commonly in short, broken, and interrupted Speeches; corresponding to the violent and desultory emotions of the mind."[33] Thus sensibility's moral aesthetic alters the novelist's role; he or she is forced into a position which is paradoxical, if not hypocritical. In fact, the fragile balance of authority and freedom, speech and silence, completion and fragmentation, plans and spontaneity—which the aesthetic of sensibility demands—eventually brings about its own end.

Certainly it is no new metaphor to associate the construction of a text with that of a building. Words have been connected with buildings at least since the writing of *Genesis'* Babel. Spatial metaphors and the language of architecture pervade our everyday descriptions of speaking and writing: we *construct* arguments, we *frame* sentences, we plan sentence and paragraph *structure,* we *build* bridges between related thoughts—and we choose the right words just as we choose the right bricks, according to our mental blueprints.[34] But how does the builder of a text conform to an architectural aesthetic that prefers ruins to finished structures? An author who writes a work, and who intends to publish it, most likely intends to construct a work that readers will admire and want to buy. The challenge, then, is to produce a fragmented text without making the readers question their mastery of the medium and to communicate a distrust of written words without instilling in the reader a similar distrust of the author and the author's own words. We shall see how two masters of the novel of sensibility, Sterne and Goethe, try to settle these difficulties by developing techniques in the novel analogous to the anatomy of the folly. This similarity will help demonstrate the primacy of the figure of the ruin in the culture of sensibility.

Partly because of Goethe's acknowledged debt to Sterne, *A Sentimental Journey* (1768) and *Die Leiden des jungen Werthers* (1774) are similar in a number of ways, despite a radical difference in tone: although one is diaristic and the other is epistolary, each traces the travels of a young man of feeling—a sensitive soul who records and communicates his own feelings with difficulty.[35] Both novels were immensely popular, and enthusiastic audiences imitated the characters' way of dress and speech, and in the case of *Werther,* scores of readers reputedly followed the protagonist, not only in his sartorial eccentricities, but some even to suicide.[36] Both works share an ambivalent attitude towards the efficacy of language or the value of words and a narrative marked by many anti-narrative techniques, such as thoughts breaking off mid-sentence; a proliferation of dashes, asterisks, ellipses, and other lacunae; and a narrator who appears disorganized.

In both cases a protagonist not only narrates, but also "writes" his own experience; therefore, within each protagonist, an internal tension exists.

Yorick and Werther both combine the narrative drive of an author wishing to communicate a holistic experience (his own identity or essence) with the non-narrative drive of a man of feeling *cum* protagonist, interacting emotionally with the world or particular experiences around him every day. Part of the underlying question for each is: to what extent is it possible to narrate the self? Is it possible to represent the self in words without sacrificing authenticity for the sake of presenting a unified whole, particularly when narrative comes to be seen as autocratic and inauthentic? Although Sterne and Goethe ultimately differ philosophically on these points—Sterne seeing greater hope for communication and community despite words and the author of *Werther* viewing the potential for both much more skeptically, they arrive at solutions which structurally resemble each other.

While they both attribute higher authenticity and ethical value to fragmented speech, they each combine anti-narrative and narrative impulses within their novels in their attempt to allow the protagonists to represent themselves. In *Werther,* fragmentation is an inescapable part of human existence, an epitaph to transparent communication, and painful reminder of the limitations imposed by conventions upon human souls. In *Sentimental Journey,* the tonality is more comic, and fragmentation represents the quixotic pursuit of higher ideals that can only be attained fleetingly and which are generally obscured by our ever-changing emotions and constant distractions. In one, the combination of anti-narrative and narrative impulses presents a metaphysical crisis; in the other, it expresses a comic recognition of human folly and weakness, as well of occasional success.

In his *Tristram Shandy* (1760–67), Sterne struggles valiantly (and very explicitly) to overcome the inherently linear character of language identified by Condillac, and particularly the referential and communicative problems raised by Locke. In *Sentimental Journey,* Sterne combines Locke's emphasis on the dark gap between sign and meaning and Rousseau's cultural claims about the difference between "natural" and "artificial" language in his own linguistic ideas. Unlike in *Tristram Shandy,* Sterne here makes no overt references to the seventeenth-century philosopher, but one senses his presence nonetheless, especially in the emphasis placed upon the referential and communicative limitations of language. Where Tristram would directly address the issue: "'tis one of the silliest things . . . , to darken your hypothesis by placing a number of *tall, opake words,* one before another, in a right line, betwixt your own and your reader's conception," Yorick is much more likely to show sentimentally the disjunction of "tall, opake words" and true feeling, such as in the following passage: "The *pauvre honteux* could say nothing—he pulled out a little handkerchief, and wiped his face as he turned away—and I thought he thank'd me more than them all."[37] Where Tristram plays with Locke's *Essay* as a seal does with a ball upon his nose, Yorick explores sentimentally the ramifications of a single issue of his work.[38]

In *Journey,* Sterne confirms the Rousseauan notion that conventions and speech have caused the affectation (and infection) of a purer human state.

"I could wish," Yorick writes, "to spy the *nakedness* of [others'] hearts, and through the different *disguises* of customs, climates, and religion, find out what is good in them, to fashion my own by—and therefore I am come."[39] Sterne uses *ancien-regime* France, the locus of the entire novel, as a symbol of elegance, fashion, aristocratic manners—a society where the codification of manners and speech has reached new levels of complexity. In Rousseauan fashion, Sterne's Yorick interprets this as insincerity or "disguise"; he longs for transparency and natural language, free of disguise and distortion. Yet all along, he is terribly self-conscious and humorously artificial himself. Thus, when he says: "All that can be said about the French sublime . . . is this—that the grandeur is *more* in the *word;* and *less* in the *thing* . . . The French expression professes more than it performs,"[40] Yorick reflects upon the effects of manners and conventional forms of speech in general, rather than specifically on France. And yet, there is a distinct parallel drawn between the French emphasis on form in language and the French baroque style of gardening. In both cases, the *ancien regime* is connected with centralized forms of constructed meaning opposed to the ostensibly democratic and authentic spirit of sensibility.

Yorick disdains the conventional laws and expectations of society; yet he expresses his preference for following the "laws" of sentiment instead. While it is true that it is precisely because they are *not* laws that he prefers them, there is still an important irony in the fact that he humorously substitutes new laws, new hierarchies, and new grammar for the old. In his supposed rebellion, he still relies on the *ancien-regime* authoritarian model.[41] On an especially memorable occasion, Yorick decides to overturn the old and highly-codified rules of heraldry by placing a starling on his crest, largely because a caged starling has just fueled him with enough tearful sympathy to fill two chapters with a sentimental daydream. Although he turns the bird in the opposite direction from that allowed by heraldic tradition, his rebellious gesture turns out to be ineffectual. The real bird is subsequently not freed, but rather passed on from owner to owner in its cage. To make matters worse, once incorporated into his crest, the bird becomes frozen in a static, official position, and therefore just as codified, conventional, and artificial as the rest of the crest.[42]

Regardless of his ultimate success, Yorick is constantly searching for a purer, more natural, form of communication. If we remember Condillac's description of the translation of thought into language as the movement from an atemporal composite of ideas into an orderly linear sequence, we can see that Sterne, through Yorick, both accepts and refutes this idea. Yorick agrees that speech is linear, but for Yorick, as for Diderot, its linearity betrays its cold artificiality. Sterne (and Yorick) comically try to overcome language's linearity in order to recapture the rich, supraverbal, supratemporal, pictorial multivalence of pristine thoughts that have not yet been distilled by grammar and logic.[43] He seeks a language that is not encumbered by "tall, opake words" and does not force the speaker into artifice, yet he is hopelessly self-conscious. Partly in response to this attitude, "ruined" language—characterized by unfinished sentences and the breakdown of logic and conventional grammar—comes to be a sign of sincerity and of purity—that is, of sensibility. The proliferation of dashes simulates such sincere non-narration: LaFleur's "faithless mistress had given his *gage d'amour* to one of the Count's footmen—the footman to a young sempstress—and the sempstress to a fiddler, with my fragment at the end of it—Our misfortunes were involved together—I gave a sigh—and LaFleur echo'd it back again to my ear—."[44] The illusion is one of flow of feelings uninterrupted by the *censorship* of grammar and punctuation, and therefore unimpeded by reason. Lacunae render his syntax more expressive. The style approximates spoken speech, which, as we have seen, both Rousseau and Herder rank as more natural and more capable of expressing emotion than writing.[45] In speech, there can be neither revision nor erasure; accordingly, Sterne achieves the effect of uncensored, unreflective simultaneity. We feel as though Yorick records the event as it occurs, as he experiences it, since he involves us in each stage of the *construction* of his sentences rather than just presenting us with the finished product. The momentary silence represented by each dash reveals Yorick's "heart" more than his words possibly can.[46]

Just as a crumbling public edifice invites the viewer into an unseen private, interior space, Yorick's surface fragmentation invites the reader's active participation in reconstructing his feelings. Through these devices, Sterne consistently tries to conquer sensibility's Babel—however vainly—to avoid the linearity of language and yet to retain the visual and emotional impact of the scenes that he describes. As we saw, Lessing, in *Laokoön*, points out that language, because it consists of artificial signs organized in time, cannot achieve the simultaneity of the plastic arts.[47] He, like Diderot, finds language's linearity a limitation. Condillac, of course, represents the opposing view and applauds language's linearity as that which enables analytical thought, logic, and reason.[48] The moral aesthetic of sensibility would favor the view of Lessing and Diderot, who, while noting the same linearity of language, bring more attention to what is lost in translation from simultaneous impression to a linear expression. As Diderot writes: "Notre âme est un tableau mouvant, d'après lequel nous peignons sans cesse: nous employons bien du temps à le rendre avec fidélité: l'esprit ne va pas à pas compté comme l'expression. Le pinceau n'exécute qu'à la longue ce que l'oeil du peintre embrasse tout d'un coup. La formation des langues exigeait la decomposition." [Our mind is a moving picture from which we paint ceaselessly: we spend a lot of time rendering it faithfully: . . . the mind does not go step by measured step like expression. The brush executes only in the process of time what the painter's eye embraces in a flash. The formation of languages demanded the decomposition.][49] Writers of sensibility were generally engaged in a battle to regain what is lost in this "decomposition": that is part of the reason for the great emphasis on gesture and visual imagery in sensibility, as well as on the *spoken* word, which was considered less decomposed than the written.[50] Perhaps it is, in this regard, fitting that Sterne wrote *Journey* immediately following a Grand Tour to Rome. While constructing his own form of the rhetoric of ruins, Sterne is, despite his parodies, also aspiring to a universal language of nature.

By combining roles of narrator and protagonist into one character, Sterne incorporates these "unwritten" and antirational elements into *Journey;* by considering Yorick's double role, we can better understand Sterne's escape from and partial recapitulation to linearity, as well as his characteristic response to sensibility's contradictory impulses. Figure 20 from *Tristram Shandy* shows Tristram's attempt at a "tolerable straight" narrative line, comically juxtaposing the narrative and anti-narrative impulses within Tristram as he struggles to be both narrator and protagonist. The illustration could apply to the self-conscious narrator of Sterne's later novel, although with greater emphasis on anti-narration. On the other hand, Yorick self-consciously distinguishes himself from non-sentimental travelers who do travel "in straight lines," and while he does not allow linearity or rational purpose to dictate his itinerary, his narratorial duties do impose a chronological linearity upon his narration.[51] In other words, Yorick, too, attempts a "tolerable straight" line of narration, but is disrupted by the pathos of individual characters or scenes rather than by Tristram's haphazard memories. If association of ideas drives Tristram's anti-narrative curves, then the association of feelings or sympathy for others drives Yorick's.[52] Because of his double role, Yorick (unlike Werther) can distance himself from his own story enough to view his digressions *as digressions:* "As I have told this [little unrelated anecdote] to please the reader, I beg he will allow me to relate another *out of its order,* to please myself—the two stories reflect light upon each other,—and 'tis a pity they should be parted."[53] Yorick is very conscious, both of the curves, squiggles, and meanderings in his narrative sequence, as well as of the more traditional linearity.

There is only one line in each narrative graph, to represent the single most unifying factor within the novel—namely, the single voice and perspective (however fragmented and torn) of Tristram that unifies the whole. However, just as Yorick spends much effort in trying to untangle his identity in the course of the novel and is plagued by his double role as participant and narrator, observer and translator, the line is anything but orderly. The straight part of the line belongs to Yorick the master, 'author,' and man of words, while the curves belong to Yorick the man of feeling and "Sentimental Traveller." If one were to draw a similar graph for LaFleur, for example, there would be no straight segments, for LaFleur simply *feels* and has neither self-consciousness nor responsibility.[54]

If we took a close-up look at one of the curves in the graph in Figure 20, we could use it to represent the individual turns in Yorick's narrative. For example, when Yorick is just realizing that he has no passport and may be put in prison for his offense, he notices the starling in the cage, which sends him on his rhapsodic detour to the suffering inmates of the Bastille, and

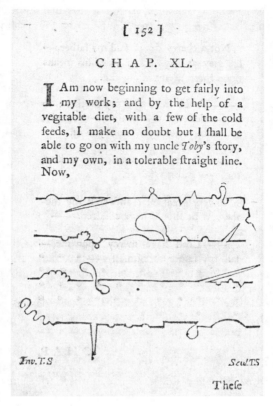

Figure 20

onward to the praises of Liberty. Just as he bursts into tears of sympathy for those who cannot enjoy liberty, LaFleur (who has not been privy to Yorick's private and silent associations) sees him crying and thinks it must be over the passport. It is Yorick's sympathetic recognition of LaFleur's connection with his "straight" line of narration that brings him back to the problem at hand. LaFleur's association reminds him of the assumptions made in public discourse. Often Yorick repeats the last phrase of an interrupted conversation or scene as he returns to the "straight" line from which he departed. Thus, the interrupted straight line also represents the interruption of public clock time in favor of Yorick's sentimental conception of private time measured by his "heart."[55]

Sterne's techniques superficially resemble modernist stream-of-consciousness narratives, yet Figure 20 again reveals the difference: the constant, self-conscious return to the straight line reveals the continued conservative reliance on a traditional narrative plot line, traditional chronology, public authority, and also *public* communication. In *Journey*, however, there is greater emphasis on Yorick's explicit role as author. For example, Yorick plays with the reader's expectation that a travelogue should begin with a preface: instead of omitting one altogether, he includes a "preface" several chapters into the book. In *Journey,* order and disorder are pursued alternately, according to whether Yorick listens more to his head or to his heart. Yorick the narrator-author provides the authoritative and orderly framework within which Yorick the participant can sentimentally meander and which brings attention to his serpentine curves. We began this chapter by exploring the conflicting impulses inherent in the general eighteenth-century fascination with ruins. By now it should be apparent that the novelistic "rhetoric of ruins" shares a similar ambivalence. The "rhetoric of ruins" in the case of both literature and landscape shows a tension between completion and incompletion, monument and ruin, narrative and anti-narrative impulses, and the desire to construct system versus the desire to particularize experience. Follies were thus constructed by authors and architects specializing in the material expression of these contradictory impulses.

In *Journey,* we find a self-conscious narrator-protagonist who has definite opinions about language—a man of feeling struggling constantly with words. In the process of his narration, fragmentation and omission function as meters of sympathy. For example, Yorick occasionally omits whole sections of dialogue: in perfect accordance with his idea that words are insignificant shells when not backed by sympathy, Yorick simply omits the monk's speech when he does not sympathize with him. In the two adjacent chapters entitled "THE MONK—CALAIS," Yorick hardly lets the monk get a word in edgewise. When the monk finally does speak, his words are elided across the transition between chapters. The second chapter thus begins with Yorick's reply to the monk's omitted speech: "—'Tis very true, said I . . ."[56] The reader still has no idea to what he is responding—we witness the fragments of a conversation, and the fragments represent Sterne's lack of sympathy with the monk. One of the multiple effects of such fragmentation is that the reader sympathetically fills the gap with imaginative scenes, allowing the reader to feel as though he or she is experiencing alongside Yorick. In this case the fragmentation also encourages the reader to sympathize with the monk, even when Yorick neglects him. (He later attempts to compensate for his failure in sympathy.)

Sterne, of course, was not the first novelist to present a fragmented text, nor the first to express the difficulty of communication. Sterne's success with the use of fragmentation and gesture in *Journey* is partially due to his ability to use and improve on techniques developed by François Rabelais, Miguel de Cervantes, Jonathan Swift, Samuel Richardson, and Tobias Smollett, among others, and employ them in the service of the novel of sensibility. Fragmentation in Rabelais and Cervantes includes a variety of mutilated manuscripts to create surface texture as well as comic effects for the reader. Their use of fragmentation has a serious side as well: "their mutilated and missing manuscripts make visible the uncertainties that mark all narrative."[57] Yet the effect of this fragmentation is very different from the type involved in the novel of sensibility, where dual impulses and the doubts about the communicative and referential powers of language play a stronger role.

TRANSLATING HAMLET

In a pure, natural state unsullied by convention, human beings would be transparent to one another, enjoying "la facilité de se pénétrer réciproque-ment" [the ease of mutual understanding];[58] however, in post-Babelian society, translation has become necessary and Yorick proclaims himself as "translator" of the world around him. This is not to say, in Sterne's fictional world, that nature has grown silent, *per se,* but rather that nature and society speak in different tongues. Ann Jessie Van Sant mentions the poignancy with which the desire for transparency is echoed throughout the culture of sensibility, formulated by Sterne's Tristram Shandy in his wish for "a *glass* in the human breast,"[59] a literally transparent body through which we could witness the workings of the inner heart.

Gestures speak to those who can understand—and translate—the language of nature. An example is Yorick's translation of a young girl's curt-sey: "—'twas one of those quiet, thankful sinkings where the spirit bows itself down—the body does no more than tell it."[60] Bodies speak, gestures speak, but they speak neither English, nor French, nor the language of reason. In fact, it could be said that these seemingly silent gestures speak whereas speech merely interprets: "There are certain combined looks of simple subtlety—where whim, and sense, and seriousness, and nonsense, are so blended, that all the languages of Babel set loose together could not express them—they are communicated and caught so instantaneously, that you can scarce say which party is the infecter. I leave it to your *men of words* to swell pages about it."[61] As Mullan indicates, "the rhetorical sug-gestion is that the signifier (the look, the gesture) can exist in all innocence, detached, for a special moment, from the words which hamper expres-sion."[62] In loudly proclaiming that he is not describing, Yorick achieves the effect of describing both the pure signified and the "opake" signifier: he preserves the moment of translation.

Willingness to translate such "looks of simple subtlety" is a sign of both sociality and sensibility in Sterne: "There is not a secret so aiding to the progress of sociality, as to get master of this *short hand,* and be quick in rendering the several turns of looks and limbs, with all their inflections and delineations, into plain words. For my own part . . . when I walk the streets of London, I go translating all the way." Such passages, however, simultaneously throw his assertions of ability into doubt: "I have more than once stood behind in the circle, where not three words have been said, and have brought off twenty different dialogues with me, which I could

have fairly wrote down and sworn to." [63] Without this ability to translate, or "decode,"[64] each human being would be isolated by language and
convention, since individual imaginations threaten a unified experience
of reading. And while solipsism still looms as one of the greatest threats
to humanity, Yorick's translation may offer the best protection (or solace)
available, even if it is momentary and perhaps illusory within the shifting
contexts of Sterne's work.

Ultimately, silence is the most sincere escape from artifice: sighs, tears,
gestures, and glances communicate more directly when untainted by words.[65]
Smollett often uses detailed physical descriptions of his characters' gestures
and stances to convey their emotion; however, Smollett's use is formulaic,
and one gesture may refer to three or four different emotions in varying
contexts. Sterne, in contrast, uses highly specific gestures that are individu-
alized and located in place and time: "There are some trains of certain ideas
which leave prints of themselves about our eyes and eye-brows; and there is
a consciousness of it, somewhere about the heart, which serves but to make
these etchings the stronger—we see, spell, and put them together without a
dictionary" (*Tristram Shandy*, 5.127). His use of gesture, corresponding to
sensibility's moral aesthetic, suggests the complexity of individual emotions
which defy verbal translation as well as traditional narration.[66] The reader
must look to the gaps between words, sentences, and chapters, for the sensible heart struggling to express itself within the confines of "artificial" language. Yorick describes how his spoken words ruin the entrancing moment
he shares with a mysterious Frenchwoman while silently staring at a remise.
His words destroy the intimate moment, as she complains: "the heart knew
it, and was satisfied; and who but an English philosopher would have sent
notices of it to the brain to reverse the judgment?"[67] In dramatically direct
opposition to its etymology, conversation severs the intimacy engendered
by silent sympathy. She concludes with "a look which I thought a sufficient
commentary upon the text," and Yorick is suitably silenced.[68]

The phrase "sufficient commentary upon the text" deserves further
consideration. According to the passage, the natural language of the body
as "text" includes its own syntax and grammar. Yorick frequently uses
the language of the written word to describe spoken and even *un*spoken
exchange, such as the words 'text' or 'translation': these borrowed terms
suggest that there is no way of speaking about conversation without falling into analogies with the written word. Ironically, such terms highlight
the inescapable similarities between the language of gesture or feeling and
the language of written words, while maintaining the superiority of the
former. In the same vein, Yorick calls his instinctive intuitions "axioms"
and uses grammatical terms to express his social interactions: "I am apt
to be taken with all kinds of people at first sight; but never more so, than
when a poor devil comes to offer his service to so poor a devil as myself;
and as I know this weakness, I always suffer my judgment to draw back
something on that very account—and this is more or less, according to the

mood I am in, and the *case,*—and I may add the *gender* too, of the *person* I am to *govern.*"[69] In these passages, Yorick also plays with analytical categories and terms like "mood," "case," "gender," "person," and "govern" that normally refer to precise grammatical relationships, and uses them to describe spontaneous, associative movement. Such passages parody the codification of sensibility—or the extent to which even the rejection of linguistic artificiality still depends on language for its mode of expression. In establishing that logic, grammar, and syntax are all inescapable, these terms also suggest the possibility of hypocrisy in the man of feeling.[70]

Names, too, are equally artificial constructs of society, tainted by the fall of the Adamic tradition. For this reason, not once do we witness Yorick asking for the name of the numerous characters he encounters. On the one hand, this means he is not fulfilling his conventional task as author; it is also an implicit critique on the generalizing or homogenizing effect of the unchecked narrative impulse. Since Yorick is narrator as well as protagonist, the reader, too, must learn to dispense with names and identify characters according to their sentiments or actions instead. Yorick will either entirely omit a name or he will mention the name much later in the novel (such as the Frenchwoman by the remise and Father Lorenzo), drawing attention to the earlier absence.[71]

When Yorick omits names, in other words, it is because he considers them inadequate representations of individuals—signifiers that require translation—to the point that he does not know what to answer when he is asked to identify himself. In a particularly illuminating scene, Yorick forgets to introduce himself to the Count—that is, in the conventional way, by telling his name; instead he tells of his love of Shakespeare, which to Yorick is a more accurate introduction. The reader discovers Yorick's omission after their long, long conversation, when the Count finally has to ask him for it. Yorick responds:

> There is not a more perplexing affair in life to me, than to set about telling anyone who I am . . . I have often wish'd I could do it in a single word—and have an end of it. It was the only time and occasion in my life, I could accomplish this to any purpose—for Shakespear lying upon the table, and recollecting I was in his books, I took up Hamlet, and turning immediately to the grave-diggers scene in the fifth act, I lay'd my finger upon YORICK, and advancing the book to the Count, with my finger all the way over the name—*Me, Voici!* said I.[72]

Yorick's "perplexing affair" stems from the great chasm that lies between knowing and naming, as well as between name and identity.

Yorick does not end with this frustrating account, however. The passage as a whole suggests that identity is both "identifiable" and potentially communicable, albeit with difficulty; it suggests the occasional concurrence of knowing, naming, and being. But why, one might ask, would *showing* the written name on a printed page signify more (or be any less "perplexing") than *speaking* the name? Is this a play on the semi-fictive protagonist-narrator of Sterne's novel, who cannot recognize himself except in yet another layer of fiction? Self-representation cannot rely on traditional narrative impulses; identity must be performed rather than told. An interactive commitment is required for self-revelation, according to Yorick's stance.

If we look closely at the passage, we notice that not only the Count, but the narrator himself conflates the two Yoricks: "recollecting *I* was in his books, *I* took up Hamlet," he says, the first "I" referring to Yorick, the king's jester in Shakespeare's play, and the second "I" referring to Yorick, the narrator and protagonist of Sterne's novel. "*Me, Voici!* said I" shows the same conflation once again. In a certain sense, such confusion is hardly new to the novel, rather, this scene crystallizes the structure of the whole novel, where, although narrator and protagonist are the same voice, it is the process of self-conscious writing that links them as well as separates them, as the following passage parodies: "I declare, said I, clapping my hands."[73] The structure of the novel equates self-representation with self-performance and simultaneously mocks this comic state of affairs.

The danger and the beauty of words, according to Sterne's (and Locke's) representation, is that while one uses them to refer to essences, they can be mistaken for the essences themselves. Yorick extends this problem one step further: one of the ironies of the man of feeling's linguistic position is that his great capacity for sympathy leads him to identify with others—he assumes their misfortunes as his own. In fact, he shapes and performs his own identity in the moments when he *identifies* with others. This is part of the reason why Yorick needs a character in a play to communicate—and establish—his own identity. "I lay'd my finger upon YORICK," he says, suggesting that he can only see himself in external manifestations—in interactions with other characters, even if they are fictive (within the novel). This is of course doubly appropriate since Shakespeare's Yorick also depended upon Hamlet's sympathetic identification of his "name" from the ruins of his body. Like the architectural ruin, which depends upon the viewer's imagination of a former state of completion, so Yorick depends upon sympathy to fill the gaps of his identity: thus, a sympathetic, literary unity is possible for the self, even when philosophical unity is not.[74] It is a risky process, however, as we see afterwards when the Count mistakes name for essence.

Sterne's conception of the self depends to a large extent upon such sympathetic connection with the external world. In a later passage, he remarks: "'Tis going, I own, like the Knight of the Woeful Countenance, in quest of melancholy adventures—but I know not how it is, but I am never so perfectly conscious of the existence of the soul within me, as when I am entangled in them." The passage also shows how previous literature and protagonists like Don Quixote, as well as Hamlet, have been reinterpreted or reclaimed, like *Genesis,* according to the demands of sensibility's moral aesthetic. On the very next page, after just such an "entanglement" with Maria, he writes: "I am positive I have a soul." [75] Shakespeare also provides such an "entanglement" by immediately arousing specific emotions and affections in the Count. [76] It is ironic that Yorick makes this connection on a verbal basis, and although he insists that there are two Yoricks, kindred only in name and association, the Count takes him literally, and introduces Yorick henceforth as the King's jester. The final and greatest irony is, therefore, that in his (painful, contorted, exaggerated) attempt at self-identification, his identity is nonetheless misunderstood.

It is important to note that, although the "Sentimental Traveller" or the man of feeling can, by definition, never be satisfied with language and convention, Yorick never gives up hope of communication and community. His attempts at making himself understood are Quixotic, not Sisyphean: each attempt is the beginning of a comic adventure in "translation." We can see, therefore, that although Sterne shares some of Rousseau's ideas about the fallen state of language, Sterne's tone has more in common with Herder's emphasis on "*Möglichkeiten*" or "possibilities."

In this regard, we can better appreciate Sterne's choice of a name for his protagonist: Shakespeare's Yorick was a silent skull from a grave to which Hamlet lends a voice—a ruined fragment, which Hamlet lovingly restores in imagination to its former glory. Hamlet, to use Sterne's word, sympathetically *translates* Yorick's silent gaze. The *new* Yorick, Sterne's Yorick, is simultaneously Yorick *and* Hamlet, ruin *and* monument, silent skull *and* eloquent interpreter, spectacle *and* storyteller. [77] This is the source of Yorick's tragicomic interpretation of the failure of words to communicate sentiments. Yet the death of spoken language is necessary, in Yorick's economy, for the discovery of the semiotics of the body. [78] If one could define, one would not need to enact; however, even this more 'natural,' visual language of gesture or facial expression must be 'enacted' through words—the process Yorick calls translation. For Yorick, the death of words enables the birth of intimacy, whether erotic or fraternal. [79]

One might ask whether Sterne's usage of gesture and fragmentation is really so different from his predecessors earlier in the century, such as Swift, Fielding, and Smollett. Fielding and Smollett, for example, also complain of the limitations of mere words to express certain poignant scenes. "O, Hogarth! had I thy pencil! then would I draw the picture of the poor Serving-man," cries the narrator in *Tom Jones* (1749). Similarly, in *Roderick Random* (1748), the protagonist-narrator laments: "It would require the pencil of Hogarth to express the astonishment and concern of Strap on hearing this piece of news." [80] Yet in adapting his use of gesture and fragmentation in *Journey* to suit the dictates of the cult of sensibility, particularly in the depiction of natural virtue and the increasing difficulty of self-representation, Sterne distinguishes himself from these authors and is the first to combine these various techniques in the service of the hallmarks of the culture of sensibility.

Sterne's fragmentation may appear even closer to that used by Jonathan Swift in *Tale of a Tub* (1697–1710), yet here, too, there is a difference in tonality and purpose. In *Tale of a Tub*'s last chapter, for example, when the Hack himself admits his "unhappiness in losing, or mislaying among my papers, the remaining part of these memoirs," Swift wishes to portray holes where arguments should be, but not because of a moral aesthetic that questions the value of argument and narrative *per se,* but rather stemming from the Hack's intellectual defects, including what Harries calls his "modern rootlessness."[81] Anti-narrative forces cause even greater uncertainty in Swift's *Tale of a Tub,* where appended fragmentary "discourses," with missing chapter numbers, rows of asterisks, a mock-preface, elaborate digressions, gaps, and lacunae mock the narrative form. In *Tale of a Tub,* as Northrop Frye and Elizabeth Harries have shown, Swift experiments with textual fragmentation, including the visual representation of lacunae with asterisks, which may at first appear similar to Sterne's technique; however, Swift has other goals in mind and does not develop the technique to the same extent. Swift does not share Sterne's goal of inspiring emotion and simultaneous, sympathetic participation in the reader; the lacunae are also overtly intentional on the part of the (fictional) author.[82] While Swift also ruminates on the problems of authorship, they are not the same problems as involved in the novel of sensibility. The important difference is that these intellectual traits are *seen by the implied reader as defects,* rather than as indicators of a competing moral aesthetic, indicating a Shaftesburian or Rousseauan natural goodness in a world filled with Hobbesian enemies to virtue.

The use of anti-narrative disruption is at least as old as Montaigne, who also used anti-narrative techniques to distinguish his text from an orderly treatise; this continues as a strong tendency in modernism, not to mention post-modern discourse. Sterne, however, applied such techniques to the novel and brought it to new heights. In fact, the emphasis on showing works "in progress" grew suddenly so popular in the 1760s and '70s that this newly refined temporal manipulation of the reading act was Northrop Frye's main criterion for distinguishing the "Age of Sensibility" from the preceding Augustan period. Richardson foreshadows this move in his style of "writing to the moment" in epistolary novels like *Pamela* (1740)—a technique which places the letter writer in occasionally ridiculous postures. What Richardson tries to effect through actual chronology and letters, Sterne achieves through syntax. In Richardson's *Clarissa* (1747–48), Richardson foreshadows some of the visually explicit anti-narrative techniques that Sterne is well known for. Within the novel, Richardson also uses asterisks, dashes, and gaps to indicate the "inexpressible" emotion of his heroine. See for example Figure 21, from an early edition of *Clarissa,* where Richardson typographically reveals the difficulty of generalizing or narrating Clarissa's subjective experience, foreshadowing her ultimate role as a ruined individual at the center of his novel. There is no obvious sequence in which her marginalia and the center text should be read. Richardson uses

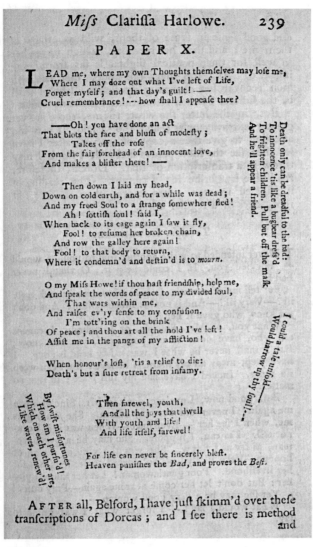

Figure 21

his experience as a master printer to create these unusual paratextual and anti-narrative devices that reveal a grief that exceeds narration.[83]

Whereas Richardson "clings desperately to his faith in man's ability to order and control life according to the conventional rules of prudent morality, to live, as Sir Charles Grandison does, strictly according to principle," the "final result of *Clarissa* is to demonstrate . . . the ultimate inadequacy of systems, and the fact that belief in them is not nearly so important as belief in the dignity and value of individual human beings."[84] Ultimately, Richardson's novels are dominated by the singular narrative drive, and the non-narrative and anti-narrative impulses that emerge from within his novels run counter to his authorial (and moral) intent. Sterne, on the other hand, begins with a more Quixotic or humanistic suspicion about the systematization of human experience. Subsequent authors of sensibility, such as Henry Mackenzie, become increasingly explicit about the combination of narrative and anti-narrative drives embodied in their literature: Mackenzie, echoing the epigraph from Diderot, for example, writes to a friend of "the Fragment Manner on which I formed my Plan [for *The Man of Feeling*]," claiming that disjointed sketches and "detach'd Essays" can "interest[-] both the Memory and Affection deeper, than mere Argument, or Moral Reasoning."[85]

Sterne takes this inexpressibility one important step further towards an increased self-consciousness, especially about the *inherent* limitations of language and their implications for the author. For Richardson, 'sentiment' and 'sentence,' meaning and the grammatical forms of language, have not yet divorced. The fragmentation of Clarissa's writing does indeed evoke a sense of her virtue as well as her distress; however, one has the sense that the fragmentation of her language has more to do with her unfortunate circumstances and the lack of a sympathetic audience than with an inescapable aspect of language. Through his unique technical innovations, Sterne succeeds in combining popular notions of the inadequacy of speech, the artifice of writing, and the suspicion of author(ity) with sentimental trust in natural virtue and sympathy.

Goethe uses slightly different techniques in his depiction of Werther's difficulty translating the world; however, the topic brings him to the unfortunate Prince of Denmark as well. For Werther, the central obstacle is not the referential capacities of language but the problem of inauthenticity. Given the growing attitude (in the mid-to-late eighteenth century) toward what Lionel Trilling calls "the inauthenticity of narration," or a growing distrust of controlled or balanced prose, omniscient narration grows incompatible with sensibility, and anti-narrative techniques proliferate. Just as follies attempt to preserve a fast eroding moment in time, precariously balanced between completion and utter destruction, the prose fiction of sensibility functions as a monument to the moment of intense feeling.

Werther's belief in the singularity of experience and the uniqueness of the moment, as well as his hatred of the censorship of emotions, is reflected in his distrust of any process of re-writing, polishing, or perfecting earlier attempts at expression. He is outraged, for example, when "Der Gesandte" (the Ambassador) suggests revisions to his written reports: "'Er ist gut, aber sehen Sie ihn durch, man findet immer ein besseres Wort, eine reinere Partikel.'—Da möchte ich des Teufels werden. Kein Und, kein Bindewörtchen darf außenbleiben, und von allen Inversionen, die mir manchmal entfahren, ist er ein Todfeind." ['It's good, but look through it: you can always find a better word, a cleaner particle of speech'—Then I get devilishly upset. No 'and,' no conjunction can be omitted, and he is the mortal enemy of all inversions that sometimes escape me.] For Werther, the initial, disjointed expression is more perfect in its authenticity than any refined, polished, grammatical revision. His dramatically morbid choice of words above ("Teufel" or devil, "Todfeind" or mortal enemy) show what mortal stakes are involved in issues of grammar.[86] According to this stance, the anti-narrative force of an utterance is proportionate to the worthiness of the speaker to narrate; to narrate experience is to demean it.

Werther frequently complains that his representation will fall far short of his experiences; in fact, these complaints form a constant refrain in his letters to Wilhelm. Werther claims to feel everything so deeply that the linearity of prose falls short—only the greatest poet could make words carry his feelings, he says: "Ich müßte die Gabe des größten Dichters besitzen" [I would need to possess the talents of the greatest poet].[87] As ironic as this is, coming from Goethe's pen, the stronger his feelings, the more reluctant Werther is to express them: "Lieber, ich mag nicht ins Detail gehn; so reizend, als es mir war, so einförmig würde es in der Erzählung werden" [Dear Friend, I don't want to go into details; it would become just as monotonous in its recounting as the experience was exciting].[88] Language flattens his emotional upheavals, with the sheer weight of its conventionality. Yet his complaints about the inefficacy of his writing are not apparent in the quantity of his actual writing (which increases rather than decreases). Underlying his constant complaints is a strain of pride. Whereas Pope, for example, in his final lines of *Eloisa to Abelard,* proudly proclaims: "He best can paint 'em [her woes], who shall feel 'em most,"[89] Werther expresses the same pride, but in an opposite direction. Werther, too, is a poet, but as a "man of feeling," he believes that those who "feel 'em most" also have the greatest difficulty communicating their sufferings.

Rather than allow reason to censor the expression of his emotion, Werther writes long, highly fragmented, disorganized paragraphs in his letters: "Dir in Ordnung zu erzählen . . . wird schwerhalten."[90] The more extreme his feelings, the greater the fragmentation, especially the proliferation of dashes, which in Werther's case should be called *Gefühlstriche* rather than *Gedankenstriche*: "daß Albert nicht so beglückt zu sein scheinet, als er—hoffte—als ich—zu sein glaubte—wenn—Ich mache nicht gern Gedankenstriche, aber hier kann ich mich nicht anders ausdrücken—und mich dünkt deutlich genug" [That Albert didn't seem so fortunate as he—I hoped—when I—believed it was—if—I don't like to make dashes, but here I can't express myself any other way—for me it seems quite clear].[91] Werther, a good student of Rousseau, assumes that if words must be used, it is more "natural" and more evocative to avoid syntactically complete sentences (recalling Rousseau's remarks that savage men gave every single word the sense of a whole proposition). The elliptical ejaculation "Klopstock!" is infinitely more personal for Werther than any sentence, such as,

"Doesn't the storm remind you of one of Klopstock's sublime odes?" ever could be. It can be a sign of intimacy and trust to allow another to fill in the gaps of one's sentence. If successful (and it is generally successful until proven *un*successful), this dynamic produces a sense of having simultaneously come upon the same thought. In other words, the breach of silence, the use of words to communicate anything, reveals in itself a distance—something yet-to-be-shared. The inappropriateness of verbal expression grows with the intensity of the feeling. "O darf ich, kann ich den Himmel in diesen Worten aussprechen?—daß sie mich liebt!" [O dare I, can I express heaven in these words?—that she loves me!][92] To force poignant feelings into words is, according to Werther, like trying to express eternity using a linear, temporal medium. Prolixity, in this context, heightens the speaker's sense of alienation from the addressee; therefore, according to the new rules of rhetoric influenced by the hallmarks of the culture of sensibility, the degree of intimacy would seem to be inversely proportional to the number of words used to express a sentiment.

After Lotte has, at the early climax of the novel, turned to Werther and uttered the word "Klopstock!" with such poignancy, he addresses the self-same poet in his imagination and hopes never to hear the name again, for fear of sullying the memory of that moment: "Edlere! hättest du deine Vergötterung in diesem Blicke gesehen, und möcht' ich nun deinen so oft entweihten Namen nie wieder nennen hören!" [Noble one! Had you seen your deification in this look, and now may I never hear your oft profaned name spoken again!][93] Only silence (or death) can preserve the utterance's purity. This connection between articulation or narrative completion and death helps drive the topos of fragmentation within the culture of sensibility. The actual death of Mackenzie's Harley, for example, coincides with the moment he finally articulates his true feelings.[94] For Werther the stakes are equally high; repetition, like convention, grammar, and logic, homogenizes and de-personalizes language and obscures the original emotions in which the utterance originated.

Werther, like Yorick, portrays himself as a translator of (his own) poignant experience into sluggish words. The difference is that while Yorick translates the outer world and its communicative gestures, Werther translates his *own* emotion. Werther's is an intensified crisis in self-representation that Goethe portrays using the greater realism of *Werther*. Werther translates his feelings into words, which to his "*Herzi*," or heart, are are like a foreign language. This attitude towards language is a symptom of an attitude towards society in general, a Rousseauan distrust of convention: it is a recognition of a fundamental irreconcilability between attention to manners and forms versus attention to feelings: the conflict between *Sittlichkeit* and *Sinnlichkeit*. Although *Sittlichkeit* might make for good neighbors and superficially pleasing social interactions, Werther's position is that rules, convention, moderation, and even narration are nonetheless all enemies of feeling. The narrative drive to represent the self has been tainted by its connection to form, manners, grammar, and tradition. The final and most extreme statement of his break with convention comes in the last letter, addressed to Lotte: "Und was ist das, daß Albert dein Mann ist? Mann! Das wäre denn für diese Welt—. . . Du bist von diesem Augenblicke mein!" [What does it mean that Albert is your husband? Husband! That then, is for this world—. . . You are from this moment mine!].[95] Eternity alone does not compromise the man of feeling.

Self-control and cheer become increasingly loathsome for Werther, and, ultimately (and paradoxically), he seeks death to preserve himself from change: "O, so vergänglich ist der Mensch, daß er auch da, wo er seines Daseins eigentliche Gewißheit hat, da, wo er den einzigen wahren Eindruck seiner Gegenwart macht, in dem Andenken, in der Seele seiner Lieben, daß er auch da verlöschen muß, und das so bald!" [O, so transient is man, that even there where he has the actual assurance of his being, there where he makes the only true impression of his presence, in the memory, in the soul of his beloved, that he even there must extinguish—and this so soon!][96] He wishes to isolate each moment in time, halting the urge to narrate, saving the original feeling from the levelling hand of storytelling. Suicide, the ultimate silence, paradoxically affords Werther the only way he can protect his feelings from the corruption of society and escape from its conventional restraints. He must die to preserve authenticity, as well as his presence in Lotte's heart and their last intimate moment together. Ultimately, language, just like nature, becomes nothing more and nothing less than an obstacle to infinity. In his final act against society's encroaching "artificiality," he destroys himself before he will allow society to tame him. In rejecting all artifice, including artifice in the service of authenticity, Werther performs the fate of the natural ruin: eventually crumbling to nothing.

FROM SYMPATHY TO SOLIPSISM

The emphasis on self-representation causes sensibility's moral psychology to be singularly theatrical—a theatricality that is both its strength and its weakness. At its best, it heightens a sense of human dignity and encourages self-knowledge as well as the 'socialization' of the passions. For Smith, for example, sensibility allows for the comic resolution of a regrettable situation: the impossibility of complete sympathetic identification between individuals leads to the necessity for us to display our emotions to others according to our conception of how we might respond to them if we were the spectator rather than the actor. Thus the theatricality of communication has its basis in the perceived crisis of self-representation. The failure of complete identification makes us strive to understand and be understood; it leads to the possibility, not only of cooperation and therefore of society, but also to the possibility of virtue itself. To use Smith's musical metaphor, as much as we naturally long for *unison,* we must recognize it as impossible; but it is because of this failure that we can achieve *harmony* instead.[97] Impossibility awakens and enlists the imagination. For better and for worse, sensibility does indeed turn those who feel into actors displaying their wares. At its worst, the actors never take off their masks, all of nature is turned into a "living Tableau" (as David Marshall warns), and sympathy degenerates into self-complacency, hypocrisy, and atomization.[98]

Could sensibility's great emphasis on sympathy be an attempt at an antidote for this intense self-consciousness? Marshall and Cox have both remarked that sensibility's constant emphasis on sympathy tends to be somewhat defensive: "the passionate assertions that universal sympathy *must* exist may well betray more than a little anxiety about the self's ability to overcome its psychic isolation, more than a little fear of solipsism."[99] Or as Mullan puts it, "the real threat is that faced with the impenetrable aspects of others, faced with the impossibility of knowing other people's sentiments except through acts of imagination, sympathy itself might be impossible."[100] In this sense, the culture of sensibility shows the profound influence of both Hume and Rousseau. On the one hand, it cherishes Hume's and Smith's vision of the social role of the passions: "We can form no wish, which has not a reference to society . . . Whatever other passions we may be actuated by; pride, ambition, avarice, curiosity, revenge, or lust; the soul or animating principle of them all is sympathy."[101] Rousseau, on the same subject of sympathy, writes that it is "obscur et vif dans l'homme sauvage, développé mais faible dans l'homme civil" [incomprehensible and vivid in the savage man, developed but weak in the civilized man].[102] Reason, in the civilized man, "replie l'homme sur lui-même" [turns man back upon himself] and makes him immune to others' sufferings, allowing him to turn his back on his natural sympathy.[103] Rousseau's description emphasizes that civilized man's sympathy is both more and less than the savage man's, because the civilized man is painfully aware of what he does *not* do for others. Together, Rousseau and Hume express sensibility's curious combination of optimism and pessimism about human nature.

Despite sensibility's relatively optimistic moral aesthetic, novels of sensibility generally reveal that feeling, just as much as reason, can turn human beings in upon themselves. When Werther first realizes that Lotte loves him, his response is striking: "Wie ich mich selbst anbete, seitdem sie mich liebt!" [How I worship myself now that she loves me!][104] It becomes increasingly evident that Werther's love for Lotte has more to do with Werther's fragile and artistic internal world and private, creative imagination than with the actual woman. In his later parody of the cult of sensibility, *Der Triumph der Empfindsamkeit* [*The Triumph of Sensibility*] (1777), Goethe ridicules just such a response. In this play the lovesick Prince, who has built a mannequin of his beloved to remind him of her when she is away with her husband, is in the end given his choice between the puppet and the real woman. Ultimately, he vastly prefers the puppet he has lovingly created with his own hands and we witness their tearful and ludicrous reunion.

The mannequin ironically conforms more closely to his ideals of intimacy and kinship.

Within Werther, we have intimations of a similarly narcissistic response: for example, when he hears a description of the beautiful woman that the farm boy loves, he responds by hoping that the exquisite creature he has created in his imagination will never be sullied by the sight of the real woman: "vielleicht erscheint sie mir vor meinen Augen nicht so, wie sie jetzt vor mir steht, und warum soll ich mir das schöne Bild verderben?" [Perhaps she would not look as good to my eyes, as she does standing before me now, and why should I ruin the beautiful picture?].[105] Yorick, too, allows his imagination to supplant reality: "I had not yet seen her face—*'twas not material;* for the drawing was instantly set about, and long before we had got to the door of the Remise, *Fancy* had finished the whole head."[106] Sensibility's imaginative creations become more important than nature herself, just as, in these novels, self-narration threatens to replace the self.

Ironically, the movement that gave new clout to the imagination, and strove to prove Johnson wrong about Imlac's "dangerous prevalence of the imagination," in the end proves him in some sense right. Both Sterne and Smith, for example, show that imagination, like sympathy, is essential for communication—to fill the gaps left by the failure of words to communicate meaning and emotion. In both of their fictional worlds, the greatest danger is not the imagination's going astray and leading to madness as Johnson, through Imlac, had warned; for them, the greatest danger would be a *lack* of imagination, which would leave individuals permanently isolated from each other. The 'sensible' imagination of both Sterne's Yorick and Goethe's Werther, however, leads them to admire the solipsistic world of madness. Werther in the end goes mad himself, much in the way described in *Rasselas.*

Ultimately, as Jane Austen so admirably parodies in *Love and Freindship* and *Sense and Sensibility,* unchecked sensibility leads not only to solipsism, but also to *in*sensibility—a deadening of the senses themselves. As the novel progresses and as Werther becomes increasingly involved in his own sensibility, he begins literally to lose his senses: when he first falls in love with Lotte he writes that "die ganze Welt verliert sich um mich her" [The whole world dissolves around me][107]; a few months later "alle meine Sinne aufgespannt werden, mir es düster vor den Augen wird, ich kaum noch höre, und es mich an die Gurgel faßt wie ein Meuchelmörder . . . Ich weiß oft nicht, ob ich auf der Welt bin!" [All my senses are stretched thin—it is dark before my eyes, I can hardly hear anymore, and it it clutches at my throat like an assassin . . . I often don't know if I am on Earth!][108]; and finally, near the end he writes, "mit mir ist es aus! Meine Sinne verwirren sich, schon acht Tage habe ich keine Besinnungskraft mehr" [It's over for me! My senses are confused, for eight days now I have been unable to think].[109] As documented in *Werther,* there is a causal connection between extreme sensibility and a lapse into insensibility. Werther's life gradually becomes a "monodrama" (the prince's favorite genre in *Triumph*): his voice replaces all other voices, and his imagination replaces the external world. He gradually loses all contact with the objects of his sensibility. He must deaden his senses in order to preserve the mental picture of the world he has created for himself. Werther loses the delicate, ironic balance that forms the rhetoric of silence and lapses, instead, into silence itself. It is in this context that we could say that madness begins where irony ends. And, because in the "monodrama" there is no separation between the narrating and narrated "I"s, the crisis of self-representation is resolved only where madness begins.[110]

Within the culture of sensibility, agony over the (im)possibility of human intimacy and communication is exacerbated by concern over human tendencies towards solipsism, so effectively illustrated by Laurence Sterne in his *Tristram Shandy*. Solipsism, in fact, becomes such a hallmark of sensibility that Keats and Hazlitt both denigrate sensibility's purposeless and solipsistic self-consciousness.[111] In a philosophical dispute that resembles a linguistic corollary to the dispute over Hobbes and natural goodness, authors were torn between the demand for intense self-consciousness on the one hand and awareness of the dangers of solipsism on the other: between self and society.

For novelists of sensibility this forms not only an intriguing philosophical problem, but also an opportunity to exercise new narrative techniques, particularly following the eccentricities of Sterne: "from the want of languages, connections, and dependencies, and from the difference in education, customs, and habits, we lie under so many impediments in communicating our sensations out of our own sphere, as often amount to a total impossibility," writes Yorick in *Sentimental Journey*.[112] Because of this concern, first-person, self-conscious narrators become much more common, largely through the work of Sterne, Tieck, and Diderot, and authors generally experiment with the self-conscious mediation of sentiment via language.

Running through the writings of the cult of sensibility is the theme of the "tender" or sympathetic heart, the most precious asset of the man of feeling, and seemingly the most valuable antidote for solipsism. Ostensibly it is precious for its ability to sympathize with others, yet these comments reveal the solipsism inherent in this admiration.[113] In fact, we must remember Yorick's preface written in the Désobligeant (a one-person chaise): the "see-saw" and "agitation" of the stationary coach that attracts the attention of at least one "inquisitive traveller" presumably stem from the masturbatory exercise that a solitary Yorick connects with writing a preface: "'Twould have been better in a Vis-à-Vis."

Yorick, however, treats the danger of solipsism with self-conscious irony and humour as the following scene displays: "The old French officer delivered this with an air of *such candour and good sense,* as coincided with my first favourable impressions of his character—I thought I loved the man; but I fear I mistook the object—*'twas my own way of thinking*—the difference was, I could not have expressed it half so well."[114] Sterne's Yorick reveals an awareness of a natural tendency to remark and love what we already know and feel, thereby often mistaking a narcissistic projection of the self for a nobler sentiment such as love or sympathy.[115] Sterne, through Yorick, also suggests an antidote: the *vis-à-vis*. Society is the only way to avoid this trap: "—Surely—surely man! it is not good for thee to sit alone—thou wast made for social intercourse and gentle greetings."[116] In order for self-representation to succeed, an audience, if not a partner, is required.

SENSIBILITY'S CIVIL WAR

In *Journey,* Sterne's Yorick takes self-consciousness and internal division to a new extreme. Yorick-the-narrator reveals that Yorick-the-participant's silent gestures and silent conversation (which supposedly represent a 'natural' and spontaneous language) are as painfully self-conscious as spoken language: for example, in one of his flirtatious encounters, he remarks "that I continued holding her hand *almost* without knowing it."[117] The telling "almost" here represents the disjunction between the two Yoricks, which prevents him from achieving a 'natural' state. The result, in *Journey,* is constant mental theatrics: "—I will not go to Brussels, replied I, interrupting myself—but my imagination went on—."[118] Both Werther and Yorick strive against all odds to be natural and both fail miserably. Each is defeated by the self-consciousness that he cannot suppress. In each man of feeling there is a separation between an observing, recording self and an acting, feeling self; an *Erzähler* (the storyteller) and an *Erzählung* (the tale). In Werther, this amounts to civil war, while for Yorick, these two selves engage in conversation.

As the novel progresses, Werther's self-consciousness increases and with it his internal discomfort. His self-knowledge gradually and uncomfortably exceeds his self-control, as he begins to ask an increasing number of questions about his own motives, observing himself as though a spectacle over which he has no control. For example, he addresses the following rhetorical question to Wilhelm: "Doch wozu alles, warum behalt' ich nicht für mich, was mich ängstigt und kränkt? Warum betrüb ich noch dich? Warum geb' ich dir immer Gelegenheit, mich zu bedauern und mich zu schelten. Seys denn, auch das mag zu meinem Schicksal gehören!"[119] [What's the purpose of all this: Why don't I keep to myself all that worries and sickens me? Why do I still distress you? Why do I always give you the opportunity to pity me and scold me? Maybe that, too, is part of my fate.] Werther follows the logic of sensibility's rhetoric to its natural conclusion: why speak or write at all? Why try to communicate the incommunicable? By asking the question, he reveals the paradoxical nature of the novel as a whole: he is the teller of his own story, but the story he wants to tell is of the hopeless artificiality of words and conventions—sensibility's second fall of Babel.

The invocation of Fate in the last line of this passage also suggests Werther's complex relation towards authority: on the one hand it accords with sensibility's disdain for attempts at control or planning—the hubris of unaided reason; on the other hand, it also seems an admission of defeat, which we encountered in Harley as well. The defeat of delicate virtue is quite central to sensibility, as Brissenden has shown; however, Werther exhibits a slightly different, newly personalized emphasis. Werther takes Yorick's self-reflexivity to new heights and combines it with Harley's pessimism about the man of feeling's potential to survive in the world. There is, however, a degree of self-disapproval and internal division, if not civil war, that we do not find in the other two characters. The internal division ("I" is both questioner and object of question) tends to suggest that Werther could possibly have avoided his fate, that he could conceivably have chosen another course of action: the questioning "I" sees options that the feeling "I" does not. The passage thus expresses Werther's growing detachment from himself and painful recognition of his own degree of control and foreknowledge—recognitions that reveal extreme forms of the tension between control and lack of control or between public appearance and private essence that characterize the culture of sensibility.

Werther's remarks about his own reading of his diary reveal more of the difficulties involved in his increasing self-consciousness: "ich bin erstaunt, wie ich so *wissentlich* in das alles, Schritt vor Schritt, hineingegangen bin! Wie ich über meinen Zustand immer so *klar* gesehen und doch gehandelt habe wie ein *Kind,* jetzt noch so *klar* sehe, und es noch keinen Anschein zur Besserung hat." [I am astonished at how consciously I went into all of it, step by step! How I saw my situation ever so clearly and yet acted as a child, . . . still see so clearly, and there is still no sign of improvement!][120] Here we see Werther suggesting the familiar conflict between head and heart, *Vernunft* and *Herz,* through the words "wissentlich" and "klar sehen" to represent reason and control, and "ein Kind" to portray uncensored, 'natural,' emotional experience. The passage shows that Werther cannot purely be a man of feeling as he defines it. His inescapably rational side demands to be heard if not obeyed. There is a great gulf between what Werther's reason forces him to see and what his heart feels, intensified by the split between two moments of time recorded within the passage. The part of Werther that sees clearly also writes clearly, while the part of him that feels most keenly inclines him towards silence and self-destruction.[121]

Goethe was, of course, not the first, even within sensibility, to use the image of internal civil war. In his *Supplément au Voyage de Bougainville* (which was written in 1772, although censored until 1796), Diderot describes civilization's deleterious effect upon the 'noble savages' of Tahiti: "Si vous proposez d'être tyran, civilisez-le. Empoisonnez-le de votre mieux d'une morale contraire à la nature; . . . embarrassez ses mouvements de mille obstacles; attachez lui des fantômes qui l'effraient; éternisez la guerre dans la caverne, et que l'homme naturel y soit toujours enchaîné sous les pieds de l'homme moral" [If you want to become a tyrant, civilize him; poison him as best you can with morality that is contrary to nature; hamper his movements with a thousand obstacles; provide him with phantoms that terrify him, . . . eternalize the conflict inside him, and arrange things so that the natural man will always be chained under the feet of the moral man].[122] Civilization brings about the civil war, for according to Diderot, as for Locke and Rousseau, the state of nature is peaceful and harmonious. Werther, too, strives wholeheartedly for a 'natural' and 'authentic' existence. This is of course his difficulty: to *strive* for authenticity is already to admit defeat. Werther cannot escape from civilization, any more than he can escape from his own rationality. As the novel progresses, the same split which Diderot describes between the 'natural man' and the 'moral man' grows within Werther. Werther chooses the 'natural man' over the 'moral man,' but ultimately, the natural man cannot survive the separation. His acceptance of this civil war spells the beginning of his ruination.

For Yorick, Harley, and the Werther of Part I, the civil war is largely external—a conflict between those of sensibility and those without, between men of feeling and men of words, between those who listen to their natural sentiments, and those who censor them with reason. In contrast, Werther of Part II internalizes this civil war. Especially in his revised version of *Werther,* Goethe emphasizes Werther's inability either to silence his reason or to control his passions. Passages such as the following show his growing self-irony: "Ich kann nicht beten: 'Laß mir sie!' und doch kommt sie mir oft als die Meine vor. Ich kann nicht beten: 'Gib mir sie!' Denn sie ist eines andern. Ich witzle mich mit meinen Schmerzen herum; wenn ich mir's nachließe, es gäbe eine ganze Litanei von Antithesen."[123] [I cannot pray: 'Grant her to me!' and yet she often seems to me as my own. I cannot pray: 'Give her to me!' For she belongs to another. I tease myself with my pain; if I were to desist, there would be a whole litany of antitheses.] Werther, both spectacle and storyteller, narrates an internal drama where his passions first overcome his reason, and his reason alternately tries to overcome his passion. Rather than an internal conversation à la Yorick, Werther shows that reason and passion are engaged in a duel unto death within himself, and he represents himself as a helpless spectator of the conflict.

If one regards Werther's central conflict as *Herz* versus *Vernunft,* one could say that he lets *Herz* direct his words as well as his actions: "ich lache über mein eigenes Herz—und tu' ihm seinen Willen" [I laugh over my own heart—and give it what it wishes] and then again, "Auch halte ich mein Herzchen wie ein krankes Kind; jeder Wille wird ihm gestattet" [I coddle my heart like a sick child; his every wish is fulfilled].[124] Werther applies the same standards to others and suggests the hypocrisy of any words and actions not dictated by the heart. Words without sympathy behind them—one of sensibility's new sins—are worse than empty for Werther; they are insupportable: "nur insofern wir mitempfinden, haben wir Ehre, von einer Sache zu reden" [Only insofar as we empathize do we have the right to speak of a matter].[125] Of course, one of the agonies of his situation is that those who feel *too intensely,* rather than those who do not feel enough, are in the end driven to silence. Reason or *Vernunft* is at home in words, while feeling or *Herz* remains forever alienated. This is what constitutes the deadly connection between Werther's too exquisite sensibility and his overriding rebellion against narration and generalization.

In his long, last scene with Lotte, when words fail both Lotte and Werther, Werther reads aloud his translation of Ossian's poetry. Ossian's unrhymed, liberated verse, "the compulsive telling over of defeat, darkness, despair, the eradication of clear outline and all degree, the world torn and scattered,"[126] its story of tragic deaths and truncated relationships, form the perfect foil for Albert's analytical reason and disdain for 'theatricality' and suicide. Part of *Ossian*'s appeal is that it deals with fourth-century Caledonians of Scotland, who were never touched by either Christianity or the Roman Empire, and were, therefore, considered more "natural." This scene places Werther in the position of protector and translator of "ruins." It is worth remembering that not only are Ossian's poems fragmentary, and thus analogous to ruins, but they are also artificial relics written by the contemporary Macpherson: they are the literal embodiment of the fake ruin. Werther is of course unaware of this irony.[127] It is parallel to the scene in *Journey* where Yorick identifies himself through Shakespeare's character by the same name: Werther also 'performs' his identity and depends upon literature and shared poetic sensibility to complete and express what he is incapable of expressing in reference to himself alone. Of course, the irony is that Werther never escapes from himself: just as his translation of Ossian remains unpublished (within the fictive world of the story, that is), destined for private consumption, "translation" remains primarily an issue of self-expression rather than a means of achieving community with other sensitive souls.[128]

Throughout Part Two, Werther contemplates his own ruin, as he narrates his anti-narrative urges. Rousseau used the statue of Glaucus to represent the pale reminders of a vibrant past; Werther similarly draws a portrait of himself as a ghost (the "ruins" of a prince) who returns to visit his ruined castle: "Kein Wink der vorigen Welt, kein Pulsschlag meines damaligen Gefühles. Mir ist es, wie es einem Geiste sein müßte, der in das ausgebrannte, zerstörte Schloß zurückkehrte, das er als blühender Fürst einst gebaut und mit allen Gaben der Herrlichkeit ausgestattet, sterbend seinem geliebten Sohne hoffnungsvoll hinterlassen hätte." [No hint of the former world, no pulse of my former feeling. It is to me as it would surely be for a spirit who returned to the burned-out ruins of the palace that, as a prospering prince, he once had built and furnished with all bounties of magnificence, and then dying, left in hopefulness to his beloved son.][129] The passage makes no distinction between a ruined world around him and his own ruin—or more precisely, his ruined "heart."

It is interesting that Werther identifies with "ghost" imagery and Yorick with "skull" imagery. In both cases, they invoke ruined remnants of individuals to invite the reader to participate in the imaginary recreation of their essences, and in both cases they invoke the same play: *Hamlet*. Yorick allies himself with the dead jester and Werther with the suffering Prince. In *Werther,* the implication is that we can detect in the earlier passages a pristine, uncorrupted Werther, and the reader's sympathies are called upon to imagine the discrepancy between the "monumental" sensibility of his heart in its prime and its current disillusionment and ruination. The reference to Hamlet is particularly interesting for the indication that Hamlet's indecision and difficulty conveying thought into action may actually be ethically superior to more decisive action.

It is interesting to note in this regard that Mackenzie, in his analysis of *Hamlet,* calls Hamlet a "man of feeling" precisely because of his tendency to split into two people. Sensibility, and its corresponding distrust of words, depends upon a degree of 'unnaturalness' and discomfort, while simultaneously idealizing an unattainable, 'natural' state. Shaftesbury similarly interprets the Delphic inscription: "Recognize yourself; which was as much to say, divide yourself, or be two." Self-knowledge, according to Shaftesbury, depends upon a "self-examining practice and method of inward colloquy."[130] We see the same emphasis upon an internal conversation in Smith's *Theory of Moral Sentiments*. (This is important in the history of Shakespearian criticism: it is at this time that Hamlet becomes interpreted as the divided, indecisive, sensitive character attractive to the ethical and aesthetic predispositions of audiences in the culture of sensibility.)

As the use of the allusions to *Hamlet* suggest, Werther exhibits the *form* of sensibility wedded to a character that gradually rejects sensibility's mode; Goethe's interjection of a note of bitter realism transforms it to something which more closely resembles Romanticism. This is largely because Werther is unwilling to accept the necessity of public speech or to acknowledge the participation of others in communication and the construction of meaning. He neglects Sternean "translation" for the sake of madness and private inspiration, so crucial to authors in the Romantic mode. Werther is unwilling to accept the irony that is Yorick's primary preoccupation, and which eventually allows Austen's Marianne Dashwood to survive.

Like the architectural ruins, language's necessary fragmentation leads to multiple interpretations as varied as Rousseau's and Herder's, Goethe's and Sterne's. It is impossible to emphasize either decay or survival in the ruins—the half that remains or the half that has vanished, yet it is nonetheless possible to emphasize one half or the other. Sterne's view, as presented in *Journey,* suggests that although language is treacherous because it can lead to solipsism, fragments are a sign of hope for intimacy *despite* words. The gaps created by verbal fragmentation and the anti-narrative drive are the gaps where sympathetic imagination can enter. Yorick's distrust of words leads to an emphasis on the shared moment of community and of imagination, which provides the only escape from solipsism.

Werther, on the other hand, shows the despair of community or intimacy that ensues from a belief in the impossibility of successful translation.

As monuments need to be excoriated in order to appeal to the aesthetic of the picturesque, Werther too excoriates himself in pursuit of an ideal. For Werther, fragments are a wrenching sign of his despair; they are gaps that seldom, if ever, can be filled. Goethe relies on the reader, however, to fill the gaps with sympathetic imagination, showing the difference between the novel as a whole and its eponymous hero—the separation between *Werther* and Werther. Werther's distrust of words leads to despair, to increasing fragmentation, to anti-narration as an end in itself, and finally to suicide and silence. Communication is for Yorick a Quixotic adventure; while for Werther it is an ultimately unendurable Sisyphean struggle.

3   Reading Ruin

We would attempt to describe the joy which Harley felt on the occasion, did it not occur to us, that one half of the world could not understand it though we did; and the other half will, by this time, have understood it without any description at all.

—*The Man of Feeling*

I leave it to your men of words to swell pages about it.

—*A Sentimental Journey*

In the epigraphs above, and in many similar passages, narrators of novels of sensibility pointedly and somewhat self-righteously lay down their (fictitious) pens. They symbolically abdicate their authority and authorship either in favor of explicitly lesser men or to illustrate the shortcomings of a world that forces a cruel and destructive separation between the man of feeling and the man of words. Multiple factors lead to this abdication of authorial responsibility, particularly the concerns about communication and self-representation explored in the previous chapter. In addition, both real and fictitious authors of sensibility express concern about their self-image and hope to present themselves in a way that will not compromise the appearance of sensibility to the reader. This latter anxiety in particular leads to great concern over the reader's freedom of interpretation as well as to elaborate techniques for controlling reader responses. These additional techniques involve perfecting the art of "accident" and creating multiple levels of fictional editing to protect the reputation of authors. Each of these techniques is designed to mask authorial control, introducing the important (and perhaps hypocritical) element of disguise. This disguise and evasion of authority affect the masking of control in both follies and novels and demonstrate how the novel of sensibility involves an altered relation between reader and author.[1]

THE ART OF ACCIDENT

On the surface, Sensibility's redefinition of authorship is, like the reclamation of *Genesis,* associated with a reaction against centralized authority, rational ordering, and the synoptic presence of an omniscient author/narrator.[2] Authors and their narrators begin adopting a more democratic approach to authorship, at least rhetorically. As Sterne's Tristram speaks of "halving the matter amicably" with his readers, Mackenzie claims to favor placing "the Pencil into their [the readers'] own Hands."[3] Such gestures indicate the desire to raise the affective powers of the work and emphasize the new dignity in uncensored human passions and "internal" sources of authority, whether in the form of Sterne's "Great Sensorium," Mackenzie's "feeling heart," Goethe's "wunderbare Empfindung," or Smith's "great Demigod within the breast." Sensibility's concern about authorship naturally affects and reflects concern about human relations with the divine—-in particular, the authority and authorship of God— both as "Author" of our being and as author of the "Book of Nature."[4] As the culture of sensibility adapts *Genesis* to reclaim the aesthetics of irregularity while also relying on the authority of an older tradition, its authors also try to reclaim a form of authorship that can allow for the tenets of its moral aesthetic—including authenticity and spontaneity in the absence of a central controlling voice.

Even the landscape gardener Uvedale Price, in his description of how gardeners need to conceal their art, makes an analogy to the need for authors of literature to conceal their own presence as authors within the work: "whenever there is any thing of natural wildness and intricacy in the scene, the improver should conceal himself like a judicious author, who sets his reader's imagination at work, while he seems not to be guiding." And the way to achieve this "natural wildness" is through disguise of explicit artifice. Using the superior example of Homer, who "Scarcely ever appears in his own person," Price complains of Fielding's tendency to appear "sometimes ostentatiously."[5] Especially if it is omniscient, authorial description needs to be vivid enough to make readers forget they are reading, just as the effect Macpherson's spurious *Ossian* had upon Joseph Warton: "who then can look at the following description and not forget almost, that he is reading words? . . . so naturally do the real objects themselves rise to our view!"[6] Authors must find new modes of narration to conform to the moral aesthetic of sensibility, all the while masking their own authorship so as not to distract from the workings of sympathy and imagination.

There is a similar authorial tension among landscapers in the picturesque English garden, between control or mastery of the garden and the attention to the authentic role of nature. The rhetoric of ruin in the novel of sensibility is parallel to the "art of accident" in landscape gardening. Gardeners would hide control, authority, and the marks of the scissors, yet between Uvedale Price and Richard Payne Knight, for example, there was active debate about the role of "accident" in landscape design. In trying to establish his difference from Repton and his followers, Knight champions "accident" as Nature's most instructive work. Knight writes of the great efforts required to achieve the effect of accident, yet he also describes how cultivated neglect differs from actual neglect:

> Those, indeed, who think only of making *fine places,* in order to gratify their own vanity, or profit by the vanity of others, may call this mode of proceeding *a new system of improving by neglect and accident;* yet those who have tried it know, that, though to preserve the appearance of neglect and accident to be one of its objects, it is not by leaving every thing to neglect and accident, that even that is to be obtained. *Profiting by accident* is very different from *leaving everything to accident;* and *improving by neglect,* very different from *neglecting.*[7]

One of the characteristic tensions within the picturesque is between the drive to achieve "artificial" mastery over the environment, so overt in baroque geometrical plantings, radial axes, and topiary, and the newer respect for "natural" accident.[8] The landscape gardener thus faces the same struggle as the artist: to what extent must he hide his own artistry (shovel as well as scissors) in order to mimic nature's authenticity, and while also claiming enough art to justify his occupation.

The language of feeling, like the language of nature, relies heavily on artifice; natural appearance is more important than how that appearance is achieved. Even so, the examples from Sterne show how "perplexing" communication can be and how much the listener or reader is involved in the process of translation. How, then, does an author control the emotional response to narrative fragmentation? Not only is there a problem of ostensive reference, but also accuracy regarding all products of the imagination: to what extent can an author trust the reader or viewer to reach the desired emotional states or conclusions? The very desire to control such responses suggests an uneasy decentralization of power on the part of authors; while pretending to "halve" the power amicably, in the absence of trust, authors return to the wish for authoritarian authorship.

Building upon the narrative drive common to both follies and novels, Thomas Whately elucidates the difficulties of interpretation. He describes the desired psychological effect of the ruins in terms of their ability to engage the viewer's imagination in a hypothetical former state:

> The representation [of fictitious ruins], though it does not present facts to the memory, yet suggests subjects to the imagination: but, in order to affect the fancy, the supposed original design should be clear, the use obvious, and the form easy to be traced; no fragments should be hazarded without a precise meaning, and an evident connexion; none should be perplexed in their construction, or uncertain as to their application. Conjectures about the form, raise doubts about the existence of the ancient structure; the mind must not be allowed to hesitate; it

must be hurried away from examining into the reality, by the exactness and the force of the resemblance.[9]

The best architects of follies are, in this sense, storytellers or authors of evocative fiction, as Capability Brown had suggested. The effects of follies are built upon the assumptions that ruins, like irregularity in general, allow for more evocative, theatrical, and interactive viewing by virtue of the gaps they offer spectators. Ruins, like tears, are studies in ambivalence: they can evoke contradictory emotions regarding the human struggle against time—either marking the sad remnants of human achievement despite time's travails, or the majestic persistence of human achievement approaching immortality. These figures both appeal to a culture that wishfully exaggerates a faith in both the human capacity for goodness and the ability to self-regulate. Both tears and ruins thus reflect the philosophical insecurities at the heart of the culture of sensibility.

At the same time, a great irony consists in the fact that the ambivalence inherent in the ruin/ fragment as symbol causes artists and authors who construct them to need to rely even further on successful communication with the reader or viewer. This dynamic relies upon the viewer's narrative drive that lends meaning to "an unmeaning heap of confusion." In other words, the freedom of interpretation that ruins' ambivalence allows can lead to the "perplexity" Whately and other artists and authors fear. The authoritarian terms of the passage (e.g. "must not be allowed," "force") thus suggest the underlying insecurity of this aesthetic stance and Whately's lack of trust in his audience. Similar to the culture of sensibility's conflicted impulses regarding human nature—the desire to believe in both natural goodness *and* the need for cultivated ethics—here we see a wavering confidence in the "natural language" of ruins. Ruins are indeed the "natural language" or "language of nature" that can communicate without words to the spectator's ready heart, and yet, without very careful arrangement on the part of the architect or gardenist, the correct response cannot be assumed. Spectators can easily become "perplexed" or "uncertain," distracted by multiple sensations, antiquarian impulses, or burgeoning intellectual curiosity, all of which are antagonistic to the desired emotive effect. Artifice and authenticity, art and nature, order and irregularity, natural language and analytic devices are all precariously balanced in the artistry of the folly. Meanwhile, the possibility of follies deteriorating into "unmeaning heaps of confusion" and generating "perplexity" in the viewer point to the frailty of ruins as a form of communication.

And although no novelist can control the temporal aspect of any reading of his or her novel, and therefore cannot 'create' silence in the way that is feasible in theater, opera, or music, Sterne comes as close as possible for a novelist to 'an empty bar of music' when he leaves us a blank page in *Tristram Shandy*. Even there, the emphasis is on how the reader will *fill* the silence—by picturing the beautiful Widow Wadman. In order for silences to function in the novel, the author must train the reader's expectations and responses so that the reader will help compose the novel while reading it.[10] And while, by definition, readers always help constitute texts by participatory reading, Sterne tailors his use of this feature of the implied reader's role to the specific demands of the culture of sensibility and the inherent conflict between the 'man of words' and the 'man of feeling.'[11]

THE SHAME OF AUTHORSHIP

The crisis of authorial authority sheds light on paradoxes that seem central to the novel of sensibility—namely, that in order to satisfy a moral aesthetic, authors are forced into a position of hypocrisy. They must mask their authorship and authority and avoid revealing their creating, ordering presence in the novel. They must hide their role as 'men of words' to protect their role as 'men of feeling,' yet ultimately the deception and artifice involved in this pretense gives rise to an even greater obstacle to authenticity and transparency. Typical male protagonists in these novels, such as Sterne's Yorick, Henry Mackenzie's Harley, and Goethe's Werther, are "men of feeling" who, although writers, self-consciously distinguish themselves from "men of letters" by exhibiting a distrust of discipline, plans, logic, grammar, straight lines, and virtue based on an obedience to law. Instead they admire the spontaneous overflow of extreme feelings— usually benevolence and tenderness, mixed with some erotic overtones. Novelists thus respond to sensibility's anxieties of authorship—such as the newly perceived disharmony between writing, speaking, and feeling subjects—by creating works that privilege the unspoken, the unwritten, and the unplanned in a number of new ways.

In other words, not only do authors of novels have to find ways to hide *their characters'* reliance upon traditional means of speech, and instead show the successful communication of feeling through the "language of nature" (frequent descriptions of look and gesture), but gradually authors begin to present *their own* narration in the "language of feeling" as well. Sterne, Goethe, and their protagonist-narrators, as well as authors of other such self-consciously fragmented narratives, *depend* upon and simultaneously *reject* the order, control, and closure associated with authors, authority, and "artificial" language in order to involve their audience in the sympathetic and imaginary completion of the more "natural" language of fragmented texts. As Tristram expresses with remarkable clarity in *Tristram Shandy,* "Writing . . . is but a different name for conversation . . . The truest respect which you can pay to the reader's understanding is to halve this matter amicably, and leave him something to imagine, in his turn, as well as yourself."[12] This corresponds to the viewer's role in the aesthetic appreciation of the picturesque. Viewers and readers do their share to ensure that the scenes (whether verbal, visual, or musical) achieve their proper emotional effect.[13] It may also be that just as Whately describes the assistance he gives the spectator in order to focus emotional attention on an interesting object, the authors of these novels also develop additional structures to direct their reader's emotions.

A narrator who is *not* self-conscious, and therefore not a participant in the action and feelings of the novel, can be seen as anonymous or heartless, randomly imposing the author's authority. Detached narration or omniscience implicitly generalizes human experience and seeks to communicate methodically and rationally; however, it ultimately leads to even greater linguistic isolation than silence, according to this aesthetic. Only spontaneous speech, 'uncensored' by strict grammatical rules and 'untainted' by practical purpose or preconceived plans, can count as authentic or sincere. According to the dominant tenets of the culture of sensibility and *Empfindsamkeit,* as we have seen, only speakers who *feel* can be trusted, and only speech that is fragmented is sincere; therefore, only an author or narrator who shows an awareness of the difficulty of expressing himself can be sympathetic. The gaps in the writing of these narrators can therefore function within the novel—within the author's grand but hidden plan—as a means of representing the narrator as an anti-author or man of feeling. And while this chapter will focus on the techniques used by Sterne, Mackenzie, and Goethe, the phenomenon affected a much wider group of authors in England, France, and Germany.

Yorick and Werther reveal different aspects of the shame and anxiety surrounding authorship. In addition to the visual fragmentation that Sterne offers on the pages of his two novels, he also provides additional techniques to display Yorick's difficulties as author in *Sentimental Journey.* Multiple chapters have the same titles; the preface is "written" after six chapters and remains in that position; and the title (*A Sentimental Journey through France and Italy by Mr. Yorick*) remains pointedly unrevised, since Yorick never reaches Italy. Sterne's unusual title displays sentimental chronology's usurpation of reason's traditional hierarchy over any sequence of moments. Rather than rising above time in an atemporal hierarchy—to the godlike foreknowledge belonging to an author revising his or her text—Sterne's title feigns a position of simple, uncensored sequence. Just as Yorick might have responded if asked at the outset of his journey, that he was heading (vaguely) for France and Italy, and might change his itinerary at any whim, so the title, too, merely records a momentary whim which is only partially materialized. Sterne takes the culture of sensibility's distrust of reason and authoritative speech to its logical (and humorous) conclusion in dethroning the title from its position of authority. According to the unspoken laws of sensibility, he must display *in*eloquence and lack of revision to prove his virtue: his fragments, half-finished sentences, and ellipses display not only his spontaneity and unconventionality, but also, interestingly, the degree of his sensibility.[14]

Another kind of narrative disjunction, which poses as an omission, serves to illustrate Yorick's denial of authorship. For example, when Yorick begins to describe a blush, he writes:

> There is a sort of pleasing half guilty blush, where the blood is more in fault than the man—'tis sent impetuous from the heart, and virtue flies after it—not to call back, but to make the sensation of it more delicious to the nerves—'tis associated.—
> But I'll not describe it.—[15]

Yorick begins to define and falters several times; then after describing it quite well in this fragmentary, disjointed way, he claims to decide not to define it at all. Again, this hypocritical declaration of silence emphasizes the irony of having to develop a "rhetoric of silence"—that is, of portraying the inadequacies of words and sentences *through words*.

There is more to this issue of definition, however: "*Eugenius,* said I . . . to define—is to distrust."[16] This remark from *Tristram Shandy* illustrates the intimate connection in Sterne's work—and in the culture of sensibility in general—between linguistic and socio-ethical concerns. It also suggests that the way to establish community and trust is not through self-conscious, analytical language, if indeed it is through language at all. It reveals the deep difficulty about the role of *public* discourse and the pursuit of shared meaning. Mullan's phrase "the tyranny of explanation"[17] is helpful in this context; it suggests the important connection between analysis and authority. Definitions, names, and categories ("tall, opake words") are artificial limitations which society imposes upon the individual. In her poem entitled *Sensibility,* Hannah More even refers to the "*chains* of definition." The sensitive soul, the sentimental traveler, the man of feeling can stand as individuals in their search for transparency above society's conventional urges to define and to control. Society's limitations and the opacity of language do not serve, however, as a source of anger for Sterne or Sterne's semi-fictive protagonists, but instead are objects of good-humored mockery and allow for the potential of additional intimacy with the reader.

Werther also reveals the painful division between narrator and protagonist through his activities as author. Goethe is careful to limit Werther's authorial positions: Werther writes only letters, rather than a public book with title, preface, and a larger intended audience. Werther writes to his 'dear friend' Wilhelm; however, his letters show that Wilhelm does not understand Werther and his sentiments. Thus the letters reveal Werther's extreme emotional isolation; Yorick's authorship is isolated geographically and linguistically, he is far less isolated emotionally. More importantly, the limited authorship reveals that Werther, a true man of feeling, neither writes with ease nor wishes to publish.

Like Yorick, Werther also exhibits the difficulties of self-representation: both experiencing as a protagonist and recording this experience as an 'author.' Werther, too feels a conflict between the drive to narrate and the need to resist the generalizing tendencies of narration. He desperately wants to represent himself authentically, and struggles to find a means to do so. Ultimately, Werther's struggles reflect his sense of isolation within society and lead to an internal civil war. The self-consciousness that seems inevitable to Yorick and humorous to Sterne spells danger, disintegration, and inauthenticity to Werther. In the end, Werther chooses suicide and his own self-ruination rather than suffering the inauthenticity of his existence within society and its rule-bound institutions, including language.

Werther's complaints that his telling will fall far short of his experiences form a constant refrain in his letters to Wilhelm. Language flattens his emotional upheavals, with the sheer weight of its conventionality. Victor Lange calls *Werther* "the record, transposed into fiction, of Goethe's own perception of the tantalizing ambiguity of words."[18] And although we will not try to judge Lange's biographical claims about Goethe's lifelong attitude toward language, it seems clear that the world portrayed in *Werther, by* Werther, is a world from which the only escape is silence. From the very beginning, the reader knows that Goethe's Werther interprets grammar and conventional forms of speech as examples of how language, while pretending to express feelings, actually obscures them: "alle Regel [wird], man rede was man wolle, das wahre Gefühl von Natur und den wahren Ausdruck derselben zerstören!" [No matter what we say, all rules destroy the authentic feeling of nature as well as its authentic expression].[19]

Convention fetters the authentic, the heartfelt; therefore, Werther must choose between a less 'authentic' and therefore compromised survival within society and 'authentic' expression which transgresses society's rules as described by Rousseau: "Avant que l'art eût façonné nos manières et appris à nos passions à parler un langage apprêté, nos moeurs étaient rustiques, mais naturelles; et la différence des procédés annonçait, au premier coup d'oeil, celle des caractères" [Before art had shaped our manners, and taught our passions to speak an artificial language, our customs were rustic but natural; differences of behavior announced, at first glance, differences of character].[20] Werther longs for just such immediate or transparent connection with other souls, and he searches for it in rustic Wahlheim. Werther emphasizes this dilemma by repeating the word authentic (das *wahre* Gefühl von Natur, der *wahre* Ausdruck): it is precisely this truth or emotional authenticity that words, being mere shadows of experience, can never hope to capture.

Werther the protagonist experiences life as a torrential stream of passions and cannot tolerate any punctuation, modification, or constriction that would make his experience any less true, even in his own recollection or recording of events. He longs for the infinite, the sublime moment, the "rapture of one great emotion,"[21] and is frustrated by any inkling of transience or limitation ("Beschränkung," or "Beschränktheit"). He yearns for the sublime, rather than the picturesque, especially in Part II of the novel. With a strong sense of nostalgia that haunts him, Werther conflates authenticity with preservation of each mood, or each moment of time; thus change itself is cruel and inauthentic for him. This trait leads Werther to some ironic extremes. For example, when someone comes and interrupts Werther as he is writing an especially tearful passage, Werther is distraught (and enraged): "Ein unerträglicher Mensch hat mich unterbrochen. Meine Tränen sind getrocknet. Ich bin zerstreut. Adieu, Lieber!" [An intolerable person has interrupted me. My tears have dried. I am distracted. Adieu, my friend!].[22] Werther cannot tolerate that even sorrow is ephemeral: ironically, he draws tragic implications even from its interruption.[23]

In this particular passage, the return to the world around him disrupts Werther's experience of infinity, which has increasingly little to do with anything other than himself. The fact that tears dry, and that individual passions wear themselves out, only to be replaced by others, are equally signs of mankind's inadequacy: "Was ist der Mensch, der gepriesener Halbgott! Ermangeln ihm nicht eben da die Kräfte, wo er sie am nötigsten braucht? Und wenn er in Freude sich aufschwingt oder im Leiden versinkt, wird er nicht in beiden eben da aufgehalten, eben da zu dem stumpfen, kalten Bewußtsein wieder zurückgebracht, da er sich in der Fülle des Unendlichen zu verlieren sehnte?" [What is man, the lauded demigod! Does he not lack the very powers he needs most? And if he lifts himself up in joy or sinks down in affliction, will he not be arrested in both just there—, returned to blunt, cold consciousness just there where he was longing to lose himself in the fullness of the infinite?][24]

The role of narration is, according to this view, not only to represent the present moment, but also to preserve the past, yet, ultimately these two purposes are in conflict for Werther as his present is ever-changing with his experiences and moods. As each word leaves his mouth or especially his pen, it ages into a hard, cold, hollow shell of meaning, no longer representing himself or his essence, and thus seems to him to be a self-prostitution.

Unlike what Diderot says about the power of sketches, Werther, an artist, has no faith in his power to represent the world visually. As a result, Werther successively gives up painting, sketching, and even writing: "Ich könnte jetzt nicht zeichnen, nicht einen Strich, und bin nie ein größerer Maler gewesen als in diesen Augenblicken" [I would not be able to draw now, not even a line, yet I've never been a better painter than I am in these moments]. According to Werther's dichotomy, drawing, like grammar, concerns itself with detail, forms, and outlines; therefore, Werther grows to prefer painting which concerns itself with the *essences* he desperately wants to express. "Lottens Porträt habe ich dreimal angefangen, und habe mich dreimal *prostituiert*" [Thrice I have begun Lotte's portrait, and thrice I have prostituted myself]. The only artistic activity which remains with Werther to the end is the enjoyment of his own, old translations of Ossian's verse.[25] The dramatic verb choice emphasizes Werther's pain at the discrepancy between his unarticulated perception and his attempts at conventional articulation, and it has its roots in Sterne's description of preface-writing as masturbatory. Both of these images suggest a shared inability to achieve lasting intimacy with others through representation. The difference between masturbation and prostitution also indicates the central danger of authorship for each protagonist: for Yorick (or Sterne) it is solipsism or selfishness; for Goethe's Werther it is inauthenticity. His nostalgic attachment to authenticity, successful mimesis, and transparency disappoint him bitterly.

The irony is that meanwhile, Goethe is relying on those very effects to work on the level of the reader of the novel. Goethe relies on the "art of accident," the successful communicative powers of the fragmented and imperfect text, while Werther despairs of them internally to the plot. In other words, while the novel itself illustrates the insecurities and 'successful failure' of the culture of sensibility, Werther fights against these principles, just as he fights against other forms of inauthenticity, progressively throughout the novel. In *Werther,* the internal conflict between the narrative structure and the ideological and anti-narrative struggles of the protagonist reveals its affinity with the philosophical insecurity of the culture of sensibility. Ultimately, where Goethe creates an ironic text, though, Werther himself refuses to accept irony and artifice in his search for authenticity. Werther refuses to accept the art of accident that Goethe has mastered. Thus while structure and narrative techniques put *Werther* squarely in the camp of sensibility, the character Werther intimates the end of the culture of sensibility, particularly in the second volume.

FRAMING THE MAN OF FEELING

If the narrative impulse is traditionally associated with utilitarianism, linearity, chronology (having a distinct beginning, middle, and end), and the maintenance of one sustained, overarching, and organizing perspective, then it is also associated with the drive to generalize, to view human experience as homogeneous or universal, and to support a centrally authorized authority—namely, the narrator (or implied author). The anti-narrative impulse, then, is non-utilitarian, purposely erratic, and non-chronological (or at least non-linear); it features multiple subjective perspectives, a higher regard for subjectivity, and the drive to sympathize with others without merging them into one's own narrative path. Anti-narrative or non-narrative (or paratextual) impulses suggest the decentralized authority of the crumbling public edifice, resulting in the exposure of interior lives. Rather than generalization, it encourages localized particularity and the resistance against codification. Narrative impulses lead us to tell or recount; anti-narrative impulses strive to perform what cannot be told. Revisions are generally subsumed within the narrative impulse—their traces erased to favor a single narrative sequence; the anti-narrative impulse encourages revision and highlights it as a decentralizing force in anti-narratives. In three-dimensional terms, narrative strives for the cumulative, incremental completion of a single monument that resists the centrifugal powers of decay; non- or anti-narrative drive does not aspire to a single monument, but rather is pulled in multiple directions, delighting in entropy and not allowing for a coherently organized whole in conventional terms. Narrative impulses strive for the monument, order, and system; anti-narrative for the ruin, irregularity, and spontaneity.

For digressions and lacunae to be noticeable, however, they must occur within a narrative framework—an assumption of a main topic or chronology that can then be effectively shaken, interrupted, or left incomplete. In the same way, a folly depends upon a tension between the desire to recreate and the desire to tear down—between the monumental and the ruined—to achieve its effect. Sensibility and the picturesque also both evince a concern for diverse subjective experiences, yet also depend partly on conventional authority, for the sake of such contrast. Sensibility's rhetoric of ruins, then, depends upon an internal tension between narrative and anti-narrative drives; it depends on the coexistence of these two drives for the construction of its narrative fiction, just as the picturesque does for the construction of follies.

As architects had to pose as archaeologists, pretending to have discovered, rather than have built, such "authentic" monuments, authors too pretend to have discovered what they actually write. Both architects and authors addressed twin goals: to create a "publishable," coherent monument or volume and also to fragment their creation and thereby mask the creator's role as well as evoke greater emotional participation in the reader or viewer. Only by studying the developments in narrative technique within this broad cultural context, can we understand the ethical stakes involved in the aesthetic demands imposed upon artists within the culture of sensibility. What is especially interesting is how Sterne, Goethe, Mackenzie, and other authors solve the problem introduced by the fake ruin—that is, the problem of presenting a fragmented text without causing the readers to lose confidence in the author's degree of mastery, and, conversely, of hiding the artfully organized character of their works so that they will appear 'authentic.'

On the one hand, the author must work to create the illusion that the text resulted from no plan of his own—that is, he must pretend to have discovered the text rather than have created it, while on the other hand, he elaborately constructs it to fit his purposes. The new structure allows the accidental, the spontaneous, the dreamt, the unintended, and the unspoken to become more significant, more credible, and more aesthetically appealing in these novels than the effects of cold reason, conscious symmetry, and planning—just as the monument is more authentic and more aesthetically appealing when it is crumbling.

An omniscient or objective narrator would have been just as unthink-able in *Journey* as in *Werther,* for it would have directly conflicted with the "unfathomableness of subjectivity" that is central to Sterne's moral psychology.[26] And yet, Sterne seems to give Yorick more narratorial authority than Goethe does Werther, since Yorick is engaged in a public act of writing. Yorick's narrative authority, though, is undermined by the fact that there is very little plot or action to report. Sterne plays with Yorick's double role as narrator and subjective participant in order partially to mask his authority as well as to depict what is lost in translation in the gulf between feeling and words. From the very beginning, Yorick makes it abundantly clear that the position thrust upon him by the moral aesthetic of sensibility necessarily leads to hypocrisy: "There are certain combined looks of simple subtlety—where whim, and sense, and seriousness, and nonsense, are so blended, that all the languages of Babel set loose together could not express them—they are communicated and caught so instantaneously, that you can scarce say which party is the infecter. I leave it to your *men of words* to swell pages about it."[27] Yorick *qua* man of feeling disdains words and their users, yet it takes Yorick, the man of words, to teach us this. Sterne achieves Yorick's rhetoric of ruins—or his art of eloquent *not*-saying—using characteristically fragmented syntax.

While it is hard to overstate the difference of tone in these two works—humor being almost as absent from *Werther* as tragedy from *Sentimental Journey*—Sterne and Goethe both use an intruding narrator to create an additional frame (or frames) of authorship in their texts and to respond to the aesthetic that distrusts yet relies upon authorship and control. In *Journey,* Yorick is the narrator as well as the central character in his travels; in *Werther,* Werther also narrates his own story—this time, in the form of letters. Goethe provides a second self-conscious narrator, the *Herausgeber* or Editor, who compiles Werther's letters and comments upon them. The *Herausgeber* forms a second narrative frame, especially noticeable since his is the first voice and the last voice of the text. All three of these narrators contribute to the fragmentary nature of the narrative because they are self-conscious about their writing and the difficulties associated with producing an organized, unified text. These complicated linguistic and narratorial requirements were not limited to these two novels, but instead exhibit responses to the central concerns of sensibility's moral aesthetic. Involved, as these techniques are, with the protection of one's reputation as a man of feeling, these authors tended to involve the implied reader in an evaluation of each man of words involved in the text. This may be one way of understanding Virginia Woolf's complaint about Sterne in her introduction to the 1928 edition of *Sentimental Journey:* She claims that the "chief fault" of the work "comes from Sterne's concern for our good opinion of his heart."[28] The reader is forced to participate in the protagonist's performance, much like the audience that Tieck creates in *Gestiefelte Kater* (*Puss in Boots*).

As Patricia Meyer Spacks writes, "Yorick's is an existence of self-display. If he does not have an immediate audience, he must imagine one . . . revealing himself on the stage of his own fantasies . . . Sensibility entails its own performance, ever demanding publicity."[29]

Henry Mackenzie's *Man of Feeling* is particularly useful for understanding the role of narrative frames for the novel of sensibility. It is hard to imagine fragmentation taking a more calculated effect in a novel. Only twenty-five out of the original (purported) fifty-six chapters remain in the text, many of them only brief fragments of the "original," which suffered the indignities of being torn, burnt, lost, shredded, or even used as wadding for a rifle by a variety of unfeeling hands. Upon examination, we can see that each of the three central voices in this novel—the three central "I"s—represents a separate "feeling heart" through its fragmentation. Although Harley does not narrate his own story, the narrators transcribe his spoken words and (somewhat unaccountably) his private thoughts at great length. At such times, Mackenzie shows his response to the demands of the culture of sensibility by sacrificing authenticity in plot for the sake of authenticity of emotion. Just as it is more important to own a Roman ruin in Sweden or the north of England than it is to explain how it arrived there in the first place, it is more important that Harley *not* be a man of words, than that the reader understands *how* the narrator could possibly have known his feelings.

On a rare occasion, Harley does write of his (unproclaimed) love: in Chapter 40, we find a pastoral poem that Harley has laboriously written; however, he promptly uses it to lift a hot teakettle, and forgetfully leaves it on the handle. The narrator, Charles, finds it there, and later records: "I happened to put it in my pocket by a similar act of forgetfulness."[30] Mackenzie will go to great, and almost comic, lengths to stress the unpremeditated nature of these men's actions; therefore, their status as men of feeling cannot be sullied with imputations of 'rational' or 'artificial' motives. The narrator-participant Charles must not think of himself as narrator during the time frame that his narration depicts, lest the reader find him cold, hypocritical, or untrustworthy. Thus, somewhat ironically, he must display a lack of foresight in order to gain the 'sensible' reader's trust. The poem embodies thematically the 'rhetoric of silence' and the pursuit of 'natural' language as the following excerpt shows:

> I term'd her no goddess of love,
> I call'd not her beauty divine:
> These far other passions may prove,
> But they could not be figures of mine.
>
> *It ne'er was apparell'd with art,*
> *On words it could never rely;*
> It reign'd in the throb of my heart,
> It gleam'd in the glance of my eye.[31]

Harley's great distrust of words (and in the same poem his painful consciousness of "tongue[s] that [are] smooth to deceive") hinders him from writing his own story, just as it keeps him from declaring his love for Miss Walton.[32] However, Harley is far from silent: Harley speaks and thinks, and both are recorded by the original narrator, whom we discover to be an intimate friend.

Through this combination of two characters—the all-important yet silent Harley, and the nearly anonymous narrator—Mackenzie is able to express the dual impulses of sensibility. Harley is allowed the silent pursuit of authenticity, with occasional quickly aborted attempts to express his feelings; the presence of his friend Charles (we learn his name on the last page) assiduously collecting Harley's thoughts and scraps of paper not only functions as a model reader and spectator for the reader (a model student of pedagogy of seeing), but also enables Harley to escape any suspicion of authority, contrivance, or authorship.

Charles repeatedly evinces traditional narratorial omniscience, but this omniscience is masked by his personal subjectivity: Charles loves Harley, and his great affection for him prevents him (according to his own account) from presenting the narrative in an orderly fashion. Charles's narration, like Harley's speech, is fragmented with dashes: "At that instant a shepherd blew his horn: the romantic melancholy of the sound quite overcame him!—it was the very note that wanted to be touched—he sighed! he dropped a tear!—and returned."[33] Charles is disorganized and writes much about the difficulties of writing: "We would attempt to describe the joy which Harley felt on the occasion, did it not occur to us, that one half of the world could not understand it though we did; and the other half will, by this time, have understood it without any description at all."[34] Mackenzie's narrators all take Tristram's lesson to heart, namely that "to define is to distrust." According to the typical paradox of the 'rhetoric of silence' and of sensibility in general, Harley's emotions are repeatedly (and paradoxically) described as surpassing description: "There were a thousand sentiments;—but they gushed so impetuously on his heart, that he could not utter a syllable. * * * *."[35] Again we find, as we did in *Journey* and *Werther,* that ineloquence is a token of depth of feeling, keenness of perception, and even virtue. The final asterisks indicate that feelings—the "thousand sentiments" that refuse analysis, sequential consideration, and linear narration—also reduce the narrator to silence.[36]

The use of fictional frames and fictitious provenances stems from the epistolary novel. Samuel Richardson is known for his innovations in the epistolary novel, especially his emphasis on "Familiar Letters, written, as it were, to the *Moment,* while the Heart is agitated by Hopes and Fears, on Events undecided."[37] He fictitiously refers to himelf as an Editor rather than author in all his major works, but does not provide the elaborate fictions of acquisition that developed in the second half of the century. His goal was also to minimize the presence of the autocratic author or the Editor in his novels—the Editor intrudes only once in *Pamela* (1740), as she is abducted, and not at all in *Clarissa* (1747–48). In the preface to *Clarissa,* he uses an interesting device to justify the anti-narrative force of the novel, excuse the length of it, and to dramatize the Editor's lack of ordering.

The Editor reports great concern over the length of the collection of letters and considers presenting them in another form, either through narrative summary or just by omitting parts to single out one narrative thread. He reports having "several judicious friends" read the letters and consult upon how they should be arranged. Some argued to "give a narrative turn" to the letters; others "insisted that the story could not be reduced to a dramatic unity, nor thrown into the narrative way, without divesting it of its warmth and of a great part of its efficacy."[38] Finally he says he will present the first two volumes to the public, and let the public decide whether or not the collection is too long. Throughout this discussion, however, it is not authenticity or the arousal of sympathy that are at stake, but rather *"instruction"* and the didactic value of the novel. This places Richardson in an ethically authoritative position, even as he is taking pains to mask his authorship. His didactic tone also distinguishes him from authors of sensibility: he publishes a table of the collected "Moral Sentiments" of *Clarissa* as an appendix to the novel, as well as an edition of Clarissa's *Meditations Collected from Sacred Books* (1749), to ensure the proper sentiments are conveyed by his novels. While avoiding the appearance of autocratic authority, Richardson waxes fairly tyrannical in his desire to control his audience's responses, especially through the use of paratextual material.[39]

Similarly, the editor of the third edition of *The Beauties of Sterne* (1782)—a compendium of the most moving scenes from both *Tristram Shandy* and *Sentimental Journey* for the "Heart of Sensibility"—expresses his difficulty in arranging the sentimental episodes and tableaux. Whereas he intended to arrange them alphabetically, he states that this would have overwhelmed the reader by too many consecutive scenes of intense pathos. So instead, the editor divides up the most pathetic scenes, so as not to overwhelm the reader of feeling.[40] Interestingly, this editor not only creates gaps in the sequence of the text in order to evoke feeling, but, confident of success, also exerts additional paternalistic control over the reader's emotions.

Frances Sheridan, in her epistolary novel *The Memoirs of Sidney Bidulph* (1761), sees fit to include multiple narrative frames, with two successive fictional editors mediating between the heroine and the historical author. While Sheridan does not focus as much on the surface fragmentation of the text, she does create many gaps when the heroine is too ill or grieved to be able to write. At those times, her nurse Patty "takes up the pen" to relate the minutiae. As in *Werther,* there is a very fine line between letters and journal entries (Sidney and Cecilia both refer to the letters as "the journal" at times in the narrative), but this time with a more sympathetic reader than Werther's Wilhelm—one who arrives in the final pages to become an active character within the story. Again, there are model readers imbedded in the text—not only Cecilia, but also her faithful servant Patty and the second nameless editor who tries desperately to discover more of Sidney's story and is disappointed to publish it as a "fragment."

Authorship flows in rapid succession between the male editor and at least four other authors; Cecilia's family history of Sidney; Sidney's own letters with multiple inset letters from others, as well as many letters written for her by Patty and others; another note from the editor; and Cecilia's final summary of events (also fragmented). With such a number of authors present in the novel, authorship is diluted and the reader is less distracted by Sidney's dual roles as protagonist and narrator of her own events. It is interesting to note that the explicit (fictional) editor is the only male author, and is the only one with the goal of publication, thus he is the only of the authors involved whose authenticity is potentially tainted, yet Sheridan makes it clear that he too is moved by Sidney's misfortunes and therefore still reliably represents the culture of sensibility.

All of Mackenzie's novels include some form of narrative frame to hide authorship and account for the mangled manuscript that lies at its center, regardless of whether the novel is epistolary or not. In the epistolary *Julia de Roubigné,* for example, the novel is interspersed with many rows of asterisks showing the missing letters and sections of letters that again, faithful editors have gathered in spite of other Hobbesian readers. Here too, sympathetic servants take up their mistress' pen to fill in gaps when their oversensitive mistress is incapable of writing herself. In addition, Julia segments her letters into miniature episodes or moments by leaving large spaces and lines between them, as she records each individual event or feeling "to the moment" in Richardsonian fashion. As a result the text has a much more fragmented surface appearance than *Sidney Bidulph.*

Finally, the editor's non-narrative impulses are made quite explicit, as the work is divided into two sections of letters—one arranged chronologically to portray Julia's fragmented but largely chronological narrative, and the other introduced as being purposely disordered: "MY Readers will easily perceive something particular in the place where the following letters of Savillon are found, as they are manifestly of a date considerably prior to many of the preceding. They came my hands assorted in the manner I have now published them, probably from a view in my young friend, who had charge of their arrangement."[41] After going back and forth as to whether or not to rearrange the two sets of letters into one whole, the editor says he decided to leave them in this order because "it is not so much on story as sentiment, that their interest with the Reader must depend."[42] Thus, for the sake of sentiment, the Editor perpetuates their non-narrative arrangement and thereby also lessens his own authorial or ordering role.

In Rousseau's preface to *Julie, ou la Nouvelle Héloïse* (1761), Rousseau conducts a dialogue between himself and an unnamed literary critic, debating the style of the letters in the novel. In the course of this dialogue,

Rousseau defends the fragmented style of the writing, saying that "a letter from an honestly impassioned lover will be loosely written, verbose, drawn out to great lengths, disorderly, repetitious." He defends the style in terms of emotional authenticity rather than instructional utility. Similarly, when he describes the composition of *Nouvelle Héloïse* in the *Confessions,* he, like Goethe, emphasizes his own lack of forethought: "Je jettai d'abord sur le papier quelques lettres éparses sans suite et sans liason, et lorsque je m'avisai de les vouloir coudre j'y fus souvent fort embarrassé. Ce qu'il y a de peu croyable et de très vrai est que les deux prémiéres Parties ont été écrites presque en entier de cette maniére; sans que j'eusse aucun plan bien formé." [At first I jotted down a few scattered letters on paper, unconnected and without sequence; and when I made up my mind to place them in order, I was often in considerable trouble. What is almost incredible but is quite true is that the first two parts were written almost entirely in this manner, without my having any well formed plan.][43] Of note here is that rather than taking elaborate strategies to mask his authorship through editorial frames, Rousseau chooses to take other strategies to protect his reputation as a man of feeling. For him, it is not as necessary to pretend that the letters were historically authentic, and instead more important to show his similarity to the characters in their shared non-narrative impulses that distinguish the man of feeling from the monarchical author, man of reason, or hack. In this way, Rousseau's approach to masking authority and authorship bears more in common with Goethe than with either Sterne or Mackenzie.

THE ARCHAEOLOGIST'S DISGUISE

Like the follies of the previous chapter, novels of sensibility combine the dual desires for monuments and ruins, artifice and nature, concealing and revealing, control and spontaneity in order to satisfy sensibility's ambivalence regarding authority and its longing for authentic communication. For the purposes of this chapter, we will take a closer look at one particularly striking folly that still exists today: the inhabitable Column House built by M. François Nicolas Henri Racine de Monville for his picturesque park in Paris, le Désert de Retz. His park included stereotypical ingredients of an English-style garden, including two classical ruins, a medieval ruin, a classical Temple, a Chinese pavilion, a Tartar tent, an obelisk, a pyramid, a tomb, a rustic bridge, a thatched-roof cottage, a hermitage, a dairy, an open-air theater, and a grotto.[44] Monville built his Column House as the centerpiece of his picturesque garden in Paris approximately in the year 1781, and it was much admired by visitors such as Thomas Jefferson, Marie Antoinette, and his good friend, the Duc d'Orléans. The structure was fifty-five feet tall, and approximately fifty feet in diameter, striking in its hill-top setting, the highest point in his estate.

Starting with comments made by visiting architects in the eighteenth-century, many commentators have remarked on the fabrique's similarity to drawings of the Tower of Babel, such as the seventeenth-century engraving by Athanasius Kircher in Figure 22. Monville, too, seems to have associated the fall of Babel with the building of ruined structures. Building upon the analogy, Diane Ketcham asserts that the upper cracks were "created to further the illusion that the structure had been blasted by God's wrath."[45] Following the traditional proportions of Doric columns, the broken ruin suggests to the viewer original columns almost 400 feet tall, supporting an even grander original classical temple. This awe-inspiring, if not threatening, spectacle may engender "Lilliputian" thoughts in the minds of spectators. "How grand the idea excited by the remains of such a column," writes Thomas Jefferson in a letter regarding his visit to the Désert de Retz.[46]

Figure 22

While purposefully ruined on the outside, with carefully planned jagged edges and long, suggestive cracks, the interior of the Column House includes five stories of carefully appointed circular and oval suites surrounding a central spiral staircase (compare Figure 23 and Figure 24). The latter was illuminated by a skylight and hung with pots of exotic plants from Monville's greenhouse. Even the fourth story above ground has carefully disguised windows: they can only be seen inside the purposefully made cracks and crevices of the tower. The Column House became Monville's principal residence, and its suites included a laboratory, library, and art galleries; Thomas Jefferson was so inspired by the interior beauty of the layout of the Column House that he copied elements of it for the Rotunda of his plans for the University of Virginia.

In short, in designing his centerpiece folly, Monville carefully disguised its artificial origin, its utility, and its internal luxury from external eyes, using fragmentation, cracks, and plantings. In addition, he went to great lengths to disguise all mechanical or practical aspects of the ruin, providing, as mentioned earlier a picturesque and extremely rickety bridge (Figure 13) as a decoy to his more useful transportation routes hidden by bushes. His original elevation drawings (Figure 25) attest to the mathematical precision and care that went into this calculated ruination. Throughout his project, Monville carefully disguised all traces of planning hands for the sake of emotional, if not historical, authenticity. Thus, as Monville constructed a building that was ruined on the outside and entirely orderly and inhabitable on the inside, the author of novels of sensibility must also invisibly combine two roles that may never be seen at the same time. On the

Figure 23

Figure 24

one hand, the author must work to create the illusion that the text resulted from no plan of his own—that is, he must pretend to have discovered the text rather than have created it, while on the other hand, he elaborately constructs it to fit his purposes.

The art of accident discloses a profound ambivalence about order and authority, which demands a medium that would simultaneously display its presence and its absence.[47] Order and closure grow suspect in the culture of sensibility, yet they still remain a symbol of an old and impossible dream. The surface fragmentation of *Journey* and *Werther* thus deliberately veils their carefully constructed nature, and thereby appeals to a view of authority that

Arrachement Géométral pour la Construction .

Coupe pour la hauteur des Planchers .

Echelle de cette partie.

Figure 25

desires strength and order, but also demands that they be invisible.[48] In all of these novels, the fragmented, 'natural' language depends upon a context of 'artificial' order for it to interrupt and punctuate: "The very act of writing *absence, ruin,* or *death* is already the beginning of a monument to them . . . The *phenomenon* of writing, even as it is stating a destruction, represents the victory of the monument over ruin."[49] In a sense, both Goethe and Sterne use self-conscious narrators to "salvage order out of seeming chaos;"[50] however the salvaging is under-cover. Werther's story is the ruin that the *Herausgeber* (his fictional editor) wants to monumentalize. Yorick, like the builder of fake ruins, seeks to assert both ruin and monument simultaneously. But the fragmentation can also be interpreted in two different ways: one pointing to the disintegration of communication and the other exhorting us to pursue the possibility of communication that still persists.

The ambivalence about authority, power, and control that accompanies the conflation of the roles of architect and archaeologist shows itself during the same period in ambivalent attitudes about the role of the novelist as creator and planner of finished texts. By transferring authorship and authority to their self-conscious narrators, Sterne, Mackenzie, and Goethe are able to combine elements of 'ruin' and 'monument,' like builders of the fake ruins of the last chapter, in an attempt to bridge the gap between men of feeling and men of words. The special technique that both Mackenzie and Goethe devise involves an additional frame of editorship and discovery. Like the architect, the author must invisibly combine two roles that may never be seen at the same time. The fragmentation and chaotic elements of the novels can therefore be attributed to the narrator agents, while the authors themselves can still maintain an invisible control over, mastery of, the text. The aim of both rhetorics of ruins, the literary as well as the architectural, is thus paradoxical: they aim for invisible control or *successful failure*. Friedrich von Schlegel could almost have been writing about the rhetoric of ruins when he wrote that "many works of the ancients have become fragments. Many modern works are fragments as soon as they are written."[51] A work that is a fragment as soon as it is written is one that succeeds in suggesting enough of its message to hint at what it fails to communicate explicitly. It must *represent* what it cannot articulate.

Ruins and passionately fragmented speech alike satisfy the need for a separation of private and public speech, of 'natural' and 'artificial' language: "Ruins too are the shapeless antithesis of the classical utterance, that well-founded speech which asserts truth clearly and publicly with the full force of antiquity's *auctoritas*. Instead, they have become components in a private language, elusive and allusive metaphors of personal grief scarcely audible at a distance."[52] The fear that feelings are "scarcely audible at a distance" is one that haunts sensibility, and encourages authors of novels of sensibility to develop techniques of portraying feelings while avoiding any appearance of "distance," control, or authority, as the picturesque seeks to erase the "marks of the scissors."

The man of feeling's crisis involving self-narration seems so central to the hallmarks of sensibility that it might at first appear that a protagonist who does not narrate his own experience could not partake of the same cultural phenomenon. Mackenzie's Harley, for example, unlike Yorick and Werther, only occasionally narrates his emotions into smatterings of poetry; he does not self-consciously narrate his own story. How, then, one might ask, can the problem of self-narration be as central for Mackenzie as for Sterne and Goethe? The difference is not as great as it may first appear; in fact, *The Man of Feeling* reveals structural and strategic similarities that are far more significant. Mackenzie's decision to leave the narrating of Harley's story to others is precisely *not* a return to an authoritative narrator, such as the one in Fielding's *Tom Jones*, for example[53]; instead, Mackenzie goes to great lengths to undermine any appearance of order, control, or objective detachment on the part of his narrators. Mackenzie's novel uses narratorial frames to mask the authorship of those whom it seeks to portray as "men of feeling"; in fact, a similar introductory and framing device is present in all his novels of sensibility. Just like Goethe's *Werther*, *The Man of Feeling* has multiple narrators, only Mackenzie uses *three* layers of editors who account for its fragmentation as well as its order.

Harley's world is the cruelest of the three fictional worlds, and his reluctance to write and speak grows in equal proportion to the misfortune he experiences. Like Werther, his disgust for society's cold conventions and his inability to adapt himself to the 'artificiality' of speech ultimately leads to his death. He is unable to propose to the woman he loves, who unlike Lotte is single and willing; this inability and unwillingness to speak becomes a way for Mackenzie to heighten the cruelty of the world which forces a man of such delicacy and promise to silence. "There are some feelings," admits Harley, "which perhaps are too tender to be suffered by the world. The world is in general selfish, interested, and unthinking, and throws the imputation of romance or melancholy on every temper more susceptible than its own."[54]

One cannot help but detect the foreshadowing of Werther's constant refrain that the world thinks he *exaggerates* when words actually force him to *understate* (and thereby abase) his feelings.[55] However, Harley lacks Werther's fiery passion and anger; he combines Yorick's good-humor with Werther's sense of isolation and natural aristocracy and surpasses both in naiveté. Like these other two men of sensibility, Harley follows his "heart" in his adventures, which leads him upon a strikingly circuitous path. Others around him, and he himself, refer to his heart as though it were synonymous with both soul and will: "You have a *feeling heart*, Mr. Harley; I bless *it* that *it* has saved my child."[56] In his death throes, he extols his heart as Werther does his. In fact, all three heroes might claim that Descartes' "cogito ergo sum" [I think, therefore I am] has been replaced by Rousseau's "je sens, donc je suis" [I feel, therefore I am].

Many of the major gaps and silences in the narrative stem from neither Charles's delicate sensibility nor Harley's distrust of words: instead their source is on another plane of narrative altogether. They are the result of the actions of "the unfeeling curate" who, as we learn in the introduction, finding Charles's story worthless, uses it as wadding for his rifle when he hunts: "the hand is intolerably bad, I could never find the author in one strain for two chapters together: and I don't believe there's a single syllogism from beginning to end."[57] An additional layer of meaning here is in the choice of the curate to be an unfeeling man of reason: because of the corruption of the modern church, sensibility's natural goodness must be reclaimed outside of traditional Christian or political institutions. Of course, the curate's objections to the narrative style reveal precisely the story's worth in terms of sensibility: a strong hand would betoken a cold heart, the love of syllogisms would reveal a blindness to the irregularities of individual experience, and more adherence to story or plot would signify insincerity. The curate's "selfish, interested, and unthinking" mangling of the document is the ostensible reason the novel begins with "Chapter XI" and has chapter headings such as "The Fragment": the narrative gaps of the manuscript function literally as wounds inflicted by a Hobbesian society upon the sensitive Shaftesburian soul.

Charles's story becomes the ruin that the second narrator not only saves from destruction, but in a sense, monumentalizes in the process. Just as one effect of ruins on the viewer is to encourage the imaginary recreation of the past and its former fullness, so the 'sight' of the suffering man of feeling will allow (equally sensitive) readers sympathetically to recreate his story. The second narrator models such behavior for the reader: in contrast to the curate's reaction, the second narrator claims "I found it a bundle of little episodes, put together *without art,* and of no importance on the whole, with *something of nature,* and little else in them."[58] The second narrator takes over at the end, as well, and in the gaps between fragments. In all of this he strikingly foreshadows *Werther*'s "*Herausgeber.*" Both editors also include occasional footnotes that carry the guise of historical objectivity as well as accuracy; however, again like the *Herausgeber,* Mackenzie's second narrator is far from objective. He reveals himself as a natural kinsman, because he too is a 'man of feeling.'

In the multiplication of narratorial tasks and the separation of 'authorial' power, Sterne, Mackenzie, and Goethe resemble one another, as well as other authors of sensibility. While Sterne's Yorick physically unites both narrator and protagonist, much of the comedy of his situation is due to his distinct opinion about the natural incongruity of these two roles, and Sterne expends great energy displaying Yorick's equal lack of control over his itinerary and his story—that is, the absence, rejection, and masking of authority. Mackenzie multiplies Yorick's difficulty by portraying three characters who share the same double duties of character-as-narrator and character-as-participant. Goethe uses the same framework as Mackenzie, reduces the narrative frames to two, yet increases the linguistic tension for the main protagonist: Werther's tormented rhetoric of ruins is initially more apparent than Harley's because he makes greater attempts to communicate by writing—the failure is more poignant because we witness his struggle to write—that is, to *represent* himself. The thematic and structural similarities imply that there is something about the form that separates narrator and participant, *Erzähler* and *Erzählung,* and which emphasizes the absence of authority as well as the difficulty of writing and self-representation that is essential to the moral aesthetic of sensibility. Non-narration alone tells no story, whereas anti-narration that punctures and challenges traditional forms of narration allows for the creative tension upon which sensibility thrives.

These structural demands affect all the speakers in the novels: not only the characters and the self-conscious narrator, but also the 'implied author.' The aesthetic requirement to protect each author's reputation—whether historical authors (Sterne, Mackenzie, or Goethe) or fictional (such as Yorick, Harley, Charles, Werther, and the *Herausgeber*)—poses additional problems within the narrative. To speak and to write is to admit separation, distance, a lack of immediate understanding; the very nature of these activities implies interpersonal gaps, yet they also represent the attempt to bridge these gaps. This is part of the reason that all 'men of feeling' and their female equivalents need to speak and at the same time to remain silent. Their dilemma is twofold: while feeling transcends words, words are still, in the novel at least, the vehicle for communicating these feelings. Similarly in the architecture of a folly, while order betokens the cold artificiality and unaided reason that are sensibility's enemies, the precious disorderly contours are only visible, effective, and, most importantly, *affective* within an orderly and carefully constructed context. A ruined monument can inspire greater emotive response than a pile of rubble, especially when the viewer is distanced from the moment of destruction, free of any aspiration to historical precision, and able to (re)construct the original monument imaginatively.

In order to accomplish this masking of their authorship and authority, Sterne and Goethe both encourage a conflation of the narrator and the author. This has led to a tradition of criticism that devotes itself to untangling the autobiographical and the fictional elements of their novels.[59] Similarities between events in Werther's life and Goethe's have, consequently, been exhaustively researched.[60] There are indeed many similarities, and Goethe emphasizes them by, among other things, giving Werther the same birthday as his own: August 28th. Sterne also complicates matters in *Journey,* by giving the narrator a name that is not only the name of a character in *Tristram Shandy,* but also his own, well-established pseudonym.[61]

By conflating their roles as *Erzähler* and *Erzählung,* as the one who represents and that which is itself represented, Sterne and Goethe both, in effect, portray themselves portraying the narrative. They become characters within the fictional world of the novel, as well as its creators. Just as the narrator takes on *authorial* responsibilities by ostensibly composing the story, the authors themselves become subjects of their own works. Monville, too, was both architect/choreographer of and inhabitant/actor in his folly at the Désert de Retz. The conflation of implied author and narrator works alongside the additional authorial frame to camouflage the author's control. Even in their portrayals of themselves, these authors dodge all appearance of authority in order to protect themselves against the charge of being 'men of words' and therefore *not* 'men of feeling.'

In *Dichtung und Wahrheit* [*Poetry and Truth*], Goethe tells of his state of mind when writing his youthful *Werther,* describing himself as a man of feeling, heavily influenced by the moral aesthetic of sensibility. Goethe claims to have composed *Werther* in a brief, exuberant period of "leiden-schaftlich Bewegung" [passionate emotion]: "Ich hatte mich äußerlich völlig isoliert, ja die Besuche meiner Freunde verboten, und so legte ich auch innerlich alles beiseite, was nicht unmittelbar hierher gehörte . . . Unter solchen Umständen, . . . schrieb ich den 'Werther' in vier Wochen, ohne daß ein Schema des Ganzen, oder die Behandlung eines Teils irgend vorher wäre zur Papier gebracht gewesen. [I had completely isolated myself externally, indeed forbidden the visits of my friends, and in the same way I even laid everything inward aside that did not immediately pertain to this . . . Under such circumstances, . . . I wrote 'Werther' in four weeks, without having brought a plan of the whole or a treatment of any part of it to paper.][62] Rather like Coleridge in his preface to *Kubla Khan,* Goethe claims that *Werther* came to him in inspiration and was uncensored by reason, plans, or system, and yet its organization as well as his own admission of plans seem to suggest otherwise. Goethe's emphasis upon his feverish speed in composing *Werther* also sits uncomfortably with the fact that the version commonly read today is the much revised one which he did not complete until 1787, thirteen years after the publication of version one.[63] The point is, that as much as Goethe claims to have been *like* Werther, and plants autobiographical analogies in the novel to encourage readers to *identify* the two, Goethe, as Tobin Siebers astutely remarks, "could not have created Werther if [he] had been a Werther."[64]

'FIXING' NATURE

Narrative frames not only protect the "reputation" of each man of feeling who presumes to write, they also enable the man of feeling to avoid responsibility and self-control. Since he defines feeling in opposition to institutions and authority, sensibility's man of feeling tends to be a powerless victim and an outsider, by definition.[65] Werther's avowed helplessness does not, therefore, in itself constitute a reaction against sensibility. On the contrary, the inability to control oneself becomes a token of both sensibility and virtue within the culture of sensibility. Over and over again, Werther displays his keen sensibility (his receptivity to nature) by emphasizing that he is physically drawn to Lotte like a piece of metal to a magnet: "ich bin zu nah in der Atmosphäre—Zuck! so bin ich dort" [I'm too close in the atmosphere—Zip! I'm over there] and again: "Wutsch! bin ich drauß" [Whoosh! Now I'm outside].[66] In Harley and Yorick, we see the same helplessness. Yorick, for example, remarks: "—but I am govern'd by circumstances—I cannot govern them."[67] Such an emphasis on helplessness, passivity, and resignation to fate poses important political and moral problems about responsibility and potential for action; the distinction between authentic victimhood and an aestheticized self-victimization is dangerously tenuous. As a result, it seems that every man of sensibility must be protected and supported either by a woman of sense or by a Sancho Panza figure.[68] Werther's mother sends him money to feed and clothe him; others find him a job and protect him; yet another tells his story. Werther's 'failures,' however, provide the narrator's opportunities, and establish Goethe's success as well.

The narrative frame that Goethe provides thus not only illustrates the structural demands that sensibility makes in order to mask the authority of authors, but it also suggests the weaknesses inherent in sensibility's role in the public world of decisions and action—a role that will ultimately help bring it to a close in cultish extremes. The crisis of moral authority and philosophical insecurity that inspires sensibility remains fundamentally unresolved. Reason has been dethroned, yet there is no new authority to take its place. The irony built into the structure of the novel of sensibility reveals the painful fact that silence generally goes unheard when unannounced, just as rubble does not communicate ruin as well as truncated monuments: silence depends upon surrounding words that it can dramatically punctuate. Since it is potentially even more ambiguous than words, silence depends upon context to suggest a meaning. Werther cannot accept this inauthenticity: he will tolerate no strategy, no dual impulses, no self-conscious rhetoric of silence. And because Werther is fundamentally unironic, he finally chooses eternal silence and ruination, rather than have to compromise himself in a worldly existence.

The aesthetic component of this framing is clearer in the context of the history of the picturesque. As an aesthetic category, the 'picturesque' developed within the framework of the debate over the sublime and the beautiful that Edmund Burke so memorably formulated in his *A Philosophical Enquiry into the Origin of our Ideas of the Sublime and Beautiful* (1757), a work that served as a basis for aesthetic debate for half a century. Burke bases our perception of these two qualities on two natural and opposing instincts: self-preservation, which is connected with pain, and self-propagation, which is connected with pleasure. Sublime objects are immense, rugged, obscure or impenetrable and evoke in the viewer a sense of infinity, difficulty, or fear, while beautiful objects are gentle, smooth, and round and evoke pleasing, gentle sensations in the viewer. A beautiful woman, for example, affects the viewer in the following physical manner: "The head reclines something on one side; the eyelids are more closed than usual, and the eyes roll gently with an inclination to the object, the mouth is a little opened, and the whole body is composed, and the hands fall idly to the sides. All this is accompanied with an inward sense of melting and langour." On the other hand: "Whatever is fitted in any sort to excite the ideas of pain, and danger, that is to say, whatever is in any sort terrible . . . is a source of the *sublime;* that is, it is productive of the strongest emotion which the mind is capable of feeling." Burke emphasizes the direct influence of objects upon the passions (via the senses and natural instincts), without any involvement of (or censorship by) the conscious mind or reason; however, Burke must also account for the differences between the reactions of any two viewers to the same object. The "physical causes" are "always proportioned to the degree of beauty in the object, and of sensibility in the observer." Disagreements over the "standard" of taste can therefore, according to Burke, not be resolved without evaluation of the *sensibility* of the viewer, leaving the door open for the elitism of sensibility. [69]

The aestheticians of the picturesque took Burke's definitions of the sublime and the beautiful and assigned a name to the qualities that neither term could comfortably admit. The picturesque thus becomes an intermediary category for that which is irregular yet pleasing—neither smooth nor overwhelming.[70] In 1794, in his *Essay on the Picturesque,* Sir Uvedale Price firmly established the picturesque as a third aesthetic category alongside the sublime and the beautiful, and gives musical examples of all three: A chorus of Handel, because of its vastness and obscurity, exhibits the sublime; "Corelli's famous pastorale" is beautiful because of its smoothness and gentleness, and "a capricious movement of Scarlatti or Haydn" is picturesque because of the "roughness and sudden variation joined to irregularity" of form, or, in this case, sound.[71] Price contends that the picturesque is ugly until one learns to appreciate it—again evoking the emphasis on connoisseurship which becomes marked in both "cults."

Within Burke, there is a seldom noticed model for this third category. Burke assigns special significance to the word "delight," which he uses to describe the feeling, akin to, but not identical with, the pleasure which we have when we are *separated* from pain or *relieved* from danger: delight describes a safe distance from terror, not far enough removed, however, to become indifference: "When danger or pain press too nearly, they are incapable of giving any delight, and are simply terrible; but at certain distances, and with certain modifications, they may be, and they are delightful."[72] Delight, therefore, can serve as an unnamed picturesque—a combination of irregularity and obscurity with a sensation of momentary safety. We might call it a form of framed or domesticated wildness. One could say that it resembles the desire to secularize the destruction of *Genesis;* it also provides the frame within which the man of feeling has the freedom to indulge in passions without sacrificing structure or sympathy.

With the picturesque, qualities such as obscurity, which Burke had located in the sublime, take on a newly domesticated role: whether in painting, landscape, or poetry, "obscurity" stimulates the reader's or viewer's imagination,[73] for as he says, "we yield to sympathy, what we refuse to description."[74] For Burke, however, the "sublime" is anything but calm or social: it is a strong, destructive, antisocial force. The aesthetic category of the "picturesque" combines his emphasis on obscurity with a new confidence in a positive and socially beneficial role. Burke himself seems to be interested in achieving this effect, for in Burke's long and interesting section on "Words" at the end of his *Enquiry,* his main purpose seems to be to emphasize that the natural *obscurity* of words demands that we participate in each other's feelings and imagine sympathetically in order to understand one another. Burke, along with Hume and Smith in moral philosophy, and Reynolds in aesthetics, thus finds sympathy and imagination central not only to the aesthetic experience, but to communication, *per se.* Therefore, after Burke, sensibility and the picturesque transform "obscurity" into the 'non finito' that can satisfy sensibility's contradictory impulses: it can ensure both the social and the educative functions of art, without sacrificing its emotional appeal.

The picturesque, as it grows out of Burke's and Price's discussions to a broader principle of aesthetics, can represent something that is threateningly close to the state of nature: a domestication of the sublime that threatens to reassert itself when the picture frame is removed, or the viewer's head is turned. It tames the wild aspects of the sublime, yet simultaneously seeks to conceal the authority that tames it.[75] Its dual impulses thus echo Knight's art of the accident and the rhetoric of ruins established by Whately and others. This is the source of the awkward position in which the picturesque finds itself: stemming from an Italian word for a painterly style, it must rely on artificiality (the picture frame) while it seeks authenticity (the natural, undisturbed, irregular, potentially terrifying scene). Although it tacitly admits the need for the 'picture frame' or that which can tame, domesticate, or temporarily remove the danger, the picturesque tends to mask the frame, as the novels of sensibility mask authority and authorship.[76] The picturesque, then, demonstrates a similarly curious ambivalence towards authority, reason, and order. Just as gardenists seek to hide the marks of the scissors and architects mask their own hands in architectural follies, authorial contrivances are masked in the novel as well. In this section, we discover that the additional editorial frames that develop in the novel of sensibility are required because of a characteristic ambivalence about authority: editorial frames are necessary to articulate the dual vision of the culture of sensibility.

One of the most curious and symbolically appropriate inventions of picturesque landscape gardeners is the "ha-ha." According to Hussey, Vanbrugh was the first to popularize this device, which was a type of fortified ditch, lined with stone or brick, although Dézallier D'Argenville and others claim it originated in France. The side closer to the great house was generally built higher to camouflage the ditch and to assist in creating a "boundless estate" from garden to park. Without visually breaking the estate into partitions, the ha-ha was also designed to control the grazing of livestock or keep out neighboring peasant children without destroying the scenic prospect, as carefully composed as a still-life painting. Ha-has thus attempt to maintain order and prospect while also hiding the traces of the landscape gardener's hands (and the owner's fences).[77] They protect the random, natural appearance while actually keeping disruptive or unsightly forces at a safe distance; at the same time, they seek to avoid the appearance of linearity and overtly imposed order.

The dual needs for authenticity and artifice evident in the ha-ha, as well as in the narratorial frames of the novel of sensibility, easily translate into a paradoxical combination of primitivism and luxury, and result in humorous arrangements, especially in landscape gardens and their architecture. These arrangements include not only ha-has and fake ruins, but additional forms that stem from the desire to mask authority and portray the domesticated, *inhabitable* wildness of Nature. Figure 26 shows an example of the fetishized huts (often "pilgrim's houses" or "hermitages") that adorned so many landscape gardens.[78] Built in the 1790s, Hirschfeld's *"Köhlerhütte"* is covered with bark on the outside to imitate a hermit's impoverished and provisional attempt at shelter. Its triangular form suggests a tent or teepee, rather than a permanent structure. Inside, however, it is opulently decorated and contains, among other luxuries, a Turkish sofa, paintings, mirrors, and an excellent library. In fact, the 'tree stump' that protrudes from the roof is actually a chimney to ensure the inhabitant's comfort in all seasons.[79] Such hermitages reveal a prevalent ambivalence, not only towards finished, orderly structures, but also towards civilization's luxuries. Such structures suggest that the culture of sensibility's preference for primitivism as a spectacle never quite translates into a practical alternative. The culture of sensibility and the picturesque both exhibit a high threshold for irony— so much so, in fact, that their artifacts teeter precariously on the brink of hypocrisy. The movements thus prove themselves ripe for aesthetic, ethical, and socio-economic satire.

The picturesque, like sensibility, is not entirely what it makes itself out to be. There is a rational, orderly, and artificial aspect to each movement. Just as the novels of sensibility try to camouflage their orderly external structures, the picturesque, especially as formulated by Gilpin, finds itself in a similar quandary, using artifice and reason to achieve what its artists know is beyond reason to achieve.[80] The picturesque, as it becomes codified, leads to a habit of viewing nature with a certain amount of the connoisseur's detachment, according to how good a given scene might look as a painting. Viewers should carry a mental picture frame as they travel and evaluate nature's composition. As Marshall writes, the stage-like descriptions of picturesque prospects emphasize this artificiality: "from the outset the question of aesthetic distance informs the very concept of the picturesque. The construction of amphitheaters, the arrangement of trees to frame natural scenes like the wings of a stage, and the use of mirrors to fill the gallery

Luſtſchlöſſern, Landhäuſern, Gartengebäuden ꝛc. 353

worinn ſich Kamin und Rauchloch befinden. Die Lage und äußere Geſtalt der Hütte erſcheint in dieſer Vorſtellung.

Nicht weit davon liegt der ſogenannte amerikaniſche Garten, die reichſte und vollſtändigſte Sammlung von ausländiſchen Bäumen und Sträuchern, die wir in Deutſchland beſitzen, *) nach dem linneiſchen Syſtem geordnet, in einem ſchönen Bezirk. Man ſieht hier die ſeltenſten Arten, und freut ſich, viele Gewächſe aus den entlegenſten Gegenden, ſelbſt aus den Inſeln der Südſee, in dem glücklichſten Fort-

*) Ein Verzeichniß davon, das nicht verkauft wird, iſt 1780 zu Stuttgard in 8. auf 253 Seiten gedruckt. Es enthält bloß die lateiniſchen Namen mit den deutſchen und franzöſiſchen. Man findet darinn 850 verſchiedene Geſchlechter und Arten aufgeführt, ohne die mancherley Abarten. — Schon im Sommer 1783, als ich Hohenheim ſah, war die Sammlung noch über 400 Arten und Abarten mehr hinaufgeſtiegen.

V Band.   Yy

Figure 26

of nature with *tableaux* were only literal manifestations of the point of view the beholder of the picturesque was supposed to internalize."[81]

It is noteworthy, in this regard, that the notorious tours in search of officially picturesque sights and locations, conducted by the gentry and aristocracy in the second half of the eighteenth century, involved not only the obligatory sketchbooks and watercolors, but also such devices as Claude glasses and convex mirrors, to "miniaturize," "fix," "station," and "compose" the untamed landscapes. Paraphernalia associated with the picturesque movement further supports its growing over-codification as well as its acceptance of artificiality. The picturesque ideals became fixed even in their palette, for it spawned a new kind of lens called the "Claude-Glass," tinted in just the yellow shades of one of Claude Lorrain's sunsets.[82] The word 'compose' reinforces the (uncomfortable) authorial role that such viewers assumed, in pretending to have *found* the picturesque in nature rather than to have *created* it. The paraphernalia and vocabulary of these tours suggest not only the desire to dodge any suggestions of 'authorship,' but also a desire to enjoy nature's wildness from a safe distance. Picturesque travelers could travel from scene to scene, carrying Claude glasses, a Gray's glass, or a camera obscura, and add the finishing touch to a compositionally perfect sight.

The Claude glass and other convex tinted mirrors, for example, tended to create oval images on paper. Many of Gilpin's illustrations were oval, replicating the effect of the convex mirrors that tend to exaggerate foreground and provide a protective barrier for the viewer. Frequently, such scenes would include some foreground desolation, ominously pointing towards the more peaceful background. In a memorable passage, Gilpin himself describes the experience of looking out the window of a chaise with Claude glass in hand: "A succession of high-coloured pictures is continually gliding before the eye. They are like the visions of the imagination, or the brilliant landscapes of a dream. Forms and colours in the brightest array fleet before us; and if the transient glance of a good composition happen to unite with them, we should give any price to fix, and appropriate the scene."[83]

In this scene, Gilpin is doubly separated from the natural scenery he is viewing—first by the window frame of the chaise, and secondly by the tinted Claude glass through which he is viewing nature as though it were a film. His use of the words "fix" and "appropriate" also suggests that nature is a commodity to be consumed. In addition, in order to use a Claude glass appropriately, one must actually have one's back or shoulder to the natural scene, in order to compose it. Such paraphernalia reveals the separation from reality to which this rigidly codified way of seeing ultimately leads; it also underscores a great, inescapable irony inherent in both "cults." The emphasis on seeing and feeling, as well as a general receptivity to nature and to one's surroundings—goals which served to distinguish these movements as linked with the culture of sensibility—eventually leads to its reverse, a greater *separation* from nature and others.[84]

As these examples show, the picturesque eventually falls from its exalted status, as does sensibility, when each becomes over-codified and ripe for such satires as Combe's and Rowlandson's in Figure 27. Both movements fall from precariously balanced contradictory impulses regarding authenticity and artifice and tip irretrievably towards hypocrisy and artifice. By the time William Combe writes his poem *Doctor Syntax* in 1819, to accompany the illustrations by Thomas Rowlandson, the two men are able to parody both the novel of sensibility and the pursuit of the picturesque within the same volume. Literary critique and aesthetic critique merge in the Doctor Syntax and Doctor Prosody stories. Combe and Rowlandson reveal that the artificially domesticating tendencies of the picturesque could blind its tourists to the real nature around them.[85]

In Figure 27, ivy-covered follies spell out the first three letters of the word 'picturesque'--an architectural find that stimulates the artist's narrative impulses, his ambition toward authorship. However, as the C teeters precariously, demonstrating the limits of artifice in construction of follies and threatening the ruin of his ruin, Dr. Syntax succumbs to his narrative urges and etches the remainder of the word into a nearby boulder. (This is probably also an allusion to the forgeries of ancient scripts by Macpherson, Chatterton, and others.) In the background, several well known ruins, including Tintern Abbey, dot the horizon in exaggerated proximity. Combe and Rowlandson's frontispiece shows the thin line between painter and writer, between observing or imitating nature and imposing one's own wishes, as well as the eager attempt to make nature conform to preconceived ideals. Combe reveals the traveling tourists' eagerness not only to *read* nature, but also to *read into* nature, and even to *compose* nature according to the demands of their own fixed aesthetic categories. These artists abiding by picturesque principles experience the same discomfort over authorship and denial of authority as we witnessed in the novels of sensibility.

> With curious eye and active scent,
> I on the picturesque am bent.
> That is my game; I must pursue it,
> *And make it where I cannot view it.*

The last phrase in particular emphasizes the thin line between finding and creating, and should remind us of sensibility's redefinition of authorship, of architects posing as archaeologists, and of the numerous painters (such as Hubert Robert and Fragonard) who assisted landscape architects in designing prospects and suitably evocative follies. The picturesque's masking of order and control ultimately leads it to the inescapable artificiality we found with the fake ruins and which played a significant role in bringing sensibility to an end or in converting a culture into a cult.[86]

Curiously, the caricatured Dr. Syntax is equally reminiscent of Gilpin and another traveling pastor, Laurence Sterne. In addition, there is also a resemblance to a fictional traveling pastor, Yorick, Sterne's alter ego. While generally taken to be a portrait of William Gilpin, other factors suggest

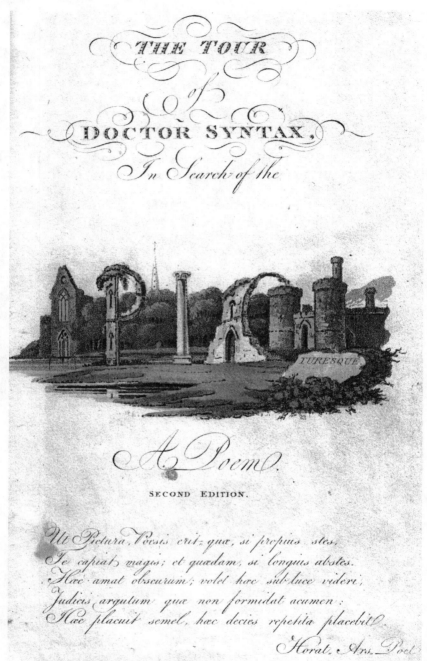

Pub.¹ᵗ May 1812 at R. Ackermann's Repository of Arts 101 Strand London.

Figure 27

a more literary origin—particularly the linguistic terms used to name Dr. *Syntax* and Dr. *Prosody,* the appearance of Dr. Syntax himself, and the content of the volumes. As a result of this recurring connection between landscape innovations and literary experimentation, both sensibility with its fractured syntax and the picturesque with its calculated love of irregularity, are held culpable for the distance they erect between natural causes and artificial responses.

THE PEDAGOGY OF SEEING

As the literature of sensibility flourishes, the ethics of feeling continues to dominate, as evidenced by: the emphasis on intense friendship or ardent romantic love as indicators of the ability to feel, continued emphasis on expressivism, and growing use of narrative techniques to affect emotion in the audience. While the Augustan tendency towards didacticism does not fade fully in England until the nineteenth century, the nature of the didactic lessons changes, and authors manipulate readers' emotional responses in order to achieve a sentimental education of the audience, presumed immune to the effects of direct argumentation, and eventually, of omniscient narration.

While their purposes and tonalities differ greatly, both Goethe's *Werther* and Sterne's *Journey* teach the reader how to become an imaginative translator of the world by becoming an imaginative participant in the novel and an interpreter of nature. The novels function as literary analogues to Gilpin's published tours of the English countryside. Just as Gilpin teaches his readers how to find, view, and describe picturesque sights, Sterne and Goethe also travel and respond to evocative tableaux, such as the scenes involving Werther's friendship for the farm boy, and children in general, as well as his reactions to landscape. The authors teach readers how to respond sympathetically to and alongside their protagonists in the multiple tableaux of sensibility that we witness.

Ethics, like art collecting or traveling in pursuit of the picturesque, become sthe realm of the connoisseur. The novelists of sensibility treat their readers as connoisseurs, and they also portray the sensibility of their protagonists through their aesthetic taste—especially their responses to visual sights. The man of feeling (and virtue) must show an ability to see with taste, whether beholding the various spectacles in an English garden, reconstructing a folly, recording his reactions to a Grand Tour through the Alps and Rome, witnessing the plight of a suffering human being, reminiscing over the fictitious remnants of Ossian's poetry, or admiring the delicate simplicity of a sensitive mimosa plant.[87] As a result of this emphasis on the art of seeing, sensibility's visual and literary art was replete with representations of seers seeing and thereby functioning as pedagogical models. Since sensibility's central hallmarks equate virtue with the ability to feel delicate emotions, one could *train* one's emotional reflexes through picturesque sights.

As we have seen, the picturesque's pictorial appreciation of nature applies to several art forms; Christopher Hussey claims "poetry, painting, gardening, architecture and the art of travel may be said to have been fused into a single 'art of landscape.'"[88] The emphasis is on spurring the imagination and training the emotions to respond to various scenes, whether human, botanical, or architectural. Most of the books on the picturesque, in fact, were travel guides to help travelers identify and appreciate "official" picturesque spots. To Hussey's list of arenas influenced by the picturesque, I would add prose fiction as well, since novels of sensibility also function as guides to traveling and models for responding to situations and spectacles. *A Sentimental Journey,* in particular, functions as a guidebook for learning not only how to travel 'sentimentally,' but also how to behave sentimentally in all situations.

Once again, Sterne builds upon tradition to emphasize sensibility's traveling motif: most directly Sterne responds to—and ridicules—Tobias Smollett's *Travels through France and Italy* (1766).[89] Yorick defines himself in contradistinction to Smollett (the splenetic Smelfungus), and lists him among the inferior kinds of travelers, declaring his own determination to be a "sentimental" traveler instead: "I pity the man who can travel from *Dan* to *Beersheba,* and cry, 'Tis all barren—and so it is; and so is all the world to him who will not cultivate the fruits it offers. I declare, said I, clapping my hands chearily together, that was I in a desart [sic], I would find out wherewith in it to call forth my affections."[90] Sterne combines the travelogue with the rage for sensibility and the picturesque by creating a journey where destinations are determined by gentle faces and pitiable sights and where nothing is barren if the traveler be sentimental.

The new dangers involved in Alpine travel helped spur the market for engravings and prints of Roman ruins, prominent in illustrated chapbooks, volumes of miscellanies, and circulating libraries. Gilpin's tours of the English countryside, published as guidebooks with helpful illustrations to explain picturesque principles, appeared from 1782, promoting domestic travel as well as literacy in the picturesque aesthetic and its corresponding cant. These developments made the picturesque tour more available to the middle classes or lower gentry—indeed, it is illustrated by Elizabeth Bennet's proposed tour of the Lake Country in *Pride and Prejudice.* Touring landscape, abbeys, and castles becomes an increasingly popular sport among middle and upper middle classes, providing the practical experience with objects required of the "picturesque eye." Therefore, those who owned no estates to transform into picturesque style, or who did not have the luxury of travel, were able nonetheless to travel vicariously through Gilpin's tour books, or through his and others' etchings, published prints, plans of English gardens, and even novels of sensibility, which frequently replicate a picturesque aesthetic through the narrative techniques and mode of sentimental traveling that they portray.

Unlike "Mundungus" (Samuel Smart), who "travell'd straight on looking neither to his right hand or his left, lest Love or Pity should seduce him out of his road,"[91] the sentimental traveler eschews straight lines and predetermined destinations, just as he does the formal restrictions of logic, grammar, and etiquette. This principle finds its parallel in the aesthetic of the picturesque, where horizontal and vertical lines are taboo and considered "unnatural." (Compare the English garden at Hohenheim in Figure 28 with the Avenues at Hampton Court in Figure 10). As Julie declares of her garden in *Julie, ou la nouvelle Héloïse* (1761), "Vous ne voyez rien d'aligné, rien de nivelé; jamais le cordeau n'entra dans ce lieu; la nature ne plante rien au cordeau." [You will see nothing aligned, nothing leveled, no straight lines in this place; nature plants nothing in rows.][92] Yorick is in complete agreement, although he claims it is out of his control: "I think there is a fatality in it—" cries Yorick, "I seldom go to the place I set out for."[93] Yorick travels through France, then, translating all the way, encountering poignant, picturesque scene after scene, very much like the spectator in one of Hirschfeld's parks, and each scene moves in him the appropriate sentiments. Yorick the Protagonist's "picturesquely" unpredictable itinerary as well as Yorick the Narrator's plot line curiously resemble the narrative graphs which Sterne visualizes in *Tristram Shandy* (Figure 20).

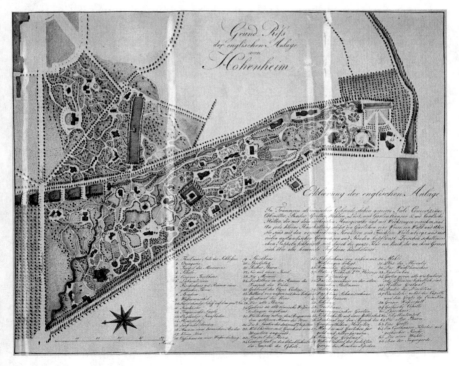

Figure 28

As novels of sensibility encourage readers to follow the serpentine windings of the narrative—witnessing its fractures, responding to its emotive tableaux, and participating in the responses of the protagonists—so too the English gardens across Europe provide carefully constructed views designed to rouse emotional responses in the reader. Seifersdorfer Tal, an English garden in Germany, for example, originates as an emblematic garden and is later transformed to accord with current tastes for sensibility. By the 1780s, it sports a series of temples, monuments, inscriptions and busts featuring characteristic icons of sensibility, including: "Goethe's young Werther, Petrarch's passion for Laura, Edward Young's *Night Thoughts,* Sterne's Yorick on his sentimental journey, . . along with altars to Truth and Virtue, an open temple dedicated to the joys of country life, and a monument to Gothic friendship."[94] Generally seats or benches are placed in opportune, private locations, to enable the spectators to indulge in the appropriate sentiments in comfort. Goethe himself was profoundly influenced by his 1776 visit to Franz's English garden Wörlitz at Anhalt-Dessau (and by the subsequent publication of the Wörlitz guidebook in 1782); he encouraged Duke Karl August to engage in similar landscaping around Weimar.

As the rhetoricians seek to describe the language of nature in order to recreate it, gardenists of the eighteenth century were also engaged in learning nature's language in order to recreate an Eden suitable for the man of feeling, supposedly driven by feelings and associations rather than by erudite references, elaborate topiary, or (explicit) displays of wealth and grandeur. Hirschfeld, one of the first to write a guide to *Theorie der Gartenkunst* [Theory of Garden Art] (1779–1785), describes the "natural" language with which the garden architect controls the responses of the viewer: "Der Mensch steht also in einem so nahen Verhältnisse mit der Natur, daß er ihre Einwirkungen auf seine Seele nicht verläugnen kann . . . Der Gartenkünstler soll alle Wirkungen der natürlichen Lagen der Landschaft kennen, um solche auszuwählen, die der Bestimmung eines Gartens gemäße Bewegungen hervorbringen, und ihnen eine solche Verbindung und Anordnung zu geben, daß diese Bewegungen in einer harmonischen Beziehung auf einander folgen." [Man is, then, in such a close relationship with nature that he cannot deny her influence on his soul . . . The garden architect should know all of the effects of the natural situations of the landscape in order to select those that evoke movements particular to the requirements of a garden, and to give them such an association and order that these movements follow one another in a harmonious relationship.][95]

Hirschfeld's lengthy descriptions of garden scenes and the emotions they evoke constitute a "grammar" of the language of nature.[96] He describes both vocabulary and syntax, showing how each variation in physical terrain produces certain emotional states in the onlooker: "Die Vertiefung ist die Wohnung der Einsamkeit und der Ruhe; sie ist melancholischen Anlagen und Scenen günstig . . . Der Character von Gebirge ist Erhabenheit und feyerliche Majestät." [The hollow is the dwelling of solitude and quiet; it is favorable for melancholy structures and scenes . . . The character of mountains is grandeur and solemn majesty.][97] He even provides pictures to illustrate the correlations between mood and natural scenes, choosing among the standard garden vocabulary, which includes shepherd's hut, cloister, Nero's tombstone, hermit's dwelling, Gothic ruin, and classical colonnade. Hirschfeld instructs the reader in the appropriate sequence (syntax) of these scenes, and suggests that "the *Gartenkünstler* could, by staging specific human responses to nature, make nature's language clearer."[98] The implication is that the language of nature retains its communicative ability and the close connections to human emotions that spoken language has lost; as long as it is manipulated well, viewers can avoid "perplexity."

Generally, an English garden in picturesque style on a large estate would have several follies of great variety. In his map of the gardens at Hohenheim, for example, Hirschfeld provides a list corresponding to its sixty-six picturesque and poignant scenes (Figure 28), each arousing a specific emotion and together creating a smorgasbord of sensibility—an emotional obstacle course geared for veteran spectators with malleable hearts. The more sentimental the garden visitor, the more keenly would he or she feel each emotion, suggesting that sensibility can be gauged by the ability to *read* nature and to translate its visual symbolism into emotion. He provides a botanical analogue to the novel of sensibility's similar "pedagogy of seeing," also in response to the philosophical insecurity of the culture of sensibility: again we see a natural language that needs to be learned, cultivated, or achieved through artifice.

In *Die Theorie der Gartenkunst,* Hirschfeld records his response to the ruins of Hohenheim: "Nirgends sind wohl Ruinen schöner gezeichnet und ausgeführt, als hier . . . Die Ruinen sind das herrlichste, was sich in dieser Art von Nachahmung denken kann . . . *Alles ist wahr* und überraschend." [Nowhere are ruins more beautifully drawn and executed than here . . . The ruins are the most delightful that can be imagined in this type of imitation . . . *All is authentic* and surprising.][99] The surprising word in Hirschfeld's description is the word "wahr": he claims that the delight of the experience lies in how true or authentic the ruins are, knowing full well of their recent origin and attempted imposture. This remark suggests that there is an authenticity involved with the appreciation of follies that overshadows the importance of historical authenticity. Perhaps it is the perfectly picturesque adaptation of structure to landscape that enables a suspension of disbelief and therefore—in some sense—an authenticity of emotional response.

The author or narrator has to hide the "marks" of their scissors in narrative form to achieve the desired evocative and didactic effect. There are suggestions that authors were self-aware of this pedagogy of seeing—that is, of the sentimental novel's responsibility to evoke emotions in the reader. Henry Mackenzie, for example, writes to a young reader, warning him about the proper way to read *The Man of Feeling*: he warns him not to read the chapters where virtue is in the greatest distress, "till you have a mind to indulge those Feelings which it endeavours to produce."[100] Readers and authors alike have responsibilities to produce the novel's sympathetic participation, which begins where speech ends. This sympathetic participation and self-conscious evocation of feeling, nature's "language," thus form an essential part of the general moral aesthetic of sensibility, as exhibited in both landscape gardening and the novel.

The locus of the ruin drama thus shifts gradually inwards to the sensitive soul of the viewer. Even in the English gardens, dotted as they are with interesting and ruined objects, the benches grow to be the most significant architectural features and the locus of the real drama. Spectators feature as the main actors in sensibility's theatricals. Whereas at first, spectators focus on recreating proper literary allusion suggested by engravings in the emblematic garden, subsequently they engage in the nostalgic recreation of the past, invited by ruination. The focus becomes private associations and poignant experiences of private loss. Finally, one might conclude that this loss transforms itself into a joyful confidence in one's own exquisite capacity to feel. Ludwig Tieck parodies the growing importance of the audience in his play *Gestiefelte Kater* [*Puss in Boots*] (1796), where he literally places the audience *on stage* to participate in the unfolding of (and especially the reaction to) events. Gradually the audience assumes increasing authorship, while retaining the guise of 'pure' spectatorship—of viewing, rather than effecting or creating. This individual reception was the key to virtue and art, as well as pleasure.

Again, Wilhelm Tischbein's life-size portrait of Goethe helps further elucidate the psychology (Figure 4): the aim of the painting is not only for us to see Goethe, but more importantly to see Goethe *seeing* the classical ruins. This dynamic reveals the narcissism inherent in the cult of sensibility, which bases virtue on one's ability to feel and thus turns those who feel into actors displaying their wares. In Goethe's own account of the character of his enjoyment of similar scenes in the Campagna, he travels with his eyes (rather than his feet) with minimal effort and maximum sensual pleasure. He speaks of the ruins of Rome, in picturesque fashion, as though the scene were a stationary, two-dimensional painting that he could observe at his leisure and from a comfortable distance. When the ruins cannot otherwise be conveniently fixed, he brings them home to survey in private: "Ich habe mich nicht enthalten können, den kolossalen Kopf eines Jupiters anzuschaffen. Er steht meinem Bette gegenüber, wohl beleuchtet, damit ich sogleich meine Morgenandacht an ihn richten kann." [I was not able to keep myself from acquiring the colossal head of a Jupiter. It stands across from my bed, well lit, so that I can immediately direct my morning devotion to it.][101] In these passages, one detects that the sensual sounds and architectural sights are unified and glorified not only by their appropriation, but also by their *reception* and *appreciation* in the connoisseur's 'sensible' soul.[102] Many paintings can therefore be found of artists eager to be *seen seeing* in order to prove their aesthetic sensibility or instruct the

Figure 29

viewer about the worthiness and evocative character of the scene within the scene (Figures 29, 30, and 31).

The technique is similar to Michael Fried's descriptions of French painting after 1750, when he said new techniques were used to seduce the viewer. According to Fried, painters begin to attract viewers' gaze and hold them in stopped time; however, they can only achieve this by negating the viewer's own presence. Instead of using frontal figures, artists turn figures with their backs to the viewer to invite the viewer to engage sympathetically in viewing the scene.[103] Such paintings, encouraged by contemporary critics Denis Diderot and Melchior Grimm, secure their appeal by hiding their artifice. In picturesque landscape paintings too, as Michasiw describes it, the evocative landscape is achieved through "the representation's implication of multiple prospects available only to those *within* the frame."[104] In other words, in engravings such as the one of Nicholas Revett in Figure 29, and in paintings such as those by Thomas Hearne and James Lambert in Figures 30 and 31, the painted spectator mediates between the scene and the (implied or historical) viewer, just as the fictional editor mediates between the protagonist's suffering and the (implied or historical) reader.

In all three cases, a tableau is established, nature is 'fixed,' an emotive source is safely framed and presented, and the reader or viewer is indirectly instructed about the appropriate response to a scene. The Nicholas Revett drawing dramatizes the contrast between the static 'fixing' of the artist

Figure 30

and the unruly nature he seeks to 'fix' by framing the artist from within a grotto and by including a horse-taming scene in the external frame. The grotto frames the exterior activities, just as the horse tamers seek to tame

Figure 31

the horses, and the artist attempts to fix nature on paper. The artifice of painting becomes explicit, yet at the same time it is also naturalized. The two paintings are very effective in showing the looming and inspiring force of monumental ruins, and both use a similar composition with ruins towering above and to the right of the artists. In all three cases, artifice and nature are intertwined, so that it is difficult to ascertain where vegetation and rocks end and ruin begins. Like the protagonist-narrator, the illustrated artist has dual roles—he is simultaneously a spectator moved by the sight and also an artist recording it on paper or canvas.

This dynamic is especially striking when the artist portrayed is the same as the artist painting the actual painting, as is the case with Lambert (Figure 31) as well as with Revett. Just as Sterne and Goethe introduce autographical elements into their novels of sensibility, the layer of self-referentiality adds an additional frame of authorship. The painter is doubled into two characters—both of whom are participants and narrator/recorders—Erzähler and Erzählung. The ultimate effect is not so much to mask authority *per se,* since the brush is not disguised, but rather to highlight the painter's authentic involvement in nature and thereby mask his artificiality. The techniques suggest painters' emotional involvement in painting the scene as men of feeling, taste, and virtue.

Within the novels of sensibility that we have examined, not only do Sterne and Goethe portray themselves portraying the narrator (and portray the narrator portraying himself portraying the man of feeling at the center of the novel!), but throughout the novels, including Mackenzie's *Man of Feeling,* there are inset scenes which show how characters react to a series of spectacles. Yorick, Harley, and Werther all serve as models for the reader of how to see and respond emotionally to scenes around them ("training the imagination to feel with the eyes"). The reader is to respond as a man of feeling (regardless of gender) according to the pedagogy of seeing that the novel establishes. Thus Gilpin and Yorick both serve as models of traveling for the reader, and, more literally, Werther serves as a model reader within his novel. Just as Werther is a model reader of Ossian, transported by his moods, the Editor is a model reader of Werther's letters, and we implied readers are to model our reactions accordingly, spurred on by the editor's marginalia. One of the results of this dynamic is that external events, including episodes with other minor characters, function as stimuli for delicate emotions in the observing 'heart': minor characters, and indeed all external phenomena, become means to a private end. Thus we find, for example, that all the chapter headings in *Journey* refer to apparently insignificant stimuli, such as "A Remise" or "The Passport" that are lent significance because of the private emotions they inspire in a feeling heart. This dynamic works two ways: it can glorify the unnoticed, the commonly ignored; however, it can also trivialize that which is significant independent of the viewer or as an end in itself, by reducing everything to *spectacle.*[105]

Within novels of sensibility, we can perceive a similar dynamic between the dramatized narrators and the implied reader. As early as the preface of *Werther,* the *Herausgeber* invites the *rare and worthy reader* to join the elite group who can sympathize with Werther. Frequently, the *Herausgeber*'s notes (and asterisks) imply a similar point: feeling hearts have no need of words, and those who have no feeling heart, would not understand the words anyway, since only the imaginative sympathy of the rare individual can fill the gaps left by words' impotence.

Sensibility evokes a strong division between the singular man of feeling and all the rest of the world; the reader is enlisted to pronounce him or herself as a member of this natural aristocracy based on feeling rather than conventional standards. The fate of Harley's papers informs the reader before the story has even begun that Harley is too delicate, too virtuous, for common understanding; he therefore relies upon the sympathy of a precious few to preserve his story.[106] Mackenzie uses many inset scenes— internalized tales within the novel—to separate the sympathetic auditors and spectators from the heartless masses. By implication, he weeds out unsympathetic readers as well. In *Werther* there are no auditors who fully understand and appreciate Werther, including even the addressee of his many letters. The reader must fill in the gap of sympathy, therefore, and feel ennobled by the role. Sterne's Yorick, too, writes: "there is so little true feeling in the *herd of the world,* that I wish I could have got an act of parliament, when the books first appeared, that none but wise men should, look into them."[107]

Inherent in the structure of the novel of sensibility, given its dual impulses, is the flattery of the reader, whose participatory role in the novel doubles both as a rescue mission as well as a self-assertion of virtuous sensibility (since sympathy is both expression and self-representation). The sympathetic reader is, by definition, *neither* of the "herd of the world," *nor* cold and unfeeling—as long as the reader is also uncritical of the text, its protagonists, and its author. Filling in the fragmentation of the rhetoric of silence (or imaginatively completing the rhetoric of ruins) draws one into the community of those who recognize the insufficiency of language, those who need no external authority to achieve consensus, and those who can ostensibly communicate without sullying their feelings with words. As the editor says of Harley: "There are some feelings which are perhaps too tender to be suffered by the world. The world is in general selfish, interested, and unthinking, and throws the imputation of romance or melancholy on every temper more susceptible than its own."[108] The 'reader of feeling' represents, as it were, natural human goodness in a cold and decadent world.

This sentimental education (or seduction) of the reader is not without a price, however, for the eighteenth-century 'reader of feeling.' This reader had to survive the accompanying pressures of a mechanistic approach to the picturesque, which measured potential for feeling by the appearance of grief (or the number of tears shed), and established canonical barometers of feeling, such as responses to the writings of Richardson, Sterne, Goethe, Mackenzie, and Ossian. Frequently the author's name alone sufficed to elicit the desired response. The *Monthly Review* (May 1771), for example, describes the natural effect of Mackenzie's *Man of Feeling* upon the reader of feeling: "The reader, who weeps not over some of the scenes it describes, has no sensibility of mind."[109] Diderot writes about the appropriate tearful reactions to a perusal of Richardson's *Clarissa.* And Lady Louisa Stuart worried that she would not cry enough when reading Henry Mackenzie's *The Man of Feeling* "to gain the proper credit of proper sensibility."[110] Debates over the historical authenticity of Ossian were not as relevant as its undisputed emotional authenticity: in fact, Ossian, too, was used to judge the merit (or sensibility) of individual readers. Boswell wrote in a letter to Erskine, 17 December 1761, for example: "take my word for it, [the Highland bard] will make you feel that you have a soul."[111]

Boswell also records that Erskine and Sheridan "talked very well upon the poems of Ossian whom Sheridan said he preferred to all the poets in the world . . . He said that Mrs. Sheridan and he had fixed it as the standard of feeling, made it like a thermometer by which they could judge of the warmth of everybody's heart."[112] Such codified reactions became so standard that a nineteenth-century edition of *The Man of Feeling* "follow[s] the author's intent" by including an "Index to the tears shed (chokings, etc., not counted)." The list contains entries such as the following:

Eye wet with a tear	Page 127
Tears, face bathed with	130
Dropped one tear, no more	131
Tears, press-gang could not refrain them	136

The list illustrates the parallel between Hirschfeld's botanical version of the emotional obstacle course and the literary one exemplified by Mackenzie or Sterne; the index also epitomizes the eventual over-codification of sensibility and the self-conscious artificiality it encourages in its readers.

The narrators and fictional editors of novels of sensibility nearly define their reader out of existence. Recurring phrases deny worth or membership to readers who do not feel the appropriate degree of interest in the protagonists' plights or who do not feel the right emotion to the right degree at the right time. Readers who do not pass the editor's tests are considered sub-human, alien to this world, unworthy, cold hearted. Sterne's Yorick momentarily speculates whether "tone and manners have a meaning," yet he quickly and defensively responds to himself: "certainly they have, unless to hearts which shut them out," again defiantly expressing optimism alongside the potential for despair. Mackenzie's editor, too, bemoans that "some feelings [are] too tender to be suffered by the world." And Austen's fictional editor warns more directly: "These sweet lines, as pathetic as beautifull [sic] were never read by any one who passed that way, without a shower of tears, which if they should fail to excite in you, Reader, your mind must be unworthy to peruse them." Whereas Mackenzie's fictional editor claims that only "one half" of the world need not be told the story that they already understood, these and other phrases suggest the haunting fear that humanity as a whole is less easily moved to sympathy than the authors of novels of sensibility would like to believe.

What begins in the distrust of authorities ends in the distrust of readers and consumers (and perhaps humanity itself). Similarly, the democratic solution of shared authorship and shared responsibility between author and reader fails in light of the authors' inability to trust the reader's interpretive role. Ultimately, the avoidance of overtly authoritarian structures leads to a disguised tyranny, as well as new structures and regulations, perhaps even more dangerous in their pretence of liberalism. The eagerness to disguise the editor, author, or architect's role thus ultimately substitutes a masked tyranny in place of a more explicit one founded on rationalist Enlightenment confidence.

4   Constructing Human Ruin

With what a moral delight will it crown my journey, in sharing in the sickening incidents of a tale of misery told to me by such a sufferer? To see her weep!

—Sterne, *A Sentimental Journey*

Amidst all my Lamentations for her (& violent you may suppose they were) I yet received some consolation in the reflection of my having paid every Attention to her, that could be offered, in her illness. I had wept over her every Day—had bathed her sweet face with my tears & had pressed her fair Hands continually in mine—

—Austen, *Love and Freindship*

I would give the world for your picture, with the expression I have seen in your face, when you have been supporting your friend.

—Wollstonecraft, *Mary, a Fiction*

THE PLEASURES OF PITY

One has to admit that there is something about other people's grief that naturally excites curiosity. This human characteristic causes great debate during the eighteenth and nineteenth centuries, often revealing profound doubt about the possibility of natural goodness. Depending upon one's perspective, this natural interest in others' grief may reveal a heartwarming fact about human nature or quite the reverse. Smith, Rousseau, and others during the eighteenth century interpreted curiosity about others' suffering (our "brother on the rack") as a natural spring of human sympathy.

In addition, Smith claims that sympathy actually works to alleviate pain: "Sympathy . . . alleviates grief by insinuating into the heart [of the sufferer] almost the only agreeable sensation which it is at that time capable of receiving." Smith assumes such sympathy to function in conversation whenever the sufferer finds a person who will listen to the "cause of their sorrow": "in relating their misfortunes, they in some measure renew their grief . . . Their tears accordingly flow faster than before, and they are apt to abandon themselves to all the weakness of sorrow. They take pleasure, however, in all of this, and, it is evident, are sensibly relieved by it."[1] Spectators' curiosity thus allows for a cathartic effect upon the sufferer.

Pity or sympathy, in fact, was elevated to the status of a "moral sentiment" by Smith, and viewed as a virtue by others, alongside more traditional virtues such as charity, courage, and justice. Others, such as Samuel Johnson, Austen, and other more traditional Christian thinkers, had less faith in human sympathy and innate human goodness, but the tide of the culture of sensibility strongly favored those who felt that sympathy was not only proof of human goodness, but that virtue could be measured by the number of tears one shed or the ease with which one could shed them. Since the culture of sensibility stems partly from egalitarian desires to notice the downtrodden and the unheard, such as children, animals, the wounded, the homeless, and the insane, there is a distinctly moral and didactic component to these descriptions of sensibility. The ability to perceive instantly what others leave unnoticed is a key feature of all heroes and heroines of novels of sensibility.[2]

It is very difficult to separate sensibility's emphasis on feelings from its emphasis on those who feel—to separate sympathizer from sufferer, spectator from spectacle. The emphasis on the often theatrical demonstrations of sympathy again reveals sensibility's philosophical insecurity and the fear of a human tendency towards solipsism or narcissism. Werther, for example, extols his heart as the root of his delicate sensibility: "dies Herz, das doch mein einziger Stolz ist, das ganz allein die Quelle von allem ist, aller Kraft, aller Seligkeit und alles Elendes. Ach, was ich weiß, kann jeder wissen—mein Herz habe ich allein." [This heart, which is my only pride, is the lone source of everything—every power, every blessing, and every misery. Ah, anyone can know what I know—but my heart is mine alone].[3] While extolling his excruciatingly delicate perception of the world around him, the remarks and emphasis on *possession* reveal that ultimately his sensibility turns him inward and causes him to congratulate and admire himself at the expense of his surroundings and ultimately his senses.[4] Sterne in a letter from 1761 makes a strikingly similar remark: "praised be God for my sensibility! Though it has often made me wretched, yet I would not exchange it for all the pleasures the grossest sensualist ever felt."[5] One of the interesting problems here is that of Sterne's complex eroticism: Sensibility's dominion over the nerves, rather than muscles (leading to tingles rather than action), actually allows Sterne to preserve a purity or chastity in Yorick that he would otherwise not maintain, and which separate him from "the grossest sensualist." In a sense, his actions are filial and remain at least technically chaste, while his nerves are erotic and self-indulgent.

The definition of 'sensibility,' as we have seen, took on multiple meanings including readiness to respond physically and emotionally to sensory stimuli. The additional problem here is that the keen and physical response could be stimulated by either *beauty* or *suffering:* in other words, 'sensibility' takes over not only aesthetic terrain but also the moral terrain of charity. As sympathy and sensibility replace charity, the emotions in the spectator become more important than any actions that this virtuous observer might take to alleviate the suffering. Personality and spontaneous, overflowing feeling replace character, plans, discipline, and, eventually, action; nerves and glands come to bear greater ethical significance than muscles. This crucial shift in ethics and aesthetics affects the representation of sensibility's protagonists, who increasingly prioritize feeling over action and sympathy over charity as the movement progresses.

As we have seen, authors of novels of sensibility return to first-person narrations of distress as opportunities for the simultaneous expression of sympathy and assertion of sensibility. To weep at another's grief is to evince one's aesthetic and moral status as a man or woman of feeling. The fact that this grief must be vicarious stems from the desire to confirm a selflessness in human nature, and yet, the spectatorial necessity of another's suffering to prove one's own merit or to satisfy one's own sense of virtue is problematic. As the epigraphs above indicate, sympathy may not be so selfless after all when it performs its theatrical role within the culture of sensibility. The narcissistic and hypocritical, if not sadistic, potential of these scenes of pathos becomes especially questionable when coupled with the novel of sensibility's masking of authorship. Authors and protagonists write, record, and experience these scenes of suffering while denying any responsibility for their existence, let alone offering assistance to the injured parties. Thus, the purposeful constructions of scenes of distress and ruination within the culture (and especially cult) of sensibility become fodder for its critics. Uvedale Price, for example, in his *Essay on the Picturesque,* does not limit his examples of picturesque sights in nature to landscape and animals, but instead he interweaves examples of the human picturesque: "beggars, gypsies, and all such rough tattered figures as are merely picturesque, bear a close analogy, in all the qualities that make them so, to old hovels and mills, to the wild forest horse, and other objects of the same kind."[6] In this way, human poverty, age, and signs of suffering—human ruin, in short—is enabled by, if not authorized and encouraged by, sensibility's moral aesthetic. This disturbing fact is exploited by opponents of sensibility—such as Bernard Mandeville and the Marquis de Sade—for their own purposes.[7]

Van Sant discusses the ways in which novelists of sensibility, such as Richardson, can be seen to adapt a trend in natural science to narratives. Scentific experiments frequently focused on the bodily manifestations of feeling, and taking this to an extreme, inflicted pain on animals in order to study the physical results; Van Sant persuasively argues that Richardson's narrator in *Clarissa,* for example, acquires a larger role after the rape, somewhat sadistically helping the reader observe her pain and death in minute detail.[8] I would argue that because of the self-narration in the novel of sensibility, this focus on the infliction of and response to pain can be seen as masochistic as well. This can be another explanation of the need for editorial frames for the protection of reputation. Not only can these editorial frames help maintain the fiction and ideal of sympathy, protecting men of feeling from accusations of sadism, but they also disguise protagonists' control over their own suffering in order to avoid the appearance of masochism. In both cases, the narrative structure helps preserve the reader's sense of the virtuous or elite displays in which he or she vicariously participates.

While this study focuses on the narrative prose fiction of sensibility, Wordsworth's first publication, a sonnet entitled "On Seeing Miss Helen Maria Williams Weep at a Tale of Distress" (1786), rather succinctly exemplifies sensibility's moral psychology and its emphasis on receptivity or sensitivity to external behavior and sights, whether the landscape garden, the Alps, or the sight of human suffering at home.

> She wept.—Life's purple tide began to flow
>   In languid streams through every thrilling vein;
> Dim were my swimming eyes—my pulse beat slow,
>   And my full heart was swell'd to dear delicious pain.
> Life left my loaded heart, and closing eye;
>   A sigh recall'd the wanderer to my breast;
> Dear was the pause of life, and dear the sigh
>   That call'd the wanderer home, and home to rest.
> That tear proclaims—in thee each virtue dwells,
>   And bright will shine in misery's midnight hour;
> As the soft star of dewy evening tells
>   What radiant fires were drown'd by day's malignant pow'r,
> That only wait the darkness of the night
>   To cheer the wand'ring wretch with hospitable light.

There are at least four loci of distress in this poem: (1) an unknown party's distress that forms the content of the "tale of distress," (2) the distress displayed by Miss Williams as a sympathetic listener, (3) the poet's distress as a sympathetic viewer, and (4) the adventures of the historical Williams, a well-known icon of sensibility.[9] The use of a historical figure and icon of sensibility invites the reader to attribute to Wordsworth the sensibility exhibited by the narrating voice of the poem—an author's indirect testimony to himself as a man of feeling, as we saw with Goethe and Sterne. By the third line, we know that the subject of the poem is the self-image and delight of the second-hand spectator, rather than Miss Helen Maria Williams herself. Another is suffering, yet the topic of the description is the sympathizer/admirer's own bodily functions: the poet/spectator's sensibility is beautifully exemplified using sensibility's physical hallmarks, including blood, tears, pulse, fainting, and sighing. The sonnet reveals nothing about the original source of distress nor the one(s) who suffer: the initial source of pain is all but forgotten in the poet's reverie. And of the portrait or tableau of Miss Williams, we only see her weeping and hear a sigh. The poet/specta-tor's weeping is at a triple or quadruple remove from the source of suffering and only the last line suggests any benefit to the suffering individual.

The poem also involves the glamorization and eroticization of the sufferer, the substitution of tears for aid, and the substitution of narration for experi-ence. On at least four levels in Wordsworth's poem, spectators eroticize the spectacle of suffering and glamorize their own ability to perceive it and feel it vicariously. Claudia Johnson takes a similarly voyeuristic and self-gratifying phenomenon as the starting point of her book-length study of sentimental-ism: she records Edmund Burke's description of the attack of Marie Antoi-nette in her bedchamber, where he intersperses remarks on his own emotional responses. Burke is moved to exemplary tears by his own description: "Tears came again into my Eyes almost as often as I looked at the description. They may again."[10] Similar to the seats or benches in English garden that allow the viewer to indulge in the appropriate emotional responses, victims are required in order to allow spectators to glorify their own sympathy and tears. Words-worth complies with this tendency to eroticize "dear, delicious pain" and to describe the pleasure of witnessing purity *au naturel,* virtue in distress, the pleasing cracks of the crumbling monument, a human tableau unencumbered by traditional decorum or reserve.[11] Of course, the trajectory of the cult of feeling described here culminates in the sadistic tendencies most notoriously developed and distributed in the narrative fiction of the Marquis de Sade, whose name was adopted to describe the psychological urge.

In a passage from a short epistolary story entitled "Jack and Alice," written when she was 11 or 12 years old, Jane Austen spoofs the problem of self-conscious sympathy and eroticized victimization within the extreme forms of sensibility. Laura, the heroine, recounts an event to the young reader of her letters, a scene that two characters find most "interesting":

> A lovely young Woman lying apparently in great pain beneath a Citron-tree was an object too interesting not to attract their notice. Forgetting their own dispute, they both with sympathizing tenderness advanced towards her & accosted her in these terms.
>
> "You seem fair Nymph to be labouring under some misfortune which we shall be happy to relieve if you will inform us what it is. Will you favor us with your Life & adventures?"
>
> "Willingly Ladies, if you will be so kind as to be seated."

She proceeds with her lengthy history of woes, but neither does the narra-tor mention, nor do the characters seem to notice, that she has a bloody broken leg, caught in "one of the steel traps so common on gentlemen's grounds." Several pages later we learn that she had been screaming at the top of her lungs until a servant released her from the trap, and she has still been lying on the ground with her bloody and "entirely broken" leg while recounting several pages' worth of life and adventures.[12]

The phrase "Life and adventures," reminiscent of a subtitle of an eighteenth-century novel, suggests also the entertainment value of the lady's narrative—and thereby of her distress. "At the melancholy recital, the eyes of all were suffused with tears." Finally, however, Lady Williams thinks to set the leg, which she does with great dexterity "the more wonderfull on account of her never having performed such a one before." The explicit delay in providing medical attention emphasizes the fact that narrative impulses were stronger than the desire to relieve her pain. Experiencing the stranger's self-narrated past distress was more pressing than eliminating her present distress. It is also unclear what bearing her physical appearance has on the degree to which her story "interests" her interviewers/ spectators. She is a "fair nymph," "lovely" and picturesque, sitting under a citron tree—portrayed detachedly, as a picture. Austen's implication seems to be that her situation "interests" the viewers only because of a combination of beauty, rank, and distress, and this "interest" piques the desire for immersion in a narrative.[13]

Since, within the culture of sensibility, ethics becomes a matter of connoisseurship, the rational, tranquil, and conventional can never please aesthetically, as the following foil from *Love and Freindship* demonstrates:

> She was very plain and her name was Bridget . . . Nothing therefore could be expected from her—she could not be supposed to possess either exalted Ideas, Delicate Feelings or refined Sensibilities—She was *nothing more than a mere good-tempered, civil & obliging Young Woman;* as such we could scarcely dislike her—she was only an Object of Contempt—.[14]

The common, pleasant, Anglo-Saxon Bridget can be neither "delicate" nor "refined" and is even worthy of "contempt." In the same story, the heroine assumes Janetta's father must "have no soul" because "he had never read the Sorrows of Werter [sic],"[15] again pointing to the totemic value of sensibility's signifiers, even when the signifiers are literary artifacts themselves. Elsewhere in *Love and Freindship*, a respectable gentleman is deemed beneath the notice of the heroines because of one dreadfully unromantic habit: "His Behaviour . . . was entirely of a piece with his general character; for what could be expected from a Man who possessed not the smallest atom of sensibility, who scarcely knew the meaning of sympathy, & who actually snored—."[16] In *Sense and Sensibility,* Austen plays further with these strict aesthetic codes, when she has Marianne object to Colonel Brandon's waistcoat.

In such passages, Austen parodies the over-codification and decay of sensibility—where it becomes an esoteric cult and its members aesthetes, who take Shaftesbury's equation of taste, feeling, and virtue as an excuse to indulge in feeling at the expense of any consideration of others—a far cry from sensibility's original impulses to celebrate sympathy as a central human virtue that overcomes societal divisions.[17] With the aestheticizing of human worth, sympathy is only afforded to those who satisfy the aesthetic requirements of the 'interesting': they must be beautiful; distressed; of rank, if possible; and, generally, amenable to erotic overtures.[18]

In Figure 32, Thomas Rowlandson parodies the potentially self-serving definition of the interesting: a lecherous man of feeling accosts a young woman, "interesting" in her solitary situation. This is inspired particularly by Laurence Sterne's unusual combination of eroticism and charity, brotherly and not-so-brotherly love in his version of sensibility and universal kinship. Poignantly, the man illustrated is also a parson, and his church is in the background of the picture. The caricature points to the difficulty of channeling the "social emotions" to good ends, or of distinguishing sympathy and self-indulgence.

THE MAN OF FEELING.

Figure 32

Elsewhere in *Love and Freindship,* Austen again parodies this ubiquitous story-telling feature of the novel of sensibility: scenes of distress evoke pity and also entail the narration of personal histories, frequently seeming (to the critical and unfeeling eye, of course) to place vulgar curiosity above humane sympathy. Laura recounts "the lucky overturning of a Gentleman's Phaeton" and the sight that the heroines saw:

> "Two Gentlemen most elegantly attired but weltering in their blood was what first struck our Eyes—we approached—they were Edward and Augustus—Yes . . . they were our Husbands. Sophia shrieked & fainted on the Ground—I screamed & instantly ran mad—. We remained thus mutually deprived of our Senses, some minutes, & on regaining them were deprived of them again—. For an hour & a Quarter did we thus continue in this unfortunate Situation . . . No sooner did we hear my Edward's groan than postponing our Lamentations for the present, we hastily ran to the Dear Youth and kneeling on each side of him implored him not to die—."

What does she say to him? She asks him to recount his life story since the time they last met: "Oh! Tell me Edward (said I) tell me I beseech you before you die, what has befallen you since that unhappy Day in which Augustus was arrested & we were separated—."[19]

These situations parody a culture in which the hobby of ruin-hunting has expanded from architectural ruin to human ruin as well. Even the aestheticization of architectural ruins caused by war can cause a similar ethical dilemma. We might recall, in this light, Gilpin's wish for just a little more "lightness of parts" in Tintern Abbey, a beloved monument for later Romantics. He explained that if it were only just a little *more* ruined, it could achieve the best visual effect—that is, be a little more picturesque.

> What share of picturesque genius Cromwell might have had I know not. Certain however it is, that no man since Henry VIIIth, hath contributed more to adorn this country with picturesque ruins. The difference between these two masters lay chiefly in the style of ruins in which they composed. Henry adorned his landscapes with the ruins of abbeys, Cromwell with those of castles. I have seen many pieces by this master, executed in a very grand style.[20]

Austen, no doubt with Gilpin in mind, wryly comments in her *History of England,* that "nothing could be said in vindication [of Henry VIII], but that his abolishing Religious Houses and leaving them to the ruinous depredations of time has been of infinite use to the landscape of England in general."[21] Playing upon the picturesque tendency to rely upon a safe distance from (and therefore enjoyment of) danger or ruin, both authors poke fun at the finding of beauty in the destruction of war and hatred, even though their playful representations also risk a similar culpability. In both cases, the authors attribute aesthetic *purpose,* composition, and *agency* of ruin where Cromwell and King Henry VIII would have denied it. In this inversion of the "art of accident," Cromwell and Henry VIII's moral culpability is compounded by a dependence upon ruination for the achievement of their aesthetic (or otherwise authoritarian) goals, as well as by their unwillingness to accept responsibility and direct agency. The passage thus reflects some of Austen's central concerns about the masking of authority common to the picturesque aesthetic and the culture and novel of sensibility: the denial of responsibility and heedless pursuit of aesthetic purity that can have inhumane results.[22]

RECLAIMING FEMALE NARRATION

Most of the authors and protagonists we have dealt with thus far have been male; such a focus on male authors seems strange when one considers that most of the novels written in the eighteenth century, according to Patricia Meyer Spacks, were written by women.[23] While not exclusive to male authors, the masking of authority through multiple narrative frames seems to be most common among male authors. Somewhat different problems arise with female authors, not only of the novel of sensibility, but also of the novel itself, which was gaining cultural respectability as a relatively new genre in the second half of the eighteenth century.[24] Eighteenth-century female authors, in contrast, tend to assert their authorship with apologies. Authors such as Charlotte Lennox and Elizabeth Boyd offer "weakness, harmlessness, youth, ill health, lack of ambition, financial need—in short, femaleness—as excuse for [the] presumption" of authoring fiction.[25] The apologies seem simultaneously to assert weakness and identity; to assert their authorship in a non-threatening way, perhaps more appealing to audiences unsure about the relationship between authorship and femininity.

Scholars differ as to the effect the culture of sensibility had on female readers and authors. G. J. Barker-Benfield, for example, claims that sensibility's cult of feeling empowered women and their favored discourse, by preferencing feeling and individual experience; Nancy Armstrong similarly argues that the rise of the novel and the emergence of female authority are "elements of a single historical event."[26] Adela Pinch is less optimistic in her interpretation: Pinch argues that the culture of sensibility restricts and confounds women's access to their own desires and experiences, by emphasizing sympathetic responses to others. Claudia Johnson offers perhaps the most nuanced, if controversial, interpretation of the effect of sensibility upon gender: Johnson argues that exaggerated male sensibility is detrimental to women's status, as it casts women in the roles of victims, while elevating the male suffering gaze higher than that of the victims themselves. In effect, however, she finds that the response of women writing in the

1790s (such as Burney, Wollstonecraft, and Austen) is to create "equivocal beings"—beings ambiguous in their sexuality, who overcome the weaknesses of sensibility's sentimental men of feeling without returning to more traditional gender roles. I argue that the equivocality she describes extends to style and narrative technique as well: it is a way of describing a response to sensibility's philosophical insecurity.[27]

Van Sant also argues persuasively that sensibility defines a new male rather than a new female character type. One could argue that 'woman' and 'woman of sensibility' might have been thought synonymous. For a man to be so defined by delicacy was noticeable enough to require a label; the sentimental characteristics coincide, on the other hand, with cultural expectations for women. Van Sant argues that the role of physical responses to external stimuli in narratives of sensibility makes the existence of female heroines of sensibility socially difficult. For a woman to embark on a man-of-feeling plot, she would be perceived as an adventuress. "Though Mackenzie's heroine can report her own experience, sensibility did not represent new modes of expression for women, nor was it fully available to them. Despite the fact that the body of sensibility is defined by a reference to a nervous system conceived as feminine, it does not represent a woman's body."[28]

Pierre Carlet de Marivaux illustrates some of the intricacies of gendered authorship and authority in mid-century France, in his relentlessly "feminine" novel *La Vie de Marianne* (1731–41), who is herself "furieusement femme."[29] His example makes it clear that self-effacing apologies and framing can coexist as narrative techniques, and may have more to do with the conventions of gendering the voices within the narrative than with the gender of the author. Aurora Wolfgang, in a recent study of gender in the French eighteenth-century novel, notes Marivaux' historical and economic incentive: "feminine-voice novels," regardless of the gender of the author, "represent the modern novel of this period" and the public seemed insatiable for examples of "more personal and idiosyncratic forms of literary expression."[30] The "feminine-voice novel" as Wolfgang describes it, is characterized by a "natural and transparent writing style" based in an epistolary tradition and, in France, the oral tradition of *salons*. She also notes that with the rising psychology associated with sensibility, "subjectivity became immanently female."[31]

Wolfgang's study centers on the ways in which Marivaux assiduously "erases" all traces of masculinity from his writing as he represents several layers and sources of women's writing in his novel. Although not noted by Wolfgang, it is of interest here that Marivaux uses a fictional editor who finds, peruses, appreciates, and publishes Marianne's letters, but also that this fictional editor is the only male voice among the "authors" of the novel. In his short note, the editor notes that the document is "une écriture de femme" [a woman's writing], and apologizes that "cette histoire n'intéresse personne" [this story will interest no one], again using the divided audience trope to challenge the reader to demonstrate his or her sensibility by enjoying the book.[32] Interestingly, Marivaux' editor also explicitly denies and limits his own authorship: "Voilà tout ce que j'avais à dire: ce petite préambule m'a paru nécessaire, et je l'ai fait du mieux que j'ai pu, car je ne suis point auteur, et jamais on n'imprimera de moi que cette vingtaine de lignes-ci." [That is all I had to say: this little preamble seemed necessary to me, and I made the best of it I could, since I am no author and no one would ever publish more than my twenty or so lines.][33] In an "avertissement" later attached to the novel, the fictional editor again apologizes: this time for the fact that Marianne's letters include too much thought. In an attempt to reclaim Marianne's feminine sensibility, the editor stresses that the reflective sections of the letters are just a product of varying moods ("suivant le goût qu'elle y a pris").[34]

In other words, the growing distrust of reason and omniscient narration that shaped, yet also gradually grew incompatible with sensibility, was most closely associated with male authors. A male narrator who was *not* self-conscious, and therefore not a participant in the action and feelings of the novel, could be seen as anonymous, heartless, and bringing a random imposition of the author's authority. Only spontaneous speech, 'uncensored' by strict grammatical rules and 'untainted' by practical purpose or preconceived plans, could count as authentic or sincere. Traditional masculine narrative is equated with cold-hearted rationality and worldliness, especially if the narrative is dominated by a central omniscient narrator addressing a public audience and exhibiting the conscious intent of publication. Both male and female voices in the novels (regardless of historical genders) must still conform to the gendered expectations of sensibility, associated with the "feminine voice."

The focus here is upon the narrative strategies that result from compromised authorship. It is not the object here to decipher whether or not they result from a situation peculiar to female authors, arise because of changing attitudes towards political authority at large, or simply reflect the culture of sensibility's general skepticism about the moral or aesthetic benefits of unmasked authority or authorship. It may be that as male authors strive to fragment and punctuate their narratives and defer their authorship in order to appear men of feeling, female authors such as Jane Austen and Mary Wollstonecraft seek to assert their authority in a way that requires less masking. "In an era when fashionable male subjectivity veers toward the luridly sentimental, and sympathy—or fellow-feeling—becomes the unifying cry of male philosophers, women seem to gain in the sphere of reason what they may have lost in their traditional dominance in the field of feeling."[35]

In other words, male authors mask their authority, building narrative follies to achieve the conventional expectations of sensibility; in contrast, many female authors are trying to escape their own sense of ruination, while relying on societal discourses that dictate feminine weakness. In particular, Austen contrives, through her use of free indirect discourse, to create a style of narration that is more compatible with intimacy and sensibility's humane goals, and which serves her didactic purposes.[36] Austen turns the masking to a syntactic level: she uses free indirect discourse as a way of simultaneously asserting and not asserting, narrating and not narrating, combining omniscience and subjectivity, establishing and denying her own authority.

Barbara Benedict also sees in Austen's narrative strategies a "dialectical tension." According to Benedict, it arises in the contrast between an audience desiring an immersion in private and authentic, if vicarious, feelings and a fear among English society about the ramifications of ungoverned feelings upon susceptible female readers devouring stories of unchecked passion in the vulnerable privacy of their own rooms. As Benedict perceives it, the dialectical tension results in the censorship and framing of tales of feeling by conventional morality and tradition.[37] For Benedict, the dialectical tension thus comes from a conflict between the culture of sensibility and more traditional British culture and moral didacticism at large; I would instead argue that the culture of sensibility inherently relies upon tension between conservative and utopian forces, between skepticism and optimism, between narration and anti-narration. For Benedict, pedagogy intrudes upon the cult of feeling, whereas I would argue that the novel of sensibility develops, alongside the picturesque, not only a characteristic moral aesthetic, but also a characteristic pedagogy of its own—training its readers to feel and respond to a variety of spectacles, following the example of model readers or viewers purposely imbedded in the texts. Sensibility's masked urge to instruct is, in fact, one of the most powerful expressions of its philosophical insecurity.

Interestingly, conventional eighteenth-century assumptions about the inherent qualities of the female mind or of female speech are not terribly different from some contemporary (often essentialist) feminist conceptions of female discourse or female narration. Conventionally, eighteenth-century women's discourse was considered disorganized and impulsive: it "circles around the subject self with its tumbling, unordered phrases and imprecise language"; it challenges the central singular authority of objective narration, long considered a masculine style, through its "value for multiplicity and feeling."[38] This discourse can be described in negative terms as "disorderly, disorganized, incoherent, illogical, irrational,"[39] or in more positive terms as "less analytic than synthetic, more intuitive than logical, more complex than simple; in other words . . . having an appearance of disorder that conceals a particularly complex mode of order."[40] The most general features are non-linearity, resistance to traditional (male, omniscient, public, detached) narration, and the pursuit of innovative means to replicate the immediacy of experience, uncensored by reason, resulting in a preference for fragmentation, subjectivity, and private discourse over linearity, objectivity, and public discourse. Accordingly, the most popular form of prose fiction for eighteenth-century female authors is the epistolary novel, which conveniently eliminates the narrator and emphasizes the female protagonists' immediacy of experience. In other words, the central difference between "male" and "female" discourse echoes the difference between the language of authoritative detachment and the language of immediate experience, between narration and anti-narration, between public discourse and private discourse.

Part of the difficulty surrounding detached narration stems from the fact that, as Benedict states, "Eighteenth-century fiction accords detachment moral power, the right to decide who and what is valuable. This detachment . . . is conventionally prohibited to women because it is structured by a narrative point of view founded on models of masculine writing which are informed by a neoclassical preference for generality," one form of overt authorial contrivance.[41] This tension between detachment and experience, or between generality and particulars, is central to the culture of sensibility as a whole and to its epistemological suspicion of knowledge as it is associated with authority, even when not explicitly connected to issues of gender.

In practice, the novel of sensibility in the latter half of the eighteenth century champions the ambivalent, rather than the radical. Not yet espousing purer forms of the unchecked language of immediate expression (such as the modernist stream-of-consciousness style of Virginia Woolf), the culture of sensibility still requires the tension between those who experience immediacy and those who merely record it, whereas Woolf's narrators themselves record and "publish" without needing the assistance of a less feeling editor to organize their experiences. In fact, even the hope or desire for such organizational force has been lost in post-WWII disappointments. If, in other terms, sensibility's ambivalence is a tension between the neoclassical and patriarchal tradition of literary order, closure, and monument on the one hand, and the feminized literary culture with a new value for fragmentation, chaos, and ruin, on the other, then it could be argued that ruination is another word for non-linearity or for the "feminization" of the novel.

In order to appeal to sensibility's contempt for overt authoritative detachment and omniscient narration, male authors use 'female' narrative style in order to hide their public authority as authors; they effectually cross-dress using a stereotypically female avoidance of narration, in order to appeal to their audiences. Male and female characters must vie for the greater sensibility, the greater responsiveness, the greater passivity—and ultimately the greater victimization and failure within the novel of sensibility. The extremes of sensibility, including its 'feminized' heroes, thus become open fodder for parody and ridicule by the end of the century.

Within the novel of sensibility, the need for narratorial frames can be seen as analogous to the picturesque desire to hide the "marks" of authorship and construction; narrative frames also reveal sensibility's insecurity regarding omniscient narration and the moral authority it seems to wield. The epistolary tradition characteristically appeals to the authority of experience by highlighting the specific circumstances of individual experience and promoting an ethics of sympathy, whereas the tradition of more omniscient narration provides greater distance from individuals and the possibility of comparing and evaluating situations philosophically, promoting an ethics of comparison and abstraction. The frames within the novel of sensibility allow it to champion the authority of experience over the authority of narration, just as an epistolary novel does, yet it also explicitly protects the experiential quality of the novel by delegating narrative urges (and commercial interests) to other fictional "authors." Authors of sensibility must negotiate the Scylla and Charybdis of excessive subjectivity (narcissistic solipsism) and excessive objectivity (generalization, moralism, disregard for individuals), taking into account the benefits of each form of authority. Ultimately, suspicion against detachment propels sensibility's novelists (and their self-conscious protagonists) towards 'monument' as well as 'ruin,' towards the desire to narrate their experience as well as to preserve the immediate authentic experience in its unordered state. The result is the delicate balance that the term 'monumental ruin' suggests; however, as we see above, the balance easily degenerates into hypocrisy, abdication of responsibility, or self-absorption, as well as attraction to sadism.

Passages such as the above sections of "Jack and Alice" as well as *Love and Freindship* have been taken by critics such as Marilyn Butler as a sign that Austen renounces sensibility; however, close attention to the themes presented in her novels tend rather to reveal not only her intimate and formative experience with the culture, literature, and moral aesthetic of sensibility, but also her genuine attachment to many of its central tenets. The force and economy of her parody may be directly proportional to the attachment and acquaintance Austen had with the culture before it deteriorated to cultish extremes. In other words, Austen attacks only the sensibility that becomes *in*sensible to others, to nature, and even to its adherents through excessive codification, elitism, victimization, or narcissism, and which encourages human ruin.

Sensibility's revision of authority and authorship, along with its dual impulses, thus profoundly affects even a writer who, in many ways, defines herself in opposition to it. In her own narrative innovations, Austen discovers a way effectively to combine the strengths of Fielding's central narrative voice with the demand for the authenticity of uncensored individual experience, championed among male authors by Richardson and Rousseau. She combines the balanced prose of the Augustan essayistic tradition (authors such as Addison, Steele, and her beloved Dr. Johnson) with the immediacy of the female epistolary tradition—a form which figures prominently (in fact, almost exclusively) in her earliest writings, intended for family entertainment rather than publication. In the process of adjusting her writing to a public audience and reclaiming female authority, Austen adjusts the female epistolary tradition to new ends, attempting to avoid sensibility's cultish extremes. A closer look reveals that her characteristic innovations in narrative style actually reflect her own ambivalence regarding authority, as well as her own dual impulses, and her desire to reclaim sensibility from its more extreme forms. Basing her innovations on the narrative fragmentation and editorial framing characteristic of the novel of sensibility, Austen both reflects and rejects the culture of sensibility, based partly on her thorough knowledge of the authors in the previous pages. In her innovations and revisions of *Sense and Sensibility*.

Austen shows the limits of both forms of moral authority. The authority based on individual experience is unreliable, especially since it lacks distance, perspective, and objectivity; the authority of narration must also be chastened of its claims to objective knowledge in order to allow the coexistence of multiple perspectives. In order to reform the expectations of an audience steeped in the culture of sensibility, Austen uses familiar structures from the culture of the picturesque and from the culture of sensibility to develop a narrative style that can reclaim authority, public discourse, and narrative detachment without returning to older masculine ideals of rational detachment, omniscient narration, and univocal objectivity. In *Sense and Sensibility,* for example, Austen retains twenty-two letters that mark its epistolary origins,[42] and develops her innovative use of free indirect discourse and narrative perspective to establish a dominant voice that allies the reader with Elinor's more mature, but not omniscient, perspective.

Observation is a key human ability that is under debate, even internally within *Sense and Sensibility,* as Austen revises sensibility's pedagogy of seeing for her own purposes. For Adam Smith in his *Theory of Moral Sentiments,* observation allows for sympathetic and imaginative interaction with other individuals, and bridges the chasm between individual experiences, separated as we are by our own bodies. As Smith describes it, observation gains value primarily in so far as it trains and authorizes the "demigod within the breast" to sympathize with others, particularly in their suffering. Observation, however, is also key to a more Enlightenment-based rational value for general observation, allowing one to gain philosophical perspective and detachment by separation from others and even from one's own immediate situation. This latter understanding also implies an authority—earned through observation and reflection—to judge others' behavior (Benedict's concern). In Austen's hands, the two roles for observation are melded: observation serves the purposes both of sympathy and comprehension; individual ethics need not be sacrificed, as Marianne initially thinks, for the sake of determining propriety or virtue.

Recognizing its dangers and potential hypocrisy, Austen tries to revise sensibility's pedagogy of seeing to accord with a sense of individual responsibility, an engagement in the community at large, an admiration of tranquility and self-control, and the possibility of community, all of which tend to be absent from its cultish extremes. [43] Austen is particularly concerned about the moral consequences of purposeful ruination, especially when ruination involves the victimization of real trees, real abbeys, or especially real human beings, sacrificed to suit a fleeting fashion—when self-narration becomes a vehicle for another's self-promotion, and, as in the epigraph from Sterne, "sickening incidents of a tale of misery" provide "moral delight." In *Sense and Sensibility,* Elinor's teasing question to Marianne "Confess, Marianne, is there not something interesting to you in the flushed cheek, hollow eye, and quick pulse of a fever?" actually signifies a much greater issue within the culture of sensibility—namely, the enjoyment of other people's suffering for the sake of an aesthetic principle. The focus here will be to uncover Austen's own version of the multiple narrative frames we saw in Sterne, Mackenzie, and Goethe, a technique that Austen adapts to train her reader in the ethics of 'translation,' the possible abuses of authority and authorship, and the potential decadence of the fascination with ruination and primitivism.[44] If Yorick portrays sensibility's characteristic ambivalence regarding authority and authorship, and Werther shows the mortal stakes involved in authorship, and authentic self-representation, then Marianne and Elinor Dashwood, as Austen portrays them, redeem both authorship and the possibility of public speech.

Especially in her main novels, Austen turns issues of sensibility and picturesque codes onto her narrative techniques, not only by applying earlier novelists' use of narrative frames to her own work, but also by using them as a didactic technique to encourage similar growth in her reader. One central goal for her protagonists is successful self-representation in a Hobbesian world despite limitations of language and a fallen nature. In response, Austen builds a style of narrative representation that combines both narrative and anti-narrative impulses in one character, manipulating narrative sympathy and the reader's participation, while reclaiming a form of authority and authorship that is compatible with sensibility, as well as with self-control and responsibility, all the while aiming at a reconciliation of public discourse and private intimacy and the edification of an implied reader imbued with the novel of sensibility.

AUSTEN'S FEMALE WERTHER

William Godwin once called Mary Wollstonecraft a "female Werter": she was one of the rare people, he wrote, "endowed with the most exquisite and refined sensibility, whose minds seem almost too delicate a texture to encounter the vicissitudes of human affairs, to whom pleasure is transport, and disappointment is agony indescribable."[45] While not calling Marianne Dashwood directly a "female Werter," Austen draws upon allusions to Werther to ally Marianne with traditional heroes of sensibility. She also relies on the broader aesthetic (particularly as it relates to language, fragmentation, and the half-spoken) to identify Colonel Brandon and Edward as heroes or men of feeling. Strangely enough, despite the fact that Austen makes overt references to Goethe's *Werther* in her writings, very little has been written about the role of this extremely popular novel in Austen's literary imagination.[46]

Not only is Marianne Dashwood a female counterpart to Werther, but Austen's portrayal of Marianne also helps us understand both her affinities with the culture of sensibility and her domestication of its extreme forms. Austen creates explicit parallels between Werther and Marianne in characterization, on the level of plot, and in the structure of their respective novels—focusing particularly on Werther and Marianne's self-ruination and refusal to accept their own public authority.

Like Werther, Marianne is spirited, idealistic, and inflexible. Just as Werther narrates his choice between 'inauthentic,' and therefore compromised, survival within society and 'authentic' expression that transgresses society's rules, Marianne also fancies herself in the same heroic struggle. Her thinking follows the same circuitous route as Werther's: the principle that to *resist* sorrow is to be inauthentic leads to the idea that for sorrow to *cease* is inauthentic and finally to the paradoxical moral obligation to *nourish* her sorrow (artificially) for the sake of its authenticity. Like Werther, she chooses to "court[-]. . misery" and "to augment and fix her sorrow by seeking silence, solitude, and idleness."[47] The word "fix" here, also used by Gilpin, is reminiscent of the artificial framing that is useful for capturing a picturesque composition. In *Sense and Sensibility,* Marianne similarly "fixes" her sorrow to preserve the authenticity of the moment she experiences. The use of picturesque vocabulary emphasizes the aesthetic component of her emotional life: Marianne, like Werther, does not wish to disturb her own riveting tableau of the self. In a sense, each of these characters is his or her own artistic creation according to principles of sensibility and the picturesque.[48] They artificially nourish their unhappiness, as Thomas Whately artificially builds and maintains ruined edifices for aesthetic purposes—only, for Marianne and Werther, the stakes are moral, if not mortal, as well as aesthetic.

From Marianne's first encounter with Willoughby, their entire relationship is governed by a code of sensibility: their kinship is as instantaneous as Werther's with Lotte, their degree of intimacy inversely proportional to the number of words they need to achieve it, and the conventional gauges of intimacy, such as time, are irrelevant to them. Marianne disdains conventional rules of etiquette, which fade away in comparison with the intense, 'natural' bond she feels with Willoughby. Just as Werther feels that natural genius should not be held to the standard rules of convention, Marianne also believes that her sensibility allows her to transcend manners and ritual.

Even the structure of Marianne's sub-plot is strikingly similar to Werther's story. In fact, Marianne's falls naturally into two parts as well. In the first, we encounter Marianne absorbed in nature; however, we quickly learn that she is as proprietary of her trees as Werther was of "mein Wald." Both Werther and Marianne derive ownership according to sensibility. They claim ownership of nature because they believe only *they* can truly appreciate it: "now there is *no one* to regard them," Marianne complains when she leaves her trees at Norland.[49] Echoing Sterne and others, Edward playfully intimates that Marianne shares the elitism of the man of feeling: "And books! Thomson, Cowper, Scott—she would buy them all over and over again; she would buy up every copy, I believe, to prevent their falling into unworthy hands."[50] (Sterne's Yorick, for example, also suggests that only the feeling should be allowed to read his novel: "there is so little true feeling in the *herd* of the *world,* that I wish I could have got an act of parliament, when the books first appear'd, 'that none but the wise men should look into them.'"[51]) Edward's remarks on the commercial results of any wealth accrued by the Dashwoods thus highlight the theme of appropriation that we first saw in relation to ruin hunting and Tischbein's portrait of Goethe (Figure 4), and which also becomes a leitmotif in later novels of sensibility.

In the first part of her story, Marianne, like Werther, is loquacious; however, both stammer feelingly in their appreciation of nature, especially when they fall in love. She is wild in her enthusiasms and "excessive sensibility."[52] There are continual hints that Marianne is more taken with her conception of Willoughby, however, than with the real man, and that she forces him to conform to her ideal, just as Werther does to Charlotte. Both Marianne and Werther reveal that their loves are narcissistic projections of themselves: "Wie ich mich selbst anbete seitdem sie mich liebt!" [How I worship myself now that she loves me!][53] In the second half of her story, Marianne's beloved marries another, and, as with Werther, the result is isolation, increasing insensibility (blindness and deafness to others), silence, and (near) suicide: "Had I died, it would have been self-destruction."[54] As with Werther, Marianne's initial, self-conscious appreciation of nature and general benevolence in Volume I eventually turns to something approaching misanthropy in Volume II, and her self-nourished grief takes her, in Werther's footsteps, to illness and the brink of madness and death.

Like Werther (and Harley), Marianne's reluctance to write and speak grows as the novel progresses. She consistently seeks words that are worthy of the supposed sublimity of her feelings and when she finds none, chooses silence instead: "I detest jargon of every kind, and sometimes I have kept my feelings to myself because I could find no language to describe them in but what was worn and hackneyed out of all sense and meaning."[55] Her stance here again almost parodies that of the 'man of feeling,' for, as we saw, Mackenzie too uses silence to heighten the cruelty of the world that can force a man of such delicacy and promise to retreat from words. Harley, rather immodestly, agrees with the narrative voice: "There are some feelings," admits Harley, "which perhaps are too tender to be suffered by the world, . . . [which] throws the imputation of romance or melancholy on every temper more susceptible than its own."[56]

In her pursuit of authenticity and ruination, the inexpressibility of Marianne's emotions becomes a source of pride, as does her inability to be comforted. In this emphasis on proud helplessness, she resembles all three 'men of feeling' of the preceding chapters. As Werther proclaims his inability to resist his attraction to Lotte ("Wutsch! bin ich da"), Marianne (proudly) explains: "misery such as mine has no pride. I care not who knows that I am wretched. The triumph of seeing me so may be open to the world. Elinor, Elinor, they who suffer little may be proud and independent as they like . . . but I *cannot*. I *must* feel—I *must* be wretched—."[57] Marianne measures sensibility according to lack of self-control, missing the fact not only that deep feeling can (and *must,* in Austen's world) coexist with reason and "exertion," but also that self-control can be an expression of feeling. Austen brings attention to the fact that an aesthetic of ruination leads these protagonists to crumble as they glorify victimization and demonstrate their virtue (sensibility).[58] They implicitly rely on editors and others to tell their story. As Goethe both represents the culture of sensibility and also challenges it with his brutal realism in sections of *Werther,* Austen too both represents and critiques sensibility—particularly within the character of Marianne.

In general, Marianne's words flow very freely, but not as freely as she would like to think. As Edward successfully parodies (in a rare, eloquent moment), Marianne's romantic vocabulary limits her. Edward playfully tells her that he does not subscribe to the same aesthetic rules and vocabulary—namely the 'picturesque' and the cult of sensibility: "Remember I have no knowledge in the picturesque, and I shall offend you by my ignorance and want of taste if we come to particulars. I shall call hills steep which ought to be bold; surfaces strange and uncouth which ought to be irregular and rugged; and distant objects out of sight which ought to be indistinct through the medium of a hazy atmosphere."[59] Marianne, confident that her great sensibility lets her experience nature more directly and express it more freely and spiritedly, shows herself to be quite the reverse.[60] She is stubborn and fixed where she ought to be free; blind where she ought to perceive. The fixity of her rigid code of life keeps her from being open to experience and enables her to see only what fits into her pre-existing categories. Like Yorick and Werther, Marianne strives against all odds to be 'natural' and fails miserably. Like Werther, she is impatient with the language available to suit the grandeur of her emotions. In the end, she, like Werther, is defeated by her own self-consciousness, for, like Werther and the heroines of Austen's juvenilia, Marianne is in love with her own grief: "Mine is a misery which nothing can do away."[61] Ultimately, Marianne's failure is the failure of the picturesque art of seeking fashionably natural appearances by design.

Marianne follows the example of countless heroes and heroines of sensibility by measuring her own sensibility according to lack of self-control. In the end, Marianne's sensibility is little better than the mechanistic approach to sensibility which measured potential for feeling by the number of tears shed. She expresses sensibility's perversion of the concept of 'virtue in distress' into 'the virtue *of* distress.' The former state of emergency invites rescue where the second disdains it. Ruination becomes a worthy goal in itself. Although her agency is masked (even to herself), she indulges in self-ruination and "torrent[s] of unresisted grief" to prove her genius, feeling, and taste, as well as to establish herself as a rare Shaftesburian soul suffering in a Hobbesian universe.[62] Werther, of course, takes self-ruination several steps further: he combines the roles of actor and dramaturge, victim and agent, as he coolly arranges for his death tableau, maximizing its effectiveness in every visual detail.

In addition to establishing the striking resemblances between Marianne and Werther, Austen also uses style of speech to place male characters in *Sense and Sensibility* in relation to the traditional hero of sensibility—the man of feeling. In doing this, Austen, like the authors of the novel of sensibility, purposely invites the participation of the reader for didactic effect. Both 'heroes' of *Sense and Sensibility*—Colonel Brandon and Edward—are remarkably poor speakers and resemble, in this regard, the men of feeling of the preceding chapters. Colonel Brandon stammers when he tries to express his feelings and confesses himself to be a "very awkward narrator."[63] His speech is punctuated with dashes and characterized by unfinished sentences. In one particular episode, it takes the Colonel over one hundred words to hint at what he is trying to say to Elinor: "My object—my wish—my sole wish in desiring it—I hope, I believe it is—is to be a means of giving comfort;—no, I must not say comfort—not present comfort—but conviction, lasting conviction to your sister's mind . . . ," and so he continues. He completes not a single sentence, but Elinor manages to understand him and promptly summarizes what he intended to say in fifteen words: "'I understand you,' said Elinor. 'You have something to tell me of Mr. Willoughby, that will open his character farther.'"[64]

Edward, too, is "no orator,"[65] as he repeatedly admits and as all his friends acknowledge with varying degrees of compassion and disappointment. His presence is frequently "silent and dull."[66] Even in the final scenes, when he has been disburdened of his secret engagement to Lucy and arrives to Barton Cottage to propose to Elinor, he first responds to Mrs. Dashwood's greetings by "[stammering] out an unintelligible reply," then slumps into a silent "reverie, which no remarks, no inquiries, no affectionate address . . . could penetrate," and finally flees from the drawing room "without saying a word."[67] The reader cannot come to love the two heroes of this novel through charming speeches, for unlike Willoughby, for example, they cannot charm others, including the reader, with their readiness of conversation.

The power to speak, and to speak well, belongs primarily to the cold-hearted characters in *Sense and Sensibility*. As early as the second chapter of the novel, the reader knows to beware of words because they can be abused by anyone who, like John and Fanny Dashwood, have a degree of sense without "the strong feeling of the rest of the family."[68] In addition to the abuse of promises, willful deception also runs rampant in the novel. Not only one, but *both* of the heroes have secrets—one a secret engagement, and the other, a secret ward resulting from a previous (and also secret) attachment. The most deceitful characters manipulate words to achieve their goals, as Lucy Steele, the most cunning of all the characters, does in her conversations with Elinor and in her letter to Edward. The rampant deception and reticence within the novel create gaps within the narrative, leaving room for the imaginative participation of readers, as more blatant narrative omission and fragmentation function in the novel of sensibility and in the rhetoric of ruins. Readers must attempt acts of translation, in Yorick's sense, alongside the fictional characters, since self-representation is so flawed and self-articulation so difficult. The sympathetic men, in particular, are represented as uttering ruined speech that the reader is trained sympathetically to complete.

In this way, the reader participates in the authorship of the text, and the text relies upon the reader's sympathy and narrative urges. It is only if the reader learns to distrust the charms of free-flowing language that he or she can not only forgive, but even admire those in the novel whose speech is constrained. Yet the reader must also share the curiosity and desire for completion (narrative urge) to fill gaps. In this way Austen adapts the narrative techniques of sensibility to suit her own didactic purposes. To admire Colonel Brandon and Edward Ferrars is to adopt the moral aesthetic of sensibility—a belief that intense and benevolent feeling, unappreciated in the unsympathetic and even cruel external world, leads these men to silence—that these 'men of feeling' are admirable and virtuous not *despite* their ineloquence, but *because* they are not 'men of words.' Yet, using Elinor, Austen shows that sensibility need lead neither to the abdication of authority and responsibility nor to self-victimization.

Like the novelists of sensibility of the previous chapter, Austen places great weight on extra-lingual communication, especially on the significance of gesture and vision. As did Rousseau and Herder, and authors within the culture of sensibility in general, Austen emphasizes that, because of its frequent abuse and inherent limitations, verbal evidence is generally less reliable—and further removed from true feeling—than visual evidence: "On parle aux yeux bien mieux qu'aux oreilles" [one can speak better to the eyes than the ears].[69] Austen's suspicion of verbal evidence results from the crisis of self-articulation that we have been following in the preceding chapters. The cause here is somewhat different, however: it results from the social separation of the sexes (that is, it is conventional or situational rather than inherent). As a result, unlike other authors of sensibility, Austen retains a greater element of hope in the possibility of human intimacy. In some sense, all her characters need to learn to represent what they cannot articulate directly. They must learn to combine the roles of *Erzähler* and *Erzählung* as they struggle to represent themselves authentically. The theatrical nature of communication thus becomes an easy target for good actors, and suggests the danger of extreme linguistic isolation.

But Austen's novels show that there is a measure of hope and opportunity as well, in learning to observe and discern carefully—in learning to become a good reader of one's surroundings. In a sense, Austen's novels teach that we all necessarily rely on the observation and sympathetic imagination of spectators to fill in the gaps of our stories, to recreate monuments from the shabby ruins we display, to "translate" our spoken comments into emotional coherence. To establish her pedagogy of seeing, she frequently avails herself of the technique of imbedding exemplary observers within her novels, such as Mr. Knightley of *Emma* or Anne Elliot, and eventually Wentworth, of *Persuasion*. Love produces a keenness of perception, a natural aptitude for Sternean translation, a sensibility inaccessible to those whose loves are merely narcissistic projections of themselves. Translation, then, comes quite close to Mr. Yorick's definition: the sympathetic participation in (re)constructing private meaning obscured (and/or partially revealed) by another's public utterance or attempt at self-representation.

The 'true' lovers in all Jane Austen's novels tend to watch their objects from afar rather than hang about them, chattering as the 'false' lovers do.[70] Colonel Brandon, in the narrator's telling formulation, visits the Dashwoods in order to "look at Marianne and talk to Elinor."[71] If his silence to Marianne leads us to believe that he loves Elinor more than Marianne, we are falling into the trap of trusting words over sight, as Elinor is tempted to do: "[Colonel Brandon's] open pleasure in meeting [Elinor] after an absence of only ten days, his readiness to converse with her . . . might very well justify Mrs. Jennings' persuasion of his attachment . . . As it was, such a notion had scarcely ever entered [Elinor's] head except by Mrs. Jennings' suggestion; and she could not help believing herself the nicest observer of the two; she watched his eyes while Mrs. Jennings thought only of his behavior."[72]

Whereas one of the fundamental ideas of the cult of sensibility was suspicion of rational detachment and objective stances, Austen portrays detachment in the service of feeling and even of intimacy.[73] Rather than always leading to a loss of objectivity, sympathy can benefit from the ethical and rational benefits of detachment, through the desire to see one's beloved in context, at a distance; this social sensibility thus tends to express itself through a rhetoric of ruins or of silence. Where the vocal suitor conversing and exchanging ideas with the object of his admiration is self-conscious about presentation and pleasing, the silent suitor who watches is turned outward.[74] Truly seeing is sympathizing; and by observing the loved one interacting with others, one learns more about the community to which the other belongs. The establishment of community through silence is an aspect of sensibility's moral aesthetic that Austen adopts for her own, more social, purposes.

Marianne, in her adamant opposition to detachment, poses a greater challenge to sensibility than any other of Austen's heroines. She, like Werther, represents Diderot's internal "civil war" between the natural and the moral; in other words, she is divided against herself rather than against society. It is quite apt, in this regards, that Willoughby reads *Hamlet* aloud during his early visits with the Dashwoods, and that he never completes the play.[75] In the end, Marianne discovers that she has been playing a role, reading a script based on the strict codes of the degenerated cult of sensibility; she discovers the hypocrisy to which sensibility can lead. Eventually, she, like Werther, discovers the internal division between aesthetic requirements and moral requirements, which Yorick and the complete man of feeling never recognize. For Werther, the "civil war" remains one between himself and the society that oppresses him. He will not allow the ironic acceptance of dual impulses that, in the end, enables Marianne to survive as well as to accept her own public role and authority.

FRAMING THE PICTURESQUE HEROINE

It is difficult to determine Elinor's stance in relation to the culture of sensibility because of her status within the novel. The strong identification of the narrative voice with Elinor has led critics, such as Angela Leighton and others, to assume that the narrative voice sympathizes *entirely* with Elinor.[76] If this is the case, then Elinor is associated with (and complicit in) authority and authorship—that is, suspect according to the cultural code of sensibility. In examples above where Elinor adeptly summarizes Colonel Brandon's rambling and fragmented speech, or where she fills the conversational gaps created by Edward's awkwardness, Elinor shows herself to be an ideal reader of the novel of sensibility, a translator in Yorick's sense, participating imaginatively and sympathetically to create a whole image out of fragments, or transcend the limitations of public discourse. Following the culture of sensibility's pedagogy of seeing, Elinor shows her sensibility in her sympathetic spectatorship—like Werther's editor, Elinor functions as an ideal reader imbedded in the narrative. There is, however, a danger attached to this performance: in her verbal acts of heroism and perspicacity, Elinor risks seeming a woman of words. And, as we will see, this is in fact how Marianne interprets her behavior.

Austen avails herself of her audience's familiarity with *Werther* by extending the allusions beyond Marianne: in addition to Marianne's resemblance to Werther, Austen portrays Elinor as a female Albert. Like Albert, Elinor reminds her sister of issues of justice, convention, prudence, and manners, risking the appearance of insensibility. While Albert never approaches centrality in *Werther,* however, Elinor is generally considered the central protagonist of *Sense and Sensibility,* causing confusion among readers and critics as to what degree of sympathy they should feel for the two older Miss Dashwoods. Let us take the passage where Marianne and Elinor debate the beauty of the autumn leaves: "'Oh!' cried Marianne, 'with what transporting sensations have I formerly seen them fall! How have I delighted, as I walked, to see them driven in showers about me by the wind! What feelings have they, the season, the air altogether inspired!'" Marianne delights in the picturesque vision, and it is clear that (true to the picturesque style and the culture of sensibility) the emphasis is on *her* perception of the

leaves, and the feelings that the leaves inspire *within her* are most important. Meanwhile, Elinor coolly responds, "It is not every one . . . who has
your passion for dead leaves."[77] In line with the preference for ruination and
decay common in both the picturesque and sensibility, particularly in their
most codified versions, dead leaves are more picturesque than living ones,
and the latter are no more able to inspire admiration than the practical and
ethical Bridget did above.

On the one hand, the narrator seems to applaud Edward and Elinor's
playful teasing of Marianne's fixed aesthetic codes, yet at the same time,
Marianne shows her appealingly youthful love of nature, her warmth of
spirit, and her local attachment through such outpourings. We know, from
her brother Henry's short biography, that "at a very early age," Jane Austen "was enamoured of Gilpin on the Picturesque; and she seldom changed
her opinions either on books or men."[78] This would seem to suggest that
the author and perhaps the implied author may have greater sympathy for
Marianne's position than the simple equation with Elinor would allow.
Without conflating the narrative voice and the implied author, one can still
observe that the authorial sympathy and authority that generally appear
to accompany Elinor, may actually not be quite so clearly identified with
Elinor after all. Or is it that Elinor is more than what she represents herself—in speech—to be?

Part of the difficulty Austen discovers within sensibility's dual impulses
is the difficulty of accurate self-representation or communication within
the parameters of narration or public speech. Just as the 'rhetoric of ruins'
can connote either optimism or pessimism—that is, monuments mournfully half-decayed or gloriously half-remaining—linguistic fragmentation,
unfinished sentences, and silences built into a narrative can express either
the tragic emptiness of language or the comic fullness of silence. A negative silence can emphasize the contamination of convention and the artificiality of language: characters who exemplify this type of silence (such
as Harley of *The Man of Feeling* or Werther of Part II of *Die Leiden des
jungen Werthers*) withdraw from speech reluctantly or rebelliously. A positive silence, on the other hand, (as we witness in Yorick of *A Sentimental
Journey* or the Werther of Part I), emphasizes the communication beyond
words, the silent flourishes of imagination and sympathy which linear
speech (although it facilitates them) cannot contain. Negative silence tends
towards isolation while positive tends towards society. As we saw in the
preceding chapter, although *Journey* emphasizes the comic and social and
Werther the tragic and isolated, the novel of sensibility, like its architectural counterpart the folly, depends upon the conjunction of the meanings—upon the multivalence of silence, fragmentation, and ruination.

Many interpretations of Austen have ignored her indications of the multivalence of language or her distrust in the powers of self-representation;
therefore, they have tended to oversimplify her position. Such critics as
Elaine Bander, Sandra Gilbert and Susan Gubar, Claudia Johnson, Mary

Poovey, Gene Ruoff, Clara Tuite, and especially D. W. Harding and Marvin Mudrick, have all emphasized Austen's portrayal of the crumbling decay of the old order—whether in social, political, architectural, or linguistic terms. On the other hand, critics such as Marilyn Butler, Alistair Duckworth, A. Walton Litz, and Jane Nardin have tended to emphasize Austen's comic and traditional perspective.[79] Because there were Jacobin and anti-Jacobin reasons for silence, critics are similarly divided along political readings. She has been portrayed as arch conservative (Butler and Duckworth), liberal feminist (Johnson and Gilbert/Gubar), or counter-revolutionary *conspiratrice* (Ruoff). Even in terms of her relations to landscape, there have been those authors who have allied her closely with public monument and traditional authority, and those who ally her with the most innovative fragmentation and Reptonian "improvement."

Just as Elinor's "exertions" to speak are portrayed as physical heroism, Marianne's final exertions toward public speech, and away from her shrieks of misery, are similarly praiseworthy. Marianne's movement from sickness to health is marked by a movement from "private inarticulateness" to "public speech,"[80] as Marianne's statements near the end of the novel reveal: "'There, exactly there'—pointing with one hand, 'on that projecting mound,—there I fell; and there I first saw Willoughby . . . I *can* talk of it now, I hope, as I ought to do.'"[81] "Not without effort,"[82] Marianne has resolved to speak, confide in Elinor, and give up her narcissistic projections by allowing them to be tempered, "rectified," to return to Condillac, by the process of converting them into rational statements. [83]

The double meaning of the final "as" in the above passage is telling: it suggests that simple dualisms might no longer govern Marianne—that no longer does she see the world in terms of cold-hearted reserve *versus* passionate, ungoverned expression, or cold-hearted, empty speech *versus* passionate, ungoverned silence. Not only does Marianne learn to speak, but she learns to speak *as* she ought to: the prepositional phrase takes circumstance, community, context into account. One cannot speak as one ought without observing what—and who—is around one. This is not necessarily a movement to the generalization so feared by sensibility, but rather a movement towards attention to immediate context—an alteration in Marianne's frame of reference. Speaking 'as one ought' requires great sensibility and is itself an act of love. She learns that words, like conventions, "need not be limitations: they are a resource, not a restraint, for the human spirit."[84] Marianne acknowledges both her responsibility and *authorship* of her own ruination, whereas earlier she masks or denies her own agency. Austen, through Marianne, reclaims post-Babelian speech for the expression of sensibility and for self-representation, despite its conventionality, weaknesses, and inescapable artificiality.

One might argue that while Marianne's transformation constitutes a gain in terms of civic and individual responsibility, it is also a loss in terms of sensibility and feeling. For many readers, there is a lingering feeling that something has been lost in the taming of Marianne—a loss that perhaps hampers the reader's full enjoyment of Elinor's final triumph. Does Austen sacrifice the intimacy of experience for the sake of generality, or for the didacticism associated with detachment and narration?[85] Is there not something within the novel that trains the reader to depend upon Marianne's "wildness" and "violence" even for our enjoyment of Elinor?

Angela Leighton's approach to the problem of sympathy in the novel will help us further understand Marianne's structural role, the role of the picturesque in the novel, and the narrative burdens placed upon Elinor:

> Although both heroines retreat into Silence at various points, it is the Silence of Marianne which remains problematic, because it is not incorporated into the narrative, like Elinor's. Elinor's Silences have Austen's approval; they signify heroic reticence and control, and are contained by the language of Sense. Marianne's Silences signify emotions which have escaped control, and which are therefore in opposition to Austen's art.[86]

There is some truth to Leighton's observations regarding the dynamics of sympathy and narratorial authority in the novel, but I would differ with her conclusions. It is precisely because they are presented within the careful *control* of Austen's art, and Elinor's "censorship," that Marianne's silences *can* "signify emotions which have escaped control." It is Elinor's explicit authority and authorship that allow Marianne to deny her own authorship of her situation. Narrative and anti-narrative forces are thus divided between the sisters to the detriment of both: one sacrificing likeability and sympathy, the other responsibility and health. Austen's structure might remind us of the 'rhetoric of ruins' and is another version of the late eighteenth-century's delicately balanced dual impulses which I have been describing. There is indeed important "opposition" within Austen's art, but rather than constituting a flaw, it helps to further her redemption of sensibility. In fact, one could say that Elinor acts as a frame for Marianne, much in the way that the double roles of the narrators worked to achieve the liberation of the man of feeling in the preceding chapters.

Time after time, we experience Marianne's (rigorously) ungoverned passion: "Marianne continued incessantly to give way in a low voice to the misery of her feelings, by exclamations of wretchedness"; she is attracted to "something more of wildness"; we experience the repeated "violence of her affliction," her "violent oppression of spirits," and so forth. [87] This "violence" or "wildness" seems to equate Marianne, like Goethe's Werther, with the Burkean sublime, by the anti-social, unruly nature of her passion. One of the ways Austen emphasizes this is through Marianne's association with "fire." Not only does Marianne associate fire with genius in her judgment of others ("His eyes want all that spirit, that fire, which at once announce virtue and intelligence"), but she is also fascinated with the actual burning flames of the fireplace. Unlike "cold, cold

Elinor," as Marianne calls her, the younger sister languishes "by the fire in melancholy meditation," spends "every night" gazing into "the brightness of the fire," and sits "by the drawing-room fire . . . , without once stirring from her seat or altering her attitude, lost in her own thoughts and insensible to her sister's presence."[88]

The fireplace is Marianne's counterpart to Werther's and Ossian's cliffs; however, Austen makes Marianne's folly clear as well. Austen's partial parody of Marianne becomes clear particularly in the latter passage, where Marianne is transfixed by the fire: her fascination with the fire does not lead her to sublime action or to awe; instead, Marianne grows increasingly apathetic and simply retreats from life. It is ironic that Marianne's absorption with the burning flames, which symbolize her passionate nature (or at least her absorption with her own passions), leads her instead to apathy and insensibility. Accordingly, the flames grow weaker and are no longer able to sustain her as the novel (and her illness) progresses: She leans "in silent misery, over the small remains of a fire," and later spends "a day . . . in sitting shivering over the fire with a book in her hand which she was unable to read."[89]

Meanwhile, we learn that Elinor loves to paint screens—*fire*place screens, appropriately enough—which allow for the fire to be enjoyed more indirectly.[90] Elinor paints screens both metaphorically and physically: the verb "screen" also appears twice in her interactions with Marianne. Elinor attempts "to screen Marianne from particularity" and again later as she "trie[s] to screen [Marianne] from the observation of others, while reviving her with lavendar [sic] water."[91] Marianne's excesses place narrative burdens on Elinor, who converts her unsought authorship into artistry. Elinor, who has been forced to have restraint enough for two, spends most of her energy arranging Marianne's representation to others, as well as her own, striving to retain—or achieve—surface order. The same dynamic is repeated elsewhere in the novel as well, without specific reference to the word "screen": "At breakfast [Marianne] neither ate nor attempted to eat anything; and Elinor's attention was then all employed, not in urging her, not in pitying her, nor in appearing to regard her, but in endeavouring to engage Mrs. Jennings's notice entirely to herself."[92] Ironically, the appearance of Elinor's pair of firescreens gives Marianne the opportunity for a display of just the unmasked emotion that Elinor feels the need to screen.

Elinor is, in effect, the *editor,* the *Herausgeber* of the public version of Marianne's and her own story. Unlike Yorick and Werther, however, Elinor does not write.[93] The pen is not in her hands, but the paintbrush is, and she covers over as many as she can of her sister's flaws. Just as in the moral aesthetic of sensibility, Elinor purposely obscures her own authority, and is more lovable for doing so, because she does not obscure it in order to avoid responsibility: she desires order, but allows it to be, perhaps not quite as invisible as sensibility requires, but aesthetically pleasing nonetheless. This would place Elinor in a similar position to Werther and Yorick. She is not a narrator-protagonist *per se,* but she does have to reconcile narration and experience. The narrative impulse to paint the firescreens is not dissimilar to the task of disguising the marks of the scissors in landscape gardening—an attempt to balance nature and artifice.[94]

In this sense, the picturesque is actually triumphant as a narrative structure in this novel, as in the other novels we have examined. Just as the *Herausgeber* allows Werther to focus on and indulge in his solipsistic vision of the world, Elinor's framing and screening ironically allow Marianne to indulge in her "violent" excesses and selfish sensibility. Just as every 'man of feeling' is protected by either a woman of sense or a Sancho Panza figure, Elinor protects and supports Marianne, who is (by her own inclination) helpless against her own inclinations.[95] Structurally, Elinor provides the safe distance from Marianne's sublime extremes that allows, in Burke's terms, the opportunity for "delight."[96]

However, the picturesque raises problems of sympathy that arise elsewhere in the text. Near the end of the novel, Elinor's forgiving, sympathetic reaction to Willoughby, "whom, only half an hour ago she had abhorred,"[97] affirms the Burkean (and Smithian) principle that delight and sympathy come from the safe distance from peril.[98] In a similar way, Elinor's framing, screening, controlling presence heightens sympathy for Marianne, perhaps at Elinor's own expense. When Marianne grows ill, then subdued, and later chastened, the reader, like Elinor, forgives her for her past offenses and she becomes dearer, almost, than she should. In other words, if Elinor's steadiness allows Marianne's wildness, does it also to some extent sacrifice Elinor's attractiveness as a character? According to Benedict, the problem with Austen's "sympathetic portrayal of Marianne and the unflagging praise for her opposite, the "sensible" sister Elinor" is that this conflict "shakes the reader's faith in Austen's narrative control" and "weaken[s] the authority of the narrative voice."[99] I would argue instead that the burdens of narration, authorship, and framing make Elinor's role seem more "masculine," authoritarian, and therefore more suspect, according to the hallmarks of the culture of sensibility. It is this difficulty of representing oneself—of being simultaneously a participant and an observer in a situation that so puzzles eighteenth-century authors and readers.

To counteract this impression, Austen gives the reader many 'feminizing' clues that Elinor cannot speak freely either. At moments of intense feeling, she, like the heroes and heroines of sensibility, grows speechless. When Edward arrives at Barton Cottage at the end of the novel, Elinor "saw her mother and Marianne change colour; saw them look at herself, and whisper a few sentences to each other. She would have given the world to be able to speak—. . . but she had no utterance."[100] Like a true 'woman of feeling,' Elinor loses her ability to speak when she feels most deeply.[101] Generally, however, Elinor either will not or cannot indulge her spontaneous emotions, and thus differs from Yorick and Werther, and instead approximates

Harley's isolation from his unsympathetic surroundings. Unlike Yorick, however, her silences are generally not exuberant and seldom erotic.

Whereas Elinor generally uses "balanced, periodical phrases that resemble those of the essayists Austen admired: Addison and Steele, and Samuel Johnson,"[102] the depth of Elinor's emotions is revealed through a proliferation of dashes and the suddenly more fragmented syntax of the narrative voice when it represents her point of view at especially poignant moments.[103] At such moments, the narrator's syntax alters—associating the anti-narrative with Elinor's unexpressed interior world: "The comfort of such a friend at that moment as Colonel Brandon—of such a companion for her mother,—how gratefully was it felt!—a companion whose judgment would guide, whose attentions must relieve, and whose friendship might soothe her!—as far as the shock of such a summons *could* be lessened to her, his presence, his manners, his assistance, would lessen it."[104] Such dramatic and syntactically fragmented passages are "preceded and followed by passages of 'normal' prose"; they also represent "the power of feelings almost beyond her control."[105] They are *framed*, picturesquely, between passages in her almost pedantically composed Augustan prose. By the end, Elinor, absolved of her narrative burdens on behalf of Marianne, indulges in fancy, becomes speechless, and "almost runs out of the room, and as soon as the door [is] closed, burst[s] into tears of joy."[106] She finally expresses the feelings which she cannot narrate. In other words, Austen creates a second frame of editorship in *Sense and Sensibility*. Whereas the first frame (Elinor's editing of Marianne) allows Marianne to indulge in her grief unencumbered by narrative burdens of self-representation, the second frame (the narrator's representation of Elinor) eventually allows Elinor to separate herself from detachment without abdicating responsibility for her own self-representation. By the end, both sisters learn to carry authority and to recognize the responsibilities inherent in the authorship of their own public images.

Critics like Leighton who do not recognize the picturesque, ironic element to the structure of the novel, also do not recognize the layers of representation within the novel (characters representing themselves, characters representing each other, and the narrator's representation of the characters, as well as the author's representation of the narrative voice. Leighton, for example, tries to divorce Marianne's story from Elinor's—in order to gain access to the 'authentic' Marianne, uncensored by either Elinor or the narrator. As a result, she presents a vastly oversimplified view of Elinor. As in *Werther,* the hero's own version of the story cannot be separated from the frame through which his story is presented. To make this mistake is to follow in the footsteps of both Marianne and Mrs. Dashwood, neither of whom, despite their protestations, understands the picturesque. The problem of sympathy for Elinor can be understood in terms of a problem of framing or the picturesque, since both mistake "Elinor's *representation* of herself" for Elinor's actual internal state. [107] Mrs. Dashwood, we learn, "had been misled by the careful, the considerate attention of [Elinor], to think [Elinor's] attachment, . . . much slighter in reality than she had been wont to believe . . . under this persuasion she had been . . . almost unkind to Elinor."[108]

Mrs. Dashwood, like Marianne, shows herself to be incapable of irony, and therefore incapable of one of the essential arts of living and speaking in Jane Austen's world: the ability to speak on two levels simultaneously or to distinguish private meaning within public utterance. Marianne, Mrs. Dashwood, and the reader who explicitly trusts Elinor's words may not recognize that Elinor knows no private discourse: her sister's behavior forces her into public discourse even in her own home. By the end of the novel, Austen has reclaimed female narration from its own tendency towards self-victimization or extinction: by the end of the novel, both heroines recognize and acknowledge their own authorship and their individual and civic responsibilities. In addition, by depicting Elinor's dual impulses, Austen not only rehabilitates the concept of civility, but she also succeeds in challenging sensibility's false dichotomy between the woman of words and the woman of feeling. Austen does not deny the central connection between words and artifice, but she does challenge the assumption that artifice must come at the expense of virtue, intimacy, and beauty. Austen redeems a degree of artifice both in terms of landscape and human relations: the picturesque landscape at Pemberley in *Pride and Prejudice* does not suffer from the artificial damming of its rivers, nor does individual authenticity necessarily suffer from the artifice and 'rectification' entailed by a degree of civility.[109]

ACTING AND THE PROBLEM OF THE INTERESTING

In *Sense and Sensibility,* Austen acknowledges the limitations of self-representation and the necessarily theatrical nature of communication, giving preference to the testimony of the eyes over the testimony of words. The testimony of the eyes is, however, highly subject to interpretation and error, particularly when all are not equally free to give visual expressiveness to their feelings, and some have no scruples regarding feigning them. Paul Hazard has shown that "les mouvements de l'âme" were not metaphorical in "an age committed to the belief that every phenomenon was the effect of a physical cause . . . the passions were said to move as the fibers of our body moved."[110] As I have sought to show above, the urge to find physical sources for thought and emotion also relate to the fall of disengaged reason and the ethical significance of rational detachment from its earlier prominence. One of the results of these changes was added credence in the popular science of physiognomy, particularly within the culture of sensibility.

In 1746, Aaron Hill wrote a work in honor of the visual expressiveness of Richardson's novel *Pamela,* and in it he claimed as the basis of his study that "Every Passion marks the Face" and ultimately gives "the right expressive GESTURE to the Body." Ironically, at least to twenty-first-century audiences, his study was entitled *The Art of Acting*.[111] Such irony, however, was not generally perceived within the culture of sensibility, for acting, or indeed the ability to read literature aloud "with feeling" (an ability that figures prominently in the novels of Jane Austen), was commonly viewed as evidence of a soul's sensibility or ability to sympathize with the plights of others who suffer, albeit fictitiously.

One of the most curious examples of sensibility's dual vision is apparent in the odd position of acting in the moral aesthetic of the time.[112] Practicing gesture or expression is a form of exercise, building malleability and sensibility, rather than the capacity to deceive. The subtitles of Hill's book make it clear that he sees acting skills as capable of aiding daily conversation as well. This points to the sad but pervasive eighteenth-century fear that, because of the fallen state of natural language, training may be required to convey emotions that one already feels. Another problem that Hill suggests is the difficulty of distinguishing between authentic feeling and simulated feeling. For Austen's heroines, this is tantamount to the distinction between heroes and villains, between a fulfilling marriage or a disastrous union.

In addition to providing training for sensitive actors and actresses and to providing insight into the natural language of feeling, theater also provides opportunities for audiences to practice their own abilities to be sympathetic spectators. Within Laurence Sterne's fictional world, this activity is, as we have seen, called "translation" of visual gesture into emotion, or looks into words. Recalling Rousseau's conception of convention and artifice, Sterne's Yorick proclaims himself as translator of the world around him, rendering "looks and limbs" into "plain words."[113] Like Rousseau, he suggests that in a pure, natural state unsullied by convention, human beings would be transparent to one another, enjoying immediate and mutual comprehension ("la facilité de se pénétrer réciproquement")[114]; however, in sensibility's dual vision of post-Babelian society, translation has become a skill as well as a necessary burden. Nature and society now speak in different tongues, and only the "man of feeling," the "sentimental traveller," or, ironically, *the actor* can speak the language of nature—the "language of real feeling."

In other words, the significance of acting, in conjunction with the moral and aesthetic importance of one's reaction to spectacles of suffering, suggests that the image or sight of sympathy comes dangerously close to usurping the importance of the feeling of sympathy—in danger of becoming a substitute for the emotion itself. Within the novels of sensibility this can be seen in what Janet Todd has dubbed "philanthropic postures."[115] A character in Mary Wollstonecraft's novel *Mary, a Fiction,* for example, exclaims to Mary that "I would give the world for your picture, with the expression I have seen in your face, when you have been supporting your friend."[116] An aestheticized tableau depicting virtuous sympathy deserves immortalization—and complete divorce from the ugly facts that originally spurred the feeling. In fact the "picture" may ultimately be more important to the speaker than Mary is herself.

One actual "picture" or portrait of sensibility will serve to illustrate this point further. George Romney, close friend of Laurence Sterne and illustrator of Sterne's writings, painted a portrait entitled *Sensibility,* which summarizes this new ideal (engraved by Caroline Watson in 1786; Figure 33). He portrays a young woman staring with kind and sympathetic eyes at a sight beyond the canvas. At her side is a delicate mimosa plant, in fuller view in the original Romney painting. She is absorbed and sympathetic; she is moist-lipped, tender, young, and seemingly uncorrupted by society. Her mouth is open, but in a singularly unverbal manner: she looks as though, if she emitted sounds, they would be sighs rather than words. The *illuminatio* effect, together with her bonnet, which resembles a halo, heightens the atmosphere of purity.

The presence of the mimosa plant as a cultural symbol also reinforces the notion of a physical basis of virtue. The mimosa was also called the "sensitive plant," because its leaves would recoil and seem to shrivel at the slightest touch. Erasmus Darwin anthropomorphizes the plant, conveying the ideals of the culture of sensibility—innocent weakness combined and the ability to perceive what other, coarser souls ignore:

> Weak with nice sense, the chaste Mimosa stands,
> From each rude touch withdraws her timid hands;
> Oft as light clouds o'erpass the Summer-glade,
> Alarm'd she trembles at the moving shade;
> And feels, alive through all her tender form,
> The whisper'd murmurs of the gathering storm.[117]

A character from Henry Brooke's *Fool of Quality* (1766–70) also uses the mimosa to argue the physical basis of conscience: "His blushing here demonstrates his sensibility; his sensibility demonstrates some principle within him, that disapproved and reproached him for what he had committed . . . It is therefore from the fountain of virtue alone that this flush of shamefacedness can possibly flow; and a delicacy of compunction, on such occasions, is as a sensitive plant of divinity on the soul, that feeling shrinks, and is alarmed on the slightest apprehension of approaching evil."[118] Thus the mimosa personifies sympathy as well as the feminization of weakness.

Interestingly, Watson's engraving reveals several of the weaknesses emphasized by sensibility's subsequent parodies: most importantly, the focus of the portrait is the sympathetic observer, a focus which places the spectacle in a clearly secondary position, important only for the emotions it rouses in the "sensible" viewer. This emphasis becomes ethically questionable since the spectacles of sensibility are generally people in distress. Yet what she sees, the source of her distress, the person relaying

Sensibility.

Engraved by Caroline Watson (engraver to Her Majesty) from the original Picture

Published April 14th 1809 by Thomas Payne, Pall Mall

Figure 33

or suffering distress, and the nature and content of the distress are all unknown to the viewer, and presumably have little bearing on her status as Sensibility personified. Her response alone serves to distinguish her, regardless of the stimulus. In addition, the woman of sensibility looks as though in the next frame she were more likely to fall backwards on a couch in a swoon, than to rush forward to aid someone in distress: it becomes evident that the ideal heroine in the cult of sensibility is ultimately as incapable of action and foresight as she is of syntactically complete expression. Finally, there appears an incongruity between the cause of the emotion and its degree of dramatic expression, which eventually leads to accusations of inauthenticity. In this sense the culture of sensibility authorizes personal ruin alongside architectural decay, for the sake of its aesthetic ideal. Whatever is actually suffering or moving in the picture is secondary in importance to the viewer and she who feels sympathy and evinces sensibility. Sensibility has become a means of display, rather than feeling, and is entirely involved with the image of the person who would like to be considered "feeling."

Most importantly for the point here, Romney made no secret of the fact that *Sensibility* was also one of his series of portraits of Emma Hart, the later Lady Hamilton, who was admired not only for her beauty, but also her ability to *act*. Romney's biographer William Hayley describes why Romney liked to paint her: "Her features, like the language of Shakespeare, could exhibit all the feelings of nature, and all the graduations of every passion, with a most fascinating truth, and a felicity of expression."[119] As a result of "her eloquent features," Emma Hart Hamilton inspired a full-length Circe, a Calypso, a Magdalen, a Wood Nymph, a Bacchante, the Pythian Priestess on her tripod, and a Saint Cecilia in addition to the portrait of Sensibility. Later in her life, she became famous as a sort of walking *tableau,* for posing in her "attitudes" in the court of Naples: these were a series of "poses plastiques," where, just as in her portraits with Romney, she would represent a series of classical and other figures.[120]

As we see, one of the incipient dangers within the culture of sensibility (that ultimately leads to its degeneration into cultish extremes) is that the images of emotion begin to be equated with or even preferred to the sentiments themselves. This is consistent with Diderot's call for *tableaux* in the new genre of bourgeois drama (*genre sérieux*): according to Diderot, well chosen frozen attitudes may have the greatest effect upon spectators of the spectacle (similar to what had already been demonstrated in "absorptive painting," the realist mode connected with Greuze and Chardin at mid century). As Thomas Sheridan, master rhetorician, writes: "Let any one who has seen Mr. Garrick perform, consider how much he was indebted to the language of his eyes, and there will be no occasion to say more, to give him an idea of the extent and power of expression to which that language may be brought."[121] The stage actor Garrick is a model for the natural language of feeling to imitate, as the pose of Emma Hart is a model of sensibility's virtuous sympathy for the suffering.

Like an English garden with a variety of interesting monuments that are each designed to invoke distinct emotions as one travels from sight to sight, such visual tableaux are also opportunities for adherents of the culture of sensibility to demonstrate their spectatorly prowess. The pedagogy of seeing and feeling emphasized both in landscape gardening and the novel of sensibility thus responds to the new need to *cultivate* feelings rather than suppress them. These examples suggest that the culture of sensibility values the ability to communicate emotion, regardless of whether this emotion is authentically felt. The most important factor is whether the spectator viewing this "picture of sympathy" feels emotionally aroused. In this way, the two movements develop a parallel emphasis on distress and ruination—sensibility focusing on human suffering and distress while the picturesque emphasizes crumbling ruins in architecture and landscape. The emphasis throughout the culture of sensibility is on spurring the imagination as well as on training the emotions to respond to various scenes, whether human, botanical, or architectural. They also both involve on-lookers traveling from sight to sight, seeking the views and situations that fit particular aesthetic criteria and that evoke the appropriate emotions. As we have seen, eventually both movements share the dubious distinction of pursuing such ruination *voluntarily,* for the sake of entertainment and self-image. The result is, for a decade or two, a seemingly hypocritical national pastime of seeking grief and ruination to prove onlookers' own sensibility and virtue.

Just as the visitor to Hirschfeld's gardens at Hohenheim, Monville's Désert de Retz, or the Kew Gardens are aware of what type of participation, admiration, and affect is required, the 'reader of feeling' also encounters an approach to the picturesque that measures potential for feeling according to visual displays. Austen echoes the pressure on implied readers in "Frederic and Elfrida," when the narrator proclaims, in reference to a ridiculous little epitaph: "These sweet lines, as pathetic as beautifull [sic] were never read by any one who passed that way, without a shower of tears, which if they should fail to excite in you, Reader, your mind must be unworthy to peruse them."[122] The reader of the novel of sensibility must fill in the narrative gaps with sympathy or even tears and feel ennobled by the role.

As we have seen, both the culture of sensibility and the picturesque favor the inclement, the ruined, the irregular, the decaying, and the suffering for the sake of their aesthetic criteria. Thomas Rowlandson parodies this trait in his illustration of an artist working hard to locate the picturesque in all sorts of inclement weather (Figure 34). The artifice of this artist, supposedly pursuing natural vistas, is highlighted by the sheer volume of equipment that he carries. He nonetheless has a hand to carry an umbrella and shield himself from the rain, showing that he cares about his own comfort almost as much as he is fanatical about the "picturesque." He is bent over and haggard, completely uninterested in what surrounds him— both natural vistas and the "interesting" plight of a young mother with her three children. The young family (who have no umbrella amongst them) look inquisitively at the man. In short, the artist is portrayed as allowing a fanaticism with the picturesque to blind him to both nature and humanity. And while he thinks of himself as braving weather for aesthetic pursuits, he

Figure 34

does not consider that others may have to endure it less willingly, making his distress a "luxury" indeed.

In Marianne's initial terms, "twisted trees" are better than straight, and suffering from "violent fever" is better than having to wear a waist-coat against catching a cold. Monuments are more picturesque when they are decayed, and people are more "interesting" (and allow greater oppor-tunities for exhibiting sensibility) when they are suffering. When com-bined with the strict aesthetic codes associated with sensibility and the picturesque, this preference for ruination at times amounts to a mode of entertainment. As it happens, the English garden transitions from a locus for reflection, to an opportunity to express sympathy, to a stage for the performance of sensibility, and finally to pleasure grounds for entertain-ment and novelty. In this sense, the English garden is a forerunner of the modern amusement park, as Figure 35 and 36 show. Figure 35 shows plans for a variety of "rides" where one can display oneself to advantage, and Figure 36 depicts a forerunner of the modern roller coaster. The tran-sition from sentiment to amusement also raises some disturbing issues. When applied to the dynamic of sympathy, only those who are "interest-ing" (or entertaining) deserve attention, just as the characters in Austen's

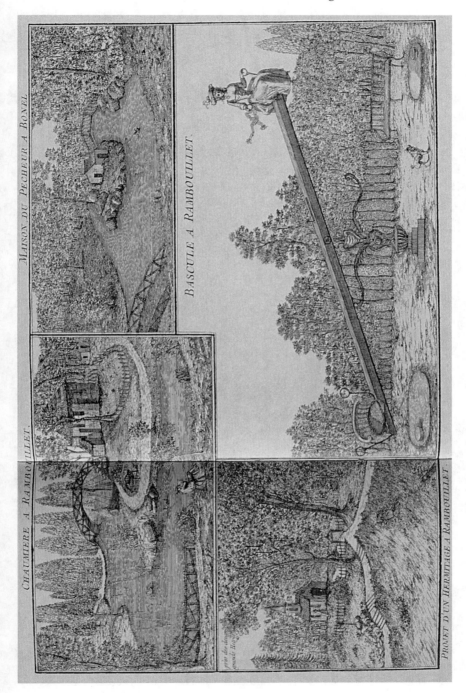

Figure 35

Figure 36

juvenilia have to *earn* the interest of others by conforming to specific picturesque criteria.

Sensibility's ethical problem is reflected in the changing meaning of the adjective "interesting." As Patricia Meyer Spacks has also shown, the older meaning "of importance" waned by the beginning of the nineteenth century, and a newer meaning was introduced in the mid-eighteenth century: "adapted to excite interest, having the qualities which rouse curiosity . . . or appeal to the emotions." The older meaning refers to piquing the intellect according to an externalized standard; the newer meaning to stimulate subjective emotions. For our purposes, it is significant that the *Oxford English Dictionary* lists the earliest occurrence of this newer affective meaning in Sterne's *A Sentimental Journey* (1768); the history of this word is thus imbedded in the history of the novel of sensibility. Within the context of sensibility, the word "interesting" narrows substantially in its meaning, attributing strong importance given to distress, ruination, and rusticity, and gradually becoming a code word for identifying whether or not a scene or an individual conforms to the aesthetic requirements of the picturesque or sensibility. In addition, the word bears feminine connotations, because of the association with the usage "to be in an interesting condition," a phrase which was also coined in the mid-eighteenth century meaning "to be pregnant."[123] In other words, if only the "interesting" can interest spectators, sensibility has lost its original, egalitarian aspirations. The Bridgets of the world have little sympathy to hope for, unless they find themselves elevated by rank, beauty, or suffering (or pregnancy) to provide a suitably "interesting" and evocative tableau. "Interesting" women are also by definition vulnerable—since positions of power are, at least for women, *un*interesting according to this aesthetic code. This is part of the meaning implicit in Thomas Rowlandson's satire on the "man of feeling" above (Figure 32): the parson, no doubt invoking Yorick's benevolent fellow-feeling in his *Sentimental Journey,* takes advantage of the isolated woman to indulge in his objectivizing sensuality.

In *Sense and Sensibility,* Austen parodies the cult of the "interesting" through Marianne and Willoughby, both of whom find the other in "interesting" situations, invoking novelistic clichés. Marianne, the narrator informs us early on, is "sensible and clever; but eager in everything; her sorrows, her joys, could have no moderation. She was generous, amiable, *interesting:* she was everything but prudent."[124] At their initial meeting, Marianne, out walking in the woods, sprains her ankle and is rescued by an "uncommonly handsome" "gentleman carrying a gun, with two pointers playing round him" who "r[uns] to her assistance" in the midst of "animating gales of an high south-westerly wind" and "a driving rain"; he literally sweeps her off her feet, rescues her, and carries her to her home.[125] Mrs. Dashwood, Marianne's twin in sensibility, finds Willoughby's entrance equally "interesting": Willoughby "apologized for his intrusion by relating its cause, in a manner so frank and so graceful, that his person, which was uncommonly handsome, received additional charms from his voice and expression. Had he been even old, ugly, and vulgar, the gratitude and kindness of Mrs. Dashwood would have been secured by any act of attention to her child; but the influence of youth, beauty, and elegance, gave an *interest* to the action which came home to her feelings."[126]

Again, interest is earned, not merely through a virtuous act, but particularly through "youth, beauty, and elegance." In contrast to such superficially evocative situations, Marianne stubbornly refuses to interest herself in the man who, of all the characters, has experienced the most romantic past: Colonel Brandon had a youthful love affair, was forbidden from marrying the girl he loved, witnessed the decline and death of his beloved, took her child as a secret ward, and finally fought a duel with the man who seduced and betrayed her. Despite all these off-stage heroics and a life of bravely endured suffering, Colonel Brandon does not earn Marianne's *interest* because he wears a waistcoat and is in his mid-thirties. Austen exposes the degree of selection that is involved in responding to others and their distress—or the moral responsibility involved in determining who is "interesting" and who deserves sympathy or love.

Part of what makes Willoughby so "interesting" to Marianne is the way in which he flatters her, conforming himself and his opinions to her aesthetic code. In this way he resembles another chameleon, Henry Crawford of Austen's later *Mansfield Park*. Willoughby also shows an ability to make words serve his own interests. Willoughby is an excellent actor; he adopts the language of those he would like to please—that is, those who can please *him*. Even in his first conversation with Marianne, he shows he can play the role she assigns him; he can appear to be what she wants to behold: "Their taste was strikingly alike"; "if any difference appeared, any objection arose, it lasted no longer than till the force of her arguments and the brightness of her eyes could be displayed. He acquiesced in all her decisions, caught all her enthusiasm."[127] Willoughby copies Marianne's vocabulary just as, at the end of the novel, he copies his wife's letter and sends it to Marianne. By the end, he demonstrates that he has mastered so many people's idiolects that he hardly knows how to express his own emotions:

> When the first of [Marianne's notes] reached me . . . , what I felt is, in the common phrase, not to be expressed; in a more simple one—perhaps too simple to raise any emotion—my feelings were very, very painful.

Every line, every word was—in the hackneyed metaphor which their dear writer, were she here, would forbid—a dagger to my heart. To know that Marianne was in town was—in the same language—a thunderbolt. Thunderbolts and daggers! What a reproof would she have given me! Her taste, her opinions—I believe they are better known to me than my own, and I am sure they are dearer.[128]

Before finishing each sentence, he deliberates about which effect he would like to achieve upon his audience, and he shows the shortcomings of each language he speaks. But Willoughby (bending like a 'willow' in winds of social pressures and temptations) has never learned to speak his native tongue—that is, he has spent so much time flattering and conforming himself to others' opinions that he neither knows nor cares to develop his own.

Marianne's fault is that she does not acknowledge her own authorship—not only of her own grief and distressed tableaux, but also her authorship of Willoughby, who gladly conforms (at least superficially) to her fiction in dialogue, if not to the narrative trajectory she imagines. From their first encounter, the narrator uses an analogy to novels to underscore Marianne's authorial tendencies: "His person and air were equal to what her fancy had ever drawn for the *hero of a favourite story;* and in his carrying her into the house with so little previous formality, there was a rapidity of thought which particularly recommended the action to her. *Every circumstance belonging to him was interesting.* His name was good, his residence was in their favourite village, and she soon found out that of all manly dresses a shooting-jacket was the most becoming. Her imagination was busy, her reflections were pleasant, and the pain of a sprained ankle was disregarded."[129] In this way, the novel serves Austen's didactic reclamation of authority and individual responsibility from the extremes of the cult of sensibility. Here again, Marianne bears resemblance to Werther, who reads himself into the motivations of the lovesick farm boy, particularly when he goes mad. Werther and Marianne both *author* fiction rather than *translate* the world around them; yet because they do not admit their agency, they refuse to bear responsibility for their narcissistic interpretations. Although technically not a narrator-protagonist like Yorick, Harley, or Werther, Marianne nonetheless writes her own story and masks her authorship—even from herself.

The strict aesthetic code and jargon of the picturesque and of sensibility thus form a subset of a larger moral concern for Austen, relating to "occupational hazards" of novel-reading itself. Many of the same human traits that attracted people to the cult of sensibility and cult of the picturesque in mid-to-late-eighteenth-century Europe and Britain are also what attract readers to novels in general.[130] These traits include a curiosity about others' lives, a love of novelty, the exhilaration of romance, and the excitement and glamour of danger and suffering (especially when vicarious). James Gillray's *Tales of Wonder* (Figure 37) parodies the reception of the first edition of M. G. Lewis' controversial Gothic novel *The Monk* (1796): the readers experience rapt terror as they read the book aloud; the picture shows a girl carried off to rape and slaughter; even the ornaments on the mantle are horrified. The illustration suggests that an occupational hazard of reading novels (whether they are Gothic, sentimental or otherwise) is the temptation to read life as a novel and thereby blind oneself to one's actual surroundings. Gillray portrays the slightly masochistic psychology through the closed curtains and the fact that the ladies are reading in the dark by candlelight, purposely enhancing their suspense and titillating fear through voluntary isolation and darkness.

Accordingly, most, if not all, of Austen's major novels include at least one warning about the danger of imagining or creating the "interesting" scene and human ruination for our own pleasure or momentary thrill—another literary corollary to pursuing ruination or danger. Instead of heightening perception, such imagining or authoring of dramatic scenes actually deadens perception. Austen warns readers to distinguish themselves from Marianne and her mother, who "must always be carried away by her imagination on any interesting subject," while simultaneously relying on such tendencies for generating readers' "interest" in her own novels.[131] Austen returns again and again to this theme and poses it as a danger both to oneself and to others.

Figure 37

We need only recollect Henry's stern lecture to Catherine in *Northanger Abbey,* after she has indulged in transforming Northanger Abbey in her imagination into an Italianate melodrama with a bloody history that might even satisfy the author of *The Monk:* "Consult your own understanding, your own sense of the probable, your own observation of what is passing around you."[132] Meanwhile, Catherine loses her ability to assess "what is around her"—*including* the real dangers, folly, and vice that are present in Northanger Abbey and her world in general. Leaving aside for the moment how dangerous her own world actually is, in succumbing to the temptation to glamorize, Catherine temporarily loses her ability to be an independent spectator and moral agent. Until Catherine recognizes her own authorship of the laundry-list she finds in the guest bedroom at Northanger, she cannot understand the world around her, and she will remain incapable of seeing her friends for who they really are.

There is generally one character in each of Austen's novels who is dead to *real* intrigue because she prefers to create her own; she wishes to be an author of her *own* novel according to the fashions of the day. Other characters in her novels also reveal the dangers of masked authorship: Emma Woodhouse exhibits such traits in her stubborn insistence on seeing romantic potential in Harriet Smith rather than Jane Fairfax, much as Marianne chooses to prefer her scripted intrigue with Willoughby over the actual potential for romantic interest in Colonel Brandon. This kind of authorship is not limited to women: Wentworth, too, in *Persuasion,* must acknowledge his own authorship of the past before he can reunite with Anne Elliot; symbolically, he drops "his pen" at the moment of this recognition.

> "We shall never agree upon this question," Captain Harville was beginning to say, when a slight noise called their attention to Captain Wentworth's hitherto perfectly quiet division of the room. It was nothing more than that his pen had fallen down; but Anne was startled at finding him nearer than she had supposed, and half inclined to suspect that the pen had only fallen because he had been occupied by them, striving to catch sounds, which yet she did not think he could have caught.[133]

When he lifts his pen again, it is in full recognition of his earlier self-victimization and denial of responsibility. What follows, and is reflected in the style of the letter he composes, is a co-authorship of the letter (and by extension, their futures) with Anne. The content of the letter responds to her commentary at the windowsill, as though in dialogue with Anne. The Roger Michell film adaptation of *Persuasion* (1995) portrays this narrative technique quite effectively using non-diegetic voice-overs of *both* Anne and Wentworth reading the letter—first Wentworth's voice alone, then alternating lines with Anne in briefer and briefer intervals, until they both read in unison by the end of the letter, symbolically culminating the letter in co-authorship.[134]

Beginning and ending as it does with Sir Walter and his volume on the Baronetage, a volume which he carefully edits, and in which he is delighted to see his own image, *Persuasion* provides reflection on male authorship. As Anne complains in her debate with Captain Harville, she will not "allow books to prove anything" since men have had more opportunities for authorship and books therefore tend to reflect men's subjective opinions rather than reality as a whole: "Education has been theirs in so much higher a degree; the pen has been in their hands." And while Wentworth's relinquishing (and sharing) of his pen suggests hope for the democratization or socialization of the authority associated with authorship, this is not necessarily true for society at large. Sir Walter, for example, accepts Anne's marriage by a reversion to his authoritarian and self-referential authorship: Wentworth's good looks and "well sounding name" "enable[-] Sir Walter, at last, to prepare his pen, with a very good grace, for the insertion of the marriage in the volume of honour."[135] The reclamation of authorship for Austen works better at the individual level than the societal; her primary concerns are psychological rather than political. Perhaps therefore, in addressing the culture of sensibility, Austen is concerned with the occasions where the denial of authority leads to the forsaking of responsibility. In this way, Austen balances the limits of authority with the recognition of its inescapable necessity.

In chastening the cult of sensibility, Austen instead offers a new kind of heroism—dramatically different in the context that she is writing. This new heroism of daily life applies to readers as well. Austen stresses the courage and strength it takes to achieve moderation, the "exertion" that it takes to achieve civility towards fools and enemies, the heroism that can be involved in the expression of "good Cheer," or the difficulty of achieving "tranquility." (The latter themes are prominent in *Pride and Prejudice* and *Persuasion*.) Austen's new heroism challenges the culture of sensibility without rejecting it, yet it also marks a return to some of sensibility's core impulses. Only by pursuing the common or by paying attention to the ordinary details of daily life, can one preserve the societal bonds that unite us, whether friend or foe, despite the limitations of language and our own solipsistic tendencies. Austen's is a heroism of the "common"—a critical word in *Northanger Abbey,* where it is used in opposition to Isabella's favorite word "amazing." The intoxicated pursuit of amazement, horror, the sublime, the picturesque, sensibility, or even charm, wit, or vivacity, will blind us to each other and cause us to lose our perceptive powers—the key to our independence. In this sense, Austen's project was a return to sensibility's goal of encouraging the keen observation of others necessary to feel sympathy—a pedagogy of seeing, purged of connections to the cult of the "interesting."

By using readerly expectations to achieve a complex dynamic between narrator and implied reader, Austen forces readers to recognize their expectations of the novel, particularly their concept of the "interesting."[136] Ultimately the reader is again challenged to perceive sensibility in the heroine who does not initially fit the category of the interesting or picturesque. Austen's attempted reformation of sensibility is limited by the fact that our admiration for Elinor is inherently linked to her degree of suffering. The two heroines never actually remove themselves from sensibility's trope of competing for misery and simultaneously for the sympathy of the reader. In *Persuasion,* Austen finds a better solution to this problem, further removing herself from the ethical dilemmas of sensibility. Suffering and prudence are united in one character, Anne Elliot. And Anne's portrayal, devoid of Marianne's tableaux by the fireplace and at the window, is singularly un-visual. Since Anne is largely unobserved, she is also no one's spectacle. Appropriately enough, as Austen struggles to find a way to revise her didactic impulses to accord with her moral philosophy, we readers are taught a basic lesson in sympathy ourselves.

Afterword
The Luxuries of Distress

The culture of sensibility partly functioned as an urban society's fanciful celebration of utopian rural simplicity. If we can judge from the number of 'hermits' hired to feign poverty and isolation and to inhabit the English gardens of the 1770s and '80s, however, sensibility remained a beautiful and intriguing *spectacle,* rather than a practical alternative: "The practical man produced the impractical model."[1] The courtly politician and the nomad meet in the silent spectacle of the philosophical hermit, hired to provide a romantic flair to estates. The hermit might live then in carefully constructed, yet flimsy-appearing hermitages of the period that imitate a rusticity that is less evanescent and less accidental than it appears. All the conveniences of modernity could be combined with the authority and mystique of the past. Both modernization and rustification carry status, and their combination in such paradoxical constructions as follies and hermitages are the height of fashion for at least two decades.

This study has been an attempt to understand the psychology behind such a fashion that attempts both to call forth and halt the process of deterioration—to exert control over decay itself in freezing the moment in perpetuity. It would be wrong, however, to relegate such paradoxical impulses to the dustbins of history. In fact, the turn of the twenty-first century in Europe and the United States shares much of the philosophical insecurity that characterized the mid-nineteenth century: its simultaneous wish for decentralization, immediacy, transparency, and universal kinship, while also haunted by fears that these ideals cannot be achieved in the current atomistic society.

In 2002, an ad appeared in the on-line *Reuter's* News in England: "Wanted: Professional Hermit for Cave-Dwelling Duty." The ad generated considerable interest, as it was supposedly the first hermit ad to be seen in Britain since the early nineteenth century.[2] The duties included occupying a cave on the 900-acre English garden of the Shugborough estate in Staffordshire, as well as "acting as a sage" and "frightening walkers" out for a stroll.[3] The ad generated responses from over 200 individuals, including many actors and even a few monks, eager to escape from urban life to the nostalgic seclusion of the past (and to be paid £600 for the effort). The return to hiring a hermit suggests an urban society's fanciful and somewhat nostalgic celebration of rural simplicity not terribly dissimilar to that evidenced in the late eighteenth century.[4]

One of the regulations generally found in hermit contracts of the eighteenth century was that of silence: hermits were not allowed to speak, particularly in the presence of any guests to the estate. When hired hermits proved inconvenient, expensive, or excessively chatty, stuffed mannequins were used instead. The hermits were desirable as spectacles only; no actual human contact was desired. It is an example of sensibility's privileging imagination over reality—aesthetic principles over individual concerns. In fact, it seems strangely appropriate that the man whose estate the modern hermit was to inhabit is the royal photographer Lord Patrick Lichfield, and also that the purpose was part of a larger art project, or 'installation' of sorts. Another age would have called it a tableau.

While the hired hermit was a self-conscious spectacle and an imitation of an eighteenth-century tradition, there are other aspects of contemporary life that less self-consciously echo the culture of sensibility. The hermit in Figure 38 was a neighbor of Jane Austen's. He is seen here in robes and a shepherd's staff, his hat mimicking the maximally non-rectilinear shape of the hut. The cross on top symbolizes the early Christian symbolism frequently associated with hermits and primitivism.

It may be valuable to acknowledge the pursuits of ruination that are still pervasive today, as well as a suspicion of authority that persists in twentieth- and twenty-first-century culture and continues to shape our architecture,

Figure 38

our literature, our gardens, our clothing, and our furniture, not to mention our minds. In literary theory, deconstruction, whose name seems to invoke purposeful ruination, also glories in contradictory impulses, crumbling (intellectual and institutional) edifices, and exposed suffering. The name itself combines both the narrative or monumentalizing urges (construction) and the opposing anti-narrative urges that prefer the ruin (destruction). It, too, particularly as formulated by Jacques Derrida, reacts to perceived limitations of language,[5] and glories in the use of punctuation to fragment the act of reading. In the case of the syntactic style generally practiced in deconstruction, individual words are frequently perforated with punctuation marks in order to represent their instability as signifiers, engaging the reader in a non-linear game of self-conscious meaning-making. At least initially, deconstruction would seem to embrace ambivalence in a way that is similar to sensibility, since "If anything is destroyed in a deconstructive reading, it is not the text, but the claim to unequivocal domination of one mode of signifying over another."[6] However, deconstruction is far more univocal in its normative assertions of ambivalence or of inconclusion as the *only* mode in language as well as in contemporary society. While self-consciously referring to play, *jouissance* is an end in itself, and ultimately less playful, I would argue, than the culture of sensibility's dual impulses. Deconstruction's playfulness is limited by its resignation to the human isolation and solipsism so feared by authors in mid-eighteenth-century Europe. In short, deconstruction exhibits the same fears without the accompanying (or compensating) exuberance, the appreciation of ruination without the ambivalence generated by a lingering and defiant esteem for monuments.[7]

And yet, deconstruction, like sensibility, has spawned a style of architecture that similarly exhibits a rich cross-fertilization between disciplines of study or art forms. Figure 39 shows one in a series of architectural structures, still unfinished, installed in a public garden in Paris, designed by Bernard Tschumi. Interestingly enough, the project, upon which Derrida consulted, is self-consciously referential to the culture of sensibility and to the history of the English garden, for the structures are called "*folies*" or follies (also meaning "madness" in French). Dozens of red metal structures are erected at uniform distances in a grid-like pattern in Parc de la Villette; each one is different in design: "multiple, dissociated, and inherently confrontational elements—aimed at disrupting the smooth coherence and reassuring stability of composition, promoting instability and programmatic madness."[8]

Although Tschumi's project has not yet been completed, neither the bare metal beams nor the final, intended structures make any attempt to conform to their natural surroundings—they resist nature and narrative alike. "My pleasure," writes Tschumi, "has never surfaced in looking at buildings . . . but rather in dismantling them."[9] Like the earlier follies, functionality is hidden if not entirely avoided, and it is intellectually playful but in a way that does not invite human story-telling impulses. To tell a story would be

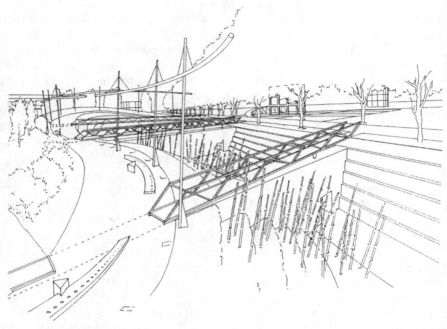

Figure 39

to invite narrative impulses and the wish for meaning, or for future conclusion or resolution.[10] Such logocentric desires are to be avoided, as the frame with no completion in Figure 39 poignantly suggests.

In an early manifesto of deconstructive architecture, Wolf D. Prix and Helmut Swiczinky, founders of the Austrian architectural group co-op Himmelblau, write: "We are tired of seeing Palladio and other historical masks, because we don't want architecture to exclude everything that is disquieting . . . Architecture should be cavernous, fiery, smooth, hard, angular, brutal, round, delicate, colorful, obscene, voluptuous, dreamy, alluring, repelling, wet, dry and throbbing."[11] This could almost be a return to Ledoux and Mézières in the anthropomorphizing of the architectural structure and the assertion of its dramatic role; in fact, the affective influence upon the viewer is again paramount. Architecture should "discomfort and unbalanc[e] . . . expectations."[12] Similarly, the Parc de la Villette project, according to Tschumi, "can be seen to encourage conflict over synthesis, fragmentation over unity, madness and play over careful management . . . subvert[ing] a number of ideals that were sacrosanct." These encouragements are made in the name of authenticity, or the lack of "historical masks": for the "nostalgic pursuit of coherence . . . ignores today's social, political, and cultural dissociations."[13]

This emphasis on *dis*comfort (along with the functional requirements of architecture as consumer good) invites the hypocritical constructions of sensibility where primitive huts are actually comfortable on the interior, for example, or where a cold column could actually host luxurious suites.[14] This brings us back to the hypocrisy at the extremes of (or perhaps at the heart of) sensibility—namely, the uncomfortable combinations of primitivism and luxury that we saw in Robert Lugar's "Design for Cottage and Ruin" (Figure 19) or in Monville's Column House at the Désert de Retz (Figures 23 and 24). Such structures again underline the culture of sensibility's preference for primitivism as a spectacle that never quite translates into a practical alternative, as well as the hypocritical desire to have the benefits of luxury in the guise of primitivism. As sensibility moves farther and farther away from a focus on virtue and suffering towards glamour and frivolity, such paradoxes become painfully apparent and result in the fashionable enjoyment of "luxurious" grief at the expense of those who grieve in earnest, as well as self-absorption posing as humane sympathy. I would argue that similar trends exist in society today, perhaps stemming from the admirable desire to sympathize with or identify with the downtrodden, yet these attempts may perversely culminate in the commodification of ruin and distress, and thus both diminish the possibility for actual human sympathy and distract us from actual attempts to alleviate distress and poverty.

The political ramifications of these seeming contradictions within sensibility were certainly quite apparent to eighteenth-century audiences, partly through the extravagancies of Queen Marie Antoinette. The Queen built her own dairy in her favorite section of the Trianon at Versailles (1787)—a whole miniature village, in fact, with mill, dairy, aviary, barn, and farmhouse. The Queen would enjoy visiting her dairy wearing pretty frocks and pretending to live a rural and simple life, while at the same time dining on dishes designed by Sèvres. She also had a second dairy at Rambouillet, built by her husband Louis XVI; there again, the interior belies the rustic pretense of the exterior, since upon entering the doors, one is greeted with lavish mosaics, marble, and almost life-size sculptures. The King's "pastoral retreat" for the Queen included a real sheep farm for merino wool; the Queen, however, preferred the other dairy, where there was no offending smell of animals. A look at the cross-section of the dairy at Rambouillet reveals some of the facets of this decadent primitivism: not only is the inside extremely lavish, but it also includes a grotto and waterfall. There is the need to evoke "nature" even inside the building through this elaborate mechanism: in order for the dairy to fulfill its associative goals, it cannot give away entirely to overt luxury.

The purposefully primitive still commands a cachet, and even a higher price tag, in the culture of the twentieth- and twenty-first-century United States. Furniture producers paint furniture white, only to tear off patches of paint in order to achieve a "distressed" look. Leather is purposely stretched roughly and unevenly to appear "worn." Grunge clothing purposely imitates the clothing and hairstyles of the homeless and disenfranchised; and denim is washed with stones and elaborately torn in order to provide the desired fashion statement. As long as it is fashionable, people pay more for clothing and furniture that has been partially destroyed, in their eagerness to imitate the downtrodden and to mask (and paradoxically flaunt) their wealth. Newly constructed malls with brick exteriors are painted with faded paints to resemble mills that were deserted and then rehabilitated, while actual rehabilitated mills demand higher rent than new spaces. These are the contemporary "luxuries of distress."[15]

The "man of feeling" in the contemporary world is not so much pitted against the "man of the world" or the "man of letters" as was the case in sensibility: he is instead defined in opposition to the "business man," who represents finance, power, and the cold unfeeling heart of the corporate world. He (or she) still conceives of himself (or herself) as the materially innocent Shaftesburian soul in a cruel, selfish Hobbesian universe, and accessorizes accordingly. Authority itself is suspect because of its ties to commercial enterprises as well, and business is anathema to genuine artistic pursuit, according to contemporary codes. Just as the eighteenth-century man of feeling is a self-defined outsider, the contemporary *innocent* must struggle to remain an outsider—on principle. Sensibility, too, is a reaction against civilization, its unnatural hierarchies, and artificial aristocracies; on the other hand, it paradoxically also establishes a new, elaborate, and exclusive aristocracy of its own called the "interesting." We can see the same dynamic at work today, and curiously, it is still defined in terms of successful failure.

In fact, definitions of the "shabby chic" style of decorating explicitly (and unconsciously) invoke the language of the picturesque as well as the paradoxical terms of the culture of sensibility. The language of advertising thus helps reveal the unconscious degree to which we daily imbibe an aesthetic that bears many similarities with the eighteenth-century culture of sensibility. A brief foray through the advertising campaigns of Rachel Ashwell, who originally coined the phrase "shabby chic,"[16] as well as of others who have since imitated her, reflects the paradox inherent in the name itself. Through this style of décor, one can have rich elegance ("sumptuous settings") without the embarrassing ostentation of overt order, newness, or effort: it is "a style that evokes a comfortable, lived-in feeling"; "unpretentious, yet truly exquisite"; through it, "entertaining need not be expensive or intimidating."

The favorite adjectives associated with shabby chic are "worn," "faded," and "rumpled," satisfying the simultaneous demands for luxury and egalitarianism that help define contemporary American culture: "instead of replacing the worn floor with carpet, they installed lower-grade lumber for an old-fashioned look. The knots and imperfections only add to the aura of the home." The result is a form of masked wealth, analogous to the masked authority and authorship we found in the culture of sensibility. Wealth is less "intimidating" if you incorporate "flea market finds" into your décor.

The phrases also suggest a longing for history, regardless of whether or not it is authentic: "Place something elegant and chic next to something aged with time"; "wrinkled fabrics only add to the charm"; "upholstery should not appear pressed, but rather *worn*"; "paint your furniture white with a chipped or crackled finish, or simply use a white garage sale find that already appears worn!" This modern antiquarian impulse even encourages the incorporation of ruined objects such as "concrete column bases, iron corner brackets, old mantles, and more." The ruination or fragmentation of an object is an added attraction: "a broken item can still function . . . Bringing these things into a room gives it another sense of history that wasn't there originally." The haphazard appearance and avoidance of symmetry in shabby chic décor also serves to deemphasize the agency of the decorator, once again echoing sensibility and the picturesque's preference for finding over creating, since finding involves less obvious contrivance and effort.

"Ruined by design," then, refers not only to the self-conscious pursuit of ruination—or fragmentation—in the novel and garden architecture associated with sensibility and the picturesque, but is also meant to indicate the potentially hazardous side of sensibility. Ironically, sensibility's cherished emphasis on the keen perception and delicate emotions that allow for sympathy—sensibility's central hope for humanity—decays into a compelling, yet uncomfortably narcissistic self-consciousness, and ultimately into hypocrisy. Few people who have felt real distress would think it a "luxury." It is only when the distress is optional, voluntary, and either vicarious or affected that one could consider it luxurious. Eventually, the viewer overshadows the view, and ruin (whether human or architectural) serves as a vehicle for the reassurance of one's capacity to feel. Not only used as theatrical proof of virtue or an attempt to communicate one's delicate, Shaftesburian soul, the ruin also serves as a means to self-portrayal, self-promotion, or, at its worst, sadistic enjoyment of others' pain. In the modern world, too, the ruin serves as a means of commodifying the suffering of others.

As we have seen through the excesses of the cult of sensibility, a principal danger involved with the suspicion and masking of authorship is that they encourage a deferral or disavowal of responsibility. This is frequently done in the name of authenticity. Yet, it is nearly impossible not to author words, letters, literature, and even oneself, since experience and representation are nearly always separated in time and by selection or other ordering principles, even if they are calculated attempts to reproduce the effects of randomness. Like Werther, contemporary audiences often try to fool themselves out of rational detachment—to regain the "left side of the brain" for aesthetic purposes or to achieve a sense of immediacy. Composition classes refer to "writing from the gut," or brainstorming, as though the brain were a Bastille, better taken by storm than allowed to maintain its predatory, authoritarian grip on thoughts. Contemporary audiences relish the disjointedness of thoughts as evidence of their freshness, and deplore those who still use outlines for composition to be as dull as a Bridget. Hacks, like Anthony Trollope, who diligently produced a fixed number of pages per day in order to earn a living, are disregarded in favor of the myth of more passionate authors whose prose flows unchecked and uncensored from their pens. Narration and closure are perceived as a form of intellectual violence, an authoritarian imposition, just as we might have heard Werther complaining about the impositions of grammar upon his uncensored speech and writing. Glamour, in other words, is still associated with the fragmented, the passionate, the uncontrolled, even when the appearance of these qualities has to be pursued using artificial techniques. It is the unwillingness to accept our own complicit artifice that places us in a similar position to the hypocrisy frequently displayed by authors writing within the cult of sensibility.

Are we resigned to the primacy of chaos? It is perhaps useful to recognize the hypocrisy that leads contemporary thinkers to treat chaos as an organizing principle of art on the one hand and the despair that leads them to insist on the univocal acceptance of the lack of absolutes on the other.[17] The concept that disorder is a more natural or authentic state of being is expressive of an aesthetic stance, if not a political one. Authenticity cannot be aimed at directly—cannot become a goal in its own right. As much as we might wish to, we cannot escape *in*authenticity, because we will never cease to reflect, to plan, nor to desire order. We cannot escape authenticity either, since we are *naturally* divided beings. Yet authenticity must be a by-product of daily living rather than a "lifestyle" or a fashion statement; otherwise the pursuit of authenticity becomes another superbist Tower of Babel. The irony of course is that once building *ruined* towers becomes a goal, then there is ultimately no difference from the rationalist tower building in *Genesis*.

Notes

NOTES TO THE PREFACE AND ACKNOWLEDGMENTS

1. D. J. Enright, "William Cowper'" *Pelican Guide to English Literature*, ed. Boris Ford (Harmondsworth, UK: Penguin, 1957); Janet Todd, *Sensibility, an Introduction* (London and New York: Methuen, 1986), 142.
2. Jerome McGann, *The Poetics of Sensibility: A Revolution in Literary Style* (Oxford: Clarendon Press, 1996), xi.
3. Marilyn Butler, *Romantics, Rebels, and Reactionaries: English Literature and its Background, 1760–1830* (New York: Oxford University Press, 1982), 29; Enright, "William Cowper," 391–392.
4. Marshall Brown, *Preromanticism* (Stanford: Stanford University Press, 1991), 99; Robert W. Jones, "Ruled Passions: Re-Reading the Culture of Sensibility," *Eighteenth-Century Studies* 323 (1999): 400.
5. Jones, "Ruled Passions: Re-Reading the culture of Sensibility," 401.
6. "Preromanticism, or Sensibility: Defining Ambivalences," in *Companion to European Romanticism*, ed. Michael Ferber (London: Blackwell, 2005), 10–28.
7. "The Adventures of a Female Werther: Austen's Revision of Sensibility," *Philosophy and Literature* 23, 1 (April 1999): 110–126; "Masculinity, Sensibility, and the 'Man of Feeling': the Gendered Ethics of Goethe's *Werther*," *Papers on Language and Literature* 35, 2 (Spring 1999): 115–140; and "Words 'Half-Dethron'd': Jane Austen's Art of the Unspoken," in *Jane Austen's Business*, ed. Juliet McMaster and Bruce Stovel (London and New York: Macmillan and St. Martin's Press, 1996), 95–106.

NOTES TO THE INTRODUCTION

1. Chevalier Louis de Jaucourt, "Sensibilité," in *Encyclopédie ou Dictionnaire raisonné des sciences, des arts et des métiers*, ed. Jean-Bapiste René Robinet (Paris: Briasson, 1751–65), 15.52. Unless otherwise noted, translations are mine.
2. Many scholars diminish the unusual characteristics of sensibility by labeling it Pre-romanticism. Definition through hindsight has a long tradition, including the term "Middle Ages," yet even if it is true that Preromanticism "preceded and anticipated Romanticism," as Gary Kelly writes, can one not say that any period which precedes generally also anticipates subsequent periods? ("Pre-Romanticism: Britain," in *Encyclopedia of the Romantic Era: 1760–1850*, ed. Christopher John Murray [New York and London: Fitzroy

Dearborn, 2004], 904–5.) We can certainly find anticipation of Romantic literary notions and style as early as Plato, Montaigne, or Cervantes, if we choose to call them anticipation. Charles Rosen, for example, cites many 17th-century analogues to Preromantic traits in music. In French literature, Lafayette, Racine, and Scudéry all bear resemblances to the sentimental impulses of Preromantic literature, or to the literature of Sensibilité.

3. The eventual elitism and over-codification of sensibility led to its designation as a "cult": see Barker-Benfield, *The Culture of Sensibility: Sex and Society in Eighteenth-Century Britain* (Chicago: University of Chicago, 1992), 258, n.135.

4. Kelly, "Pre-Romanticism: Britain," 904–5.

5. More recently, cultural historians have come to see sensibility as "the specifically cultural aspect or expression of a broad, late-eighteenth-century movement for social, economic, or political reform" (Kelly, "Pre-Romanticism: Britain," 904–5).

6. Interestingly, this work is also sometimes categorized under the movement "Empfindsamkeit."

7. The situation is further complicated by nomenclature, with some authors speaking of a first and second Romanticism. Michel Baridon, for example, refers to Preromanticism as "premier romantisme," (*Les Jardins: Paysagistes, Jardiniers, Poètes* [Paris: Robert Laffond, 1998}, 929).

8. Another confounding element in discussions of sensibility in England and beyond is its relation to sentimentalism. Sensibility became a dominant aspect of Preromanticism, distinguishing itself from sentimentalism (a much broader term, preferred by Janet Todd) in its combination of assumptions about human psychology and anatomy. There is scholarly dissent regarding this matter as well: Jerome McGann sees the discourse of sensibility as a precursor to the discourse of sentiment (McGann, *Poetics of Sensibility,* 4, 7), while in *Framing Feeling: Sentiment and Style in English Prose Fiction, 1745–1800* (New York: AMS Press, 1994), Barbara Benedict sees sentimental literature as a transitional and ambiguous cultural mode.

9. Robert J. Frail, "Pre-Romanticism: France," in *Encyclopedia,* ed. Murray, 907. In music, representatives of sensibility would include Haydn and Mozart; in painting, Constable, Turner, Claude, Poussin, Greuze, and Piranesi; and in landscape gardening, the Englishmen Gilpin, Repton, and Whately.

10. For further information about the intertextual relations of the work and its successors, see Jean Marie Goulemot, "Un Roman de la Révolution: *Le voyageur sentimental en France sous Robespierre* de François Vernes," *Europe: Revue Littéraire Mensuelle* 659 (1984): 80–88.

11. Henry Mackenzie, *The Man of Feeling* (Oxford and New York: Oxford University Press, 1987), 93; henceforth, *Man of Feeling.*

12. Marilyn Butler writes that the "tendency towards relativism . . . becomes conscious and explicit" in the novels of the 1760s and 1770s and claims that this change grows naturally in the novel, because of its form which naturally emphasizes the individual and his or her independent worth. In saying this, Butler draws on Ronald Paulson's claim that given its concentration on explaining the motives of individual protagonists, the ethics of the novel are naturally more relativist than satire, for example (Butler, *Romantics,* 11).

13. On self-reflexivity and the theatrical impulses of sensibility, the best work to date is David Marshall's *The Figure of Theater: Shaftesbury, Defoe, Adam Smith, and George Eliot* (New York: Columbia University Press, 1986). Additional works in this area include: Michael Bell, *Sentimentalism, Ethics, and the Culture of Feeling* (Basingstoke and New York: Palgrave, 2000);

Syndy McMillen Conger, *Sensibility in Transformation: Creative Resistance to Sentiment from the Augustans to the Romantics: Essays in Honor of Jean H. Hagstrum* (Cranbury, N.J.: Associated University Presses, 1990); Stephen D. Cox, *"The Stranger within Thee": Concepts of the Self in Late-Eighteenth-Century Literature* (Pittsburgh: University of Pittsburgh Press, 1980); Michael Fried, *Absorption and Theatricality: Painting and Beholder in the Age of Diderot* (Berkeley, Los Angeles and London: University of California Press, 1980); Morris Golden, *The Self Observed: Swift, Johnson, Wordsworth* (Baltimore: Johns Hopkins University Press, 1972); John Mullan, *Sentiment and Sociability: the Language of Feeling in the Eighteenth Century* (Oxford and New York: Clarendon Press; Oxford University Press, 1988); Charles Rosen, *The Romantic Generation* (Cambridge: Harvard University Press, 1995); and Charles Taylor, *Sources of the Self: The Making of the Modern Identity* (Cambridge: Harvard University Press, 1989).

14. McGann, *Poetics*, ix.

15. This is true especially in French and English versions of Preromanticism; the German example is more complicated. The Sturm und Drang movement was more involved in the sublime, storms, and darker, emotional concepts including a fascination with death, in comparison with the French and English versions of sensibility. Although contemporaries like E. T. A. Hoffman called all three composers "romantisch" ("Beethovens Instrumental-musik," *Fantasiestücke in Callots Manier: Blätter eines reisenden Enthusiasten*), Mozart and Haydn can be considered Preromantic, whereas Beethoven can be seen to represent Romanticism because he opens up the realms of the monstrous and immeasurable.

16. Connections between landscape gardening and the literature of feeling have also generally focused on poetry rather than the novel. See, for example, John Dixon Hunt's excellent *The Figure in the Landscape: Poetry, Painting, and Gardening during the Eighteenth Century* (Baltimore: Johns Hopkins University Press, 1989).

17. Quoted in Christopher Hussey, *The Picturesque: Studies in a Point of View* (London: Frank Cass and Company, Ltd., 1967 [1927]), 137–38. Such discourse is the main focus of Lipking's *The Ordering of the Arts in Eighteenth-Century England* (Princeton, N.J.: Princeton University Press, 1970).

18. John Barrel, *The Idea of Landscape and the Sense of Place, 1730–1840: An Approach to the Poetry of John Clare* (Cambridge and New York: Cambridge University Press, 1972), 48.

19. Hussey continues: "The picturesque phase through which each art passed, roughly between 1730 and 1830, was in each case a prelude to Romanticism. It appeared at a point when an art shifted its appeal from reason to imagination." (*The Picturesque*, 4; see also 32).

20. See Katherine Haskings, *Picturing Britain: Time and Place in Image and Text, 1700-1850* (Chicago: University of Chicago Library, 1993), 12, 21; Hussey, *The Picturesque*, 151–185. The best treatment is perhaps Michel Baridon on the gardens of the man of sensibility in *Les Jardins*, 801–937. Baridon displays an awareness of the broad cultural affinities of sensibility and the picturesque, but the study remains an overview of the history of the garden. Michasiw mentions the strong connections with the culture of sensibility in passing: Kim Ian Michasiw, "Nine Revisionist Theses on the Picturesque," *Representations* 38 (1992): 87, 93–95.

21. John Dixon Hunt, *The Picturesque Garden in Europe* (London: Thames and Hudson, 2002), 8.

22. Martin Price claims, on the one hand, that "moral or religious grounds" are initially absent from the picturesque, and that once it is given such grounds, it moves towards the sublime (Price, "The Picturesque Moment," in *From*

Sensibility to Romanticism: Essays Presented to Frederick A. Pottle, ed. Frederick W. Hilles [New York: Oxford University Press, 1965]: 262–63). He also claims in the same article, however, that the "dissociation of . . . generally aesthetic elements from other values" is a "late" requirement within the picturesque (Price, 260–61). His ambivalence here seems important. I have argued that the picturesque was influenced by sensibility's conflation of ethics and aesthetics—its 'moral aesthetic.'

23. These characteristics of sensibility are further developed in my essay "Preromanticism, or Sensibility: Defining Ambivalences."

24. Locke divides "Experience" into "Observation" of both "external, sensible Objects" and "internal Operations of our minds" (John Locke, *An Essay Concerning Human Understanding*, ed. Peter H. Nidditch [Oxford: Clarendon Press, 1975], 105). The sensations and passions do not themselves rule thought or reason, but they come first in the process and provide thought with its fodder. Most scholars agree that for Locke, "disengaged reason" nonetheless still rules supreme and provides the only way we gain our rightful place in the providential order; cf. Charles Taylor, *Sources of the Self: The Making of the Modern Identity* (Cambridge: Harvard University Press, 1989), 265. Or as Hans Aarsleff writes, "To Locke all men are by nature rational and God 'commands what reason does'" (*From Locke to Saussure: Essays on the Study of Language and Intellectual History* [Minneapolis: University of Minnesota Press, 1982], 175). See also A. D. Nuttall, *A Common Sky: Philosophy and the Literary Imagination* (Berkeley: University of California Press, 1974), 13–19, for a discussion of the eighteenth-century interpretations of the implicit solipsism in Locke's teaching, as well as Locke's foreshadowing of nineteenth- and twentieth-century existentialism.

25. Shaftesbury, *Characteristics of Men, Manners, Opinions, Times* (London: 1727), III.2.177. "Be persuaded," Shaftesbury wrote elsewhere to one of his students, "that wisdom is more from the *heart* than from the *head. Feel* goodness, and you will see all things fair and good," quoted in Louis I. Bredvold, *The Natural History of Sensibility* (Detroit: Wayne State University Press, 1962), 12. Bishop Butler protested that conscience could not survive without judgment, discipline, authority, or a standard which stood outside and opposed itself to the individual, and suggested that such thinking as Shaftesbury's offered no protection against human weakness and vice. Voices such as Bishop Butler's and Samuel Johnson's, however, were outnumbered by those who had greater faith in the "internalization" of virtue.

26. David Hume, *A Treatise of Human Nature*, ed. L. A. Selby-Bigge and P. H. Nidditch (Oxford and New York: Clarendon Press; Oxford University Press, 1978), 470. Cf. "I shall endeavour to prove *first,* that reason alone can never be a motive to any action of the will; and *secondly,* that it can never oppose passion in the direction of the will" (Hume, *Treatise,* 413).

27. Hume, *Treatise,* 484.

28. Jean-Jacques Rousseau, *La Profession du Foi du Vicaire Savoyard,* (Paris: J. Vrin, 1978), 26.

29. Cf. Wendy Motooka, *The Age of Reasons: Quixotism, Sentimentalism, and Political Economy in Eighteenth-Century Britain* (London and New York: Routledge, 1998).

30. This "disengagement" or "externalized" view of reason is inherently unstable because of the multivalence of the external stance: one can be detached, in the sense of *dis*interested, objective, and capable of *good* judgment—or one can be detached in the sense of *un*interested and unassociated.

31. An example would be David Marshall's analysis of Hume's 1757 essay, "On the Standard of Taste": Marshall reveals Hume's defensive position within the

essay. Hume's rhetorical choices reveal his philosophical insecurity; Hume is desirous of avoiding any reliance on externally imposed authorities (critics) for a standard of taste, yet insists upon the existence of a popularly conceived standard of taste. Yet his own argument undermines this certainty and he finds himself torn between anarchy and tyranny in his attempt to achieve a democratically based, "naturally occurring standard by which choices may be evaluated" (*The Frame of Art : Fictions of Aesthetic Experience, 1750–1815* [Baltimore : Johns Hopkins University Press, 2005], 176–196).

32. See John O'Neal, *The Authority of Experience: Sensationist Theory in the French Enlightenment* (University Park, Pa.: Pennsylvania State University Press, 1996).

33. Examples in the literature of sensibility abound: for example, the man who destroys Harley's manuscript is a "strenuous logician" (*Man of Feeling,* 4); similarly, in Goethe's *Die Leiden des jungen Werthers* [*Sorrows of Young Werther*], Albert's use of traditional logic in his argument with Werther over suicide shows he cannot comprehend matters of true feeling. See *Die Leiden des jungen Werthers* in *Goethes Werke:* Hamburger Ausgabe, ed. Erich Trunz (München: C.H. Beck, 1989); henceforth *Werther.*

34. This connection has received little attention. The one exception is Douglas Den Uyl's interesting work *The Virtue of Prudence* (New York: P. Lang, 1991). Den Uyl traces prudence's fall from a position as one of the four cardinal virtues, to a position of disrepute, almost amounting to a vice.

35. *Man of Feeling,* 40.

36. Michel-Jean Sedaine, *Le philosophe sans le savoir* (Durham: University of Durham, 1987 [1765]).

37. Each in a different context, Edward Young, Jean-Jacques Rousseau, and Johann W. von Goethe, all wrote about the importance of originality and the corrupting and diminishing effects of society, draining individuals of their authenticity. In his *Discours sur les sciences et les arts* (1750), henceforth *First Discourse,* Rousseau complains of the homogenizing effect of society upon our passions: "Avant que l'art eût façonné nos manières et appris à nos passions à parler un langage apprêté, nos moeurs étoient rustiques, mais naturelles" [Before art had shaped our behavior, and taught our passions to speak an artificial language, our morals were rude but natural] (*Œuvres Complètes* [Paris: Gallimard, 1968], III.8). Nine years later, in his *Conjectures on Original Composition in a letter to the author of Charles Grandison* (London: A. Millar and J. Dodsley, 1759), Edward Young similarly complains of the contemporary lack of originality in a society that seems to require uniformity: "Born Originals, how comes it to pass that we die Copies?" (42). With a memorable line that could almost be a paraphrasing of Young's credo, Rousseau opens his *Le Contrat Social* (1762): "L'homme est né libre, et partout il est dans les fers" [Man was born free, but he is everywhere in chains] (*Œuvres Complètes* [Paris: Du Seuil, 1971], I. 518). And in his *Werther,* Goethe's eponymous protagonist shows fictionally the fate of those who try to remain authentic originals despite the pressure of society to conform to regulations and homogenizing expectations, whether in terms of social conventions or ethical standards: his struggles bring him to the brink of madness and, ultimately, to suicide.

38. Shaftesbury, *Characteristics* (London, 1727), I.4.129–30. Francis Hutcheson, following suit, speaks of "subtle Trains of Reasoning, to which honest Hearts are often wholly Strangers" in *An Essay on the Nature and Conduct of the Passions and Affections with Illustrations on the Moral Sense* (London: J. Darby and T. Browne, 1728), 4. The attempt to guide action by reasoning is taken as cunning or calculation, which must be opposed to 'true' virtue 'of the heart': "while some men are willing to wed virtue for her personal charms, others are

engaged to take her for the sake of her expected dowry." William Melmoth the younger wrote these words in 1742: *The Letters of Sir Thomas Fitzosborne, On Several Subjects* (London: R. Dodsley, 1750), XVIII.79.

39. Mary Wollstonecraft, *The Cave of Fancy* in *Posthumous Works,* ed. William Godwin (New York and London: Garland Publishing Inc., 1974), IV.135.

40. Mary Wollstonecraft, *The Wrongs of Woman, or Maria; A Fragment: to which is added the First Book of a Series of Lessons for Children* in *Posthumous Works,* ed. William Godwin (London, 1798), I. 69.

41. For further discussion of Whig and Tory interpretations of sensibility see Markman Ellis, *The Politics of Sensibility: Race, Gender and Commerce in the Sentimental Novel* (Cambridge and New York: Cambridge University Press, 1996). For Whig and Tory interpretations of the picturesque, see Stephen Copley and Peter Garside, *The Politics of the Picturesque: Literature, Landscape, and Aesthetics since 1770* (Cambridge and New York: Cambridge University Press, 1994), and Nigel Everett, *The Tory View of Landscape* (New Haven: Yale University Press, 1994).

42. Claudia L. Johnson, *Equivocal Beings: Politics, Gender, and Sentimentality in the 1790s: Wollstonecraft, Radcliffe, Burney, Austen* (Chicago and London: University of Chicago Press, 1995), 4–19.

43. While scholars of the 1990s frequently stress one political side or another—either the undercover Tory politics of the picturesque and its implicit promotion of aristocratic estates at the expense of the public, or (more rarely) its Whig effects on liberating the middle classes—the approach here is consistent with a more recent set of interpretations, such as David Marshall's "Problem of the Picturesque" and Gary Harrison and Jill Heydt-Stevenson's volume of essays in *The European Romantic Review* 13, 1 (2002). In the introduction to their collection, Harrison and Heydt-Stevenson forward a "self-contradictory politics of the picturesque" and a "dialectical view of the picturesque" that emerges from the essays: in recognition of the "playful" origins of the picturesque aesthetic, the essays as a whole note the seemingly contradictory impulses embodied within the picturesque aesthetic. One essay notes that the picturesque, while seemingly controlling viewers, also liberates their eyes; another that it forwards both utilitarian and non-utilitarian aesthetics; a third that it provides a balancing of objective and subjective impulses; a fourth that the picturesque effect of surprise can erode its illusions of authority; and finally that the picturesque characteristically shifts between the beautiful and the sublime (Gary Harrison and Jill Heydt-Stevenson, "Variations on the Picturesque," 4, 6). These critics contribute to the understanding of the paradoxical forms and potentially unstable underpinnings inherent in the picturesque: "The picturesque . . . is a subversive genre in its own right because it contains its own ability to self parody, adapt, and resist control. That is, like nature, the picturesque is always threatening to undermine structures we place upon it" ("Variations on the Picturesque," 9–10).

44. Thomas Hobbes, *Leviathan: Or the Matter, Forme, and Power of a Commonwealth Ecclesiasticall and Civil,* ed. Michael Oakeshott (New York and London: Collier, 1962), 100. Michael Gassenmeier traces an attempted Puritan reframing of sensibility in *Der Typus des man of feeling* (Tübingen: Max Niemeyer Verlag, 1972).

45. David Hume, *Enquiries Concerning Human Understanding and Concerning the Principles of Morals,* ed. L. A. Selby-Bigge and P. H. Nidditch (Oxford: Clarendon Press, [1748, 1751]1975), 226.

46. Cf. the following passages by Sterne: "REASON is, half of it, SENSE; and the measure of heaven itself is but the measure of our present appetites and

concoctions" and "L'amour n'est rien sans sentiment. Et le sentiment est encore moins sans amour." The first is from *The Life and Opinions of Tristram Shandy, Gentleman,* ed. Ian P. Watt (Boston: Houghton Mifflin, 1965), 7.13.494, and the second from *A Sentimental Journey through France and Italy by Mr. Yorick,* ed. Gardiner Stout Jr. (Berkeley: University of California Press), 153; henceforth *Journey.*

47. *Journey,* 128–9.

48. R. F. Brissenden also views this paradoxical situation as central to sensibility. In fact, it is the inspiration for the title of his book *Virtue in Distress* (e.g., 21): *Virtue in Distress: Studies in the Novel of Sentiment from Richardson to Sade* (New York: Barnes and Noble, 1974).

49. See Bredvold, 24–25; and Brodey, "The Adventures of a Female Werther," 110–126.

50. *Man of Feeling,* 69.

51. Basil Willey once wryly described mid-eighteenth-century English thought as "intrepid in speculation and conservative in practice" (*The Eighteenth Century Background: Studies on the Idea of Nature in the Thought of the Period* [London: Chatto & Windus, 1940], 119). Although only made in passing, this remark rather aptly describes the philosophical insecurity or conflicting impulses of the culture of sensibility in England, Germany, and to a lesser extent, also in France. In his *Origins of the English Novel* (Baltimore: Johns Hopkins University Press, 1987), Michael McKeon also speculates whether the growth of the novel in the eighteenth century might function as the "adjudication" of historical change in the aftermath of the Glorious Revolution, which could result in a similar ambivalence to that described by Willey.

52. A series of older, etymologically-based studies attempted to make sense of sensibility's characteristic ambivalence (dual impulses) by studying the strange history of phrases like 'common sense.' According to C. S. Lewis, in his *Studies in Words,* eighteenth-century authors simultaneously minimized and put great new emphasis on the phrase 'common sense': ironically, the phrase "stooped to conquer," as Lewis puts it, during the first half of the eighteenth century, in "the age which of all others made *sense* or *good sense* or *common sense* its shibboleth." "The implication of the whole Augustan attitude," Lewis writes, "is 'We're not asking much. We're not asking that poets should be learned, or that divines should be saints, or that courtiers heroes, or that statesmen should bring in a heaven on earth . . . We ask only for rationality'" [Cambridge and New York: Cambridge University Press, 1990], 154–5). The rhetoric of sensibility can be seen as continuing the same tendency simultaneously to minimize and idealize; however it is in relation to perception rather than common sense.

53. For all its vocal self-conscious contrast to Hobbes, there is a strong resemblance here to Hobbes' own perspective, at least as understood by Michael Oakeshott: Hobbes too acknowledges that there is a "radical conflict between the nature of man and the natural condition of mankind: what the one urges with hope of achievement, the other makes impossible . . . [I]t is neither sin nor depravity that creates the predicament; nature itself is the author of his ruin" (Oakeshott, *Leviathan* introduction, 36).

NOTES TO CHAPTER 1

1. Thomas Burnet, *Sacred Theory of the Earth: Containing an Account of the Original of the Earth, and of All the General Changes Which It Hath Undergone, or Is to Undergo till the Consummation of All Things* (London: R.N. for Walter Kettilby, 1697), I: 67–68.

2. Marjorie Hope Nicolson, *Mountain Gloom and Mountain Glory: The Development of the Aesthetics of the Infinite* (Ithaca, N.Y.: Cornell University Press, 1959); Elizabeth Wanning Harries, *The Unfinished Manner: Essays on the Fragment in the Later Eighteenth Century* (Charlottesville: University Press of Virginia, 1994).

3. Nicolson describes at length how the attitude towards the irregularities of nature showed itself in the changing view of mountains: Nicolson, *Mountain Gloom*, 2 ff.

4. Whereas these seventeenth-century authors tend not to limit God's authority, Jean-Jacques Rousseau reverses the causality of *Genesis*' ruination. In the *Discours sur l'origine et les fondements de l'inégalité parmi les hommes* [1755], he writes: "Semblable à la statue de Glaucus: que le temps, la mer et les orages avaient tellement défigurée qu'elle ressemblait moins à un dieu qu'à une bête féroce, l'âme humaine altérée au sein de la société . . . a, pour ainsi dire, changé d'apparence au point d'être presque méconnoissable" [Like the statue of Glaucus, which time, sea, and storms had so disfigured that it looked less like a god than a wild beast, the human soul, altered in the bosom of society . . . has, so to speak, altered its appearance to the point of being nearly unrecognizable] (*Œuvres complètes* [Paris: Gallimard, 1966] III.122); henceforth, *Second Discourse*. Modern man is a ruin, but his ruined state is not desirable for Rousseau. By stressing God's authorship of a ruined or picturesque world, His authority is lessened, or at least made less threatening.

5. Hobbes, *Leviathan*, 80, 100, 157.

6. John Locke, *Second Treatise of Government*, ed. C.B. McPherson (Indianapolis and Cambridge: Hackett, [1690]1980), 18, 42.

7. Rousseau, *Second Discourse*, III.133.

8. Roland Barthes, *Mythologies* (Paris: Edition du Seuil, 1957), quoted in Syndy McMillen Conger, *Mary Wollstonecraft and the Language of Sensibility* (London and Toronto: Associated University Presses, 1994), xix.

9. Cf. Nicolson's extensive treatment of Burnet's claims in chapters 5–7 of *Mountain Gloom and Mountain Glory*; see also Hussey, *The Picturesque*, 56, 83–127.

10. Cf. Erwin Panofsky, "Et in Arcadio Ego: On the Conception of Transcience in Poussin and Watteau," in *Philosophy and History: Essays Presented to Ernst Cassirer*, ed. Raymond Kilbansky and H.J. Paton (Oxford: Clarendon Press, 1936); Laurence Goldstein, *Ruins and Empire: The Evolution of a Theme in Augustan and Romantic Literature* (Pittsburgh: University of Pittsburgh Press, 1977), 31; and Rose Macaulay, *Pleasure of Ruins* (London: Thames and Hudson, 1953), 183.

11. Cf. Goldstein's discussion of Dyer, Cowper, Goldsmith, and Wordsworth; cf. Hussey, *Picturesque*, on Dyer (18), Thomson (32ff.), and Young (102ff.).

12. Denis Diderot, "Salon of 1767," in *Œuvres complètes de Diderot*, XI. 227.

13. *Man of Feeling*, 64.

14. See Anne F. Janowitz, *England's Ruins: Poetic Purpose and the National Landscape* (Cambridge, Mass.: Blackwell, 1990), 14; Macaulay, *Pleasure*, 48.

15. Barbara Maria Stafford, "'Illiterate Monuments': The Ruin as Dialect or Broken Classic," *The Age of Johnson: A Scholarly Annual* 1 (1987): 26.

16. Dr. Francis Walsh, *The Antediluvian World; Or, a New Theory of the Earth: Containing a Clear Account of the Form and Constitution of the Terrestrial Globe before the Universal Deluge; Proving It to Be Quite Different from What It Is at Present. And Also of the Origin and Causes of the Said Deluge, Subterraneous Cavities, Seas, Islands, Mountains, Etc.* (Dublin: Printed by S. Powell, 1743), 55.

17. Anonymous, *The Beauties of Nature and Art Displayed, in a Tour through the World* (London: Printed for J. Payne at the Feathers, Pater-Noster Row, 1763–64), Vol. IX.

18. E.g., Rev. W. Derham, *Physico-Theology: a Demonstration of the Being and Attributes of God from His Works of Creation* (London: Printed for A. Straham; T. Cadell Jun.; and W. Davies in the Strand, 1798).

19. William Drysdale, *Sacred Scripture: Theory of the Earth from Its First Atom to Its Last End* (Newcastle upon Tyne, 1798).

20. William Hooper, M.D., *Rational Recreations, in Which the Principles of Numbers and Natural Philosophy are Clearly and Copiously Elucidated by a Series of Easy, Entertaining, Interesting Experiments* (London: Printed for B. Law and Son, Ave-Maria Lane and J. Robinson, Pater-Noster Row, 1794), Vol. IV: 155.

21. Ludwig Trauzettel, "Wörlitz: England in Germany," *Garden History* 24, 2 (1996): 221–236.

22. Maiken Umbach, "Visual Culture, Scientific Images, and German Small-State Politics in the Late Enlightenment," *Past and Present* 158 (February, 1998): 116.

23. Umbach, "Visual Culture," 132.

24. Quoted in Macaulay, *Pleasure,* 191–92. Macaulay emphasizes the personal effect of the Grand Tour on various well-known eighteenth- and nineteenth-century figures throughout her work. See also Michel Baridon, *Les Jardins,* 808, for a discussion of the "idée-image" of England as a new Rome, which helped inspire the combination of classical and Gothic elements in the ruin collecting of the time.

25. Cf. Stafford, "Illiterate Monuments," 26–8. The following two passages (one from John Dennis and one from Edmund Burke) suggest the enormous change in aesthetics that was required in the redemption of ruin. The late-seventeenth-century critic John Dennis had written that "the Work of every reasonable Creature must derive its Beauty from Regularity; for Reason is Rule and Order, and nothing can be irregular either in our Conceptions or our Actions, any further than it swerves from Rule, that is, from Reason. Nature is nothing but that Rule and Order and Harmony, which we find in the visible Creation . . . And nothing that is Irregular, as far as it is Irregular, ever was, or ever can be either Natural or Reasonable" (*The Critical Works of John Dennis,* ed. Edward Niles Hooker [Baltimore: Johns Hopkins University Press, 1939], 335). The question was whether Nature had been perverted at the Fall, and whether its irregularity is a token of a depraved condition. In contrast to Dennis, Edmund Burke, writing in the mid- eighteenth century, refers to artificial lines and angles of buildings in gardens, openly discarding a reliance upon proportion as a principal source of beauty: "Nature has at last escaped from their discipline and their fetters" (*A Philosophical Enquiry into the Origin of Our Ideas of the Sublime and Beautiful* [London: Routledge and Paul; New York: Columbia University Press, 1958], 71–6).

26. According to Jeffery Whitelaw, the first folly may have been built as early as 1579 (Freston Tower in Suffolk); however, the original purpose—and extent—of the building is unclear. See Whitelaw, *Follies* (Malta: Gutenberg Press, 2005), 4–5.

27. Janowitz, *England's Ruins,* 4.

28. The terms folly and *fabrique* refer to a much wider range of artificial architecture than just fake ruins (see Figure 17 for examples). *Fabrique* can also refer to the very popular Chinese pagodas, hermitages, and other exotic buildings inspired at the same period. For the purpose of this study, I am limiting my use of follies to purposely ruined and antiquated monuments, whether inhabitable or not. These fake ruins have received surprisingly little

critical attention, especially in the literary context of sensibility. Macaulay, Hussey, Goldstein, McFarland, and Janowitz all have written interesting accounts of the cultural and literary significance of the general fascination with ruins in the late-eighteenth and early-nineteenth centuries, but none has dealt adequately with the added complications of the artificial ruins. Each has tended to isolate one particular symbolic meaning of the ruins (e.g. Janowitz tends to focus on the glorification of the past for political purposes), or assign one reading for each author or painter, rather than address the inherent multivalence of the rhetoric of (especially fake) ruins. One of the best treatments of the multivalence of follies is Michael S. Roth, Claire Lyons, and Charles Merewether, *Irresistible Decay: Ruins Reclaimed* (Los Angeles: Getty Research Institute, 1997).

See John Dixon Hunt's *The Picturesque Garden in Europe* for the most thorough account of the dissemination and adaptation of the English garden style and picturesque taste throughout Europe. See also Stephanie Ross, *What Gardens Mean* (Chicago and London: University of Chicago Press, 1998); Jane Brown, *Art and Architecture of English Gardens* (New York: Rizzoli, 1989); and Michel Baridon, *Les Jardins* (Paris: Robert Laffond, 1998).

29. For a list of extant British follies as well as historical descriptions and directions, see *Follies*, edited by Hugh Casson (New York: Taplinger Publications, 1965).
30. Barbara Jones, *Follies and Grottoes* (London: Constable, 1953).
31. The location is not clear in the King James translation of *Genesis:* "And the LORD God planted a garden eastward in Eden; and there he put the man whom he had formed. And out of the ground made the LORD God to grow every tree that is pleasant to the sight, and good for food; the tree of life also in the midst of the garden, and the tree of knowledge of good and evil."
32. Prest, *The Garden of Eden: The Botanic Garden and the Re-Creation of Paradise* (New Haven and London: Yale University Press, 1981), 96–7.
33. Walpole composed this epitaph in a letter to William Mason, Feb. 4, 1783; quoted in H. F. Clark, "Eighteenth Century Elysiums: The Role of 'Association' in the Landscape Movement," *Journal of the Warburg and Courtauld Institutes* 6 (1943): 184.
34. Martin Price, "The Picturesque Moment," in *From Sensibility to Romanticism,* ed. Frederick Hilles and Harold Bloom (New York: Oxford University Press, 1965), 259.
35. Alpine interests long predate Gilpin, as the example from Burnet's *Sacred Theory* suggests.
36. Gary Harrison and Jill Heydt-Stevenson, "Variations on the Picturesque: Authority, Play, and Practice," *European Romantic Review* 13, 1 (2002): 3.
37. Ann Bermingham in *Landscape and Power* (Chicago: University of Chicago, 1994) makes excellent comparisons between landscape and government that reveal similar ideas regarding the picturesque. In her *Landscape and Ideology: The English Rustic Tradition, 1740–1860* (Berkeley: University of California Press, 1986), Bermingham connects the developments of the picturesque to changes in agriculture, class division, and the nouveaux riches. Tom Williamson connects economics, politics, and perceptions of personal identity as reflected in eighteenth-century landscape gardens in *Polite Landscapes, Gardens, and Society in Eighteenth-Century England* (Baltimore: Johns Hopkins University Press, 1995). John Dixon Hunt has been the most prolific author in this area: his works include *Gardens and the Picturesque* (Cambridge: MIT Press, 1992), *The Figure in the Landscape: Poetry, Painting, and Gardening During the Eighteenth Century* (Baltimore: Johns

Hopkins University Press, 1989), and *The Picturesque Garden in Europe* (London: Thames and Hudson, 2002).

38. William Gilpin, *Three Essays: On Picturesque Beauty; on Picturesque Travel; and on Sketching Landscape: To Which is Added a Poem, on Landscape Painting* (London: R. Blamire, 1792), I: 8.

39. There has been a considerable number of scholarly works focusing on the picturesque in the last decade, particularly in relation to consumerism, tourism, and political ideology. The following sources have been most helpful in this study: Malcolm Andrews, *The Search for the Picturesque: Landscape, Aesthetics, and Tourism in Britain, 1760–1800* (Stanford: Stanford University Press, 1989); Ann Bermingham, *Learning to Draw: Studies in the Cultural History of a Polite and Useful Art* (New Haven: Yale University Press, 2000), 77–126; Stephen Copley and Peter Garside, eds., *The Politics of the Picturesque: Literature, Landscape and Aesthetics Since 1770* (Cambridge: Cambridge University Press, 1994); Nigel Everett, *The Tory View of Landscape* (New Haven: Yale University Press, 1994); John Dixon Hunt, *Gardens and the Picturesque: Studies in the History of Landscape Architecture* (Cambridge: Harvard University Press, 1992) and *The Picturesque Garden in Europe*; Christopher Hussey, *The Picturesque: Studies in a Point of View* (London: Frank Cass and Company, Ltd., 1967); David Marshall, "The Problem of the Picturesque," *Eighteenth-Century Studies* 35, 3 (2002): 413–37; Kim Ian Michasiw, "Nine Revisionist Theses on the Picturesque," *Representations* 38 (1992): 76–100; Stephanie Moss, "Gardens and the Picturesque: Studies in the History of Landscape Architecture," *Journal of Aesthetics and Art Criticism* 52, 2 (1994): 252–4; Martin Price, "The Picturesque Moment," in *From Sensibility to Romanticism*, edited by Harold Bloom (New York: Oxford University Press, 1965); and Sidney K. Robinson, *Inquiry into the Picturesque* (Chicago: University of Chicago Press, 1991).

40. As Gilpin explains, the love of irregularity and masking of order or human contrivance helps explain the popularity of ruins in picturesque landscaping: "The solid, square, heavy form we dislike; and are pleased with the pyramidal one, which may be infinitely varied; and which ruin contributes to vary." Quoted in William D. Templeman's *The Life and Works of William Gilpin* (Urbana: Univ. of Illinois Press, 1939), 145.

41. Samuel Kliger, "Whig Aesthetics: A Phase of Eighteenth-Century Taste," *English Literary History* 16, 2 (1949): 135–150.

42. Washington Irving, *Christmas at Bracebridge Hall* (New York: David McKay, 1962). Quoted in Kliger, 138.

43. Joseph Addison, "No. 161," in *The Tatler,* ed. Donald F. Bond (Oxford: Clarendon Press, 1987), 398. According to Baridon, the equation of rectilinearity with tyranny and the serpentine curve as "the sinuous line of freedom" was widespread: "la ligne droite est le signe du despotisme; la ligne sinueuse, celle de la liberté. L'argument est caricatural mais c'est justement sa force" (Baridon, 812).

44. Filippo Pizzoni, *The Garden: A History in Landscape and Art* (New York: Rizzoli Press, 1999), 130–1. Cf. John Prest, *The Garden of Eden,* 94.

45. John Dixon Hunt, *The Picturesque Garden in Europe,* 151.

46. Humphry Repton, *A Letter to Uvedale Price, Esq.* (London: G. Nicol, 1794), 9.

47. James Thomson, *Liberty, a Poem* (Glasgow: Robert & Andrew Foulis, 1774), V.164–6, 681–2.

48. Marshall, "Problem of the Picturesque," 436 n.13.

49. Hunt uses this term derived from Diderot and Whately, among others.

50. *Genesis,* 11.1.

51. *Genesis*, 11.4.
52. *Genesis*, 11.5–8.
53. Hobbes, *Leviathan*, 33–34, my emphasis.
54. Sterne, *Journey*, 168.
55. Goethe, *Werther*, 58.
56. Jean-Jacques Rousseau, *Julie, ou la Nouvelle Héloïse* (Paris: Hachette, [1761] 1925), II.59.
57. *Man of Feeling*, 114–5.
58. Timothy Reiss, "Perioddity: Considerations on the Geography of Histories," *Modern Language Quarterly* 62, 4 (2001): 425–452.
59. Samuel Johnson, *The Idler* (London: J. Parsons, 1793), II.49–50.
60. Riskin does an excellent job of demonstrating the legacy of the Enlightenment at work in the culture of sensibility: Jessica Riskin, *Science in the Age of Sensibility: The Sentimental Empiricists of the French Enlightenment* (Chicago and London: University of Chicago Press, 2002).
61. James Thompson, *Between Self and World: The Novels of Jane Austen* (University Park: Pennsylvania State University Press, 1988), 92.
62. Cf. Hans Aarsleff, *The Study of Language in England, 1780–1860* (Minneapolis and London: University of Minnesota Press; Athlone Press, 1983) and Ralph Cohen, *Studies in Eighteenth-Century British Art Aesthetics* (Berkeley: University of California Press, 1985).
63. Joseph Addison, *Spectator* 416 (London: J. Bumpus Holburn-Bars, 1819 [June 27, 1712]).
64. William Wordsworth, "Lines Composed a Few Miles Above Tintern Abbey," lines 75–6. Cohen describes how the emphasis shifts from language's importance as representation of nature's order (waning at the turn of the eighteenth century), to an emphasis on language's role as expression of ideas (first half of the eighteenth century), to a concern primarily about the communication of feeling and the social context of language (second half of the eighteenth century). Aarsleff shows that similar changes occur in France and Germany as well as England; he describes the change in terms of changing ideas of "natural" and "artificial" language, an idea to which I return below. Martin Elskey also provides an illuminating study of changing attitudes towards language. Elskey focuses on the debates between Humanists and Scholastics beginning in the late Middle Ages, and draws interesting conclusions applicable to the conflict between speech and writing in later periods as well. Although he treats some eighteenth-century figures, he does not represent the specifically eighteenth-century debate and its permutations of the problematic relationship between speaking and writing, which must take into consideration the new moral psychology. Not considered in these and other studies of changing attitudes towards language is sensibility's corresponding moral psychology based on the newly elevated position of feeling.
65. Cf. Aarsleff, *Study*, 15–16. See also Foucault on "Classifying," in *The Order of Things: An Archaeology of the Human Sciences* (New York: Pantheon Books, 1971), 125–162. This is called the Adamic tradition, as it is based directly on the function of Adam's naming of animals in the King James *Genesis*: "And out of the ground the LORD God formed every beast of the field, and every fowl of the air; and brought *them* unto Adam to see what he would call them: and whatsoever Adam called every living creature, that *was* the name thereof" (*Genesis* 2.19).
66. There was neither separation of word and thing, sign and referent, nor of names and meanings: 'sentence' and 'sentiment' had not yet been divorced. As Foucault writes in his study of this document: "The fundamental task of classical 'discourse' is to *ascribe a name to things, and in that name to*

name their being . . . When it named the being of all representation in general, it was philosophy: theory of knowledge and analysis of ideas. When it ascribed to each thing represented the name that was fitted to it, and laid out the grid of a well-made language across the whole field of representation, then it was science—nomenclature and taxonomy" (Foucault, *The Order of Things*, 120).

67. "On ne sait pas encore, ce me semble, combien la langue est une image rigoureuse & fidèle de l'éxercice de la raison" [We do not yet know to what extent language is a rigorous and faithful image of the exercise of reason], writes one representative of this hybrid profession, Jean-Bapiste René Robinet, "Encyclopédie," in *Encyclopédie, ou Dictionnaire raisonné des sciences, des arts et des métiers,* ed. Jean-Baptiste René Robinet (Paris: Briasson, 1751–65), 5: NA9.

68. William V. Holtz, *Image and Immortality; a Study of Tristram Shandy* (Providence: Brown University Press, 1970), 61.

69. Locke also intimates the rise of the passions in authority by claiming that immediate sensory experience is much more effective than words for conveying the taste of pineapple, for example, or describing the shape of a horse: "He that thinks otherwise, let him try if any words can give him the taste of pine-apple, and make him have the true idea of the relish of that celebrated delicious fruit" (Locke, *Essay*, 424). The arbitrariness of words, names, or signs also casts further doubt on the referential power of language: "our distinguishing substances into species by their names, is not at all founded on their real essences; nor can we pretend to range and determine them exactly into species according to internal essential differences" (Locke, *Essay*, 449). One might speculate whether the practice of capitalizing nouns ended in English during the course of the eighteenth century partly because of increasing doubt about ostensive reference. Capitalizing nouns suggests a privileged status of the *naming of things* that never disappeared from German; it also suggests a parallel with proper nouns—that nouns for all persons, places, and things evoke equally specific, clear, and communicable referents as do proper nouns, like 'Samuel Johnson,' or 'Antigua.' The capitalization of nouns thus serves as visual tribute, it seems, to the Adamic tradition, which equates nouns with names.

70. Locke, *Essay*, 386.

71. Locke, *Essay*, 476.

72. Words, according to Locke, "interpose themselves so much between our Understandings, and the Truth, which it would contemplate and apprehend, that like the *Medium* through which visible Objects pass, their Obscurity and Disorder does not seldom cast a mist before our Eyes, and impose upon our Understanding," (Locke, *Essay*, 488). In fact it hearkens back to Hobbes, who wrote: "A man can have no thought, representing any thing, not subject to sense." In fact, there are many chapters in Hobbes where he demotes reason and language (logos), as well as the human pride of self-sufficiency. It is ironic that so much of late-eighteenth-century thought, while pretending to spurn him, is in a way accepting his assumptions and just challenging his conclusions regarding the need for centralized authority (Hobbes, *Leviathan*, 31–32).

73. Locke, *Essay*, 402.

74. Locke actually wanted an illustrated dictionary of natural science: "Words standing for things which are known and distinguished by their natural shapes should be expressed by little draughts and prints made of them" (Locke, *Essay*, 3.11).

75. Locke, *Essay*, 408.
76. Borrowing a term from Destutt de Tracy, Aarsleff writes, "in so far as words communicate adequately, they do so only because they are submitted to a constant process of 'rectification' in the social intercourse of speech" (Aarsleff, *From Locke*, 375–76). "I shall imagine I have done some service to truth, peace, and learning," Locke writes, "if, by any enlargement on this subject, I can make men reflect on their own use of language" (*Essay*, 436).
77. Étienne de Condillac, *Essai sur l'origine des connaissances humaines*" in *Œuvres* (Paris: Baudouin Freres, 1827, [1746]), I. 436b.
78. Condillac, *Essai sur l'origine des connaissances humaines*, in *Œuvres*, I. 403b.
79. Denis Diderot, *Lettre sur les sourds et muets*, in *Œuvres complètes de Diderot*, ed. J. Assezat (Paris: Garnier Frères, 1875), I. 369.
80. Diderot, *Lettre sur les sourds et muets*, in *Œuvres*, I. 369.
81. Van Sant makes excellent observations on the perceived opposition between narrative and sentiment within the culture of sensibility. Narrative coherence or continuity "exists in the reader's experience, not in narrative form. The episode becomes the height of narrative achievement, its immediate effect registered on the reader's interior structures . . . [P]lot is thus potentially undermined when sensibility governs narrative structure" (115–118).
82. Rousseau, *Second Discourse*, III.133.
83. Arthur M. Melzer, *The Natural Goodness of Man: On the System of Rousseau's Thought* (Chicago: University of Chicago Press, 1990), 280.
84. Rousseau, *Second Discourse*, III.133.
85. Melzer, *Natural Goodness*, 286–7.
86. Rousseau, *Second Discourse*, III.132–33.
87. Jean-Jacques Rousseau, *Essai sur l'origine des langues: ou il est parlé de la mélodie et de l'imitation musicale*, ed. Jean Starobinski (Paris: Gallimard, 1990), 65, 138.
88. See the following related passage: "L'amour, dit-on, fut l'inventeur du dessein. Il put inventer aussi la parole, mais moins heureusement; Peu content d'elle il la dédaigne, il a des maniéres plus vives de s'exprimer" (Rousseau, *Essai sur l'origine des langues*, 60). Such a hierarchy is arguably much older than Rousseau—at least as old as Vico. I am bracketing for further study the marked differences between this interpretation of Rousseau and Derrida's influential reading in *Grammatology*.
89. Rousseau, *Essai sur l'origine des langues*, 79.
90. Denis Diderot, "Le rêve de D'Alembert," in *Œuvres*, II.180–1.
91. Denis Diderot, "Pensées détachées sur la peinture," in *Œuvres*, XII.77.
92. Johann Gottfried Herder, *Abhandlung über den Ursprung der Sprache: Text, Materialien, Kommentar* (München: Reclam, 1983), 9.
93. Herder, *Abhandlung über den Ursprung der Sprache*, 6–7, my emphasis.
94. Murray Cohen documents this change in the popular linguistic writings of Britain—that is, where "words . . . come to function less referentially or logically and more affectively" (*Sensible Words: Linguistic Practice in England, 1640–1785* [Baltimore: Johns Hopkins University Press, 1977], 109).
95. John Herries, *The Elements of Speech* (London: E. and C. Dilly, 1773), 247.
96. Hugh Blair, *Lectures on Rhetoric and Belles Lettres* (Edinburgh: W. Strahan, T. Cadell, and W. Creech, 1783), I. 101.
97. Murray Cohen also notes a similar trend towards printed visualization, phonetic alphabets, and transcriptions of spoken language (Cohen, *Sensible Words*).
98. Locke also recommended visual aids, particularly for an illustrated dictionary of natural science: See note 74 above.

99. Thomas Sheridan, *A Course of Lectures on Elocution (1796)* (Delmar, New York: Scholars' Facsimiles & Reprints, 1991), x-xi.

100. Thomas Sheridan, *Lectures on the Art of Reading. In Two Parts: Containing Part I, The Art of Reading Prose and Part II, The Art of Reading Verse* (London: J. Dodsley and C. Dilly, 1787), 88.

101. Thomas Sheridan, *A Complete Dictionary of the English Language, Both with Regard to Sound and Meaning, One Main Object of Which Is, to Establish a Plain and Permanent Standard of Pronunciation: To Which Is Prefixed a Prosodial Grammar* (Dublin: Pat. Wogan and Pat. Byrne, 1790), lviii.

102. Blair, *Lectures on Rhetoric and Belles Lettres,* II. 231.

103. Hugh Blair, John Walker, John Herries, James Beattie, Adam Smith, Thomas Sheridan, Lord Monboddo, as well as Rousseau and Herder, all contributed to this heightened regard for natural language, whether it was by comparing modern language against ancient, European language against "primitive," human against animal, or prose against poetry. The natural in each case represents a past ideal from which we have degenerated. For Monboddo and Sheridan, the corruption is a fall from classical perfection; for Rousseau and Herder, it is the fall from a purer state of nature that is reenacted daily. Seen in this way, both Classicism and primitivism have their roots in the growing moral aesthetic of sensibility.

104. Blair, *Lectures on Rhetoric and Belles Lettres,* II. 232.

105. The analogous actress in France was Mlle. Clairon, who not only contributed Encyclopedia entries on aspects of acting, but also wrote an essay, after she had retired from the stage, condemning the exaggerated use of make-up in favor of more 'natural' pantomime of expressions. See Kirsten Gram Holmström, *Monodrama, Attitudes, Tableaux Vivants: Studies on Some Trends of Theatrical Fashion, 1770–1815* (Stockholm: Almkvist and Wiksell, 1967), 28.

106. Smith, *Theory of Moral Sentiments,* ed. D.D. Raphael and A.L. Macfie (Indianapolis: Liberty Press, 1982), 9.

107. Smith, *Theory of Moral Sentiments,* 11.

108. Samuel Jackson Pratt, *Sympathy, a Poem* (London: T. Cadell, 1781), II.55.

109. Sheridan, *A Course of Lectures on Elocution,* 121.

110. Sheridan, *A Course of Lectures on Elocution,* 136.

111. For a modern comparison, consider usage of emoticons such as :) and :(in contemporary e-mail messages, attempting to ensure that tone is transmitted correctly to counterbalance ambiguity—or rather to "fix" the affect of the written word.

112. Sheridan, *A Course of Lectures on Elocution,* 120–121.

113. Sheridan, *A Course of Lectures on Elocution,* 147–154.

114. Sterne, *Journey,* 162.

115. There is a similar claim in relation to landscape viewing in the picturesque style: that the appreciation of picturesque views requires a "picturesque eye." Once again, such claims raise the vexed issue of whether sensibility's moral aesthetic relies on naturally occurring abilities or ones that need careful cultivation.

116. Laurence Sterne, *The Sermons of Mr. Yorick* (Stratford-upon-Avon: Shakespeare Head Press, 1927), II. 239–40.

117. Victor Lange describes a simultaneous faith in and doubting of the powers of language among authors of the late-eighteenth-century cult of sensibility; he claims that they were "deeply committed" to "all the rhetorical strategies of speech" and yet "return again and again to the haunting experience of linguistic insufficiency" (Victor Lange, "The Metaphor of Silence," in *Goethe Revisited: A Collection of Essays,* edited by Elizabeth Wilkinson [London and New York: Calder, Riverrun, 1984], 133).

118. Sterne, *Journey,* 277–8. The idea of God as "omnipotent awareness infinitely extended through time and space" and "the motion of the universe as a divine 'sensorium' had been put forward by Newton, discussed vigorously in the Clarke-Leibniz correspondence, and commented upon at length by Addison in the *Spectator,* no. 565" (Brissenden, *Virtue in Distress,* 48). Hagstrum also points out that Hartley anticipates Sterne by deriving the term from Newton as well: Jean H. Hagstrum, *Sex and Sensibility: Ideal and Erotic Love from Milton to Mozart* (Chicago: University of Chicago Press, 1980). See also Christopher Nagle, "Sterne, Shelley and Sensibility's Pleasure of Proximity," *ELH* 70, 3 (Fall, 2003), 840, n.4. In the passage from Sterne, it is not clear whether the "Sensorium" is another name for God the creator, or whether it is a name for the internal physiological sources of individual sensibility.
119. "Are not two sparrows sold for a farthing? And one of them shall not fall on the ground without your Father. But the very hairs on your head are numbered. Fear ye not therefore, ye are of more value than many sparrows," *The Gospel according to St. Matthew* 10.30, King James version.

NOTES TO CHAPTER 2

1. Quoted in Nicolson, *Mountain Gloom,* 319.
2. Macaulay, *Pleasure,* 100.
3. Goldstein, *Ruins and Empire,* 5.
4. Marcia Allentuck uses the term to mean the artistically and intentionally unfinished: "In Defense of an Unfinished *Tristram Shandy:* Laurence Sterne and the Non Finito," in *The Winged Skull,* ed. Arthur H. Cash (Kent: Kent State University Press, 1971), 147. See also Eric Rothstein, "'Ideal Presence' and the 'Non Finito' in Eighteenth-Century Aesthetics," *Eighteenth-Century Studies* 9, 3 (1976): 308.
5. Cf. Rothstein, "Ideal Presence," 309; Michael Fried, *Absorption and Theatricality.*
6. "Pourquoi une belle esquisse nous plaît-elle plus qu'un beau tableau? C'est qu'il y a plus de vie et moins de formes. A mesure qu'on introduit les formes, la vie disparaît" (Denis Diderot, "Salon of 1767," in Œuvres, XI. 245).
7. See also Hussey for the crucial importance of irregularity to the cult of the picturesque, 211 ff.
8. Gilpin, *Three Essays,* 49–50.
9. Hussey, *The Picturesque,* 24.
10. In an 1804 letter quoted in Macauley, 192–93.
11. Diderot, "Salon of 1767," in Œuvres, XI. 227. Famous literal examples include Hubert Robert's painting of the Louvre in ruins and William Chambers' plans for a mausoleum for the Prince of Wales. See Sophie Thomas, "Assembling History: Fragments and Ruins," *European Romantic Review* 14, 2 (2003): 183.
12. Thomas Whately, *Observations on Modern Gardening, Illustrated by Descriptions* (London: T. Payne and Son, 1777), 132.
13. Gilpin, *Three Essays,* I. 7–8.
14. Whately, *Observations,* 72, 131.
15. Whately, *Observations,* 134.
16. For a discussion of the "cult of the colossal" in France, see Hussey, 200.
17. With the notable exception of Erwin Panofsky's article "Et in Arcadia Ego" and a few intimations in Robert Rosenblum's *Transformations in Late Eighteenth Century Art* (Princeton, N.J.: Princeton University Press, 1967), 112–115, cultural historians and literary critics have tended artificially to

isolate one or the other of these aspects of ruins, thereby ignoring their inherent multivalence. Goldstein claims that the eighteenth-century fascination with ruins is due to "an undeniable mania for physical representations of decay" (Goldstein, 3). I think, however, that this is inaccurate. Unlike the later Romantic fascination with general decay and crumbling peasant-cottages (which Jane Austen parodies so well through Marianne Dashwood), the interest in ruins in the 1760s and 1770s was not an interest in decay *an sich*, but rather was dependent upon this juxtaposition of the monumental and the ruined, which uniquely corresponded with ambivalent attitudes towards authority.

18. "Many works of the ancients have become fragments. Many modern works are fragments as soon as they are written" (August Wilhelm von Schlegel and Friedrich von Schlegel, *Athenaeum, eine Zeitschrift* [Berlin: Bey F. Vieweg dem Älteren, 1798], Fragment No. 24).

19. Susan Buck-Morss, *The Dialectics of Seeing: Walter Benjamin and the Arcades Project* (Cambridge and London: MIT Press, 1989), 212.

20. Cf. Elizabeth Wanning Harries, *The Unfinished Manner: Essays on the Fragment in the Later Eighteenth Century* (Charlottesville: University Press of Virginia, 1994), 85. See also Thomas, *Assembling History,* for a description of "the ways in which ruins function more generally and reveal aspects of the ruin's necessarily *constructed* relationship to questions of history, and its importance in the creation of the present" (181 ff.)

21. Jacques-François Blondel, *Cours d'architecture, ou traité de la decoration, distribution & construction des bâtiments; contenant les leçons données en 1750, & les années suivantes* (Paris: Desaint, 1771–1777), 373.

22. Blondel, *Cours,* 411, 413, 418.

23. Claude Nicolas Ledoux, *L'Architecture considérée sous le rapport de l'art, des moeurs, et de la législation* (Paris: Hermann, 1997), 11.

24. Ledoux, *L'Architecture,* 14.

25. G. L. Hersey, "Associationism and Sensibility in Eighteenth-Century Architecture," *Eighteenth-Century Studies* 4, 1 (1970): 75.

26. Quoted in Hersey, 75 and 89.

27. See Louise Pelletier "Nicolas Le Camus de Mézières's Architecture of Expression, and the Theater of Desire at the End of the Ancien Régime; or the Analogy of Fiction with Architectural Innovation", (Ph.D. diss., McGill School of Architecture, 2000).

28. In Rousseau, too, we can find the philosophical analogy to this spectatorly and sympathetic interaction with ruins. Civilization, according to Rousseau's portrayal, is a ruin; it is always incomplete, unsettled, and unsatisfactory because it is located—not temporally, but ontologically—between the perfect satisfaction of "l'homme sauvage" and the utopian, moral, rational society that we can imagine. One of the primary goals of the *Second Discourse* is to awaken readers to the fundamental fragmentation of their condition and to encourage us to envision the better state accessible through our imagination. He draws our attention to our ruined state, enlists our human *perfectibilité,* and invites us to complete the monument. Therefore, even though Rousseau's emphasis is on the catastrophic side of the story, the recognition of failure (just as with Smith and Hume) is not the end, but instead a point of departure. It represents another of sensibility's compensatory successes that rely upon a more foundational sense of failure.

29. Robert Lugar, *Architectural Sketches for Cottages, Rural Dwellings, and Villas, in the Grecian, Gothic, and Fancy Styles, with Plans, Suitable to Persons of Genteel Life and Moderate Fortune* (London: J. Taylor, 1805), 23.

30. William Gilpin, *Observations on Several Parts of England, Particularly the Mountains and Lakes of Cumberland and Westmoreland, Relative Chiefly to Picturesque Beauty, Made in the Year 1772* (London, 1808), 73, 74.

31. Edward Stephens, *A Poem on the Park and Woods of the Right Hon. Allen Lord Bathurst* (Cirencester: printed for the author, 1748), 8–9.

32. Saint Preux uses this quotation from Marini in a letter describing Julie in Rousseau's *Julie, ou la nouvelle Héloïse.*

33. Blair, *Lectures on Rhetoric and Belles Lettres,* II. 510.

34. It is true that many of these verbs could apply to sculpture as well as architecture (cf. Cleanth Brooks and "well-wrought" urns); however, as the Tower of Babel illustrates and Locke suggests in his writings, language is more than an artifact that we admire upon a shelf or in a display case. We inhabit language, just as we imaginatively and temporarily inhabit the world which the reader helps the novelist 'build.'

35. For thorough discussion of the difficult and much debated question of which techniques Goethe adopted from Sterne and which arose independently out of a similar philosophy and aesthetic, see Wilhelm Robert Richard Pinger, *Laurence Sterne and Goethe, University of California Publications in Modern Philology* (Berkeley: University of California Press, 1920), X.1.

36. For a discussion of the semiotics of Werther's clothing, see Daniel L. Purdy, *The Tyranny of Elegance: Consumer Cosmopolitanism in the Era of Goethe* (Baltimore: Johns Hopkins University Press, 1998). My thanks to Eric Downing for this suggestion.

37. Sterne, *Tristram Shandy,* 3.20, my emphasis; Sterne, *Journey,* 134. This is not to say that this treatment is absent in *Tristram:* the silently sentimental scenes with uncle Toby work in much the same way as *Journey.* It is striking that precisely those scenes were the ones in *Tristram* which received the most critical acclaim. For this reason, Sterne's later novel is more useful for the themes pursued here. *Journey* became a symbol of the cult of sensibility, partly because Sterne self-consciously tried to make it match the public taste for sentimentality.

38. My thanks to the late Saul Bellow for his insight on this issue. There is no hint of such sentimentalism or nostalgia in Locke, unlike what John Sitter has suggested in referring to Locke's "nostalgia for things and ideas untouched by words" (Sitter, 156). Sitter is applying a later nostalgic interpretation to Locke's conclusions. (See Nuttall, Chapter One, for a discussion of the discrepancies between Locke's view of his own work and later perspectives.) For a perceptive analysis of the often exaggerated influence of Locke on Sterne, see Mullan, *Sentiment and Sociability,* 164–170.

39. Sterne, *Journey,* 217–218, my emphasis. Cf. also Laurence Sterne, *The Sermons of Mr. Yorick,* II. 239–40: "Nature has assigned a different tone, look of voice, and gesture, peculiar to every passion and affection we are subject to . . . We are not angels, but men cloathed with bodies, and, in some measure, governed by our imaginations, that we have need of all these external helps which nature has made the interpreters of our thoughts."

40. Sterne, *Journey,* 159.

41. With the eventual over-codification of sensibility, they do, in effect, become laws and bring themselves to an end.

42. Sterne, *Journey,* 205–6 and notes. This is the scene to which Austen alludes in *Mansfield Park,* chapter 10, during the visit to Sotherton. Maria complains: "But unluckily that iron gate, that ha-ha, give me a feeling of restraint and hardship. 'I cannot get out,' as the starling said." See Brodey, "Papas and Hahas: Authority, Rebellion, and Landscape Gardening in Mansfield Park," *Persuasions* 17 (December 1995): 90–96, for further treatment of the role of the ha-ha and reference to Sterne in this scene.

43. This is parallel to the emphasis on potential energy in Lessing's *Laokoön*. Painting, Lessing writes, can transcend a given moment in time by imitating bodies at their most "pregnant moment": "aus welchem das Vorhergehende und Folgende am begreiflichsten wird" (G. E. Lessing, *Laokoön,* ed. Hugo Blümner [Berlin: Weidmannsche, 1880], 251). See also Rothstein, "Ideal Presence," 317–18.

44. Sterne, *Journey,* 256.

45. For further discussion of Sterne's use of dashes, see Wolfgang Iser, *Laurence Sterne: Tristram Shandy,* (Cambridge and New York: Cambridge University Press, 1988), 61, and for Sterne's punctuation in general, see R. B. Moss, "Sterne's Punctuation," *Eighteenth-Century Studies* 15, 2 1981–1982): 179–200.

46. "The comic use of association, Lockean or otherwise, is usually taken as Sterne's chief way of attacking logic," Frank Brady, "Tristram Shandy: Sexuality, Morality, and Sensibility," *Eighteenth-Century Studies* 4.1 (Autumn, 1970): 47. But the sentence structure also attacks logic and the hegemony of unaided reason, just as it attacks Cartesian dualism.

47. Cf. Holtz, 63.

48. Quoted in Aarsleff, *From Locke to Saussure,* 157.

49. Denis Diderot, *Lettre sur les sourds et muets,* in *Œuvres,* I. 369.

50. Even Addison admitted that "colors speak all languages, but words are understood only by such a people or nation" (Addison, 159).

51. Yorick's feelings dictate the pace, as well as content, of the novel. When he first meets LaFleur, Yorick sees him advance three steps: "from that single *trait,* I knew his character as perfectly, and could rely on it as firmly, as if he had served me with fidelity for seven years." The movements of Yorick's heart, which determine all his actions, cannot be measured by the clock, any more than his feelings could be expressed in conventional essay form. After several chapters and at least two sentimental episodes, all of which take place in Calais, "Lord!" Yorick exclaims, "hearing the town clock strike four," and recollects "that [he] had been little more than an hour in Calais—" (Sterne, *Journey,* 193). Time can expand or shrink depending upon the affections of the heart; and while this in itself is not a new observation, Sterne devises syntax and narrative structure that ensure the reader intimately follows the beating of Yorick's heart.

    On time and the rapidity of "sentimental commerce," see Stout's note, 91–92, on Sterne's letter to Elizabeth Vesey (Letters, No. 76, June [?1761], 137–138). For a discussion of Sterne's indebtedness to Locke's analysis of duration, see John Traugott, *Tristram Shandy's World: Sterne's Philosophical Rhetoric* (Berkeley: University of California Press, 1954), 34ff. On Sterne's portrayal of time, see also Jonathan Lamb, *Sterne's Fiction and the Double Principle* (Cambridge and New York: Cambridge University Press, 1989), and Stuart Sherman, *Telling Time: Clocks, Diaries, and English Diurnal Form, 1660–1785* (Chicago: University of Chicago Press, 1996).

    It may not be inappropriate to draw the analogy to the pocket watch, which had just been appearing in the years before Sterne wrote *Journey.* The pocket watch not only creates "private" time—a portable, personal authority compared to the clock on the church tower in the town square—but it is also worn on the chest. Its position, together with the ticking sound, make it analogous to the heart. Yorick's private pace is guided by the beating of his own heart, and external time is irrelevant to his progress.

52. Note also that some points extend into the past or future, suggesting anti-chronological narration; in the bottom left corner, there is also a reference to Hogarth's serpentine line of beauty.

53. Sterne, *Journey*, 80, my emphasis.
54. If there were straight segments in an analogous graph for Werther in his eponymous novel, they would be the digressions that cruelly distract him from the wanderings of his heart. Werther, too, is an author and has similar dual roles to Yorick, yet his letters do not attempt to form a sustained narrative: his goal is authentic representation of a series of immediate moments.
55. For Werther, in contrast, interruption forces a return to his authorial role—and to his unwanted self-consciousness.
56. Sterne, *Journey*, 73.
57. Harries, *Unfinished Manner*, 26–7.
58. Rousseau, *First Discourse*, III.8.
59. Sterne, *Tristram Shandy*, I.82, quoted in Van Sant, 60–62.
60. Sterne, *Journey*, 189.
61. Sterne, *Journey*, 168, my emphasis. We return in the next chapter to the irony of Yorick's last claim, considering he has just "swollen" his own page.
62. Mullan, *Sentiment and Sociability*, 171.
63. Sterne, *Journey*, 171–2.
64. Mullan, *Sentiment and Sociability*, 171.
65. See Mullan, *Sentiment and Sociability*, 170–71, for an excellent description of this effect in *Tristram Shandy*.
66. William V. Holtz, *Image and Immortality; A Study of Tristram Shandy* (Providence: Brown University Press, 1970), 41–59.
67. It is interesting that just as the French gardener is presumed guilty of excessive artificiality in gardening, the English philosopher is presumed guilty of excess ratiocination in philosophy.
68. Sterne, *Journey*, 96–7.
69. Sterne, *Journey*, 107, 124, my emphasis.
70. The revised rules of rhetoric which accompany the moral aesthetic of sensibility signify a recognition that speech is indispensable for public use as well as that it is not only inherently flawed, but also inevitably abused. The late-eighteenth-century linguists wish to discard nomenclature, syntax, and the tyranny of explanation, while still expressing a longing for order, taxonomy, and rules of rhetoric. As a result of these contradictory impulses, authors frequently use the terms of the model they are replacing: Sterne and others make reference to terms such as 'the grammar of sentiment,' 'the syntax of feeling,' or 'the logic of feeling,' suggesting that feeling, accent, tone, and gesture can be systematized as well as words in a dictionary.
71. Sterne, *Journey*, 108, 102. It is constructive to compare this technique with the opening of *Tom Jones*, for example, where names and descriptions of each character precede their words and actions. For Fielding, names and descriptions hamper identification neither *of* nor *with* the characters.
72. Sterne, *Journey*, 220–223.
73. Sterne, *Journey*, 115.
74. Cf. Holtz, 135–37.
75. Sterne, *Journey*, 270, 271.
76. This passage is in all likelihood a self-conscious echo of the Rousseauan phrase "je sens, donc je suis." See also Austen's *Love and Freindship* where a "sensible, well informed man" has "no soul" because he "had never read the sorrows of Werter" (Austen, *Minor Works*, 93, my emphasis). Cf. also Shaftesbury's interpretation of the Delphic inscription: "Recognize yourself; which was as much to say, divide yourself, or be two," in *Characteristics* (Basil, 1790), I.2.147. Self-knowledge, according to Shaftesbury, requires a "self-examining practice and method of inward colloquy" (*Characteristics*,

I.3.282). We see the same emphasis upon an internal conversation in Adam Smith's *Theory of Moral Sentiments*.

77. For a somewhat different interpretation of the skull metaphor, see Lamb, 108.

78. "The failure of linguistic communication," Iser writes, "is only a step towards a new discovery: a semiotics of the body, which represents a final link between self and the world" (Iser, *Laurence Sterne*, 45).

79. Interestingly, Sterne employs a similar technique for exegesis in his sermons. In *Sermon XX* on *Luke* 15 and the prodigal son, Sterne exemplifies the act of sympathetic reading, emotively entering into the complaints of both father and son, and drawing a visual tableau for his parishioners, down to specific details of gestures and nerves: "——I see the picture of [the prodigal son's] departure:—the camels and asses loaden with his substance, detached on one side of the piece, and already on their way:——the prodigal son standing on the fore ground, with a forced sedateness, struggling against the fluttering movement of joy, upon his deliverance from restraint:——the elder brother holding his hand as if unwilling to let it go:——the father,——sad moment! with a firm look . . ." Laurence Sterne, *The Complete Works of Laurence Sterne*, ed. David Herbert (Edinburgh: William P. Nimmo, 1872), 312.

80. Henry Fielding, *The History of Tom Jones, a Foundling* (London: A. Millar, 1749), IV.64. Also cited in Holtz, 42–44.

81. Swift, *Tale*, 100.

82. See Martin C. Battestin, *The Providence of Wit* (Oxford: Clarendon Press 1974), 215–69, on the distinction between Swift and Sterne.

83. Richardson also inserted a musical score into the pages of *Clarissa*, to ensure that the experience of the novel could be carried forth beyond its pages. For an analysis of Richardson's paratextual innovations, see Janine Barchas, "The Engraved Score in *Clarissa*: An Intersection of Music, Narrative, and Graphic Design," *Eighteenth-Century Life* 20, 2 (1996): 1–20.

84. Brissenden, *Virtue in Distress*, 122.

85. Henry Mackenzie, *Letters to Elizabeth Rose of Kilravock* (Münster: Verlag Aschendorff, 1967), 5 July 1769, 16.

86. In a letter of August 15, Werther shows that even *poetic* improvement will not justify alteration of original expressions, suggesting that the moral considerations of authenticity are ultimately of greater importance than the aesthetic, tipping the scale irretrievably toward ruination. Society's eternal search for the "better word" or for grammatical or syntactic completion destroys the immediacy of experience (Goethe, *Werther*, 61, 51).

87. Goethe, *Werther*, 18.

88. Goethe, *Werther*, 73.

89. Alexander Pope, "Eloisa to Abelard," in *Letters of Abelard and Heloise, to Which is Prefix'd a Particular Account of Their Lives, Amours, and Misfortunes by the Late John Hughes, Esq. To Which Is Now First Added, the Poem of Eloisa to Abelard by Mr Pope* (London: W. Johnston, B. Law, T. Lownds, and T. Caslon, 1765), 180.

90. Goethe, *Werther*, 19.

91. Goethe, *Werther*, 82.

92. Goethe, *Werther*, 38.

93. Goethe, *Werther*, 27.

94. Mackenzie, *Man of Feeling*, 96. This exemplifies Peter Brooks' psychoanalytic reading of narrative, where it is at the moment of death that narrative becomes transmissible: *Reading for the Plot: Design and Intention in Narrative* (Cambridge: Harvard University Press, 1993), 28.

95. Goethe, *Werther*, 117.

96. Goethe, *Werther,* 83.
97. "What [others] feel, will, indeed, always be, in some respects, different from what he feels, and compassion can never be exactly the same with original sorrow; because the secret consciousness that the change of situations, from which the sympathetic sentiment arises, is but imaginary, not only lowers it in degree, but, in some measure, varies it in kind, and gives it a quite different modification. These two sentiments, however, may, it is evident, have such a correspondence with one another, as is sufficient for the harmony of society. Though they will never be unisons, they may be concords, and this is all that is wanted or required" (Smith, *Theory of Moral Sentiments,* I.I.36).
98. See Marshall, "Problem of the Picturesque," 414.
99. Cox, *"Stranger within Thee",* 45.
100. David Marshall, *The Surprising Effects of Sympathy: Marivaux, Diderot, Rousseau, and Mary Shelley* (Chicago: University of Chicago Press, 1988), 181.
101. David Hume, *A Treatise of Human Nature,* ed. L. A. Selby-Bigge and P.H. Nidditch (Oxford and New York: Clarendon Press; Oxford University Press, [1739–40] 1978), 363.
102. Rousseau, *Second Discourse,* III.155.
103. Rousseau, *Second Discourse,* III.156.
104. Goethe, *Werther,* 38.
105. Goethe, *Werther,* 19.
106. Sterne, *Journey,* 92.
107. Goethe, *Werther,* 28.
108. Goethe, *Werther,* 55.
109. Goethe, *Werther,* 100.
110. For the definition of a monodrama, see Holmström, *Monodrama, Attitudes, Tableaux Vivants,* 40–41. Rousseau invented the genre with his one-act play *Pygmalion,* written in 1763, and first performed in 1770. The monodrama, as invented by Rousseau, is a combination of drama, musical score, recitation, and pantomime. A "phrase musicale" introduces every "phrase parlée" to compensate for the failing of spoken language, and in moments of extreme emotion, all words cease, and instead pantomime set to a musical score ensues.
111. See comments by Keats and Hazlitt in *Sterne: The Critical Heritage,* ed. Alan B. Howes (London: Routledge & Kegan Paul, 1974).
112. Sterne, *Journey,* 13.
113. Stephen Cox writes about the "education of [self-] consciousness" in readers and authors of sensibility, who measure their own emotional responses against an ideal. He gives the example of Burke, who "was proud that he could pass the test of his own description of the suffering queen of France: 'Tears came again into my Eyes almost as often as I looked at the description. They may again'" (Stephen D. Cox, *"The Stranger within Thee,"* 68).
114. Sterne, *Journey,* 181.
115. Cf. Sterne, *Journey,* 207 n. 19–20; 181 n. 34–35.
116. Sterne, *Journey,* 167.
117. Sterne, *Journey,* 90, my emphasis.
118. Sterne, *Journey,* 147: "[T]hought and self-analysis," as Todd writes, "are dramatized and externalized" in *Journey* (Todd, 107).
119. Goethe, *Werther,* 77.
120. Goethe, *Werther,* 44, my emphasis.
121. Deirdre Vincent also finds similar importance in Werther's growing awareness of his inescapable, but impotent, rationality: "the conflict is actually intensified by his new clarity; this rational self asserts its existence and its

helplessness here at one and the same time" (*Werther's Goethe and the Game of Literary Creativity* [Toronto; Buffalo, N.Y.: University of Toronto Press, 1992], 155).

122. Diderot, *Supplément,* in *Œuvres,* II. 246–7.
123. Goethe, *Werther,* 87.
124. Goethe, *Werther,* 75, 10.
125. Goethe, *Werther,* 48.
126. Lionel Trilling, *Sincerity and Authenticity* (Cambridge: Harvard University Press, 1972), 51.
127. Cf. Cox, "*The Stranger within Thee,*" 53–54.
128. Nicholas Boyle seems to be thinking of just such a distinction when he describes the difference between the English and German forms of sentimentalism. He claims that the English were primarily influenced by Locke and therefore focused on "a philosophical concern with the knowledge our sensibility might provide about things and minds other than ourselves" and subsequently cared about its overt manifestations, social consequences, and social penalties, while the Germans, in Leibnizian fashion, focused on a "philosophical concern with the unity of the soul" and on the inner processes of sensibility which lead to isolation and destruction (Boyle, *Goethe: The Poet and the Age* [Oxford and New York: Oxford University Press, 1991], I.32).
129. Goethe, *Werther,* 76.
130. Shaftesbury, *Characteristics* (Basil, 1790), I.2.147, I.3.282.

NOTES TO CHAPTER 3

1. Patricia Meyer Spacks also relates the presence of fragmentation to a distrust of centralized authority and provides explicit historical events that could have stimulated or encouraged this distrust. The use of "fragmentary structure [. . .] reflect[s] a troubled and troubling social situation, thus enabling the development of the sentimental novel" (Spacks, *Novel Beginnings,* 282–283). Other abuses and abusers of authority in her account include Tory landholders, the moneyed middle classes, the burst of the South Sea bubble, the American colonies, and the British "natural" dominion over France. These abuses are reflected in falsified and borrowed letters and documents in the novels of sensibility (Spacks, *Novel Beginnings,* 147–151).
2. There is an interesting parallel in late-eighteenth-century landscape images: lateral perspectives tended to replace the bird's-eye view that had dominated seventeenth-century depiction of landscape. Accordingly, landscapes too are portrayed to deemphasize a hierarchical universe, replacing centralized authority with greater importance on individuals' subjective experiences, just as novels make a shift from an impartial narrator's objective view to protagonists' psychological subjective views, shared more directly with the reader.
3. Henry Mackenzie, *Letters to Elizabeth Rose of Kilravock on Literature, Events, and People 1768–1815,* ed. Horst W. Drescher (Münster: Verlag Aschendorff, 1967), 29.
4. The term authorship carries religious connotations that affect its later history. There was a tradition of referring to God as an author, such as in Addison's "Supreme Author of our being" (*Essays in Criticism and Literary Theory,* ed. John Loftis [Northbrook, Illinois: A.H.M. Publishing, 1975]) or in Hobbes' Preface to *Leviathan,* where he describes his own authorship, as well as a king's authority over a state, as microcosms of God's authorship of the Book of Nature.

5. Uvedale Price, *An Essay on the Picturesque, as Compared with the Sublime and the Beautiful* (London: J. Robson, 1796–8), I. 344–45.
6. Warton, *An Essay on the Genius and Writings of Pope* (London, 1782): II, 165.
7. Richard Payne Knight, *The Landscape: A Didactic Poem in Three Books Addressed to Uvedale Price, Esqu.*, 2nd ed. (London, 1795), 48 n. (Also quoted in Michasiw.)
8. Michasiw, "Nine Revisionist Theses," 83. Michasiw's concern is whether accident can be subsumed under rule, and therefore expected or anticipated by the viewer. Or does accident always challenge the viewer's ability to create a cohesive whole? Does accident rely on viewers' noticing its non-conformity?
9. Whately, *Observations*, 132. In this regard, Tintern Abbey is an especially effective model for building follies, according to Whately: "if any parts are entirely lost, they should be such as the imagination can easily supply from those which are still remaining. Distinct traces of the building which is supposed to have existed, are less liable to the suspicion of artifice, than an unmeaning heap of confusion. Precision is always satisfactory; but in the reality it is only agreeable; in the copy, it is essential to the imitation" (Whately, *Observations*, 134). Precision, a word so inimical to the anti-analytic fervor associated with the culture of sensibility, is here invoked again to ensure the highly artificial success of the natural, showing the paradoxical stance or dual impulses involved in the building of follies.
10. In addition, Sterne tauntingly passes the responsibility for the bawdiness of his jokes from himself to Yorick to the reader. The most famous technique of such fragmentation is Sterne's use of aposiopesis, such as the last lines of *Journey:* "So that when I stretch'd out my hand, I caught hold of the Fille de Chambre's —END—" (*Journey*, 291).
11. This crucial issue of Sterne's writing and the cult of sensibility in general has received surprisingly little critical attention. The best treatment of this subject is to be found in Mullan, *Sentiment and Sociability* (e.g. 171).
12. Sterne, *Tristram Shandy*, 83.
13. Northrop Frye, in his pioneering article on "Sensibility," identifies its emphasis on revealing the process of creation, rather than just the result, as its most characteristic feature. This notion of "process" and participation applies equally well to the picturesque landscapes.
14. For an illuminating contrast, see Austen's *Emma*, where the fragmented, unclear speeches of Mr. Elton characterize him as a hypocrite.
15. Sterne, *Journey*, 234–335.
16. Sterne, *Tristram Shandy*, 3.31.
17. Mullan, *Sentiment and Sociability*, 182.
18. Victor Lange, "The Metaphor of Silence," in *Goethe Revisited: A Collection of Essays*, ed. Elizabeth Wilkinson (London and New York: Calder, Riverrun, 1984), 137.
19. Goethe, *Werther*, 15.
20. Rousseau, *First Discourse*, III.8.
21. Hagstrum, *Sex and Sensibility*, 261.
22. Goethe, *Werther*, 75.
23. Goethe expresses a similar sentiment in a letter to Charlotte von Stein, dated January 9, 1779: "Einen guten Morgen von Ihren stummen Nachbar. Das Schweigen ist so schön dass ich wünschte es Jahre lang halten zu dürfen." Like Werther, Goethe here longs for the perpetuation of his state of mind and of silence. Such passages (despite their epistolary context) suggest that emotional authenticity is of greater importance than intimacy or communication.
24. Goethe, *Werther*, 92.

25. Goethe, *Werther,* 9, 41, my emphasis.
26. Iser, *Laurence Sterne,* 56.
27. Sterne, *Journey,* 168, my emphasis.
28. Virginia Woolf, "Introduction," in *A Sentimental Journey through France and Italy* (London: Oxford University Press, 1965), xiv.
29. Spacks, *Privacy,* 83.
30. Mackenzie, *Man of Feeling,* 113.
31. Mackenzie, *Man of Feeling,* 115, my emphasis.
32. One could protest that it is not this overwhelming "grammophobia" that prevents Harley from declaring his love to Miss Walton, but instead her superior social status. I would argue, however, that these two points are inseparable: since he believes in the superiority of natural aristocracy—or aristocracy of feeling—it is not that he deems himself hopelessly unworthy, but rather that in both cases, he fears that it is impossible for nature to win in the battle with artifice and societal convention.
33. Mackenzie, *Man of Feeling,* 113.
34. Mackenzie, *Man of Feeling,* 69.
35. Mackenzie, *Man of Feeling,* 105.
36. Swift also uses two fictional narrative frames in *Tale of a Tub* (the "Hack's" and the "Editor's") to "explain" the omissions in the text: "Here is pretended a defect in the manuscript; and this is very frequent with our author either when he thinks he cannot say any thing worth reading, or when he has no mind to enter on the subject, or when it is a matter of little moment; or perhaps to amuse his reader (whereof he is frequently very fond) or lastly, with some satirical intention." Swift's fictional authors openly draw attention to and acknowledge the artifice involved in these pretended "Defects"—they are not due to external, Hobbesian, unfeeling forces.
37. Samuel Richardson, *The History of Charles Grandison* (Oxford and New York: Oxford University Press, 1986), 4.
38. Samuel Richardson, *Clarissa, or the History of a Young Lady* (Harmondsworth, Middlesex, England: Viking and Penguin, 1985), 35–6.
39. For more on Richardson's didactic use of paratexts, see Janine Barchas, "*Grandison*'s Grandeur as Printed Book: A Look at the Eighteenth-Century Novel's Quest for Status," *Eighteenth-Century Fiction* 14, 3/4 (2002): 673–714.
40. "I intended to have arranged them alphabetically, till I found the stories of *Le Fever,* the *Monk,* and *Maria,* would be too closely connected for the *feeling reader,* and would wound the bosom of *sensibility* too deeply: I therefore placed them at a proper distance from each other" (*The Beauties of Sterne: Including all his Pathetic Tales, and Most Distinguished Observations on Life, Selected for the Heart of Sensibility* [London, printed for T. Davies et al, 1782], viii). This example is cited in Van Sant, 52.
41. Henry Mackenzie, *Julia de Roubigné, a Tale in a Series of Letters* (London: W. Strahan, T. Cadell, 1777), II.v.
42. Mackenzie, *Julia de Roubigné,* II.vii.
43. Jean-Jacques Rousseau, *Les Confessions,* in *Œuvres Complètes,* ed. Bernard Gagnebin and Marcel Raymond (Paris: Gallimard, 1959), I. 431.
44. Diana Ketcham, *Le Désert De Retz: A Late Eighteenth-Century French Folly Garden, the Artful Landscape of Monsieur De Monville* (Cambridge and London: MIT Press, 1994), 3–4.
45. Ketcham, *Désert,* 7.
46. Ketcham, *Désert,* 6–7. While the tower certainly bears suggestions of ancient grandeur, and the ruins are magnificent enough to inspire the imagination and feeling to complete the imaginary monument, Ketcham has argued that

Monville's Column House reverses the usual role of the picturesque, not enhancing the viewer's sense of physical and intellectual power, but rather forcing upon the viewer a sense of smallness, insignificance, and even terror.

47. See Rosenblum's interesting discussion of the *tabula rasa* mentality of this period, an ambivalent attitude towards authority that evinces itself in the simultaneously constructive and destructive impulses of the French Revolution (Rosenblum, *Transformations in Late Eighteenth Century Art*, 146–91).

48. It is interesting in this regard that Goethe destroys the drafts of *Die Wahlverwandtschaften* in order to conceal the structure of the work.

49. Michael Riffaterre, *Text Production* (New York: Columbia University Press, 1983), 155–6.

50. Wayne C. Booth, "The Self-Conscious Narrator in Comic Fiction before *Tristram Shandy*," *PMLA* 67, 2 (1952): 164.

51. Friedrich von Schlegel, *Athenaeum*, Fragment No. 24.

52. Barbara Maria Stafford, "'Illiterate Monuments': The Ruin as Dialect or Broken Classic," *The Age of Johnson: A Scholarly Annual* 1 (1987): 29.

53. While Fielding does not explicitly flaunt his authority quite as much as Thackeray with his analogy to puppets and their puppeteer, I agree with Patricia Meyer Spacks' assessment: "Fielding more explicitly than any of his contemporaries or immediate followers acknowledges fictional artifice, directly asserting the author's power as contriver and manipulator of events" (*Imagining a Self: Autobiography and Novel in Eighteenth-Century England* [Cambridge and London: Harvard University Press, 1976], 6).

54. Mackenzie, *Man of Feeling*, 128.

55. While Werther complains about his inability to express the depth of his feelings in words, he also alludes simultaneously to the constant complaint Wilhelm and others make of him—namely, his exaggeration: "Ich werde, wie gewöhnlich, schlecht erzählen, und du wirst mich, wie gewöhnlich, denk' ich, übertrieben finden" [I will, as usual, tell it poorly, and I think you will, as usual, think I exaggerate]. The Ambassador, too, rebukes Werther for his "allzugroße Empfindlichkeit" [excessive sensibility] (*Werther*, 18, 66). The irony is, of course, that while Werther is ruing the fact that all his words sound too flat, or fall so short of the actual emotions, others call it exaggeration and claim that he already conveys unacceptably overblown emotions. What is for Werther devastatingly little is already too much in society's eyes.

56. Mackenzie, *Man of Feeling*, 69, my emphasis.

57. Mackenzie, *Man of Feeling*, 5.

58. Mackenzie, *Man of Feeling*, 5, my emphasis.

59. See Edward Fowler for a discussion of a parallel phenomenon in the Japanese novel: *The Rhetoric of Confession: Shishôsetsu in Early Twentieth-Century Japanese Fiction* (Berkeley: University of California Press, 1988).

60. See Horst Flaschka for an exhaustive study of these biographical parallels: *Goethes "Werther": Werkkontextuelle Deskription und Analyse* (München: W. Fink, 1987).

61. *The Sermons of Mr. Yorick* was published in 1760. The name "Mr. Yorick" also appears in the full title of *A Sentimental Journey through France and Italy by Mr. Yorick*. See Mullan, *Sentiment and Sociability*, 7ff. for a discussion of Sterne's use of his own letters and of autobiography in the novel. See also Nagle, "Sterne and Shelley," n. 36.

62. Johann Wolfgang von Goethe, *Goethes Werke: Hamburger Ausgabe*, ed. Erich Trunz (München: C. H. Beck, 1989), IX.587.

63. See Vincent for a book-length study that attempts to untangle the differences between versions one (1774) and two (1787).

64. Tobin Siebers, "The Werther Effect: The Esthetics of Suicide," *Mosaic* 26, 1 (1993): 20. It is well known that writing *Werther* had a purging effect upon Goethe, as he admits in *Dichtung und Wahrheit*. What is less commonly understood is that Goethe could write Werther out of his system without writing *Werther* out of his system: that is, *Werther* contains within its structure an antidote to Werther's excessive and ultimately suicidal sensibility. It may be true, as Deirdre Vincent observes, that "Goethe used his literary talent as a means to order his own inner world" (*Werther's Goethe and the Game of Literary Creativity* [Toronto; Buffalo, NY: University of Toronto Press, 1992], 234). Order is certainly not absent from the pages of *Werther*. Goethe uses the two narratorial perspectives of the novel—Werther's and the *Herausgeber*'s—to portray simultaneously the man of feeling's emotion-laden chaos and the man of words' impoverished but practical control. As a result, the message of *Werther* is implicitly even more mixed than it is in *Journey* and exhibits what Boyle describes as Goethe's "middle path between the official and the marginal, between establishment and opposition" (Boyle, *Goethe*, 39). *Werther* represents this same middle path between Albert and Werther that Boyle finds more generally in Goethe's writings.

   In an editorial note, Ernst Trunz makes a similar distinction between Werther's self-consciously chaotic existence and the degree of order within *Werther*: "Werther ist nur eine Seite von [dem jungen Goethe], und wenn man genau hinsieht, findet man auch im *Werther*-Roman den anderen Pol mit angelegt, in der Art der Darstellung, im Bericht des Herausgebers und nicht zuletzt in der harmonischen Gestalt Lottens, die, schön und seelenhaft, in ihrer Begrenztheit eine Unendliche repräsentiert" (*Werther*, 571 n. 13).

65. Inger Sigrun Brodey, "Masculinity, Sensibility, and the 'Man of Feeling': the Gendered Ethics of Goethe's *Werther*," *Papers on Language and Literature* 35, 2 (1999): 137.

66. Goethe, *Werther*, 41, 47.

67. Sterne, *Journey*, 209.

68. Lillian Furst also notices this trend in "The Man of Sensibility and the Woman of Sense," *Jahrbuch-fur-Internationale-Germanistik* 14, 1 (1982): 13–26, *passim*.

69. Edmund Burke, *A Philosophical Enquiry*, 149 and 39. In his "Introduction" (added later), which focuses on the concept of "Taste," Burke qualifies this idea: he states that Taste is based upon a combination of "sensibility" and "judgment." The want of sensibility leads to a want of taste, to indiscrimination, and the want of judgment leads to "wrong" or "bad taste." The lack of either faculty eventually leads to dullness and insensibility (Burke, *Philosophical Enquiry*, 23–24).

70. Gilpin first invents the term "picturesque Beauty" to distinguish "objects that were actually beautiful and also adapted for pictures" (Hussey, 13). Unlike Knight, Gilpin never actually divorces the picturesque and the sublime (Price, 259). The term "picturesque Sublime," interestingly enough, never becomes popular.

71. Uvedale Price writes: "[W]e no more scruple to call one of Handel's chorusses sublime, than Corelli's famous pastorale beautiful. But should any person simply, or without qualifying expressions call a capricious movement of Scarlatti or Haydn picturesque, he would with great reason, be laughed at, for it is not a term applied to sounds; yet such a movement, from its sudden, unexpected, and abrupt transitions,—from a certain playful wildness of character and appearance of irregularity, is no less analogous to similar scenery in nature, than the concerto or the chorus, to what is grand or beautiful

to the eye" ("Essay on the Picturesque as compared with the Sublime and the Beautiful" in *Essays on the Picturesque* [London, 1810], I. 45–46).

72. Burke, *A Philosophical Enquiry*, 40.

73. See James T. Boulton's introduction to Burke, *A Philosophical Enquiry*, cviii.

74. In the same passage, Burke writes that "all verbal description, merely as naked description, though never so exact, conveys so poor and insufficient an idea of the thing described, that it could scarcely have the smallest effect, if the speaker did not call in to his aid those modes of speech that mark a strong and lively feeling in himself. Then, by the contagion of our passions, we catch a fire already kindled in another" (Burke, *A Philosophical Enquiry*, 175). Intonation and gesture communicate passions where words alone are impotent.

75. Hunt speaks of the picturesque as a movement to process and tame the natural world by pictorializing it (*Gardens and the Picturesque*, 5). Stephanie Ross also notices this characteristic in a book review of Hunt's *Gardens and the Picturesque:* "The physical world could be seen more pleasantly, occupied and visited more safely, if it were thought of as a painting" (*Journal of Aesthetics and Criticism* 52 [1994.2]: 250–252).

76. In Part II, Werther flirts increasingly with the sublime, as we can see in his love of Ossian's wild and tragic fragments and his climbing the ragged cliff before he dies. His suicide may be the ultimate submission to the sublime. Part I and the *structure* of the novel as a whole, however, bear greater affinity to the picturesque—through the editing of the *Herausgeber*, we remain at a safe distance from Werther's wildness. In his later *Die Wahlverwandtschaften* [*Elective Affinities*], published in 1809, Goethe again plays with the same theme of the picturesque which politely and delicately, but also dangerously, attempts to frame nature's wildness.

   Barbara Stafford makes the point that during this period, even the portrayal of fossils and volcanoes was done in the picturesque mode; she implies that this mode of representation constrains its subjects "to speak a rational or geometrical language." That is, violent, mysterious, and wild natural occurrences were presented in an orderly and 'picture-perfect' manner. The aspect of picturesque representation which she does not mention is that the picturesque (like sensibility) also strives to conceal the very order it imposes through, for example, its strict avoidance of straight lines and right angles (Stafford, "Illiterate Monuments," 26).

77. In Austen's *Mansfield Park* (published 1814), a ha-ha plays a very important symbolic role in the "Wilderness" scene where Fanny sits by the ha-ha and watches Maria, Julia, and Henry squeeze through and hop over it, while Mr. Rushworth is running to get the keys. It is an interesting scene, in that each character reveals his or her attitude towards authority, convention, and propriety by his or her responses to the ha-ha—and therefore to society's *hidden* constraints—the realm of virtue, rather than legality. Maria also compares herself to Sterne's caged starling. (See Brodey, "Papas and Hahas.")

78. Even Longbourn, in *Pride and Prejudice,* has a hermitage.

79. "Nicht weniger ist die Köhlerhütte in einem dichten Pappelwald eine artige Erfindung, denen äußeres Ansehen das Auge täuscht, und deren Inneres mit einem feinen Kabinetchen überrascht, das eine sehr ausgesuchte Bibliothek der Frau Reichsgräfinn von Hohenheim enthält . . . ; sie lehnt sich an den Stamm einer großen, aber abgestorbenen hohlen Eiche, worin sich Kamin und Rauchloch befinden" [No less is the hut of a charcoal maker in a dense poplar wood a charming invention, whose exterior appearance deceives the eye and whose interior surprises us with a fine little chamber that contains

the Duchess of Hohenheim's highly exceptional library . . . ; the hut leans on the trunk of a great but dead, hollow oak, which contains a fireplace and chimney]. See C. C. L. Hirschfield, *Theorie Der Gartenkunst* (Leipzig: M.G. Weidmann, 1779–85), V: 351–352.

80. Jonathan Lamb identifies what he calls the "Shandean Sublime" in Sterne's writings (especially *Tristram Shandy*); this is Lamb's way of describing the paradox of purposeful fragmentation or how a "story can be written digressively and progressively at the same time" (Lamb, 23). Lamb, however, does not carry his own theory far enough, for it would carry him past the Shandean Sublime, to the "Sternean picturesque": by its nature, his question involves the multiple narrative frames, including the implied author as well as the narrator. Lamb notices what I have called Sterne's "rhetoric of ruins" except that he does not see that Sterne's ruins are really *fake* ruins, involving the masking of the author-builder's creative role. In so doing, Lamb misplaces the later Kantian sublime at the cost of ignoring Gilpin's and Price's responses to Burke's sublime. To do so is to miss a crucial part of Sterne's irony and humor. Lamb's book is, however, useful for his treatment of epistemological questions and their relation to literary structure.

81. Marshall, "Problem of the Picturesque," 419.

82. For an excellent book-length treatment of the Claude glass and additional paraphernalia of the picturesque, see Arnaud Maillet, *The Claude Glass: Use and Meaning of the Black Mirror in Western Art,* translated by Jeff Fort (New York: Zone Books, 2004). See also Andrews, *The Search for the Picturesque,* 68; Barrell, *The Idea of Landscape,* 23; Hunt, *Gardens and the Picturesque,* 171; and Bermingham, *Learning to Draw,* 87, 101–103.

83. William Gilpin, *Remarks on Forest Scenery, and Other Woodland Views, Relative Chiefly to Picturesque Beauty* (London: R. Blamire, 1791), II: 225.

84. In his seminal work on the Claude Glass, Arnaud Maillet tells also of the eighteenth-century desire to mediate natural lighting to protect the health and comfort of the viewers: "the rawness of natural light constituted . . . an anti-aesthetic effect, disagreeable to the very organ of sight, sometimes cruel to the point of engendering ocular maladies. This led to the constant recommendation to contemplate the landscape at twilight" (Maillet, 139). See also Alan Liu's notion of "arrested desire" in Liu, *Wordsworth, the Sense of History,* (Stanford: Stanford University Press, 1989), 60–61; and Raimonda Modiano's response in *The Politics of the Picturesque: Literature, Landscape and Aesthetics since 1770* ed. Stephen Copely and Peter Garside (Cambridge: Cambridge University Press, 1994), 197 n. 3.

85. Combe and Rowlandson also frequently represent the powers and dangers of nature that the picturesque never completely manages to tame. Since the picturesque represents a controlled view from afar of nature's wildness, Rowlandson's images frequently show Doctor Syntax and Doctor Prosody involved in "accidents" of nature: nearly drowned by a wave, knocked off a horse, falling off precipices, etc. Artists engaged in the domestication of wildness for the sake of the picturesque experience nature at such a distance that they are surprised by its inconveniences and dangers. Rowlandson suggests that under a very thin guise, nature is ready to reassert herself.

86. The waning of the picturesque occurred when viewers, reacting to standards of 'authenticity,' became overly conscious of the discrepancy between the picture frame and nature. For example, the picturesque fascination with fake ruins had come to an end when Sir Edward Turner would say, "Come and deplore the ruin of my ruin" (quoted in Macaulay, 31–32). While the picturesque claims to control and *compose* nature and halt time, the decay of the fake ruins reveals this to be false. The fake ruins were more fragile than real

decaying monuments, and susceptible to time in a way that the genuine product is not. The picturesque movement could tolerate an unusual degree of disguise. Hersey gives a passage from 1835, after the movement had waned, to show this change: "A barn disguised as a church would afford satisfaction only to those who considered it as a trick. The beauty of truth is so essential to every other kind of beauty, that it can neither be dispensed with in art nor in morals" (Hersey, 85).

87. Using Shaftesbury's aestheticization of virtue as a cornerstone of its moral aesthetic, the culture of sensibility establishes the equation of feeling, taste, and virtue. Because of this intimate connection between art and ethics, little distinction is made between artist and moral agent.

88. Hussey, *The Picturesque*, 4.

89. Sterne, *Journey*, 14–15 and notes.

90. Sterne, *Journey*, 115.

91. Sterne, *Journey*, 119.

92. Rousseau, *Julie, ou la Nouvelle Héloïse*, II. 234.

93. Sterne, *Journey*, 208.

94. Hunt, *The Picturesque Garden*, 176.

95. Hirschfield, *Theorie Der Gartenkunst*, I: 186.

96. James Courtney Federle, "Authenticities: Bodies, Gardens and Pedagogies in Late-Eighteenth Century Germany," (diss., University of California at Berkeley, 1991), 128.

97. Hirschfield, *Theorie*, I. 191–94.

98. Federle, 112.

99. Hirschfield, *Theorie*, V. 350, my emphasis.

100. Quoted in Todd, *Sensibility*, 91–92.

101. Johann Wolfgang von Goethe, *Italienische Reise*, ed. Herbert von Einem (München: C. Wegner, 1978), 151.

102. This movement is related to the growing cult of "genius" as well, for it was only the rare individual who was capable of such aesthetic appreciation. We can find this tone in Werther's expression of the uniqueness of his fate: "Manchmal sag' ich mir: Dein Schicksal ist einzig; preise die übrigen glücklich—so ist noch keiner gequält worden.—Dann lese ich einen Dichter der Vorzeit, und es ist mir, als säh' ich in mein eignes Herz. Ich habe so viel auszustehen! Ach, sind denn Menschen vor mir schon so elend gewesen?" [Sometimes I say to myself: Your fate is singular; count the rest lucky—no other has yet been tortured like this.–Then I read a poet of the past, and it seems to me as though I were looking into my own heart. I have so much to endure! Oh, have people before me ever been so wretched?] (Goethe, *Werther*, 88).

Goethe, too, in a letter to Sophie von La Roche, portrays himself as a rare man of feeling (i.e. genius): "You complain of solitude! . . . Alas that is the fate of the noblest souls to sigh in vain for a mirror of themselves" (quoted in Boyle, 135). Isolation is not the moral failing for Goethe and Mackenzie that it is for Sterne and later Austen: rather it is a symptom of the unappreciated genius who is too good for his surroundings.

103. Michael Fried, *Absorption and Theatricality*.

104. Michasiw, "Nine Revisionist Theses," 85–86.

105. Interesting in this regard is Williams' article on the use of illustrations within the sentimental novel of the 1780s and '90s (by authors such as William Sadler, Charles Dodd, and Courtney Melmouth). Williams identifies tableaux in these novels that signify "frozen pathos" (465); her thesis is that tableaux "serve to undercut the sense of privacy, of immediacy, and so inscribe contradiction as one of the very foundations of this genre" (465). Engravings of pathetic scenes within the novels: "represent the most important and most

pathetic moment in the story, they are referred to and *deferred* to within the narrative" (466). Such tableaux "constituted of *description* rather than *narration,* work further to garment the story's narrative and to interrupt the plotline" (468). In other words, the illustrations further sensibility's dual impulses by simultaneously decreasing and increasing readers' intimacy and sympathy with the suffering characters. They can also function as imbedded critiques—authors' warnings about their own protagonists (e.g. Goethe's warnings about Werther; Mackenzie's about Harley; or the narrator of Ann Radcliffe's *Mysteries of Udolpho* warning about the sensibility that is the dominant trait of the female protagonist).

106. Cf. Ann Radcliffe's initial description of the heroine of *Udolpho:* "uncommon delicacy of mind, warm affections, and ready benevolence; but with these was observable a degree of susceptibility too exquisite to admit of lasting peace. As she advanced in youth this sensibility gave her a pensive tone to her spirits and a softness to her manner, which added grace to beauty and rendered her a very interesting object *to persons of a congenial disposition*" (*The Mysteries of Udolpho,* ed. Jacqueline Howard [London: Penguin, 2001], 8–9, my emphasis).

107. Sterne, *Letters from Yorick to Eliza* (Altenburgh: printed for Richter, 1776), 131–2, my emphasis.

108. Mackenzie, *Man of Feeling,* 128.

109. *Monthly Review* XLIV (May 1771): 418.

110. Lady Louisa Stuart's writings reflect the trajectory of sensibility toward cultish and laughable extremes, as she monitors her own reactions to readings of *The Man of Feeling:* at the age of 14, she worried about not crying enough when reading its "Exquisite" and pathetic scenes. In 1826, audiences laugh at the same scenes: "What was exquisite becomes comical . . ." (*Selections from her Manuscripts* [Edinburgh: David Douglass, 1899], 235–36).

111. Andrew Erskine, *Letters between the Honourable Andrew Erskine, and James Boswell, Esq.* (London: Samuel Chandler, 1763), 58.

112. James Boswell, *Boswell's London Journal 1762–1763,* ed. Frederick A. Pottle (New York: McGraw-Hill, 1950), 182.

NOTES TO CHAPTER 4

1. Smith, *Theory of Moral Sentiments,* I.i.2.2–4.

2. Other authors at the time also warn of the deleterious effect of the novels of sensibility, in that they cultivate a sensitivity to suffering without the ability to act. Barbauld warns that "at length the mind grows absolutely callous" ("An Inquiry into those Kinds of Distress which Excite Agreeable Sensations," *The Works of Anna Laetitia Barbauld* (London: Longma, Hurst, et al., 1825)" II. 225). This problem of course intensifies when the ability to perceive suffering is predicated on the inability to speak or act in an effective manner. In this regard, Harkin makes an interesting argument that sensibility's fragmented speech combined with its emphasis on sympathy is an indicator of a broader sense of political helplessness (Harkin, 30–37).

3. Goethe, *Werther,* 74. The *Herausgeber,* too, writes of Werther's "wunderbare[-] Empfindung, Denkart und . . . end- lose[-] Leidenschaft" [wonderful sensibility, way of thought, and infinite passion], *Werther,* 98.

4. One might remember in this regard, Samuel Johnson's parody of the Shaftesburian stoics in *The History of Rasselas, Prince of Abbissinia* (Edinburgh: William Creech, 1789), 117: "When [the philosopher] had spoken, he looked round him with a placid air, and enjoyed the consciousness of his

own beneficence." As Donald Green writes regarding this passage, "Shaftesbury does indeed argue that one of the rewards of virtuous behavior is the pleasant awareness of your own superior virtue, such as the Pharisee in the Gospels enjoyed" (*The Politics of Samuel Johnson* [New Haven: Yale University Press, 1960], 114).

5. Sterne, *Journey*, 277.

6. Price, *Essay on the Picturesque and Sublime*, I:76. See Mackenzie's description of the "old soldier," as picturesque as his setting because of his age and weariness: "He was one of those figures which Salvator would have drawn; nor was the surrounding scenery unlike the wildness of that painter's backgrounds. The banks on each side were covered with fantastic shrub-wood. [...] A rock, with some gangling wild flowers, jutted out above where the soldier lay; on which grew the stump of a large tree, white with age, and a single twisted branch shaded his face as he slept. [...] His face had the marks of manly comeliness impaired by time; his forehead was not altogether bald, but its hairs might have been numbered; while a few white locks behind crossed the brown of his neck with a contrast the most venerable to a mind like Harley's" (Mackenzie, *Man of Feeling*, 85).

7. It is an open question as to whether these authors are opponents of sensibility or rather simply make aspects of sensibility explicit that are inherent in the culture and its literature.

8. Van Sant, 60–82.

9. Miss Williams was an icon of sensibility and a poet in her own right. In the 1780s, she was known for her rural and simple upbringing, her "modesty and candour" (*European Magazine* 1786): see for example her well-known poem "Sensibility," published in 1786, one year before Wordsworth's poem: "In Sensibility's lov'd praise/ I tune my trembling reed;/ And seek to deck her shrine with bays,/ On which my heart must bleed!" (lines 1–4). There is perhaps one additional level depending on whether one views telling a tale as separate in time, substance, or personage from the initial event.

10. Burke, *Letter to Philip Francis, Esquire* (1790). See also Stephen Cox's treatment of this feature of Burke's writing. In *Sentimental Journey*, Sterne makes the solipsism of this dynamic explicit, as Yorick bursts into tears over his own imaginings of the sufferings of a prisoner in the Bastille: "I burst into tears—I could not sustain the picture of confinement which my fancy had drawn" (Sterne, *Journey*, 204).

11. Worthy readers are even included *within* the novels as models. In *The Liberal American* (1785), the female protagonist narrates the following scene: "The book I had been reading lay by my side. He took it up, and opened it where I had marked down the page. It was wet with tears. He regarded me with a look of inquiry, then pressing the page to his lips, he exclaimed: 'Gracious heaven! What enchanting sensibility!'" Real readers, such as Lady Louisa Stuart, for example, worried that she would not cry enough when reading *The Man of Feeling*—enough, that is, "to gain the proper credit of proper sensibility."

12. Austen, "Jack and Alice," in *Minor Works*, 20–23.

13. "When in common language we say *a miserable object*, we mean an object of distress which, if we relieve, we turn away from at the same time. To make pity pleasing, the object of it must not in any view be disagreeable to the imagination. How admirably has the author of Clarissa managed this point!" (Anna Laetitia Barbauld, "An Inquiry," II. 223.

14. Austen, "Love and Freindship," in *Minor Works*, 100–101, my emphasis.

15. Austen, "Love and Freindship," in *Minor Works*, 93.

16. Austen, "Love and Freindship," in *Minor Works,* 105–6.
17. We find the same Shaftesburian sentiments parodied in *Sanditon,* Austen's last, unfinished novel, and spoken by Sir Edward Denham, who represents the 'man of feeling' turned hypocritical aesthete: "[Although] the Coruscations of Talent, elicited by impassioned feeling in the breast of Man, are perhaps incompatible with some of the prosaic Decencies of Life," Sir Edward insists that "it were Hyper-criticism, it were Pseudo-philosophy to expect from the soul of high toned Genius, the grovellings of a common mind.—" (Austen, *Sanditon,* in *Minor Works,* 398). Decency, in Sir Edward's inflated vocabulary, is common, prosaic, and altogether unsuitable for the man of genius.
18. Patricia Meyer Spacks has an excellent treatment of "The Problem of the Interesting" republished in *Boredom: A Literary History of a State of Mind* (Chicago and London: University of Chicago Press, 1995), 113–125. Although she treats some of the aspects of the interesting mentioned here, she does not address the broader ethical concerns or the question of the erotic admixture so significant for Laurence Sterne.
19. Austen, "Jack and Alice," in *Minor Works,* 24–25.
20. William Gilpin, *Observations . . . on the Mountains and Lakes of Cumberland and Westmoreland* (London, 1786), II. 122–23.
21. Austen, "A History of England from the Reign of Henry the 4th to the Death of Charles the 1st, By a Partial, Prejudiced, and Ignorant Historian," in *Minor Works,* 142. A passage from Anna Laetitia Aikin[Barbauld]'s memoirs of visiting a monastery reduced to a piteous site also reveals the delight in ruination fueled by dislike of the Roman Catholic church: "These mossy stones and scattered reliques of the vast edifice, like the large bones and gigantic armour of a once formidable ruffian, produce emotions of mingled dread and exultation. Farewell, ye once venerated seats! Enough of you remains, and may it always remain, to remind us from what we have escaped, and make posterity for ever thankful for this fairer age of liberty and light" (J. and A.L. Aikin, *Miscellaneous Pieces in Prose,* 63–5; quoted in Maurice Levy, "Les ruines dans l'art et l'écriture: esthétique et idéologie," *Bulletin de la Societé d'Études Anglo-Americaines des XVIIe et XVIIIe Siècles* 13 [1981]: 152).
22. In Van Sant's terms, the desire for mutual transparency and a glass chest to see the contents of the human heart perversely becomes the desire to open a woman's chest and see (or actually hold) her beating heart, as we see in *Clarissa*. Lovelace begins by wishing to "unlock" the secrets of Clarissa's heart, and the verb choices become more violent and intrusive until the end of the novel, when he actually has a surgeon standing by to extract her heart from her dead body for his own possession (Van Sant, 81).
23. Spacks, *Imagining a Self,* 57.
24. Armstrong, *Desire and Domestic Fiction: A Political History of the Novel* (New York: Oxford University Press, 1987), 127; see also Paul Hunter, *Before Novels: The Cultural Contexts of Eighteenth-Century English Fiction* (New York: W.W. Norton, 1990).
25. Spacks, *Imagining a Self,* 58–61.
26. Armstrong, *Desire and Domestic Fiction,* 129.
27. Heydt-Stevenson uses the picturesque to inform Austen's gender in a way that is analogous with Claudia Johnson's *Equivocal Beings:* the picturesque, according to Heydt-Stevenson, allows Austen to mediate gender between the extremes of the masculine sublime and feminine beautiful, as posited by Burke ("Liberty, Connection, and Tyranny," 261–79).
28. Van Sant, 113–115.
29. Pierre Carlet de Marivaux, *La Vie de Marianne, ou, Les aventures de Madame la comtesse de * * ** (Paris: Garnier, 1966 [1745]), 49.

30. Aurora Wolfgang, *Gender and Voice in the French Novel, 1730–1782* (Wiltshire and Burlington, Vt.: Ashgate, 2004), 1–2.
31. Wolfgang, *Gender and Voice*, 18.
32. Marivaux, *La Vie de Marianne*, 7.
33. Marivaux, *La Vie de Marianne*, 7.
34. Marivaux, *La Vie de Marianne*, 5.
35. Julie Choi, "Feminine Authority? Common Sense and the Question of Voice in the Novel," *New Literary History* 27, 4 (1996): 641–62.
36. In John Bender's terms, Austen negotiates between the "fantasy of omniscient authority," or retaining a powerful central authoritative perspective, on the one hand, and presenting the individual subjectivities of the characters on the other, but she does so invisibly, using the guise of free indirect discourse (*Imagining the Penitentiary: Fiction and the Architecture of Mind in Eighteenth-Century England* [Chicago and London: University of Chicago Press, 1987], 165, 177–180). In this way Austen negotiates between the claims of authenticity and authority.
37. Barbara M. Benedict, "Jane Austen's *Sense and Sensibility:* The Politics of Point of View," *Philological Quarterly* 69.4 (1990):One of the main differences is that, while she too claims a dual impulse among novelists of sensibility (sentimental novelists), her focus is on imbedded tales within volumes of "literary miscellanies" and their intended pedagogical effects, rather than the narrative techniques in question here, such as the multiple frames of fictional editors. Pedagogical effect, for example, is for Benedict almost exclusively the realm of conventional morality, rather than something that sensibility co-opts for its own purposes.
38. Benedict, "Jane Austen's *Sense and Sensibility*" 455.
39. Marsha Warren, "Time, Space, and Semiotic Discourse in the Feminization/Disintegration of Quentin Compson," *The Faulkner Journal* 4, 102 (1988-1989): 99–111.
40. Patrick Brady, "From Feminism to Chaos Theory," *Discontinuity and Fragmentation*, ed. Henry Freeman (Amsterdam: Rodopi, 1994), 108.
41. Benedict, "Jane Austen's *Sense and Sensibility*," 468.
42. Jan Fergus argues that *Sense and Sensibility* was first written in an epistolary format, then substantially revised, and finally became Austen's first book accepted for publication. (*Pride and Prejudice* had been submitted earlier, but was not published until after *Sense and Sensibility*, by "the author of *Sense and Sensibility*.") Jan Fergus, *Jane Austen: a Literary Life* (Basingstoke: Macmillan, 1991), 74.
43. Austen explicitly parodies sensibility and the picturesque in her juvenilia, as well as in her major novels, most of which, one must remember, were first written in the eighteenth century. *Sense and Sensibility* (started sometime before 1797, published in 1811), *Pride and Prejudice* (original version written in 1796–1797, published in 1813), *Northanger Abbey* (mostly written in 1798–99, published posthumously), and *Sanditon* (written in her last years, published posthumously with *Northanger Abbey* in 1817) have been repeatedly misunderstood because her affinities with sensibility have either been ignored, or her rejection of the movement taken more literally than her work warrants. Many elements of her novelistic world probably stem from her youthful acquaintance with the moral and cultural aesthetic of sensibility. These aspects include: an emphasis on an (initially) isolated individual, the importance of *inner* feelings, the difficulty of self-representation, a mistrust of public discourse, the importance of feeling for virtue, an emphasis on vision as a vehicle for imaginative sympathy, and the preference for ordinary and domestic experience.

The most important work to date on Austen's connection with sensibility or 'novels of sentiment' has been done by Marilyn Butler, Claudia Johnson, A. Walton Litz, and John Mullan: Marilyn Butler, *Jane Austen and the War of Ideas* (Oxford: Clarendon Press, 1987); Claudia L. Johnson, *Equivocal Beings: Politics, Gender, and Sentimentality in the 1790s: Wollstonecraft, Radcliffe, Burney, Austen* (Chicago and London: University of Chicago Press, 1995); A. Walton Litz, *Jane Austen, a Study of her Artistic Development* (New York: Oxford University Press, 1965); and John Mullan, *Sentiment and Sociability: the Language of Feeling in the Eighteenth Century* (Oxford and New York: Clarendon Press; Oxford University Press, 1988). On Austen's attitudes regarding authority, especially the authority associated with authorship, see Rachel Brownstein, "Irony and Authority," in *Sense and Sensibility and Pride and Prejudice: Jane Austen* ed. Robert Clark (New York: St. Martin's, 1994), 180–192; Deborah Kaplan, "Achieving Authority in Austen," *Nineteenth-Century Fiction* 37, 4 (1983): 531–51; Tara Ghoshal Wallace, *Jane Austen and Narrative Authority* (New York: Macmillan Press; St. Martin's Press, 1995); and William Galperin, *The Historical Austen* (Philadelphia: University of Pennsylvania Press, 2005).

44. There have been a few treatments of Austen's relation to the picturesque. The most seminal have been: Martin Price, "The Picturesque Moment," in *From Sensibility to Romanticism: Essays Presented to Frederick A. Pottle* ed. Frederick W. Hilles and Harold Bloom (New York: Norton, 1965), and *Forms of Life: Character and Moral Imagination in the Novel* (New Haven: Yale University Press, 1983), 65–89; and Alistair M. Duckworth, *The Improvement of the Estate: A Study of Jane Austen's Novel* (Baltimore: Johns Hopkins University Press, 1971), 35–80. The most important for this study are essays by Jillian Heydt-Stevenson that focus on issues of tourism and economy, such as "Liberty, Connection, and Tyranny: The Novels of Jane Austen and the Aesthetic Movement of the Picturesque," in *Lessons in Romanticism*, ed. Thomas Pfau and Robert Gleckner (Durham: Duke University Press, 1998), 261–79; an unpublished dissertation by Roberta Blackley Hannay, which draws connections between the picturesque and moral education ("Jane Austen and the Picturesque Movement: The Revision of the English Landscape"); David Marshall's insightful treatment of representation in "Problem of the Picturesque"; and Mavis Batey's broad and engaging overview of the picturesque in *Jane Austen and the English Landscape* (London and Chicago: Chicago Review Press, 1996). Batey illustrates Austen's specific familiarity with real follies, wildernesses, ha-has, hermitages, and historical landscape gardeners and theorists. More recently, William Galperin applies the picturesque aesthetic to Austen's *Sense and Sensibility* in *The Historical Austen*, 44–81: Galperin argues, as do I, that the picturesque affects Austen's modes of representation, and he offers one of the best treatments to date of Austen's ethical scruples regarding the picturesque.

45. Godwin, *Memoirs of the Author of a Vindication of the Rights of Woman by William Godwin* (London, 1798), 114–15.

46. We have no direct evidence that Austen read the English editions of *Werter* (sic), so popular during her day (most likely the 1780 version by Peter Graves or the 1789 version by J. Gifford); however, her allusions to the novel show a distinct familiarity with the plot. This could have been acquired a number of ways, since print-shops, too, were full of images of Werther and Lotte. The following passage from Charlotte Smith's *Emmeline* (for which I am grateful to Albrecht Strauss) is an example of a reference to Werther's popularity that Austen most surely read. An offensive young woman is said to be "drest in the character of Charlotte in the Sorrows of Werter," and speaking of her and her equally objectionable sister, the narrator declares, "Their air and

manner were adapted, as they believed, to the figures of those characters as they appear in the print shops; and their excessive affectation, together with the gaudy appearance of their mama, nearly conquered the gravity of Emmeline and of many in the company" (*Emmeline: Orphan of the Castle* [London: Oxford University Press, 1971], 506–7).

    The only other studies, to my knowledge, that draw connections between Werther and Marianne are my "The Adventures of a Female Werther: Austen's Revision of Sensibility," *Philosophy and Literature* 23, 1 (1999):110–126, and Lionel Trilling's *Sincerity and Authenticity* (Cambridge: Harvard University Press, 1972).

47. Jane Austen, *Sense and Sensibility* in *The Novels of Jane Austen*, ed. R. W. Chapman (Oxford and New York: Clarendon Press, 1932), 83, 104.
48. Goethe dramatizes this principle in the ending tableau of *Werther*. The *Herausgeber* reports that in his death scene, Werther carefully creates a tableau that functions as an epitaph, the contents of his room carefully arranged to indicate his priorities and philosophy of life. One such detail, the open copy of Lessing's play *Emilia Galotti* (1772), further attests to the extreme lengths to which this principle of the authenticity of the arrested moment can lead. In *Emilia Galotti*, the chaste eponymous heroine asks her father to kill her, to give rest to her teeming emotions and to preserve her virtue, rather than to let her live and potentially be seduced: "Eine Rose gebrochen, ehe der Sturm sie entblättert" [a rose, broken before the storm deprives her of her petals].
49. Austen, *Sense and Sensibility*, 88, my emphasis.
50. Austen, *Sense and Sensibility*, 92.
51. Sterne in a letter to John Eustace (February, 1768).
52. Austen, *Sense and Sensibility*, 7.
53. Goethe, *Werther*, 38, my emphasis.
54. Austen, *Sense and Sensibility*, 345.
55. Austen, *Sense and Sensibility*, 97.
56. Mackenzie, *Man of Feeling*, 128.
57. Austen, *Sense and Sensibility*, 189–90, my emphasis. It is interesting to compare this attachment to misery with the treatment of a similar theme in *Persuasion*. In the final scene where Wentworth writes the proposal letter to Anne, Anne and Captain Harville engage in a verbal competition as to whether men or women suffer most and grieve longer. The difference is that substantial loss is at stake and has actually occurred—a sister's death in his case, eight years of loneliness in hers—and also that neither one disdains rescue or relief from this grief. It is the sense of real loss and grief that leads critics to refer to *Persuasion* as "autumnal" and which also underscores the dying Austen's critique of feigned ruination and misery.
58. Cf. "Elinor saw, with concern, the excess of her sister's sensibility; but by Mrs. Dashwood it was valued and cherished. They encouraged each other now in the violence of their affliction. The agony of grief which overpowered them at first, was voluntarily renewed, was sought for, was created again and again. They gave themselves up wholly to their sorrow, seeking increase of wretchedness in every reflection that could afford it, and resolved against ever admitting consolation in future. Elinor, too, was deeply afflicted; but still she could struggle, she could exert herself. She could consult with her brother, could receive her sister-in-law on her arrival, and treat her with proper attention; and could strive to rouse her mother to similar exertion, and encourage her to similar forbearance" (Austen, *Sense and Sensibility*, 7).
59. Austen, *Sense and Sensibility*, 97.
60. Cf. Tave, *Some Words of Jane Austen* (Chicago: University of Chicago Press, 1973), 90–91.

61. Austen, *Sense and Sensibility*, 186. Cf. a scene from Mary Wollstonecraft's novel *Mary*, where Henry, the dying man of feeling, and his beloved Mary compete for the most misery: "'I have myself,' said he, mournfully, 'shaken hands with happiness, and am dead to the world; I wait patiently for my dissolution; but, for thee, Mary, there may be many bright days in store.' 'Impossible,' replied she, in a *peevish* tone, *as if he had insulted her by the supposition*; her feelings were so much in unison with his, that she was *in love with misery*'" (*Mary, a Fiction* [London: J. Johnson, 1788], 91, my emphasis).

62. Austen, *Sense and Sensibility*, 185. Marianne attests later on to her own self-ruination and the "negligence of [her] own health": "Had I died, it would have been self-destruction" (Austen, *Sense and Sensibility*, 345).

63. Austen, *Sense and Sensibility*, 204.

64. Austen, *Sense and Sensibility*, 204. It is true that Colonel Brandon's task—to vilify another man—is a difficult one; however, to respond to such a declaration is also difficult. The contrast between their styles is therefore, I would maintain, significant.

65. Austen, *Sense and Sensibility*, 289.

66. Austen, *Sense and Sensibility*, 95.

67. Austen, *Sense and Sensibility*, 359–60.

68. Austen, *Sense and Sensibility*, 5. In the following pages, they are remarkably adept at abusing the sense of the promise which John gave his father on his deathbed. In the successive stages of their conversation, the John Dashwoods convince themselves with profuse self-congratulation, and dexterous manipulation of words, that they really have satisfied the promise John made his father on his deathbed to do "everything in his power to make [his surviving family] comfortable." Their mutual observations of their excessive generosity to Elinor, Marianne, and their mother gradually substitute themselves for any real gifts of money, to the point where the actual gift shrinks from an initially intended one-time gift of £3000, to £1500, to £100 per year, to an occasional £50, to nothing at all: in a stunning reversal, Mrs. John Dashwood audaciously concludes, "*They* will be much more able to give *you* something" (8–13, my emphasis; parts of the following discussion were taken from my "Dangerous Words and Silent Lovers" in *Persuasions* 12 (1990): 134–38.

69. Rousseau, *Essai sur l'origine des langues*, 33; of interest in this regard is Mary Ann O'Farrell's *Telling Complexions: The Nineteenth-Century Novel and the Blush* (Durham: Duke University Press, 1997). O'Farrell traces the use of blushes in Austen and her successors to indicate physical and emotional truths, as well as the limitations of these visual signs as indicators of characters' inner worlds.

70. Brodey, "Dangerous Words," 136–37.

71. Austen, *Sense and Sensibility*, 169.

72. Austen, *Sense and Sensibility*, 305.

73. Austen's philosophy seems close to Adam Smith's on this point: Smith claims that communication is not necessary for sympathy, but rather, imaginative sympathy is necessary for communication (Smith, *Theory of Moral Sentiments*, 337).

74. Austen was certainly aware that this distinction might also be abused. Mr. Collins, for example, feigns inarticulacy to heighten his rhetorical effect: "Words were insufficient for the elevation of his feelings; and he was obliged to walk about the room" (Austen, *Pride and Prejudice*, 216).

75. This also raises the issue of Marianne as an Ophelia character. For an excellent discussion of Ophelia figures in the eighteenth century, see Mary Floyd-Wilson,

"Ophelia and Femininity in the Eighteenth Century: 'Dangerous Conjectures in ill-breeding minds,'" *Women's Studies* 21 (1992): 397–409.

76. Angela Leighton, "Sense and Silences," in *Jane Austen: New Perspectives,* ed. Janet Todd (New York: Holmes and Meier, 1983), 132–33.

77. Austen, *Sense and Sensibility,* 87–8.

78. Austen, *Northanger Abbey,* 7.

79. Gilbert and Gubar, *The Madwoman in the Attic;* Claudia L. Johnson, *Jane Austen: Women, Politics, and the Novel* (Chicago: University of Chicago Press, 1988); Marvin Mudrick, *Jane Austen; Irony as Defense and Discovery* (Princeton: Princeton University Press, 1952); Gene W. Ruoff, *Jane Austen's Sense and Sensibility* (New York: St. Martin's, 1992); Clara Tuite, *Romantic Austen: Sexual Politics and the Literary Canon* (Cambridge: Cambridge University Press, 2002). Examples of the more conservative interpretations include Marilyn Butler, *Jane Austen and the War of Ideas* (Oxford: Clarendon Press,1987 [1975]); Alistair M. Duckworth, *The Improvement of the Estate; a Study of Jane Austen's Novels* (Baltimore: Johns Hopkins University Press, 1971); A. Walton Litz, *Jane Austen, a Study of her Artistic Development* (New York: Oxford University Press, 1965); and Jane Nardin, *Those Elegant Decorums: The Concept of Propriety in Jane Austen's Novels* (Albany: State University of New York Press, 1973).

80. Leighton, "Sense and Silences," 138.

81. Austen, *Sense and Sensibility,* 344.

82. Austen, *Sense and Sensibility,* 349.

83. Cf. Aarsleff's explanation of Destutt de Tracy's term: "In so far as words communicate adequately, they do so only because they are submitted to a constant process of 'rectification' in the social intercourse of speech" (Aarsleff, *From Locke to Saussure,* 375–76). See also Rothstein on "modification" in *Systems of Order and Inquiry in Later Eighteenth-Century Fiction* (Berkeley: University of California Press, 1975), 20ff.

84. Jan Fergus in Jane Austen and the Didactic Novel (Totowa, N.J.: Barnes and Noble, 1983), 51.

85. Stuart Tave makes the point that Marianne's alteration is not only an integral part of Elinor's triumph, but also relieves her of her heaviest burden. Marianne, Tave claims, is not, in contrast to what many contemporary critics claim, "the girl of strong feeling whose sensibility (resisting the novelist's intention) makes her the true heroine of the novel" (Tave, *Some Words of Jane Austen,* 96). Building on Austen's audience's knowledge of the inheritance and dynamic of the novel of sensibility, Tave shows instead how both structurally and thematically, Marianne's story clearly fits *within* Elinor's. He claims that *Sense and Sensibility*'s flaw is not Marianne, but instead Edward (*Some Words,* 78). Emma Thompson's screenplay of *Sense and Sensibility* addresses this issue by adding several scenes that enable Edward to display his charm, allowing the viewer to sympathize with Elinor's love. The film, however, also domesticates Marianne to the point that the dramatic effect described in this section is entirely absent. The film version of Marianne is even able to laugh at herself—unthinkable in the novel.

86. Leighton, "Sense and Silences," 132–3.

87. Austen, *Sense and Sensibility,* 178, 305–6.

88. Austen, *Sense and Sensibility,* 17, 168, 172, 175.

89. Austen, *Sense and Sensibility,* 197 and 307.

90. Austen, *Sense and Sensibility,* 234.

91. Austen, *Sense and Sensibility,* 86, 177. Interestingly, "lavendar [sic] water" was a common eighteenth-century treatment for sun-burned skin, which becomes significant in relation to Marianne's association with fire.

92. Austen, *Sense and Sensibility*, 181. It is tempting to argue that the metaphor of the screen is especially appropriate given that historically, fireplace screens served the purpose of protecting ladies' wax-based makeup from melting in the direct heat. In that sense, Elinor's screens would serve similar 'face-saving' purposes; however, the screens in *Sense and Sensibility* are for camouflaging the empty fireplaces in summer. It may still be that this is an even more affective parody of the heatless fire within Marianne.

93. Jan Fergus' suggestion that the earliest forms of *Sense and Sensibility* were epistolary only emphasizes my point (*Literary Life*, 74).

94. See description of the Pemberley estate in note 117 below.

95. Remember that Werther's mother feeds him, others protect him, and another tells his story. See Furst, "Man of Sensibility," on this topic.

96. Marshall and Litz have each suggested hidden thematic (but not structural) emphases on the picturesque in *Mansfield Park* and *Pride and Prejudice*: David Marshall, "True Acting and the Language of Real Feeling: *Mansfield Park*," *Yale Journal of Criticism* 3, 1 (1989) 88; A. Walton Litz, "The Picturesque in *Pride and Prejudice*," *Persuasions* 1 (1979) 13, 15, 20–24.

97. Hagstrum, *Sex and Sensibility*, 273.

98. In an interesting passage, Smith shows that a sense of injustice is "planted in the human breast" to the extent that everyone wants criminals to be captured and perhaps even put to death; however, then he says that as soon as the prisoner no longer threatens us, when he is behind bars, we begin to sympathize with him—we wish him well and do not want him to die. In other words, justice naturally transforms itself into benevolence when we can "afford" it (Smith, *Theory of Moral Sentiments*, 86 ff.).

99. Benedict, "Jane Austen's *Sense and Sensibility*," 453; Austen has reached a better solution to this problem of sympathy for the character carrying the burden of authority by the time she writes *Persuasion*.

100. Austen, *Sense and Sensibility*, 358.

101. Elinor's silences are also not all similarly motivated, nor are they always similarly manifested. Elinor silences herself in two principal ways: not speaking and speaking otherwise than she feels. Not speaking is retreating into a private world in the midst of others, while speaking otherwise than she feels exhibits a public engagement. In addition, there is a lack of respect that also can induce her silence: "Elinor agreed to it all, for she did not think he deserved the compliment of rational opposition" (Austen, *Sense and Sensibility*, 252).

102. Benedict, "Jane Austen's *Sense and Sensibility*," 457.

103. Norman Page, *The Language of Jane Austen* (Oxford: Basil Blackwell, 1972), 97–98.

104. Austen, *Sense and Sensibility*, 311–2.

105. Page also notices that the "formal patterning has by no means disappeared" (Page, 98). This is important for the point below about Elinor's picturesque "framing" of Marianne.

106. Austen, *Sense and Sensibility*, 360.

107. Austen, *Sense and Sensibility*, 355: "Mrs. Dashwood [. . .] now found that she had erred in relying on Elinor's representation of herself; and justly concluded that everything had been expressly softened at the time, to spare her from an increase of unhappiness, suffering as she then had suffered for Marianne. She found that she had been misled by the careful, the considerate attention of her daughter, to think the attachment, which once she had so well understood, much slighter in reality than she had been wont to believe, or than it was now proved to be. She feared that under this persuasion she had been unjust, inattentive—nay, almost unkind, to her Elinor:—

that Marianne's affliction, because more acknowledged, more immediately before her, had too much engrossed her tenderness, and led her away to forget that in Elinor she might have a daughter suffering almost as much, certainly with less self-provocation, and greater fortitude."

108. Austen, *Sense and Sensibility*, 355–6.
109. "It was a large, handsome stone building, standing well on rising ground, and backed by a ridge of high woody hills; and in front a stream of some natural importance was swelled into greater, but without any artificial appearance. Its banks were neither formal nor falsely adorned. Elizabeth was delighted. She had never seen a place for which nature had done more, or where natural beauty had been so little counteracted by an awkward taste" (Austen, *Pride and Prejudice*, 245).
110. Herbert Josephs, *Diderot's Dialogue of language and gesture: Le neveu de Rameau* (Columbus: Ohio State University Press, 1969), 50.
111. Aaron Hill, *The Art of Acting, Part I* (London: J. Osborn, 1746), iv. Hill dedicates his work to Lord Chesterfield, and in admiration of *Pamela*. This is discussed in Marcia Allentuck's "Narration and Illustration: The Problem of Richardson's *Pamela*," *Philological Quarterly* 51 (1972): 886.
112. Theater is treated elsewhere at length in an excellent work by David Marshall, *The Figure of Theater*. See also Spacks, *Privacy: Concealing the Eighteenth-Century Self* (Chicago and London: University of Chicago Press, 2003), 55–86, on the "performance of sensibility."
113. Sterne, *Sentimental Journey*, 57.
114. Rousseau, *First Discourse*, III.8.
115. Todd, *Sensibility*, 120.
116. Wollstonecraft, *Mary, A Fiction*, 78.
117. Erasmus Darwin, *The Botanic Garden, Part II, Containing the Loves of the Plants, a Poem* (Lichfield: J.Jackson, 1789), II.25, lines 247–252.
118. Henry Brooke, *Fool of Quality*, 5 vols. (London; W. Johnston), II.ix, 100–101, 120–21 (cited in Ellis 225, n 47, 48).
119. Kristen Gram Hayley, *Life of George Romney* (Chichester: Mason, 1809), 119.
120. Lady Hamilton's attitudes were even published in a series of twelve. See William Holström, *Monodrama, Attitudes, Tableau Vivants*, 122–125.
121. Thomas Sheridan, *A Course of Lectures on Elocution* (London, 1796), 127.
122. Austen, "Frederic and Elfrida," in *Minor Works*, 9.
123. *Oxford English Dictionary Online*, Oxford University Press, 2005.
124. Austen, *Sense and Sensibility*, 6, my emphasis.
125. Austen, *Sense and Sensibility*, 42.
126. Austen, *Sense and Sensibility*, 42.
127. Austen, *Sense and Sensibility*, 47. Cf. *Love and Freindship:* "She was all sensibility and Feeling. We flew into each others arms & after having exchanged vows of mutual Friendship for the rest of our Lives, instantly unfolded to each other the most inward Secrets of our Hearts—" (Austen, *Minor Works*, 85).
128. Austen, *Sense and Sensibility*, 325.
129. Austen, *Sense and Sensibility*, 43: "His person and air were equal to what her fancy had ever drawn for the hero of a favourite story; and in his carrying her into the house with so little previous formality, there was a rapidity of thought which particularly recommended the action to her. Every circumstance belonging to him was interesting. His name was good, his residence was in their favourite village, and she soon found out that of all manly dresses a shooting-jacket was the most becoming. Her imagination was busy, her reflections were pleasant, and the pain of a sprained ankle was disregarded."
130. This observation applies equally well to sensibility and the Gothic.

131. Austen, *Sense and Sensibility*, 336.
132. Austen, *Northanger Abbey*, 197.
133. Austen, *Persuasion*, 232–235.
134. *Persuasion*, BBC/Sony: Television/theatrical release. (104 min.). Dir. Roger Michell; screenplay by Nick Dear; produced by Fiona Finlay and George Faber, 1995.
135. Austen, *Persuasion*, 234 and 238.
136. One can see this in *Mansfield Park*, for example, where Austen purposely juxtaposes a vivacious, witty, attractive character with her much less prepossessing heroine. Readers are challenged, along with Edmund, to prefer the *good* to the *interesting*—or rather, to learn to find Fanny Price more *interesting* and affecting than Mary Crawford, despite the latter's picturesque qualities. One of the arguable shortcomings of *Sense and Sensibility* emerges from a similar didactic purpose. Debates about whether Elinor or Marianne is the heroine (or whether this novel has one or two heroines) stem from Austen's desire to chasten readerly responses to sensibility, while being unwilling to give up on sensibility itself.

NOTES TO THE AFTERWORD

1. Basil Willey wrote, referring to Hume's remark that "whenever he left his study all his doubts vanished," that the eighteenth-century spirit was characterized by "intrepidity in speculation coexisting with conservatism in practise" (Willey, 119). See also John Mullan, "The Language of Sentiment: Hume, Smith, and Henry Mackenzie," in *The History of Scottish Literature:1660–1800,* ed. Andrew Hook and Craig Cairns (Aberdeen: Aberdeen University Press, 1987), II. 117–8.
2. My thanks to Marsha Huff for sending me an article about this strange cultural phenomenon.
3. "Scores Clamour to be a Hermit," BBC News, 20 August 2002.
4. The typical hermit contract was for as much as five years, with a small salary and a large sum to be offered upon completion of the term (as opposed to the one weekend sought by the *Reuter's* ad). Hermits were generally not allowed to speak, drink, smoke, or have visitors. On the other hand, they were often supplied with libraries and food. (The hermits seem to have had difficulty in completing their tenures and reaping the promised rewards. There are stories of hermits losing their jobs for a variety of offenses: being found in alehouses, consorting with milkmaids, and otherwise breaking their hermitly contracts.) Hermitages were widespread; even Longbourn, of *Pride and Prejudice,* had one, yet most were uninhabited.
5. Jacques Derrida, "The Future of the Profession, or the Unconditional University (Thanks to the 'Humanities': What *Could Take Place* Tomorrow)," Stanford Presidential Lectures in the Humanities and Arts, April 15, 1999.
6. J. A. Cuddon, *A Dictionary of Literary Terms and Literary Theory* (London: Blackwell, 1991).
7. In contemporary narrative theory, for example, the manipulation of a distinction between story and discourse loses its effect on the reader, because there is less confidence in the heuristic assumption of a "true order of events," or a constant level of structure (*fabula*) for the narrative to manipulate. As Jonathan Culler writes, "Without the assumption that there is a true order of events prior to narrative presentation, one could not claim that the lack of order was the result of point of view," ("Fabula and Sjuzhet in the Analysis of Narrative," *Poetics Today* I, 3 [1980]: 28).

8. Bernard Tschumi, *Cinégramme Folie: Le Parc de la Villette* (Princeton: Princeton Architectural Press, 1987), vi.

9. Tschumi, *Cinégramme Folie,* 16.

10. See, for example, the interesting remarks of Gilles Deleuze and Felix Guattari: "We no longer believe in the myth of the existence of fragments that, like pieces of an antique statue, are merely waiting for the last one to be turned up, so that they may all be glued back together to create a unity that is precisely the same as the original unity. We no longer believe in a primordial totality that once existed, or in a final totality that awaits us at some given date," quoted in Harries, *Unfinished Manner,* 9.

11. Coop Himmelblau, "Architecture must blaze," in *The Power of the City,* ed. Robert Hahn and Doris Knecht (Darmstadt: Georg Büchner, 1988), 95.

12. Bernard Tschumi, "The Pleasure of Architecture," *Architectural Design* 47.3 (1977): 214.

13. Tschumi, *Cinégramme Folie,* vii.

14. The deconstructionist artist also attempts to present architecture as excavation or archaeology, just as Thomas Whately and others do in the eighteenth century. Bart Van der Straeten indicates that the more contemporary analogy to archaeology is based in Freudian concepts of the uncanny. Van der Straeten describes an architectural entry by Peter Eisenman for a competition on a housing project near Checkpoint Charlie in Berlin: "Eisenman's unrealised project included more than the original assignment, a housing block next to the Berlin Wall. Eisenman wanted to raise an entire city block against the Wall that would incorporate the existing buildings in the new project. Around that block, an underground park was designed that was to be called the 'City of Excavations.' By constructing a park below ground level the architect hoped to discover archaeological relics of the old city. Still, no relics that explicitly referred to the city's history were found, but that did not seem to bother Eisenman. The essential point was not that 'real' archaeological objects could be shown, but rather that the project emphasized and drew the people's attention to the site as a pool boiling with history. That is why the City of Excavations was planned to contain a part of a wall that would serve as a merely hypothetical reconstruction of a nineteenth-century rampart" (Van der Straeten, "The Uncanny and the Architecture of Deconstruction," *Image & Narrative: Online Magazine of the Visual Narrative* 5). Just as in the culture of sensibility, historical authenticity is secondary to the desired effect upon the audience.

15. The purposeful pursuit of distress or grief, the emphasis on the intentionally impractical, and the heartless romanticization of poverty and suffering—all in the name of sympathy and sensibility—eventually troubles many authors. In *Love and Freindship,* the young Austen successfully (if somewhat broadly) caricatures such an attitude. Edward, in conversation with his sister Augusta, proudly asserts his unwillingness to seek reconciliation with and financial assistance from his father. When Augusta asks if he will not need money to provide "victuals and drink" for his wife, he responds:

> "Victuals and Drink! ([he] replied . . . in a most nobly contemptuous Manner) and dost thou then imagine that there is no other support for an exalted Mind . . . than the mean and indelicate employment of Eating and Drinking?"
>
> "None that I know of, so efficacious," (returned Augusta).
>
> "And did you never feel the pleasing Pangs of Love, Augusta? (replied my Edward). Does it appear impossible to your vile and corrupted Palate, to exist on Love? Can you not conceive the *Luxury of living in every Distress that Poverty can inflict,* with the object of your tenderest Affection?"

The phrase "the Luxury of living in every Distress that Poverty can Inflict" captures the hypocritical stance of sensibility, especially when the same characters rob others in order to maintain their own (luxurious) love of fashion and high living. Characters in novels of sensibility go to great lengths, and great artifice, to achieve the appearance of simplicity, rusticity, and spontaneity—the literary parallel to hiring hermits and playing dress-up at dairy farms and inhabiting purposely ruined structures.

16. See *www.shabbychic.com* for these phrases and more complete descriptions of the style.

17. Harries, *Unfinished Manner,* 8–9.

Bibliography

Aarsleff, Hans. *From Locke to Saussure: Essays on the Study of Language and Intellectual History.* Minneapolis: University of Minnesota Press, 1982.
———. *The Study of Language in England, 1780–1860.* Minneapolis: University of Minnesota Press; London: Athlone Press, 1983.
Addison, Joseph, and Richard Steele. *Spectator.* 1712. Reprint, London: J. Bumpus Holburn-Bars, 1819.
———. *The Tatler.* Ed. Donald F. Bond. 1709. Reprint, Oxford: Clarendon Press, 1987.
Aikin, J. and A. L. Aikin. *Miscellaneous Pieces in Prose.* London: J. Johnson, 1773.
Allentuck, Marcia. "In Defense of an Unfinished *Tristram Shandy:* Laurence Sterne and the Non Finito." In *The Winged Skull: Papers from the Laurence Sterne Bicentenary Conference,* ed. Arthur H. Cash, 145–55. London: Methuen, 1972.
———. "Narration and Illustration: The Problem of Richardson's *Pamela.*" *Philological Quarterly* 51 (1972): 874–86.
Andrews, Malcolm. *The Search for the Picturesque: Landscape, Aesthetics, and Tourism in Britain, 1760–1800.* Stanford: Stanford University Press, 1989.
Armstrong, Nancy. *Desire and Domestic Fiction: A Political History of the Novel.* New York: Oxford University Press, 1987.
Austen, Jane. *The Novels of Jane Austen.* Ed. R. W. Chapman. Oxford and New York: Clarendon Press, 1932.
Barbauld, Anna Laetitia. "An Inquiry into those Kinds of Distress which Excite Agreeable Sensations." In *The Works of Anna Laetitia Barbauld.* London: Longma, Hurst, et al., 1825.
Barchas, Janine. "The Engraved Score in *Clarissa:* An Intersection of Music, Narrative, and Graphic Design." *Eighteenth-Century Life* 20, 2 (1996): 1–20.
———. "*Grandison*'s Grandeur as Printed Book: A Look at the Eighteenth-Century Novel's Quest for Status." *Eighteenth-Century Fiction* 14, 3/4 (2002): 673–714.
Baridon, Michel. *Les Jardins: Paysagistes, Jardiniers, Poètes.* Paris: Robert Laffond, 1998.
Barker-Benfield, G. J. *The Culture of Sensibility: Sex and Society in Eighteenth-Century Britain.* Chicago: University of Chicago, 1992.
Barrel, John. *The Idea of Landscape and the Sense of Place, 1730–1840: An Approach to the Poetry of John Clare.* Cambridge and New York: Cambridge University Press, 1972.
Barthes, Roland. *Mythologies.* Paris: Edition du Seuil, 1957.
Batey, Mavis. *Jane Austen and the English Landscape.* London and Chicago: Chicago Review Press, 1996.

Battestin, Martin C. *The Providence of Wit.* Oxford: Clarendon Press, 1974. *The Beauties of Nature and Art Displayed, in a Tour through the World.* London: Printed for J. Payne at the Feathers, Pater-Noster Row, 1763–64.

Bell, Michael. *Sentimentalism, Ethics, and the Culture of Feeling.* Basingstoke and New York: Palgrave, 2000.

Bender, John. *Imagining the Penitentiary: Fiction and the Architecture of Mind in Eighteenth-Century England.* Chicago and London: University of Chicago Press, 1987.

Benedict, Barbara. *Framing Feeling: Sentiment and Style in English Prose Fiction, 1745–1800.* New York: AMS Press, 1994.

———. "Jane Austen's *Sense and Sensibility:* The Politics of Point of View." *Philological Quarterly* 69, 4 (1990): 453–70.

Bermingham, Ann. *Landscape and Ideology: The English Rustic Tradition, 1740–1860.* Berkeley: University of California Press, 1986.

———. *Landscape and Power.* Chicago: University of Chicago, 1994.

———. *Learning to Draw: Studies in the Cultural History of a Polite and Useful Art.* New Haven: Yale University Press, 2000.

Blair, Hugh. *Lectures on Rhetoric and Belles Lettres.* Edinburgh: W. Strahan, T. Cadell, and W. Creech, 1783.

Blondel, Jacques-François. *Cours d'architecture, ou traité de la decoration, distribution & construction des bâtiments; Contenant les leçons données en 1750, & les années suivantes.* Paris: Desaint, 1771–77.

Booth, Wayne C. "The Self-Conscious Narrator in Comic Fiction before *Tristram Shandy.*" *PMLA* 67, 2 (1952): 163–85.

Boswell, James. *Boswell's London Journal 1762–1763.* Ed. Frederick A. Pottle. New York: McGraw-Hill, 1950.

Boyle, Nicholas. *Goethe: The Poet and the Age.* Oxford and New York: Oxford University Press, 1991.

Brady, Frank. "*Tristram Shandy*: Sexuality, Morality, and Sensibility," *Eighteenth-Century Studies* 4, 1 (1970): 41–56.

Brady, Patrick. "From Feminism to Chaos Theory." In *Discontinuity and Fragmentation,* ed. Henry Freeman, 101–8. Amsterdam: Rodopi, 1994.

Bredvold, Louis I. *The Natural History of Sensibility.* Detroit: Wayne State University Press, 1962.

Brissenden, R. F. *Virtue in Distress: Studies in the Novel of Sentiment from Richardson to Sade.* New York: Barnes and Noble, 1974.

Brodey, Inger Sigrun. "The Adventures of a Female Werther: Austen's Revision of Sensibility." *Philosophy and Literature* 23 (April 1999): 110–26.

———. "Dangerous Words and Silent Lovers." *Persuasions* 12 (1990): 134–8.

———. "Masculinity, Sensibility, and the 'Man of Feeling': the Gendered Ethics of Goethe's *Werther.*" *Papers on Language and Literature* 35, 2 (1999): 115–40.

———. "Papas and Hahas: Authority, Rebellion, and Landscape Gardening in *Mansfield Park.*" *Persuasions* 17 (1995): 90–6.

———. "Preromanticism, or Sensibility: Defining Ambivalences." In *Companion to European Romanticism,* ed. Michael Ferber, 10–28. London: Blackwell, 2005.

———. "Words 'Half-Dethron'd': Jane Austen's Art of the Unspoken." In *Jane Austen's Business,* ed. Juliet McMaster and Bruce Stovel, 95–106. London and New York: Macmillan and St. Martin's Press, 1996.

Brooke, Henry. *The Fool of Quality or, The History of Henry Earl of Moreland.* 5 vols. 1766. Reprint, London: W. Johnston, 1792.

Brooks, Peter. *Reading for the Plot: Design and Intention in Narrative.* Cambridge: Harvard University Press, 1993.

Brown, Jane. *Art and Architecture of English Gardens*. New York: Rizzoli, 1989.

Brown, Marshall. *Preromanticism*. Stanford: Stanford University Press, 1991.

Brownstein, Rachel. "Irony and Authority." In *"Sense and Sensibility" and "Pride and Prejudice": Jane Austen*, ed. Robert Clark, 180–92. New York: St. Martin's, 1994.

Buck-Morss, Susan. *The Dialectics of Seeing: Walter Benjamin and the Arcades Project*. Cambridge and London: MIT Press, 1989.

Burke, Edmund. *A Philosophical Enquiry into the Origin of Our Ideas of the Sublime and Beautiful*. London: Routledge and Paul; New York: Columbia University Press, 1958.

Burnet, Thomas. *Sacred Theory of the Earth: containing an account of the original of the earth, and of all the general changes which it hath undergone, or is to undergo till the consummation of all things*. London: R.N. for Walter Kettilby, 1697.

Butler, Marilyn. *Jane Austen and the War of Ideas*. 1975. Reprint, Oxford: Clarendon Press, 1987.

———. *Romantics, Rebels, and Reactionaries: English Literature and its Background, 1760–1830*. New York: Oxford University Press, 1982.

Casson, Hugh, ed. *Follies*. New York: Taplinger Publications, 1965.

Choi, Julie. "Feminine Authority? Common Sense and the Question of Voice in the Novel." *New Literary History* 27, 4 (1996): 641–62.

Clark, H. F. "Eighteenth Century Elysiums: The Role of 'Association' in the Landscape Movement." *Journal of the Warburg and Courtauld Institutes* 6 (1943): 165–89.

Cohen, Murray. *Sensible Words: Linguistic Practice in England, 1640–1785*. Baltimore: Johns Hopkins University Press, 1977.

Cohen, Ralph. *Studies in Eighteenth-Century British Art Aesthetics*. Berkeley: University of California Press, 1985.

Condillac, Étienne de. *Essai sur l'origine des connaissances humaines*. 1746. In *Œuvres*. Paris: Baudouin Frères, 1827.

Conger, Syndy McMillen. *Mary Wollstonecraft and the Language of Sensibility*. London and Toronto: Associated University Presses, 1994.

———, ed. *Sensibility in Transformation: Creative Resistance to Sentiment from the Augustans to the Romantics: Essays in Honor of Jean H. Hagstrum*. Cranbury, N.J.: Associated University Presses, 1990.

Coop Himmelblau. "Architecture must blaze." In *The Power of the City*, trans. Robert Hahn, ed. Oliver Gruenberg, Robert Hahn, and Doris Knecht. Darmstadt: Verlag Press, 1988.

Copley, Stephen, and Peter Garside. *The Politics of the Picturesque: Literature, Landscape, and Aesthetics since 1770*. Cambridge and New York: Cambridge University Press, 1994.

Cox, Stephen D. *"The Stranger within Thee": Concepts of the Self in Late-Eighteenth-Century Literature*. Pittsburgh: University of Pittsburgh Press, 1980.

Culler, Jonathan. "Fabula and Sjuzhet in the Analysis of Narrative." *Poetics Today* I, 3 (1980): 27–37.

Darwin, Erasmus. *The Botanic Garden, Part II, Containing the Loves of the Plants, a Poem*. Lichfield: Printed by J. Jackson, 1789.

Den Uyl, Douglas. *The Virtue of Prudence*. New York: P. Lang, 1991.

Dennis, John. *The Critical Works of John Dennis*. Ed. Edward Niles Hooker. Baltimore: Johns Hopkins University Press, 1939.

Derham, Rev. W. *Physico-Theology: a Demonstration of the Being and Attributes of God from His Works of Creation*. London: Printed for A. Straham, T. Cadell Jun., and W. Davies in the Strand, 1798.

Derrida, Jacques. "The Future of the Profession, or the Unconditional University (Thanks to the 'Humanities': What *Could Take Place* Tomorrow)." Stanford Presidential Lectures in the Humanities and Arts, 15 April 1999.

Diderot, Denis. *Œuvres complètes de Diderot*. Ed. J. Assezat. Paris: Garnier Frères, 1875.

Drysdale, William. *Sacred Scripture: Theory of the Earth from its First Atom to its Last End*. Newcastle upon Tyne, 1798.

Duckworth, Alistair M. *The Improvement of the Estate: A Study of Jane Austen's Novels*. Baltimore: Johns Hopkins University Press, 1971.

Ellis, Markman. *The Politics of Sensibility: Race, Gender, and Commerce in the Sentimental Novel*. Cambridge and New York: Cambridge University Press, 1996.

Enright, D. J. "William Cowper." In *Pelican Guide to English Literature*, ed. Boris Ford, 387–98. Harmondsworth, UK: Penguin, 1957.

Erskine, Andrew. *Letters between the Honourable Andrew Erskine, and James Boswell, Esq.* London: Samuel Chandler, 1763.

European Magazine, 10 (August 1786): 89–93.

Everett, Nigel. *The Tory View of Landscape*. New Haven: Yale University Press, 1994.

Federle, James Courtney. "Authenticities: Bodies, Gardens, and Pedagogies in Late-Eighteenth-Century Germany." Ph.D. diss., University of California at Berkeley, 1991.

Fergus, Jan. *Jane Austen: A Literary Life*. Basingstoke: Macmillan, 1991.

———. *Jane Austen and the Didactic Novel*. Totowa, N.J.: Barnes and Noble, 1983.

Fielding, Henry. *The History of Tom Jones, a Foundling*. London: A. Millar, 1749.

Flaschka, Horst. *Goethes "Werther": Werkkontextuelle Deskription und Analyse*. Munich: W. Fink, 1987.

Floyd-Wilson, Mary. "Ophelia and Femininity in the Eighteenth Century: 'Dangerous Conjectures in ill-breeding minds.'" *Women's Studies* 21, 4 (1992): 397–409.

Foucault, Michel. *The Order of Things: An Archaeology of the Human Sciences*. New York: Pantheon Books, 1971.

Fowler, Edward. *The Rhetoric of Confession: Shishôsetsu in Early Twentieth-Century Japanese Fiction*. Berkeley: University of California Press, 1988.

Fried, Michael. *Absorption and Theatricality: Painting and Beholder in the Age of Diderot*. Berkeley, Los Angeles, and London: University of California Press, 1980.

Furst, Lillian. "The Man of Sensibility and the Woman of Sense." *Jahrbuch-fur-Internationale-Germanistik* 14, 1 (1982): 13–26.

Galperin, William. *The Historical Austen*. Philadelphia: University of Pennsylvania Press, 2005.

Gassenmeier, Michael. *Der Typus des man of feeling*. Tübingen: Max Niemeyer Verlag, 1972.

Gilbert, Sandra M., and Susan Gubar. *The Madwoman in the Attic: The Woman Writer and the Nineteenth-Century Literary Imagination*. New Haven: Yale University Press, 1979.

Gilpin, William. *Observations on Several Parts of England, Particularly the Mountains and Lakes of Cumberland and Westmoreland, Relative Chiefly to Picturesque Beauty, Made in the Year 1772*. London, 1808.

———. *Remarks on Forest Scenery, and Other Woodland Views, Relative Chiefly to Picturesque Beauty*. London: R. Blamire, 1791.

———. *Three Essays: On Picturesque Beauty; on Picturesque Travel; and on Sketching Landscape: To which is Added a Poem, on Landscape Painting*. London: R. Blamire, 1792.

Godwin, William. *Memoirs of the Author of "A Vindication of the Rights of Woman" by William Godwin*. London, 1798.

Goethe, Johann Wolfgang von. *Italienische Reise*. Ed. Herbert von Einem. Munich: C. Wegner, 1978.

———. *Die Leiden des jungen Werthers (Sorrows of Young Werther)*. In *Goethes Werke: Hamburger Ausgabe*, ed. Erich Trunz. Munich: C. H. Beck, 1989.

———. *Die Wahlverwandtschaften (Elective Affinities)*. In *Goethes Werke: Hamburger Ausgabe*, ed. Erich Trunz. Munich: C. H. Beck, 1989.

Golden, Morris. *The Self Observed: Swift, Johnson, Wordsworth*. Baltimore: Johns Hopkins University Press, 1972.

Goldstein, Laurence. *Ruins and Empire: The Evolution of a Theme in Augustan and Romantic Literature*. Pittsburgh: University of Pittsburgh Press, 1977.

Goulemot, Jean Marie. "Un Roman de la Révolution: *Le voyageur sentimental en France sous Robespierre* de François Vernes." *Europe: Revue Littéraire Mensuelle* 659 (1984): 80–88.

Green, Donald. *The Politics of Samuel Johnson*. New Haven: Yale University Press, 1960.

Hagstrum, Jean H. *Sex and Sensibility: Ideal and Erotic Love from Milton to Mozart*. Chicago: University of Chicago Press, 1980.

Hannay, Roberta Blackley. "Jane Austen and the Picturesque Movement: The Revision of the English Landscape." Ph.D. diss., Columbia University, 1985.

Harkin, Maureen. Introduction to *The Man of Feeling*, by Henry Mackenzie, 9–38. Peterborough, Ontario, Canada: Broadview Press, 2005.

Harries, Elizabeth Wanning. *The Unfinished Manner: Essays on the Fragment in the Later Eighteenth Century*. Charlottesville: University Press of Virginia, 1994.

Harrison, Gary, and Jill Heydt-Stevenson. "Variations on the Picturesque: Authority, Play, and Practice." In *European Romantic Review* 13, 1 (2002): 3–10.

———, eds. *European Romantic Review* 13, 1 (2002).

Haskings, Katherine. *Picturing Britain: Time and Place in Image and Text, 1700–1850*. Chicago: University of Chicago Library, 1993.

Hayley, William. *Life of George Romney*. Chichester: Mason, 1809.

Herder, Johann Gottfried. *Abhandlung über den Ursprung der Sprache: Text, Materialien, Kommentar*. Munich: Reclam, 1983.

Herries, John. *The Elements of Speech*. London: E. and C. Dilly, 1773.

Hersey, G. L. "Associationism and Sensibility in Eighteenth-Century Architecture." *Eighteenth-Century Studies* 4, 1 (1970): 71–89.

Heydt-Stevenson, Jillian. "Liberty, Connection, and Tyranny: The Novels of Jane Austen and the Aesthetic Movement of the Picturesque." In *Lessons in Romanticism*, ed. Thomas Pfau and Robert Gleckner, 261–79. Durham: Duke University Press, 1998.

Hill, Aaron. *The Art of Acting, Part I*. London: J. Osborn, 1746.

Hilles, Frederick W., ed. *Romanticism: Essays Presented to Frederick A. Pottle*. New York.: Oxford University Press, 1965.

Hirschfield, C. C. L. *Theorie Der Gartenkunst*. Leipzig: M.G. Weidmann, 1779–85.

Hobbes, Thomas. *Leviathan: Or the Matter, Forme, and Power of a Commonwealth Ecclesiasticall and Civil*. Ed. Michael Oakeshott. New York and London: Collier, 1962.

Hoffman, E. T. A. *Fantasiestücke in Callot's Manier: Blätter aus dem Tagebuche eines reisenden Enthusiasten*. With an introduction by Jean Paul. Bamberg: Kunz, 1814.

Holmström, Kirsten Gram. *Monodrama, Attitudes, Tableaux Vivants: Studies on Some Trends of Theatrical Fashion, 1770–1815*. Stockholm: Almkvist and Wiksell, 1967.

Holtz, William V. *Image and Immortality: A Study of "Tristram Shandy."* Providence: Brown University Press, 1970.

Hooper, W. *Rational Recreations, in which the Principles of Numbers and Natural Philosophy are Clearly and Copiously Elucidated by a Series of Easy, Entertaining, Interesting Experiments.* London: Printed for B. Law and Son, Ave-Maria Lane, and J. Robinson, Pater-Noster Row, 1794.

Howes, Alan B., ed. *Sterne: The Critical Heritage.* London: Routledge & Kegan Paul, 1974.

Hume, David. *"Enquiries Concerning Human Understanding" and "Concerning the Principles of Morals."* Ed. L. A. Selby-Bigge and P. H. Nidditch. 1748, 1751. Reprint, Oxford and New York: Clarendon Press, 1975.

———. *A Treatise of Human Nature.* Ed. L. A. Selby-Bigge and P. H. Nidditch. 1739–40. Reprint, Oxford and New York: Clarendon Press, 1978.

Hunt, John Dixon. *The Figure in the Landscape: Poetry, Painting, and Gardening during the Eighteenth Century.* Baltimore: Johns Hopkins University Press, 1989.

———. *Gardens and the Picturesque.* Cambridge: MIT Press, 1992.

———. *The Picturesque Garden in Europe.* London: Thames and Hudson, 2002.

Hunter, Paul. *Before Novels: The Cultural Contexts of Eighteenth-Century English Fiction.* New York: W.W. Norton, 1990.

Hussey, Christopher. *The Picturesque: Studies in a Point of View.* 1927. Reprint, London: Frank Cass and Company, 1967.

Hutcheson, Francis. *An Essay on the Nature and Conduct of the Passions and Affections with Illustrations on the Moral Sense.* London: J. Darby and T. Browne, 1728.

Irving, Washington. *Christmas at Bracebridge Hall.* New York: David McKay, 1962.

Iser, Wolfgang. *Laurence Sterne: "Tristram Shandy."* Cambridge and New York: Cambridge University Press, 1988.

Janowitz, Anne F. *England's Ruins: Poetic Purpose and the National Landscape.* Cambridge, Mass.: Blackwell, 1990.

Johnson, Claudia L. *Equivocal Beings: Politics, Gender, and Sentimentality in the 1790s: Wollstonecraft, Radcliffe, Burney, Austen.* Chicago and London: University of Chicago Press, 1995.

———. *Jane Austen: Women, Politics, and the Novel.* Chicago: University of Chicago Press, 1988.

Johnson, Samuel. *The History of Rasselas, Prince of Abbissinia.* 1759. Reprint, Edinburgh: William Creech, 1789.

———. *The Idler.* 1758–1760. Reprint, London: J. Parsons, 1793.

Jones, Barbara. *Follies and Grottoes.* London: Constable, 1953.

Jones, Robert W. "Ruled Passions: Re-Reading the Culture of Sensibility." *Eighteenth-Century Studies* 32, 3 (1999): 395–402.

Josephs, Herbert. *Diderot's Dialogue of Language and Gesture: "Le neveu de Rameau."* Columbus: Ohio State University Press, 1969.

Kaplan, Deborah. "Achieving Authority in Austen." *Nineteenth-Century Fiction* 37, 4 (1983): 531–51.

Ketcham, Diana. *Le Désert De Retz: A Late Eighteenth-Century French Folly Garden, the Artful Landscape of Monsieur De Monville.* Cambridge and London: MIT Press, 1994.

Kliger, Samuel. "Whig Aesthetics: A Phase of Eighteenth-Century Taste." *English Literary History* 16, 2 (1949): 135–50.

Knight, Richard Payne. *The Landscape: A Didactic Poem in Three Books Addressed to Uvedale Price, Esqu.* 2d ed. London, 1795.

A Lady. *The Liberal American: A novel, in a series of letters, by a lady.* 2 vols. London: Printed for William Lane, 1785.

Lamb, Jonathan. *Sterne's Fiction and the Double Principle.* Cambridge and New York: Cambridge University Press, 1989.

Lange, Victor. "The Metaphor of Silence." In *Goethe Revisited: A Collection of Essays,* ed. Elizabeth Wilkinson, 133–52. London and New York: Calder, Riverrun, 1984.

Ledoux, Claude Nicolas. *L'Architecture considérée sous le rapport de l'art, des moeurs, et de la législation.* Paris: Hermann, 1997.

Leighton, Angela. "Sense and Silences." In *Jane Austen: New Perspectives,* ed. Janet Todd, 53–66. New York: Holmes and Meier, 1983.

Lessing, Gotthold Ephraim. *Emilia Galotti: Ein Trauerspiel.* Ed. A. Rebhann. 1772. Reprint, Vienna: K. Graeser, [192?].

———. *Laokoön.* Ed. Hugo Blümner. Berlin: Weidmannsche, 1880.

Levy, Maurice. "Les ruines dans l'art et l'écriture: Esthétique et idéologie." *Bulletin de la Societé d'Études Anglo-Americaines des XVIIe et XVIIIe Siècles* 13 (November 1981): 141–58.

Lewis, C. S. *Studies in Words.* 1960. Reprint, Cambridge and New York: Cambridge University Press, 1990.

Lipking, Lawrence. *The Ordering of the Arts in Eighteenth-Century England.* Princeton: Princeton University Press, 1970.

Litz, A. Walton. *Jane Austen, a Study of her Artistic Development.* New York: Oxford University Press, 1965.

———. "The Picturesque in *Pride and Prejudice.*" *Persuasions* 1 (December 1979): 13–5, 20–4.

Liu, Alan. *Wordsworth, the Sense of History.* Stanford: Stanford University Press, 1989.

Locke, John. *An Essay Concerning Human Understanding.* Ed. Peter H. Nidditch. 1689. Reprint, Oxford: Clarendon Press, 1975.

———. *Second Treatise of Government.* Ed. C. B. McPherson. 1690. Reprint, Indianapolis and Cambridge: Hackett, 1980.

Loftis, John, ed. *Essays in Criticism and Literary Theory.* Northbrook, Ill.: A.H.M. Publishing, 1975.

Lugar, Robert. *Architectural Sketches for Cottages, Rural Dwellings, and Villas, in the Grecian, Gothic, and Fancy Styles, with Plans, Suitable to Persons of Genteel Life and Moderate Fortune.* London: J. Taylor, 1805.

Macaulay, Rose. *Pleasure of Ruins.* London: Thames and Hudson, 1953.

Mackenzie, Henry. *Julia de Roubigné, a Tale in a Series of Letters.* London: W. Strahan, T. Cadell, 1777.

———. *Letters to Elizabeth Rose of Kilravock on Literature, Events, and People, 1768–1815.* Ed. Horst W. Drescher. Münster: Verlag Aschendorff, 1967.

———. *The Man of Feeling.* 1771. Reprint, Oxford and New York: Oxford University Press, 1987.

Maillet, Arnaud. *The Claude Glass: Use and Meaning of the Black Mirror in Western Art.* Translated by Jeff Fort. New York: Zone Books, 2004.

Marivaux, Pierre Carlet de. *La Vie de Marianne, ou, Les aventures de Madame la comtesse de ***.* 1745. Reprint, Paris: Garnier, 1966.

Marshall, David. *The Figure of Theater: Shaftesbury, Defoe, Adam Smith, and George Eliot.* New York: Columbia University Press, 1986.

———. *The Frame of Art: Fictions of Aesthetic Experience, 1750–1815.* Baltimore: Johns Hopkins University Press, 2005.

———. "The Problem of the Picturesque." *Eighteenth-Century Studies* 35, 3 (2002): 413–37.

———. *The Surprising Effects of Sympathy: Marivaux, Diderot, Rousseau, and Mary Shelley.* Chicago: University of Chicago Press, 1988.

———. "True Acting and the Language of Real Feeling: *Mansfield Park*." *Yale Journal of Criticism* 3, 1 (1989): 87–106.

McGann, Jerome. *The Poetics of Sensibility: A Revolution in Literary Style.* Oxford: Clarendon Press, 1996.

McKeon, Michael. *Origins of the English Novel.* Baltimore: Johns Hopkins University Press, 1987.

Melmoth, William (the younger). *The Letters of Sir Thomas Fitzosborne, On Several Subjects.* London: R. Dodsley, 1750.

Melzer, Arthur M. *The Natural Goodness of Man: On the System of Rousseau's Thought.* Chicago: University of Chicago Press, 1990.

Michasiw, Kim Ian. "Nine Revisionist Theses on the Picturesque." *Representations* 38 (1992): 76–100.

Moss, R. B. "Sterne's Punctuation." *Eighteenth-Century Studies* 15, 2 (1981–1982): 179–200.

Moss, Stephanie. "Gardens and the Picturesque: Studies in the History of Landscape Architecture." *Journal of Aesthetics and Art Criticism* 52, 2 (1994): 250–2.

Motooka, Wendy. *The Age of Reasons: Quixotism, Sentimentalism, and Political Economy in Eighteenth-Century Britain.* London and New York: Routledge, 1998.

Mudrick, Marvin. *Jane Austen: Irony as Defense and Discovery.* Princeton: Princeton University Press, 1952.

Mullan, John. "The Language of Sentiment: Hume, Smith, and Henry Mackenzie." In *The History of Scottish Literature: 1660–1800,* ed . Andrew Hook and Craig Cairns, 273–89. Aberdeen: Aberdeen University Press, 1987.

———. *Sentiment and Sociability: The Language of Feeling in the Eighteenth Century.* Oxford and New York: Oxford University Press, Clarendon Press, 1988.

Murray, Christopher John, ed. *Encyclopedia of the Romantic Era: 1760–1850.* New York and London: Fitzroy Dearborn, 2004.

Nagle, Christopher. "Sterne, Shelley, and Sensibility's Pleasure of Proximity." *ELH* 70, 3 (2003): 813–45.

Nardin, Jane. *Those Elegant Decorums: The Concept of Propriety in Jane Austen's Novels.* Albany: State University of New York Press, 1973.

Nicolson, Marjorie Hope. *Mountain Gloom and Mountain Glory: The Development of the Aesthetics of the Infinite.* Ithaca, N.Y.: Cornell University Press, 1959.

Nuttall, A. D. *A Common Sky: Philosophy and the Literary Imagination.* Berkeley: University of California Press, 1974.

O'Farrell, Mary Ann. *Telling Complexions: The Nineteenth-Century Novel and the Blush.* Durham: Duke University Press, 1997.

O'Neal, John. *The Authority of Experience: Sensationist Theory in the French Enlightenment.* University Park, Pa.: Pennsylvania State University Press, 1996.

Oxford English Dictionary, 2d ed., s.v. "interesting."

Page, Norman. *The Language of Jane Austen.* Oxford: Basil Blackwell, 1972.

Panofsky, Erwin. "Et in Arcadio Ego: On the Conception of Transcience in Poussin and Watteau." In *Philosophy and History: Essays Presented to Ernst Cassirer,* ed. Raymond Kilbansky and H. J. Paton. Oxford: Clarendon Press, 1936.

Pelletier, Louise. "Nicolas Le Camus de Mézières's Architecture of Expression, and the Theater of Desire at the End of the Ancien Régime; or the Analogy of Fiction with Architectural Innovation." .Ph.D. diss., McGill School of Architecture, 2000.

Persuasion. Film (104 min.). Dir. Roger Michell, screenplay by Nick Dear, produced by Fiona Findlay and George Faber. BBC/Sony, 1995.

Pinger, Wilhelm Robert Richard. *Laurence Sterne and Goethe.* University of California Publications in Modern Philology. Berkeley: University of California Press, 1920.

Pizzoni, Filippo. *The Garden: A History in Landscape and Art.* New York: Rizzoli Press, 1999.

Pope, Alexander. "Eloisa to Abelard." In *Letters of Abelard and Heloise, to Which is Prefix'd a Particular Account of Their Lives, Amours, and Misfortunes by the Late John Hughes, Esq. To Which Is Now First Added, the Poem of Eloisa to Abelard by Mr Pope.* London: W. Johnston, B. Law, T. Lownds, and T. Caslon, 1765.

Pratt, Samuel Jackson. *Sympathy, a Poem.* London: T. Cadell, 1781.

Prest, John. *The Garden of Eden: The Botanic Garden and the Re-Creation of Paradise.* New Haven and London: Yale University Press, 1981.

Price, Uvedale. "An Essay on the Picturesque as Compared with the Sublime and the Beautiful." In *Essays on the Picturesque.* London, 1810.

Purdy, Daniel L. *The Tyranny of Elegance: Consumer Cosmopolitanism in the Era of Goethe.* Baltimore: Johns Hopkins University Press, 1998.

Radcliffe, Ann. *The Mysteries of Udolpho.* Ed. Jacqueline Howard. London: Penguin, 2001.

Reiss, Timothy. "Perioddity: Considerations on the Geography of Histories." *Modern Language Quarterly* 62, 4 (2001): 425–52.

Repton, Humphry. *A Letter to Uvedale Price, Esq.* London: G. Nicol, 1794.

Richardson, Samuel. *Clarissa, or the History of a Young Lady.* Harmondsworth, Middlesex, England: Viking and Penguin, 1985.

———. *The History of Charles Grandison.* Oxford and New York: Oxford University Press, 1986.

———. *Pamela: or, virtue rewarded. In a series of familiar letters from a beautiful young damsel to her parents.* 4th ed. 2 vols. 1740. Reprint, London: C. Rivington, 1741.

Riffaterre, Michael. *Text Production.* New York: Columbia University Press, 1983.

Riskin, Jessica. *Science in the Age of Sensibility: The Sentimental Empiricists of the French Enlightenment.* Chicago and London: University of Chicago Press, 2002.

Robinet, Jean-Bapiste René, et al., eds. *Encyclopédie ou Dictionnaire raisonné des sciences, des arts et des métiers.* Paris: Briasson, 1751–65.

Robinson, Sidney K. *Inquiry into the Picturesque.* Chicago: University of Chicago Press, 1991.

Rosen, Charles. *The Romantic Generation.* Cambridge: Harvard University Press, 1995.

Rosenblum, Robert. *Transformations in Late Eighteenth Century Art.* Princeton, N.J.: Princeton University Press, 1967.

Ross, Stephanie. Review of *Gardens and the Picturesque: Studies in the History of Landscape Architecture,* by John Dixon Hunt. *Journal of Aesthetics and Art Criticism* 52, 2 (1994): 250–2.

———. *What Gardens Mean.* Chicago and London: University of Chicago Press, 1998.

Roth, Michael S., Claire Lyons, and Charles Merewether. *Irresistible Decay: Ruins Reclaimed.* Los Angeles: Getty Research Institute, 1997.

Rothstein, Eric. "'Ideal Presence' and the 'Non Finito' in Eighteenth-Century Aesthetics." *Eighteenth-Century Studies* 9, 3 (1976): 307–22.

———. *Systems of Order and Inquiry in Later Eighteenth-Century Fiction.* Berkeley: University of California Press, 1975.

Rousseau, Jean-Jacques. *Les Confessions.* 1782. In *Œuvres Complètes.* Paris: Gallimard, 1959.

——. *Le Contrat Social.* 1762. In *Œuvres Complètes*. Paris: Du Seuil, 1971.

——. *Discours sur les sciences et les arts.* 1750. In *Œuvres Complètes*. Paris: Gallimard, 1968.

——. *Discours sur l'origine et les fondements de l'inégalité parmi les hommes.* 1755. In *Œuvres complètes*. Paris: Gallimard, 1966.

——. *Essai sur l'origine des langues: ou il est parlé de la mélodie et de l'imitation musicale.* Ed. Jean Starobinski. 1781. Reprint, Paris: Gallimard, 1990.

——. *Julie, ou la Nouvelle Héloïse.* 1761. Reprint, Paris: Hachette, 1925.

——. *La Profession du Foi du Vicaire Savoyard.* 1765. Reprint, Paris: J. Vrin, 1978.

Ruoff, Gene W. *Jane Austen's Sense and Sensibility.* New York: St. Martin's, 1992.

Schlegel, August Wilhelm von, and Friedrich von Schlegel. *Athenaeum, eine Zeitschrift.* Berlin: Bey F. Vieweg dem Älteren, 1798–1800.

Sedaine, Michel-Jean. *Le philosophe sans le savoir.* 1765. Reprint, Durham: University of Durham, 1987.

Shaftesbury, Anthony Ashley Cooper, third earl of. *Characteristics of Men, Manners, Opinions, Times.* 1711. Reprint, London: 1727.

Sheridan, Thomas. *A Complete Dictionary of the English Language, Both with Regard to Sound and Meaning, One Main Object of Which Is, to Establish a Plain and Permanent Standard of Pronunciation: To Which Is Prefixed a Prosodial Grammar.* Dublin: Pat. Wogan and Pat. Byrne, 1790.

——. *A Course of Lectures on Elocution.* London, 1796.

——. *Lectures on the Art of Reading. In Two Parts: Containing Part I, The Art of Reading Prose and Part II, The Art of Reading Verse.* London: J. Dodsley and C. Dilly, 1787.

Sherman, Stuart. *Telling Time: Clocks, Diaries, and English Diurnal Form, 1660–1785.* Chicago: University of Chicago Press, 1996.

Siebers, Tobin. "The Werther Effect: The Esthetics of Suicide." *Mosaic* 26, 1 (1993): 15–34.

Smith, Adam. *Theory of Moral Sentiments.* Ed. D. D. Raphael and A. L. Macfie. Indianapolis: Liberty Press, 1982.

Smith, Charlotte. *Emmeline: Orphan of the Castle.* London: Oxford University Press, 1971.

Spacks, Patricia Meyer. *Boredom: A Literary History of a State of Mind.* Chicago and London: University of Chicago Press, 1995.

——. *Imagining a Self: Autobiography and Novel in Eighteenth-Century England.* Cambridge and London: Harvard University Press, 1976.

——. *Novel Beginnings: Experiments in Eighteenth-Century English Fiction.* New Haven: Yale University Press, 2006.

——. *Privacy: Concealing the Eighteenth-Century Self.* Chicago and London: University of Chicago Press, 2003.

Stafford, Barbara Maria. "'Illiterate Monuments': The Ruin as Dialect or Broken Classic." *The Age of Johnson: A Scholarly Annual* 1 (1987):1–34.

Stephens, Edward. *A Poem on the Park and Woods of the Right Hon. Allen Lord Bathurst.* Cirencester: Printed for the author, 1748.

Sterne, Laurence. *The Beauties of Sterne: Including all his Pathetic Tales, and Most Distinguished Observations on Life, Selected for the Heart of Sensibility.* London: Printed for T. Davies et al., 1782.

——. *The Complete Works of Laurence Sterne.* Ed. David Herbert. Edinburgh: William P. Nimmo, 1872.

——. *Letters from Yorick to Eliza.* Altenburgh: Printed for Richter, 1776.

——. *The Life and Opinions of Tristram Shandy, Gentleman.* Ed. Ian P. Watt. 1760–7. Reprint, Boston: Houghton Mifflin, 1965.

————. *A Sentimental Journey through France and Italy by Mr. Yorick.* Ed. Gardiner D. Stout Jr. 1768. Reprint, Berkeley: University of California Press, 1967.

————. *The Sermons of Mr. Yorick.* In *The Writings of Laurence Sterne.* Oxford and New York: Shakespeare Head Press, 1927.

Stuart, Lady Louisa. *Selections from her Manuscripts.* Edinburgh: David Douglass, 1899.

Swift, Jonathan. *Tale of a Tub.* Ed. A. C. Guthkelch and D. Nichol Smith. 1704. Reprint, Oxford: Clarendon Press, 1920.

Tave, Stuart. *Some Words of Jane Austen.* Chicago: University of Chicago Press, 1973.

Taylor, Charles. *Sources of the Self: the Making of the Modern Identity.* Cambridge: Harvard University Press, 1989.

Thomas, Sophie. "Assembling History: Fragments and Ruins." *European Romantic Review* 14, 2 (2003): 177–86.

Thompson, James. *Between Self and World: The Novels of Jane Austen.* University Park: Pennsylvania State University Press, 1988.

Thomson, James. *Liberty, a Poem.* Glasgow: Robert & Andrew Foulis, 1774.

Todd, Janet. *Sensibility, an Introduction.* London and New York: Methuen, 1986.

Traugott, John. *Tristram Shandy's World: Sterne's Philosophical Rhetoric.* Berkeley: University of California Press, 1954.

Trauzettel, Ludwig. "Wörlitz: England in Germany." *Garden History* 24, 2 (1996): 221–36.

Trilling, Lionel. *Sincerity and Authenticity.* Cambridge: Harvard University Press, 1972.

Tschumi, Bernard. *Cinégramme Folie: Le Parc de la Villette.* Princeton: Princeton Architectural Press, 1987.

————. "The Pleasure of Architecture." *Architectural Design* 47, 3 (1977): 214–8.

Tuite, Clara. *Romantic Austen: Sexual Politics and the Literary Canon.* Cambridge: Cambridge University Press, 2002.

Umbach, Maiken. "Visual Culture, Scientific Images, and German Small-State Politics in the Late Enlightenment." *Past and Present* 158 (February 1998): 110–43.

Van der Straeten, Bart. "The Uncanny and the Architecture of Deconstruction." *Image & Narrative: Online Magazine of the Visual Narrative* 5 (January 2003). http://www.imageandnarrative.be/uncanny/bartvanderstraeten.htm

Van Sant, Ann Jessie. *Eighteenth-Century Sensibility and the Novel: The Senses in Social Context.* Cambridge: Cambridge University Press, 1993.

Vincent, Deirdre. *Werther's Goethe and the Game of Literary Creativity.* Toronto and Buffalo, N.Y.: University of Toronto Press, 1992.

Wallace, Tara Ghoshal. *Jane Austen and Narrative Authority.* New York: Macmillan Press, St. Martin's Press, 1995.

Walsh, Francis. *The Antediluvian World; or, a New Theory of the Earth: Containing A clear Account of the Form and Constitution of the Terrestrial Globe before the Universal Deluge; proving it to be quite different from what it is at present. And also of the Origin and Causes of the said Deluge, Subterraneous Cavities, Seas, Islands, Mountains, etc.* Dublin: Printed by S. Powell, 1743.

Warren, Marsha. "Time, Space, and Semiotic Discourse in the Feminization/ Disintegration of Quentin Compson." *The Faulkner Journal* 4, 1–2 (1988–1989): 99–111.

Warton, Joseph. *An Essay on the Genius and Writings of Pope.* 1756. Reprint, London: J. Dodsley, 1782.

Whately, Thomas. *Observations on Modern Gardening, Illustrated by Descriptions.* London: T. Payne and Son, 1777.

Whitelaw, Jeffery. *Follies.* Malta: Gutenberg Press, 2005.

Willey, Basil. *The Eighteenth Century Background: Studies on the Idea of Nature in the Thought of the Period.* London: Chatto & Windus, 1940.

Williamson, Tom. *Polite Landscapes, Gardens, and Society in Eighteenth-Century England.* Baltimore: Johns Hopkins University Press, 1995.

Wolfgang, Aurora. *Gender and Voice in the French Novel, 1730–1782.* Wiltshire and Burlington, Vt.: Ashgate, 2004.

Wollstonecraft, Mary. *The Cave of Fancy.* In *Posthumous Works,* ed. William Godwin. London: 1798.

———. *Mary, a Fiction.* London: Printed for J. Johnson, St. Paul's Church Yard, 1788.

———. *The Wrongs of Woman, or Maria; A Fragment: to which is added the First Book of a Series of Lessons for Children.* In *Posthumous Works,* ed. William Godwin. London: 1798.

Woolf, Virginia. Introduction to *A Sentimental Journey through France and Italy by Mr. Yorick,* by Laurence Sterne, ed. Virginia Woolf. London: 1928.

Wordsworth, William. "Lines Composed a Few Miles above Tintern Abbey." In *The Poetical Works,* 2: 150–4. London: Edward Moxon, 1850.

Young, Edward. *Conjectures on Original Composition in a letter to the author of Charles Grandison.* London: A. Millar and J. Dodsley, 1759.

Index

Note: Page numbers in **boldface** indicate illustrations.